OUR SCHOOL IN PAVLYSH

OUR SCHOOL IN PAVLYSH

A HOLISTIC APPROACH TO EDUCATION

Vasyl Sukhomlynsky

Translated and edited by Alan Cockerill

EJR Publishing

A catalogue record for this book is available
from the National Library of Australia

ISBN: 978-0-6485800-4-1 (paperback)

First published in 2021 by EJR Language Service Pty Ltd
Trading as EJR Publishing
9 Taralye Place, Chapel Hill, QLD 4069 Australia
https://www.ejr.com.au

Copyright © 2021 EJR Language Service Pty. Ltd. All rights reserved.
No part of this publication shall be reproduced, stored in or introduced into a retrieval system, or transmitted in any form or by any means (electronic, mechanical, photocopying, recording, scanning or otherwise), without the prior permission of the copyright owner and publisher of this book.

Cover photograph and all other archival photographs reproduced by permission of Olga Sukhomlynska

Copy-editing by Lisa Hill

Internal design with guidance from Paul Howson

This book has been published with financial assistance from the Ukrainian Studies Foundation in Australia.

Contents

From the translator   xi

Introduction   1

Chapter One — Our Staff

    Reflections on school leadership   23
    Our teachers and educators   41
    Our school council   77
    Leadership roles   82
    Professional development   84
    Collective research   96
    Our traditions   101

Chapter Two — Our School Environment

    Caring for the environment   113
    Our facilities   117
    Our school grounds   130
    Inside our school buildings   138

Chapter Three — Health and Physical Education

    Physical and mental health   157
    Hygiene and student routines   161
    Work as a means of strengthening health   169
    Physical education during lessons and sport   172
    Leisure activities   174

Chapter Four — Moral Education

    Basic values   179
    Moral understanding and moral conviction   187
    How convictions grow and strengthen   198
    Educating sensitivity and empathy   208
    Educating in a spirit of honesty and integrity   214
    Respectful relationships   219

CHAPTER FIVE — INTELLECTUAL EDUCATION

    Intellectual education and its objectives   227
    Developing a philosophy of life   229
    Developing a scientific world view   234
    The curriculum   246
    Learning and intellectual development   256
    Developing students' intellectual abilities   264
    Methods of instruction   286

CHAPTER SIX — WORK EDUCATION

    Principles of work education   305
    Work education infrastructure   314
    Organising student work activities   317
    Teaching work skills   322
    Keeping up with science and technology   338
    Developing talents, abilities, and a vocation   345
    Manual work and all-round development   358
    Self-service   363
    The role of work in a holistic education   364
    The role of example in work education   365
    Work exercises   367
    Group work projects   369
    The role of competition   370
    Work routines   371

CHAPTER SEVEN — AESTHETIC EDUCATION

    The appreciation of beauty   373
    Aesthetic education and holistic development   378
    Aesthetic appreciation and aesthetic creativity   382
    The role of the environment and of work   390

APPENDICES   397

ENDNOTES   411

RESOURCES   417

Acknowledgements

I would like to acknowledge the generous help and advice I have received from Sukhomlynsky's daughter, Professor Olga Sukhomlynska, who has supported my efforts to popularise her father's work over the past thirty years. She has granted me permission to translate her father's work, arranged access to archives and photographs, and given permission for the use of photographs. She has supplied me with copies of new publications relating to her father's work and has always been available as a sounding board when I am preparing translations for publication. Her own publications have continued to throw new light on the life and work of Vasyl Sukhomlynsky.

The Ukrainian Studies Foundation in Australia facilitated the publication of this book by providing funding for copy-editing of my translation, and I am grateful for their support, and for the generous assistance from Professor Marko Pavlyshyn in liaising with the Foundation.

I would like to thank my friend Paul Howson, a skilled designer, who has advised me on this and all my previous publications. For this book, he generously provided me with guidance on the internal design, helping me set up the parameters, while at the same time teaching me how to undertake some of the design work myself. I am very grateful for his help and for the way he has been willing to share his knowledge. Any imperfections in the design are mine and not his.

I am indebted to Lisa Hill for her thorough copy-editing of the text. I enjoyed working with her when she carried out the copy-editing of my translation of Sukhomlynsky's *My Heart I Give to Children* and was very happy when she agreed to perform the same task on this work.

My thanks also extend to the Avid Reader bookshop in Brisbane for allowing me to use their venue to launch this book, and The Really Good Bookshop for stocking my translations of Sukhomlynsky's works over the past five years.

Finally, I would like to thank my wife Hiroko and son Christopher for their patience and support while I have been working on this book.

Sukhomlynsky with students and another teacher.
School beehives are visible in the background.

FROM THE TRANSLATOR

VASYL SUKHOMLYNSKY (1918–1970) WAS THE PRINCIPAL of a combined primary and secondary school in the Ukrainian village of Pavlysh from 1948 until his death in 1970. Together with his dedicated staff, he created a holistic system of education that addressed multiple aspects of a child's development: physical, emotional, moral, intellectual, aesthetic and vocational. Sukhomlynsky wrote extensively about his experience, and thousands of visitors flocked to his school. His works have been translated into over 50 languages and read by millions of educators.

The original title of this work was *Pavlyshskaya srednyaya shkola [Pavlysh Secondary School]*. It was first published in 1969, in a Russian language edition, and has never before been translated into English. It is a proud account of how Sukhomlynsky's school functioned to provide its students with a holistic education. Another work published around the same time, *My Heart I Give to Children*, shows us how Sukhomlynsky interacted with children as a teacher. *Pavlysh Secondary School* shows us how he ran his school as a principal and how staff, parents and students cooperated to create a vibrant learning community.

This translation has been done with English-speaking educators in mind: teachers, principals and parents. The social and environmental challenges we face today require a holistic approach to education: one that develops robust physical and mental health; fosters curiosity, empathy and creativity; and teaches young people to be custodians of our natural environment. Sukhomlynsky developed such an approach.

The book is divided into chapters that address various aspects of holistic education, including health and physical education, moral education, intellectual education, work education and aesthetic education. One of the remarkable things about the educational approach at Sukhomlynsky's school was how he and his staff managed to integrate all these aspects of education into a coherent whole. Whatever their subject, all teachers kept in mind the children's health, moral development, intellectual development, vocational development and aesthetic development. Every activity could be seen through the prism of any one of these priorities and address several of them simultaneously.

Another aspect of the school's holistic approach was the way it developed an extended learning community. Teachers, parents, community members and the students themselves all played a role in educating each other, providing a striking demonstration of the notion that 'it takes a village to raise a child'. Through heart-to-heart individual and group discussions, Sukhomlynsky created a sense of common purpose among his stable cohort of staff. The first chapter of this book describes how his staff developed common convictions and worked as a team. The school's spirit of teamwork extended to parents and families, who attended twice-monthly parenting sessions at the school, led by Sukhomlynsky and other senior teachers. The school also had an extensive program of extracurricular activities that Sukhomlynsky sometimes referred to as a 'second curriculum'. Dozens of extracurricular clubs and groups operated after school, offering activities as diverse as horticulture, agriculture, animal husbandry, carpentry, metal work, mechanics, modelling, electronics, puppetry, creative writing, local history and drama. Many of these groups involved children of varying ages, and the older children played a significant role in educating the younger children. These informal, extracurricular programs were extremely important in developing children's talents, building their self-esteem and providing an experiential background for formal studies.

A third aspect of Sukhomlynsky's holistic approach was utilising the school environment as a potent educational tool, as detailed in the second chapter of this book. Vegetation was chosen to improve the air quality in the school grounds and create an environment of great beauty. The grounds were divided into various areas that allowed smaller groups of children to play quietly without being unduly agitated by the bustle and noise of large crowds. This contributed to the children's psychological equilibrium. The children themselves were heavily involved in creating and maintaining the beauty of their environment and the facilities that supported the school's various programs. The classrooms and corridors were decorated with many displays that stimulated thought and reflection.

Sukhomlynsky encouraged students to become autonomous, lifelong learners. The extracurricular program was an essential part of this approach. One of Sukhomlynsky's priorities was that both staff and students should have sufficient free time to pursue their own interests and read books that took them beyond the curriculum they had to master. He encouraged students to think independently and form their own convictions.

Sukhomlynsky prepared this book for publication at a very difficult time in his life. In 1967, he had been subjected to sustained attacks in the press by ideologues who accused him of 'abstract humanism' and not adhering to communist ideology. He had great difficulty securing the 1969 Russian language publication of *My Heart I Give to Children* and only did so by first securing its 1968 publication in the German Democratic Republic (East Germany). It is no surprise, then, to find that *Pavlysh Secondary School* contains numerous references to the Communist Party, communist ideology and canonical representatives of Soviet education such as Lunacharsky, Krupskaya, Shatsky and Makarenko. As is clear from Olga Sukhomlynska's study of the manuscripts and publishing history of *My Heart I Give to Children*, Sukhomlynsky was obliged to make frequent references to communist ideology to get his work published.

Some of these ideological references have been removed from this translation due to their irrelevance to the intended readership of English-speaking educators. I have deleted references to pronouncements at Communist Party conferences and canonical representatives of Soviet education when they clearly serve no purpose other than to appease his Soviet editors. I have cut a section on 'social orientation' from the chapter on moral education, as its terms of reference were so foreign to Western educators. I have also cut a section on 'atheistic education' from the chapter on intellectual education. This section was interesting in its own way, as it called for tolerance and tact when dealing with parents who had religious beliefs, but the discussion did not seem relevant to educators in pluralistic societies.

However, I have not deleted references to communist ideals, as these were part of Sukhomlynsky's genuine faith and motivation. He fervently believed in educating young people to be unselfish and committed to the welfare of all, and to have respect for shared public property. He wanted young people to find wealth in their appreciation of the beauty in nature, in works of art and literature and human relationships, rather than the accumulation of money or property. For example, in his chapter on moral education, Sukhomlynsky describes how he and his students laboured to create a communal grape plantation:

> Many people think we are strange, obsessed, and ask us cynically what we gain from our efforts, what benefit accrues to us. These questions do not so much offend us as concern us. Those who see everything only from the point of view of personal gain are not yet ready for the collective work of which we dream. We try to convince such people of their error.
>
> What are we making such an effort for? For people's happiness. For us, communism means happiness and joy for all people. We are making such an effort because we do not want each person to drag happiness into their own little corner, to surround it with a high fence and guard it with chained dogs, but to create it together with others, to seek it among their comrades and find it in common work.

Such ideals may be foreign in our own competitive and individualistic societies, but exposure to them may provoke reflection. Similar ideals motivated the first Christians and are inherent in many spiritual traditions.

Pavlysh Secondary School was one of a number of works that Sukhomlynsky wrote during the final three years of his life, knowing he did not have long to live. He had been severely wounded during the war and still carried shrapnel fragments in his chest that had travelled to his heart. He had a severe heart condition that had undoubtedly been aggravated by overwork and the stress he endured due to the hostile press campaign against him. By 1967 he knew he would not be alive for much longer and hastened to record as much of his experience as possible. The last three years of Sukhomlynsky's life were astonishingly productive, as he wrote his most mature and enduring works. These include *My Heart I Give to Children, The Birth of a Citizen, Letters to My Son, Pavlysh Secondary School, 100 Pieces of Advice for School Teachers, The Methodology for Educating a School Community* and *Parental*

Pedagogy. He wrote in the early morning hours before school, during holidays and in his hospital bed. Many of these works were only published posthumously.

Wanting to record his experience in detail, *Pavlysh Secondary School* contains many fulsome descriptions: lists of books students were expected to read, quotations displayed in the school corridors, equipment the students manufactured at school, topics set for creative writing throughout the school, even the books in one section of a Grade 4 reading room. While this detail may have been of interest to teachers working in Soviet schools at the time the work was written, some will clearly not be relevant to the readers of this translation and have been cut during editing. In other cases, long lists have been placed in appendices at the end of the book for interested readers to consult. As a result of my editorial trimming of ideological references and some material not relevant to English-speaking educators, a work of approximately 170,000 words has been reduced to one of approximately 150,000.

In an effort to help English-speaking readers relate to the content of this translation, I have 'domesticated' some of the terminology using what I regard as equivalent terms from our own culture. I have generally translated the terms for 'motherland' (родина) and 'fatherland' (отечество) as 'homeland'. The noun 'collective' has been translated variously according to the context, sometimes as 'school community', 'class' or 'class group', or 'staff' or 'staff group'. Russian personal names can be confusing for English readers. Russians have a given name, a patronymic (formed from their father's name) and a surname. When referring to a teacher for the first time and giving all three elements, I have translated their name in full. When a teacher is referred to by their given name and patronymic (e.g., Aleksandr Aleksandrovich), or their initials and surname (e.g., A.A. Filippov), I have generally translated this in the form of 'Mr Filippov' or 'Ms Stepanova', which conveys a similar level of politeness. I have used the first name and surname (e.g., Aleksandr Filippov) in photograph captions, although such a combination is not found in the original text.

There are some key cultural terms that I have retained. Soviet citizens referred to their involvement in the Second World War from 1941 to 1945 as 'The Great Patriotic War', and I have retained that term. I have retained references to the Pioneer movement and the Komsomol, as these are essential to understanding the school system in which Sukhomlynsky was operating. The Pioneers were a communist version of the Boy Scout and Girl Guide movement. Children joined the Pioneers during Grade 3, and every school class from Grade 3 to Grade 8 constituted something like a scout troop. As Pioneers, they were exposed to communist ideology and involved in hikes, camps and community service projects. Children in Grade 8 graduated from the Pioneers to the Komsomol (sometimes translated as 'Communist Youth League' or 'Young Communist League'), a communist youth organisation from which some members were eventually recruited into the Communist Party, usually after they turned 25. As virtually all senior students were members of the Komsomol, Sukhomlynsky sometimes refers to senior students as 'Komsomol members' (a single word in Russian). Consequently, I have sometimes translated 'Komsomol members' simply as 'senior students'.

Finally, Sukhomlynsky included a number of footnotes in the text of his book, which I have converted to endnotes that are collected together at the end of the book. I have also added some of my own endnotes to explain certain textual references that readers might otherwise find puzzling. These are all preceded by the phrase 'Translator's note' to distinguish them from Sukhomlynsky's own notes.

Although 50 years have passed since *Pavlysh Secondary School* was first published, it remains a remarkable account of a holistic system of education that was refined and developed over a 22-year period. Some readers may be put off by the fact that Sukhomlynsky developed his approach in a country that was attempting to build a communist society, while others may be sympathetic to his idealistic vision of communism. With his emphasis on developing empathy, curiosity, creativity and a sense of community, Sukhomlynsky suggests ways of countering the spirit of individualism and consumerism that tends to characterise much of the modern world. It is hard to see how many of the serious issues we face today can be overcome without reversing the trend towards ever-increasing consumption that has characterised developed societies over the past century or more, and without some move towards distributing the world's wealth more equitably. The

COVID-19 pandemic has highlighted the need for collective solidarity, cooperation and mutual support.

I hope readers will find both inspiration and food for thought in this translation. If school principals were to read only the short chapter on health and physical education and implement some of its key ideas, I believe much good would come of it. Sukhomlynsky's approach to teacher mentoring and professional development, described in chapter one, foreshadows some of the most progressive modern practices. His description of the school's extracurricular programs may lead us to reflect on how to better coordinate after-school care programs with school curricula. Studies have shown that schools that prioritise student wellbeing and inculcate positive values also perform well academically,[1] and Sukhomlynsky's work demonstrates this. Sukhomlynsky's books offer a window into the experience of an outstanding educator and invite us to reflect on our own practices.

Vasyl Sukhomlynsky

INTRODUCTION

THIS BOOK IS A SUMMARY of many years of educational experience at Pavlysh Secondary School. In describing our efforts to educate a fully developed personality, the author has attempted to show our work from all angles, to explain the methods applied and how these methods are interconnected.

The aim of our educational work is to give every young man and woman a moral, intellectual, practical and psychological preparation for work, to discover each person's individual talents, aptitudes and abilities. We strive to prepare our students for highly moral and aesthetic relationships, built on friendship and comradeship, on respect for everything that is truly human. Our collective educational work is based on the following views and convictions, which make up our pedagogical creed.

A specific feature of educational work is the fact that we, as teachers, are working for the future. What a child absorbs today is manifested in an adult's character several years and sometimes decades later.

We try to ensure our students work creatively for the good of society. From the time children lift a spoon to their mouths, they work. By the age of 10 or 12, they are harvesting fruit from a tree raised with their own hands.

As they progress, we teach our young people to have a dialectical view of work, of the relationship between humankind and nature, so the knowledge they acquire can become a genuine means of increasing work productivity. At our school, students of all ages develop their characters in an environment characterised by creative work. They see the practical necessity of acquiring knowledge for their work and become convinced, in practice, of the possibility of directing the forces of nature in accord with human reason.

The social and moral progress of a society depends greatly on how the people who make up that society view work and what they find in it, whether it is just a means of earning a living or seen as necessary for a full, rich, interesting spiritual life. That is why we have based our educational approach on the principle that a child must find joy in work, in enriching their knowledge, and in creating things of material and spiritual value for others.

We place great significance on creating an atmosphere of altruistic joy in working for society. Children take delight in work itself. They take pleasure in the work process. It is completely obvious that to create such an atmosphere, work must be intellectually challenging, and science and technology must be applied in daily work activities.

But it is equally essential that the relationships between the members of each group of students should be morally significant. Ultimately, the communist basis of work is not found in technology but in people—in their ideals and aspirations and the goals they achieve through their altruistic voluntary work. In our view, the joy of work comes from maintaining deeply humane relations between young workers, where the prime motivating principle is the creation of happiness and joy for individuals and for society. This is what gives life a higher meaning.

If a school is to fulfil its role in society, there must be a strong connection between school and life, and between students' intellectual and moral education.

As we strive to meet our educational challenges, we apply the ideas of great educators such as Comenius, Pestalozzi, Rousseau, Ushinsky and Diesterweg. These pioneers urged schools, teachers and students to study the surrounding world, to investigate and explain what people can see with their own eyes. It is important that children see the world as it is and also strive to make it better, and the instructional methods chosen by the teacher are of great significance. Diesterweg said that a poor teacher just presents the truth, while a good one teaches students how to find it. The ability to lead students on the path to knowledge, so they discover the truth for themselves, is not only a mark of educational skill. It is also a way of educating correct attitudes towards nature and society, forming firm convictions, and developing an investigative approach towards the phenomena of nature and social life, which is essential for creative work. We see our role in social development as being not just to help students acquire certain knowledge but to instil a desire to go on learning for the rest of their lives. We strive to develop the conviction that intellectual culture is essential for an interesting, valuable, spiritually rich life; that an interesting life is impossible without knowledge because creative work is impossible without knowledge. 'Labour adds oil to the lamp of life, when thinking inflames it.' These words by English economist John Bellers are quoted by Marx in *Capital*. We try to ensure that every student's aspiration to demonstrate their strength and ability, to affirm their worth, is realised through determined, persistent work to acquire knowledge.

Moral convictions are closely connected with formal education, but in some ways they are independent of it. They are independent of a person's practical readiness to create things of material value. A person may have knowledge and be able to work but be unprepared for life in a moral sense. Moral education means developing a world view and convictions while acquiring knowledge and being active, but it is also a specific form of educational work having its own principles. It requires time and involves particular ways of influencing a person's consciousness, character and behaviour.

The curriculum taught in Soviet schools affords great potential for contributing to the formation of moral character, developing decency, honesty, integrity, spiritual courage, fearlessness and steadfastness in the face of difficulties and obstacles. But the acquisition of knowledge alone will not educate such moral qualities. The ideals of integrity, spiritual courage and fearlessness, while they may be inherent in the material studied, will only touch the hearts of adolescents and young men and women when integrity, courage and fearlessness characterise their daily lives.

For example, a student may be deeply moved by the heroic conduct of Giordano Bruno, the steadfastness and determination of the Czech hero Julius Fučík, or the bravery and self-sacrifice of Alexander Matrosov. The student wishes with all their soul to test their strength in some noble, lofty endeavour. The skill and art of education is to help a student to find opportunities for such a trial of strength in real life, to ensure the spark that has been ignited in a young heart is not extinguished. If the educator cannot find these opportunities, the thought born in the student's mind will turn into a blank shot. The more of these blank shots there are, the less sensitive the student will be to the educational methods a teacher employs to influence their thinking and behaviour. We create the opportunities to ensure students acquire moral behaviour at the same time as they acquire moral understanding. These opportunities are inherent in the very structure of collective student life—in the things they do, the goals that motivate them, the type of relationships they form with each other and with adults. The moral significance of their behaviour also depends on what part teachers play in students' lives.

As well as being a mentor to students, a teacher should be a friend. One who overcomes difficulties with them, experiences the same emotions, and shares their joys and disappointments. We try to organise the collective life of our students in such a way that moral behaviour is not seen by them as some sort of exercise organised by a teacher to meet their planning objectives.

Young hearts will not tolerate artificiality. The impulse to act nobly should come naturally, flowing from the very spirit of relationships in the community. For children, the best teacher is the one who, when mixing with them, forgets they are a teacher and sees in the student a friend and like-minded person. Such a teacher knows their student's heart through and through, and their words become a powerful instrument for influencing the young person during their formative years. It is a teacher's sensitivity to students' inner worlds that makes it possible for them to create an atmosphere that encourages moral behaviour. This quality is especially important in a teacher who is educating adolescents. The main reason for difficulties in educating adolescents is they perceive the education process in all its nakedness, while the nature of adolescence is that young people do not want to feel they are being educated.

It is well known that the best form of social education combines the efforts of family and school. The family is the first school of intellectual, moral, aesthetic and physical education. The father, mother, older brothers and sisters, grandfather and grandmother, are a child's first educators during the preschool years and remain so when they go to school. A rich spiritual, moral and aesthetic family life is an important precondition for the successful education of a child at home, in kindergarten and at school. A child enters Grade 1 at the age of seven, but it is desirable that they come under the educational influence of the school two years earlier, from the age of five. Our teachers attach great significance to the moral, intellectual and aesthetic environment in which a child finds themselves from ages two to seven. During the first years of life, a decisive role in child development is played by the people surrounding the child, with all the richness and variety of their human relationships. Science is aware of 32 instances of children who have been raised in the wild by animals. When these 'wild' children were returned to human society, none were able to become fully human because their early years were spent without human company. They had no experience of human relationships during the period they were most sensitive to outside influences. This single fact, which in its own way illuminates the essence of human education, provides incontrovertible evidence that the further a person is from their birth, the more difficult it is to educate them. Nature itself has allotted the lengthy period of the 'infancy of the nervous system' for the education of children.[2] If this period is missed, nothing can be done to remedy it later. However, even in human society, not all children experience the rich human relationships that alone can guarantee the full development of a child's psyche, of their mind, thinking, will, feelings and character. That is why we consider it so important from an educational perspective that every child—every future school student—should enjoy human relationships that are as enriching as possible. We achieve this through parent education.

Cooperation between school and family allows us to give the next generation a good education while also providing an avenue for enhancing the family's moral character, by educating the father and mother. Without parents educating their children, without the mother and father's active participation in the life of the school and the constant spiritual communion and mutual spiritual enrichment of adults and children, it is impossible for the family to fulfil its role as the primary unit of society, impossible for the school to fulfil its role as the most important educational institution, and impossible for society to progress morally.

Life has decisively refuted the suggestion that the future belongs to boarding schools divorced from family life. Everything that weakens families' daily involvement in the education of their children also weakens schools. It follows that one of a school's most important functions is to give parents elementary knowledge about the education of children. The school must have close ties with the parent community. Representatives of the parent body should take a direct part in the education process as members of the school council and participate in discussions about instruction and education.[3]

Experience has convinced us that the most favourable location for a school is in natural surroundings: in a place with abundant greenery and water and not too far from where families live, so the children do not spend too much time getting to school, and parents can visit the school frequently in their spare time. Where the vegetation around a school is sparse, it is necessary to gradually create a green belt, at least in the school's immediate surroundings. One of a school's most important tasks is giving maximum attention to the children's physical education, primarily to strengthen their resistance to disease. Schools should be just as concerned to ensure children do not fall ill, that their organisms are resistant to illness, as they are to ensure their intellectual and moral development.

The power and potential of education are inexhaustible. All children without exception, as long as they have no pathological defects in intellectual development, may successfully complete secondary education. Failure in studies and the need to repeat a year are the result of poor educational work. The school's task is not only to give each person the knowledge necessary for a vocation and worthwhile social activity, but also to give each one happiness in their spiritual life. Happiness is impossible without a rich inner spiritual world, the joy of work and creativity, and a sense of inner worth, honour and pride.

Our school's educational ideal is a holistically and harmoniously developed personality, an active participant in social progress. Harmonious, holistic development means integrating many factors: work, spiritual enrichment in all areas of a person's activity, moral purity in their conduct and relations with other people, physical strength and beauty, diverse aesthetic interests and tastes, and wide-ranging social and personal interests. When a person develops their abilities, contributes, and has their needs met, they feel contented and happy. Harmonious development means that a person blossoms: as a creator of material goods and of things of value to the spiritual life of society; as a consumer of the good things of life, material and spiritual; as someone who values and carefully preserves human culture; as a social activist and citizen; and finally, as the creator of a new family, founded on shared values.

At the centre of harmonious, holistic development is a high level of moral development. We try to inspire the life of our community with lofty moral ideals and ensure relations between all members of our Pioneer and Komsomol groups are based on mutual friendship.

Implementing a program of holistic development requires a complex interweaving of intellectual, physical, moral, work and aesthetic education so all aspects of education are combined in a single process. Everything students receive, and give back in return to society, serves one ultimate aim: to educate a human being with a clear mind, noble heart and golden hands, one who respects other members of society, who values, protects and respects the work, moral worth, intellect and beauty of other people. Intellectual education aims not only to develop and enrich the intellect but also to form refined moral and aesthetic qualities: a preparedness to share one's knowledge with others, a love of work, and an appreciation of beauty in nature and in the life of society. Students enjoy and appreciate the good things created by humanity, and in turn, create new things of value, that in one form or another, are given back to society and benefit others.

For holistic development, it is very important that intellectual life is integrated with work. A spirit of creativity, research and experimentation permeates the spiritual life of our school community. Children work while thinking and think while working. Creative reflection during the work process is one of the things that leads to a love of work. One of our staff's major educational objectives is that graduates from our school should embark upon life as highly skilled workers, capable of both producing things of material value and transforming the work process.

Each stage in intellectual development corresponds to a stage in the development of work skills and work maturity. A student who solves problems involving the application of trigonometric functions during mathematics lessons has also developed advanced work skills. They have mastered comparatively complex skills in electrical circuitry and radio electronics and can operate an internal combustion engine. They can set up a metalworking machine tool, manufacture tools for working with wood and metal and have many other skills. In this integration of intellectual and vocational development, we have found a way to practically meet an important function of schooling. That is, to ensure a citizen of the Soviet Union who has received a secondary education during adolescence and youth has already acquired the broadest possible range of reasonably complex work skills, so they do not need to learn the ABC of technology as adults.

At the current time, Soviet schools are fundamentally changing their conception of a person's strengths and abilities during childhood. Students in primary school (aged 7–11) are mastering a significantly broader range of knowledge and skills than they did formerly. It is possible to begin instruction at the age of six rather than seven, and it is possible to complete primary schooling in three years rather than four. These advancements are based on integrating the development of intellectual and work skills. (A student aged nine or ten can be taught to operate a lathe, and this ability significantly widens the scope of their intellectual work.) The more complex the skills a child acquires while young, the higher the level of their intellectual development when they graduate from secondary school.

It is impossible to give a genuine education if students merely consume things of material and spiritual value that are created by society and given to the school. Education takes place in active work, in creating and strengthening educational infrastructure, in creating things of material value that are essential for life and work and intellectual and aesthetic development. Such work is an important prerequisite for the integrated development of intellectual maturity and readiness for work.

The development of science, technology and thought provides the foundation for the technological progress of our nation. It is a secondary school's task to instil in its students a love of knowledge, books and science. This task is accomplished when teachers and students have rich scientific, intellectual and creative interests.

The pathway to science begins in secondary schools and requires the creation of essential infrastructure. Every student in our senior classes has the opportunity to extend their studies beyond the curriculum in the subject that interests them most and for which they display talent and ability. In addition to the compulsory curriculum, creating a special program for intellectual and vocational development and excellence is expedient. Our teachers try to ensure that every student discovers their talent, that they find their favourite activity, master it and experience the joy of creative work.

In the future, some of our students will become scientists, thinkers or artists; others will become engineers, technicians, doctors or teachers; and others will become carpenters and lathe operators, or agricultural machinery operators. But they will all be united by one characteristic: the leading role of reason and creativity in their work. The creativity of a metal worker or lathe operator, electrician or builder, animal breeder or horticulturalist is no different to the creativity of a mathematician or designer, composer or painter. A school's task is to discover every person's talents and abilities and give them the happiness of interesting, intellectually challenging, creative work for the benefit of society. Attention to every individual, care for every student, relating sensitively and thoughtfully to every child's strengths and weaknesses—that is the bedrock of the education process.

The diversity of interests, aptitudes and abilities in a student community has many facets. This diversity cannot be made to fit a single template. Vocational studies for senior students have not worked when every student in the school has been expected to master the same vocation. Life has shown that attempts to combine general education with training in a specific vocation have harmful consequences. It leads to lower general education standards and superficial mastery of the vocation. A general education secondary school is a polytechnical school. Its main tasks are to give students deep, sound knowledge of the foundations of science; introduce them to the main branches of modern production; and combine theoretical knowledge with practical skills in such a way that individual talents, abilities and interests are fully developed.

A school educates through the atmosphere created by its interesting, multifaceted intellectual life. Not all knowledge can be applied in the workplace. Our system of educational work is founded on the principle that although each student is preparing themselves for work, not everything they learn at school will relate directly to the work in which they will ultimately be engaged. Children see the acquisition of knowledge not only as an obligation but an inner imperative. Without constant intellectual growth, their lives seem grey and uninteresting. The education of this inner imperative is very important for aligning abilities and interests. Issues relating to science and technology, to the social, moral and aesthetic development of society, are discussed by our senior students during debates, discussions and question-and-answer evenings, and very much taken to heart by our young men and women as being of great personal interest.

Holistic personal development involves the acquisition of deep knowledge, active participation in the life of society and work, and the opportunity to freely choose one's profession. All of this presupposes the integration of personal and social interests, and a profession should correspond to one's abilities and calling. This places a great responsibility upon teachers. We believe people blossom when each one is engaged in their favourite work. The more deeply they immerse themselves in that work, the more their talents and abilities are developed, and the happier their life will be.

Marx wrote, 'Without limiting one's sphere of activity, it is impossible to achieve anything of significance in any area'.[4] Our task is to ensure each of our students consciously finds themselves in adolescence and early youth and selects a path in life where their work can attain the highest degree of mastery—creativity. The key to achieving this is discerning each child's greatest strength. To find that 'golden vein' from which their individual development can flow, to ensure each child achieves outstanding success for their age in the activity that most clearly expresses their natural talents. This gradual limitation of the sphere of activity takes place against a broad background of cultural knowledge. It should not in any way be identified with early vocational training or choosing a vocation while still studying at school.

Our school staff work individually with children who show interest in a particular type of intellectual or artistic activity. In the way we organise lessons, in our system of extracurricular work and the development of the community's spiritual interests, we constantly direct our educational approach towards developing talents, educating the intellect and fostering the creative abilities of our students, who in the future will become scientists, thinkers, writers and artists. A teacher's skill is in their ability to perceive a student's giftedness, to identify an area suitable for the application of their intellectual and creative abilities, and to set them tasks in which they will overcome difficulties, facilitating the further development of their abilities. We take care to ensure students live a rich intellectual life during extracurricular activities. This is reflected in the community's spiritual life, raising the intellectual level of all students and developing the abilities of those who are less gifted.

Every individual needs free time every day to develop their gifts and talents while doing their favourite work. For this reason, we consider making free time available to students to be priceless. One of our goals in perfecting our teaching and learning during lessons is to lighten the workload required to master the compulsory curriculum so as to create more free time. We have made it one of the rules of our educational work that a child should have as much free time as they spend on lessons at school. This is especially important in the senior years. Giving students free time to spend as they choose is important for self-education. Work done voluntarily gives rise to new interests and fresh motivation.

The many-faceted spiritual life of our community of teachers and students (their work, their moral, intellectual and aesthetic development, their social involvements) is not just something managed by the teachers and the principal, but a powerful educating force in its own right. The art of education is to awaken this force, to bring it to life and then manage it. Then the spiritual life of the students will attain such a level of independence that at a certain stage, they forget the teacher is a mentor and see them more as an older friend.

It is well known that the less a child senses the teacher's intent behind any educational activity, the greater the educational effect of the activity. We consider this principle the essence of the art of teaching. It allows us to find a way to a child's heart and approach them in such a way that any enterprise they become involved in becomes their own passion, their dream, and the teacher becomes their comrade, friend and like-minded companion. The extent to which the school principal masters this skill determines the educational impulse of the school. It also determines the principal's ability to unite the educational efforts of the teachers. This skill, a love for children, and a broad education, are the main prerequisites for the successful management of the teaching staff.

Self-education takes place when, as students get to know the surrounding world, nature, work and the life of society, they also get to know themselves, evaluating their convictions, actions and behaviour from the perspective of the highest ideals. Self-knowledge and self-affirmation are unthinkable without an ideal, without a model that excites, that is admired, provokes wonder and inspires children, adolescents and young men and women. Being inspired by an ideal generates an aspiration to be good. It makes people think about themselves and teaches them to see the good and bad within themselves. Students begin to consciously test their moral strength and willpower, as if subjecting themselves to an examination.

In facilitating this stage of spiritual development, which coincides with the transition from childhood to adolescence, teachers and school administrators need to show great sensitivity, tact and enormous respect for the student's personality. Adolescents want to manage not just the organisational side of their group activities, but also the psychological processes affecting their thoughts, feelings and experience of life. We need to relate sensitively to the inner spiritual world of adolescents, not crudely imposing our opinions on them, but patiently listening to their views (even if we may disagree with them) and debating issues with them as with an equal.

Teacher management of this process of self-education is subtle, meticulous work that teaches a person self-control in childhood and adolescence so they can discipline themselves to work, follow a routine, overcome difficulties and overcome their own weaknesses. We also need to convince students that they do not need exceptional circumstances to test their strength of will. Exceptional situations can be created under ordinary living conditions through a person's own efforts, and a person can develop a strong will in ordinary work, overcoming difficulties and even overcoming their own weaknesses.

Our management of self-education takes into account that in our country, a general education secondary school is a multi-age school.[5] It is our deep conviction that this makes our educational work easier. Self-education in a multi-age school community is characterised by moral social relationships between older students and younger students. One of our important educational objectives is to ensure our senior and middle school students become educators of our junior students. Only then is it possible to fully cater for age differences.

We view this as a process of collective self-education. During the early years, moral concepts and values take root in children's minds through engaging in emotionally positive relationships. These relationships mainly form when young children and their older friends are united by friendship and interesting activities. In investing their spiritual energies in their younger friends, older students can demonstrate their abilities and also come to know themselves.

The main objective of character education (as a specific process that is to a certain extent independent of classroom lessons) is the development of consciousness: of philosophical, moral and aesthetic understanding, of attitudes, convictions and motives for moral behaviour. This development of consciousness involves converting knowledge into personal convictions and a personal interest in seeing the truth prevail.

Conviction develops when a student becomes aware of the truth during self-motivated activity—when the truth is associated with deep intellectual, moral and aesthetic feelings. The power and beauty of an idea that inspires a student makes them feel that their own soul and actions partake of this power and beauty. This process is an exceptionally important aspect of self-education. We try to organise the spiritual life of the school community in such a way that ideas make a deep impression on the minds of all our students, giving rise to strong emotions and intentions, acting as guiding lights in their personal lives. It is also important that our students have opportunities at school to put inspiring ideas into practice.

Active participation, deeds, work and overcoming difficulties are important prerequisites for conviction. However distant the scientific truths that students come across in their studies may be from daily life (such as the limitlessness of the world in time and space, or the possibility of intelligent life on other planets), we try to direct their intellectual lives so knowledge of the material that is distant from the practice of daily life still serves their earthly interests, and awakens an urge to do good works, to ensure the truth prevails.

To develop consciousness while acquiring scientific knowledge, we need to involve all spheres of a person's spiritual life in learning, especially feelings. Students admire the greatness, courage and spiritual beauty of people who have struggled for the triumph of a scientific view of the world. They develop an urge to understand the surrounding world more deeply. They closely examine everything that happens around them, including the actions of other people. They come to the disturbing conclusion that there is still much in the world that is unworthy of human beings. They see that we need to rid ourselves of social injustice, wars, the threat of nuclear self-destruction, but also things that are wrong in our daily lives. All these thoughts prompt adolescents and young men and women to do something, to find a way to express their active relationship with the world.

Knowledge becomes conviction when a student uses it to acquire new knowledge, widen their horizons and independently find answers to the many questions that arise in work, social activity and one's spiritual life.

For the formation of convictions, it is very important the knowledge acquired while studying the compulsory curriculum is widened and deepened through the extracurricular reading of supplementary scientific literature. Such reading gives children significantly more information than the curriculum requires them to assimilate, broadens their horizons, and makes further study easier as they develop new intellectual interests. The more such interests drive them to learn, explain, investigate and delve deeply into issues through reading or experimentation, the richer their spiritual lives will be, and the deeper their scientific and materialistic convictions.

One of a school's central tasks is the education of refined feelings of a moral, intellectual and aesthetic nature. Such feelings include love for our homeland, for other people, work and culture, respect for the human dignity of our citizens and every decent human being in the world, feelings of friendship and brotherhood for workers, joy in discovering and transforming the world, and taking unselfish pleasure in the cultural riches created by humanity. A genuine human being is unthinkable without kindly feelings. In essence, education begins with the development of personal sensitivity—the ability to respond with heart, thoughts and feelings to everything that happens in the world around us. Personal sensitivity provides a general background for harmonious development, against which any human quality—intelligence, industry, talent—acquires its true meaning, finds its most vibrant expression.

At our school, the education of feelings permeates everything the children do, see and hear. While children logically and intellectually evaluate everything they see or do; they also evaluate everything emotionally. Indeed, if learning is not accompanied by feeling, a child does not fully apprehend what is presented to them.

A child should experience the joy of doing good deeds as often as possible, so the moral and aesthetic satisfaction they enjoy from such deeds can give them a rich spiritual life. That is one of the main rules for the collective life of our student body. The sphere of activity in which such deeds take place is caring for other people. Emotional refinement takes place when a child brings joy to other people, and in consequence, experiences moral and aesthetic pleasure themselves. Anyone who remains indifferent to the grief or suffering of another person is not fulfilling the duty of a Soviet citizen.

A person cannot make themselves experience any particular feeling. As Konstantin Stanislavsky said, 'you cannot produce feelings on demand'. It takes skilled educational work to find, notice and sometimes create a psychological situation that will prompt an emotional response to the phenomena of the surrounding world. The richness and variety of such situations depend on how deeply the educator understands a child's psychology. It depends on their ability to awaken an emotional sensitivity to what the child sees and motivate them to express noble feelings in purposeful activity. The creation of a situation in which thoughts and ideas are deeply experienced by a whole group of students collectively is especially powerful and can lead to significant group action.

The more a goal attracts a person because of the moral ideal it represents, the stronger the feelings accompanying that person's actions. Revealing the attractiveness of an ideal, awakening moral and aesthetic feelings and inspiring students to achieve a goal is an important way to develop students' willpower. When explaining the significance of an activity, educators must encourage students to view their efforts to overcome difficulties as part of a most attractive battle to affirm their personal worth.

Adolescents strive to develop strength of will through taking on 'serious' projects, and this is even more true of senior students. It is in young people's nature to seek out difficulties that take them beyond their studies. To strengthen willpower, it is necessary to involve adolescents and senior students in work of great social significance that plays a definite role in creating and strengthening the material and technological foundations of Soviet society. We consider it exceptionally important for developing students' awareness and the education of civic responsibility that we highlight the social and civic orientation of work. Work in which students feel themselves to be active citizens and campaigners has the greatest educational value. When West German firms refused to supply the Soviet Union with pipes for a gas pipeline, the Soviet nation decided to manufacture the pipes in its own factories. Our senior students decided at a Komsomol meeting that they would collect enough scrap metal for 50 tonnes of pipes. They experienced this work as a fulfilment of their civic duty and an expression of national pride.

The moral significance of a goal elevates work, and students see it as a test and affirmation of their willpower. It is very important that the goals children set are challenging without being exhausting so they can experience the joy of success. If an educator is unable to correctly assess a child's capacity, they may either set work that is not sufficiently challenging or set an excessive amount of work that leads to physical and psychological exhaustion. In either case, the student will subsequently retreat in the face of difficulty. We must keep this in mind when challenging a student's willpower in studies or socially useful work if we wish to encourage self-education. We carefully observe the extent to which a test of willpower is appropriate to a student's inner psychological resources.

The ability to engage students' willpower in their work is a significant educational skill. Each of our teaching staff meticulously studies children's individual strengths and carefully monitors any work that challenges their physical and intellectual abilities to ensure they achieve their goal and experience moral satisfaction in doing so. It is exceptionally important when teaching children self-discipline not to allow a child to become demoralised in their studies and to teach them to waste as little of their energy as possible.

We consider it an important educational objective to help students develop useful habits and avoid harmful ones. Useful habits relate primarily to work and interpersonal relationships within the group. We associate the development of useful habits with the education of feelings and a child's emotional life in general. We organise the children's lives and work so that establishing useful habits gives rise to joyful, positive feelings and leaves a pleasant impression. Emotional and aesthetic motivation makes daily work a spiritual imperative. Only when a person feels and experiences this imperative can their own will become a source of self-education and an important factor in strengthening useful habits.

The more students' daily work activities become habitual, the more opportunities there are for further moral development, for cultivating new moral qualities, interests and involvements. In these circumstances, the educator has limitless opportunities to discover the individual gifts of each student and their vocation.

Such are the educational convictions of our staff. They have taken shape and been consolidated through our common, purposeful, creative work. Thanks to our common educational convictions, we confidently progress towards achieving our goal. That goal is to fully develop the abilities of every student who graduates from our school and embarks on life.

We strive to organise our teaching and educational work so that none of our students feels they lack ability. For example, a senior student may have a quite limited capacity for creative thought, but they may have an exceptional talent for some type of work, which just needs to be developed. We seek to ensure they achieve exceptional mastery, even perfection. For one student, it may be a talent in horticulture; for another, it may be technical innovation, building, or caring for animals. After all, the goal of education is to ensure each person experiences the joy of work, today and in the future.

In our work, we observe the principle that we should not allow a single day of school studies to pass without success, without a result. We conduct meticulous individual work with students who find study difficult. By developing these students' individual interests, we ensure each one achieves success, if not in studies then in work. This success affords moral support, inspiring the student to overcome their difficulties in study.

As a rule, none of our students repeats a year. The few cases where a student does repeat a year are due to prolonged illness (2–4 months). The following table shows the student pass rate each year for the past 12 years. These figures demonstrate that concern for children's health is the number one factor that can lift educational standards.

School year	Number of children at the school	Students repeating year	Repeating due to illness	Pass rate %
1955/56	418	15	12	96.5
1956/57	406	14	12	96.6
1957/58	407	9	6	97.8
1958/59	422	6	4	98.5
1959/60	463	6	5	98.7
1960/61	477	5	4	99.0
1961/62	516	4	3	99.3
1962/63	560	3	3	99.5
1963/64	614	3	2	99.6
1964/65	640	2	2	99.8
1965/66	630	4	3	99.4
1966/67	570	2	2	99.7

Making sure our educational work is closely connected with real life, we seek to ensure the most progressive aspects of community life are incorporated into the education process. Each of our students learns from experience that spiritual and cultural growth is only possible when one is involved in work of social significance. Further, work only becomes interesting and attractive when it is illuminated by civic feeling, intelligence and creative thought. That is why we try to introduce variety into the interests that unite children in a group. These may include interesting ideas for creative work, engaging books, issues of a social, moral and aesthetic nature that concern society and consequently concern the children, leisure activities, travel, hiking, games and so on.

We try to ensure that society's drive to harness the productive potential of science is clearly reflected in our educational work. The agricultural work conducted by our students involves experimentation and research. In our technical clubs, children's creative thought is directed to finding ways to replace manual work with mechanisation. Our young chemists are studying how to increase soil fertility with chemicals. Combining physical work with scientific thought is one way to encourage self-education during the work process.

We also connect our school with real life by instilling in our students the conviction that the main source of our material wellbeing and rich spiritual life is the labour of workers in industry and agriculture who produce metal and coal, oil and machinery, electricity and fertilisers, bread and meat. Work is the foundation of human happiness. Our whole system of moral and vocational education instils in our students (who are about to embark on independent working lives) an aspiration to create material benefits for as many members of society as possible. From an early age, our students gain satisfaction from the fact they are contributing something to others, to society, seeing in this a moral justification for all the good things they receive from the older generation.

Our staff are convinced that there can be no true education without self-education. We consider the student community an independent educational force that can only be managed by studying the surrounding environment and discovering genuine opportunities to actively participate in the life of society. The formation and development of social awareness in our school community, a feeling of collective responsibility to society, provides the foundation for independence and self-motivated activity. We do not believe in organisation for organisation's sake, subordination for subordination's sake, or management for management's sake. Independent, collective activity is impossible unless students are inspired by a single idea, unless they feel their work is part of the nation's work, that their ideals are the ideals of the nation.

Educational management of independent student activity also takes place when we utilise the many opportunities life affords for the most varied spiritual connections between students. So, within the student community as a whole, there are many groups based on common interests, activities and ideas. This is of prime importance for developing the individuality of every student.

Every person has their own spiritual requirements and interests, and no single group can fully satisfy all of these. They will only be satisfied if the spiritual life of each student takes place in several groups, each with its specific goals and sphere of activity. One group may satisfy interests associated with a student's intellectual development. In another group, the student may develop their aesthetic interests, and in a third group, they may join with friends in creative work. A fourth group may be created by the students themselves to organise leisure activities. Some groups operate at school, while others are based at students' homes. Some groups bring students of different ages together, while others involve students of the same age. The variety of these collective links guarantees genuine independence.

Staff from left: Andrei Barvinsky, Evdokiya Kolomyichenko, Vasyl Sukhomlynsky, Matrena Syrovatka, Mariya Verkhovynina, Yakim Lysak, Olga Stepanova

CHAPTER ONE

Our Staff

Reflections on School Leadership

TO LEAD A SCHOOL WELL means to have a thorough knowledge of educational theory, which should provide the foundation for a knowledge-based approach to education and instruction, and the organisation of the work of the school community—teachers and students. The principal needs to be a master of the education process, which encompasses both academic instruction and personal development, to have mastered the art of interacting with children, adolescents, and young men and women. Broadly, education is the continual spiritual enrichment and renewal of both those who are educated and those who educate. Moreover, this process is distinguished by its deeply individual nature. Any particular pedagogical principle that is valid in one case will be neutral in a second case and absurd in a third.

School principals will only be good and authoritative leaders of teachers and students if they continue to perfect their skills as teachers and educators. A good school principal is first and foremost a good organiser, educator and authority on the curriculum, for the students who attend their lessons and for every student and teacher in the school.

The great responsibility placed on the principal's shoulders leads to many demands on their personal qualities, their morality, intellect and willpower. The most important quality—without which a teacher cannot become a principal, just as not everyone can become a teacher—is a deep love for children, a natural inclination to spend time in the company of children, deep humanity and an ability to penetrate a child's inner world, to understand and feel each student's individuality.

This ability, which to a certain extent is the result of a high level of pedagogical development, is determined first and foremost by a person's ability to apprehend the world through the heart—to understand and feel the joys and sorrows of others, to respond to their pleas for help.

You cannot learn to love children from any educational establishment or book. This capacity is developed through participation in social living and interactions with other people. But, by its very nature, educational work—the daily interaction with children—deepens teachers' love for others and faith in them. A vocation for educational work is developed in schools in the process of that work.

This book is based on personal experience. It reflects the outcome of the author's 33 years of educational work at Pavlysh Secondary School, including 26 years as its principal.[6] Working in a school and educating children has become my vocation. Before entering the pedagogical institute, I worked for two years as a primary teacher and Pioneer leader. When I entered college (I studied for three years by correspondence and one year internally), I was convinced that work in a school was the most interesting and absorbing work possible.

I remember the Poltava Pedagogical Institute from which I graduated and the lecturers in pedagogy, literature and history with great warmth. For them, pedagogy was not some dry collection of findings, but a vibrant, living account of the art of education, the methods for making an impression on people's feelings and consciousness. They taught me to love language. I will never forget how we wrote descriptions of an evening sunset and a January blizzard.

After graduating from the language and literature faculty, it was with some trepidation that I crossed the threshold of a secondary school. While I taught senior high school students, I could not live without some contact with younger children. I was a leader of one of the Pioneer troops, assisted the senior Pioneer leader and went with the children on hiking trips.

Now, when I reflect on the work of a teacher, I come to the conclusion that children are drawn to those who are drawn to them, who cannot live without them and find pleasure and happiness in communicating with them. During the first years of my teaching work, of course, I did not think about this correlation. Children just gave me joy. As soon as the school year ended, I set out on hikes with them, into the fields and forests and to the river. I felt happy spending the night with the children under the bright southern stars, making porridge, telling the children stories, legends and fairy tales. That is probably why the children walked with such pleasure in the hot sun, carrying heavy rucksacks.

During the summertime, many young children were left unsupervised (at that time, there were no crèches or kindergartens in the village). I collected the little ones and played with them and organised something like today's Pioneer camps for them on the banks of a lake.

Some young adolescents wanted to go on a 'sea voyage' in the summer—to sail in a boat across the lake and down the river to land on some 'uninhabited' island. I have only just realised that I put this idea in their heads, but at the time, I thought they came up with the idea themselves, independently of my tales. But we did not have a boat, so I collected money throughout the school year, and in spring, I bought two boats from the fishermen. The parents bought a third, and our flotilla set sail. Some readers may think I am presenting these facts as evidence of my extraordinary concern for children. No, I bought the boats because I wanted to give the children joy, and their joy gave me more happiness than anything else.

I was interested in each child: I wanted to find out what made them tick, what interested and excited them, what joys and sorrows they experienced. My circle of friends widened with each passing day. My friends and, as I later understood, my students included children I did not teach in class.

As a teacher of language and literature, I was entrusted with the organisation of a literature circle. I was given a brochure with methodological guidelines, but from the very beginning, things took a different direction to those suggested by the guidelines. I began to read the children my own poems. I was not trying to awaken the children's poetic talents, but somehow we created a group of young poets and literature lovers.

On quiet spring evenings, clear sunny days, Sundays and public holidays, we went into the fields, to the banks of a lake or an oak grove, sat somewhere on the grass and composed verses and poetic descriptions of what we could see and hear, and what we were thinking. We compiled collections of these verses and stories, which we called a literary journal.

Some of the children uncovered genuine poetic talents. I remember being struck by Alyosha K.'s poems, which drew detailed pictures. Imagine my amazement when I learned Alyosha was getting failing grades in his native language and did not want to participate in mathematics lessons. It seemed grotesquely absurd. The more I got to know Alyosha, the more I was convinced that no normal person should be a failure. In each child, some ability manifested itself, and the conviction grew in me that there is no such thing as a child without ability or talentless or lazy children. I did not have a single failing student. I was surprised to hear that in some teachers' classes, children were not learning their lessons, were getting unsatisfactory grades (twos) and repeating the year. It seemed to me, the main things that should motivate a student to study are respect for the teacher, faith in their own ability, interest in learning and a thirst for knowledge.

I wanted to satisfy the various interests and aspirations of my students as fully as possible. In other words, I wanted it to be interesting for the children to live and to study.

In those years, the nation was excited by Soviet pilots' first long-distance flights, distant expeditions into the Arctic, and the construction of new cities in the taiga. The children and I wrote poems about the heroes involved in these exploits and pretended to be explorers of new lands. On the outskirts of the town was a half-ruined, abandoned peasant house. We turned it into something like a ship's cabin and called our imaginary ship the 'Northern Robinson'. Here we read books about famous explorers and drew pictures of our imaginary discoveries.

I will never forget those autumn evenings when the wind was howling outside, and the rain was beating on the glass windows—the 'portholes' of our ship. We huddled around the fire, with bated breath, living through the amazing adventures of Amundsen and

Miklouho-Maclay, struggling with them over the Arctic ice or through tropical rainforests. In the winter, we made igloos and ice hummocks and pretended to be members of the *Chelyuskin* expedition.[7]

Now, a quarter of a century later, in the same tumbledown hut (repaired but deliberately left half-ruined), the children of my first students pretend to be astronauts. The spirit of romanticism continues to permeate the 'cabin', and just as before, the wood crackles in the fire on the long autumn evenings. I am quite convinced that you cannot educate children without romance, without the opportunity for children to meet their teacher in a friendly family atmosphere, such as in our 'Northern Robinson'.

My first years of teaching (before I was appointed as a principal) were years of happy (and sometimes sad and difficult) discovery. I saw into those secret corners of a child's soul that hold hidden joy, limitless faith in adults and a trusting readiness to open up to an adult, but sometimes also opposing features—guardedness, mistrust, pain, hurt, anger, deliberate opposition and stubbornness. I was amazed by the multifaceted, sometimes completely unexpected refraction of grief and, not infrequently, anger in children's hearts. I became convinced that the most frightening thing in life—and the thing most in need of love, affection, care, attention and kindness—is the crippled, disfigured heart of a child. I encountered several children, about each of whom a book could have been written: Kolya G., who had witnessed a murder; Oksana Kh., who never knew her mother or father and was raised by a distant relative who treated her like a servant and inculcated in her inhuman attitudes towards life; Vitya K., who grew up in the family of a Kulak, imbibing misanthropic values; and Nadya Z., who belonged to 'no-one', an abandoned child who defended herself from ridicule with anger and mistrust.

I was drawn to these and other equally unfortunate children by simple human compassion, and many such difficult children became my friends during the first years of my work in schools.

And so, when I was appointed a school principal, I was already deeply convinced that education only becomes an effective force when it is founded on faith in the child. Without faith in a child, without trust, all pedagogical wisdom, educational methods and procedures will come tumbling down like a house of cards. Moreover, if children are to believe in their own powers and learn never to retreat in the face of difficulty, they must believe in their teachers and see them as models and a source of help and support.

Teachers' communication with children during lessons is only one part of their educational work. Children's education, their personal development and moral growth, largely depend on the work carried out during leisure time, unregulated by timetables and routines. Teachers only become educators when they are organisers and leaders of groups in which children's personal development takes place and their moral relationships with each other manifest. In those early years, life showed me that the Pioneer and Komsomol groups provide a potent avenue for educating active citizens.

The Komsomol organisation in the class I was responsible for in 1938 took on the challenge of growing a hectare of wheat with a yield three times higher than was usual on the collective farm. This work had a clearly expressed civic significance. We were not just working; we were demonstrating through our work that science can help people achieve heightened labour productivity. Our success (the Komsomol members achieved a yield of 3.8 tonnes per hectare) elevated us in our own eyes; we felt ourselves to be participants in socialist construction.

Every child is a unique world of thoughts, views, feelings, experiences, interests, joys and sorrows, worries and grief. Teachers should be aware of their students' inner worlds but should never approach students as objects of research. Teachers should become children's friends, take their interests to heart, experience their joys and sorrows, forgetting that they are teachers. Then children will open up to them. A school is only a centre of education when it has become a centre of joy for children, a centre of interest, inviting them to taste knowledge and learning.

When I was appointed a school principal, I was overjoyed to have the opportunity to put my convictions into practice with the rest of the staff and have each pupil as my student. That was on the eve of the Great Patriotic War. I had five years of teaching experience behind me and my whole life in front of me, which I could not imagine without children.

The Soviet school during the pre-war years had created a cultural wealth that played a huge role in the fate of our homeland. That wealth was comprised of the younger generation's love for their homeland, readiness to give their lives for it, faith in the communist ideal, industriousness and deep interest in learning. The best teachers have always considered correctly organised work to be a great educator. In our school, even before the war, every class had its own garden plot where young fruit trees were propagated, young technicians and designers worked away in our workshop and practical classrooms, and senior students worked during the summer holidays operating tractors and combine harvesters.

The moral potential of the younger generation, educated in Soviet schools, manifested itself for all to see during the years of the Great Patriotic War. Of the 147 young men and women who graduated from our school during the six years before the war, 42 gave their lives fighting for their homeland's freedom and independence. The young women who remained in territory occupied by the fascists took part in antifascist underground organisations for young people. One of them, Vera Povsha, led such a group, compiling and distributing leaflets among the population. The young woman was arrested and bestially tortured. Covered in blood, Vera still found the strength to cry out during the last moments of her life, 'Long live our homeland!'

I joined the army at the very beginning of the war, taking part in battles near Smolensk and Moscow and then on the Kalinin front. In 1942 I was seriously wounded near Rzhev and spent several months in a hospital in the settlement of Uva, in Udmurtia. When I was released from the hospital and demobilised as an invalid, I took up a position as the Uva Secondary School principal. It was a difficult time, but a year and a half at the school left me with happy memories. The staff and students formed a closely knit community that cared for each child.

As soon as our village was freed from occupation, I returned to my own school. The 29 months of occupation had left a terrible mark not only on the economy but on our spiritual life. Everything we had created with such love during the pre-war years—laboratories, a library, a flourishing orchard—was destroyed. Even the desks were burned. With great difficulty, our teachers and the senior students prepared the classrooms and laboratories for lessons and enrolled all the children of school age.

The war had brought children terrible suffering—the loss of their parents. Without genuine friendship between teacher and child, without giving school instruction a deeply moral foundation, it was impossible even to consider requiring all children to attend school. Many children's spiritual world had been deformed by the horrors of occupation, and the heartless atmosphere of apathy and indifference to others' fates that had arisen in some families. Several children whose parentage was unknown appeared in the village. They lived in pitiful circumstances. The state was not yet able to accommodate all those in need in its children's homes.

Sensitivity, friendship, collectivism—every teacher must bring these characteristics into the spiritual life of a school. I considered that my primary mission at that time was to ensure all the staff shared my educational convictions. Before the beginning of the school year and in the days that followed, I tried to impress upon them that many of our difficulties could only be overcome with genuine humanity. Many of the children who were coming to us had never known care and affection. They were wary and distrustful; some were embittered. The only teachers who could educate these children well would be those who believed they were essentially beautiful children, and the goodness in them was sure to triumph if they received the help they needed. I advised my colleagues not to alienate the children with mistrust, suspicion and doubts about their honesty and good motivation. I advised them not to interrogate children about their past lives, so as not to open old wounds, but to definitely find out as much as they could about each child, especially those who had known grief at a young age. We should find out the sources of that grief, but in such a way that the child was unaware of our inquisitiveness.

The advice I gave then has remained a statement of my educational convictions throughout my life. Faith in human beings is the most precious thing for me, and I jealously guard it against defilement by mistrust or indifference.

In difficult situations, an educator's honesty, decency and openness is especially important. I advised teachers to say directly if they have doubts about something, not to harbour those doubts in their soul, especially doubts about a child, as that is a harmful burden for an educator. If I saw in a teacher's actions or words a lack of faith in a child or in the power of education, I made every effort to convince them of their error, and I still do this. And I do mean to convince, not to take the administrative approach of forcing or coercing.

During those years, life convinced me again and again of the enormous educational force of our school community. Our Komsomol organisation 'adopted' a young student who was constantly unsupervised at home. The young people independently created a Pioneer camp during the summer.

Individual, friendly, open, heartfelt conversation is the main method in a principal's work with teachers. After all, education is a most subtle spiritual activity. I would compare an educator's influence on a student with the influence of music. 'To try and influence someone's spiritual life through force,' wrote Tolstoy, 'is like trying to catch the rays of the sun. No matter what you cover them with, they always come out on top.' I can remember thousands of conversations with teachers. Some gave me joy and some bitter disappointment. Sometimes I had to talk for one, two or three hours about a single word, even a smile or an angry glance. Once, while checking the homework in Grade 5, the literature teacher called on a weak student. She did not like the sentence he had composed. Without saying a word, she dismissed him with a wave of her hand, and the boy cried all evening. It was necessary to have a long conversation to show the teacher her mistake, to explain that her gesture was an expression of her educational views: indifference to the child, a lack of faith that he could achieve anything worthwhile, believing that a bad student will always be a bad student.

Only when I have succeeded in convincing a teacher and they begin to express their conviction in practical actions (of course, this is not achieved in a single conversation nor by conversation alone) do I consider that I have fulfilled my mission as a principal. I have never written a single direction relating to the process of education—that is a complete waste of time in a principal's work. Neither have I ever brought a difference of opinion with a teacher to a staff meeting.

Knowing each student's inner world as deeply as possible is the first commandment for both teacher and principal. A new student arrives at the school. I study them closely; I seek some means of heartfelt communication with them that might motivate their active participation, the vibrant expression of their wishes and interests. A child's behaviour must tell me what I need to know about them: that is one of the principles of educational management of a group of children.

In our school, we have dozens of educational and hobby groups, and the multifaceted spiritual life of the students flows through each of them. The principal is an active participant in these groups, and first and foremost, a friend and comrade to the students. The path to the heart of a child is through friendship, through common interests, passions, feelings and experiences. I could narrate at least ten instances when the heart of a seemingly unapproachable, secretive child opened up simply because we shared a common joy, were enthused by the same activity, book, game or journey.

I remember how an obstinate, unsettled boy, very embittered about something, entered our school in Grade 5. He did everything in defiance of his teachers. I advised the staff that we needed to find some common interest with the boy, and then his heart would open up to us, and we would learn what we needed to about him. So we began seeking out his interests. The whole staff was involved. I was convinced that somewhere we would find common ground with this obstinate Grade 5 student—in the creative writing circle, the nature study circle, the young explorers club (we met from time to time in our 'Northern Robinson'), the green laboratory, the young electricians' circle, the young mechanics, the young biochemists or the animal husbandry group.

I found common ground with him twice: the first time in the nature study group, the second time in the science fiction club (we have one of those too). For a long time, we were unable to acclimatise that noble southern plant, the peach tree, to our locality. Finally, we attempted to graft some buds of that warmth-loving tree to the frost-hardy apricot. Spring came. Each day the most impatient among us ran to the orchard to see if any buds had opened. I went to the orchard early in the morning. Then one day, I saw a boy squatting near an apricot tree. It seemed to me that he was holding his breath, afraid of harming the shining little green shoot that had just appeared from one of the buds on this sunny morning. I was so excited about this first shoot that, at first, I did not think about who had come into the orchard before me. Then I raised my head to share my joy with this other person. At that moment, he also raised his head, evidently wishing to share his joy with me. Our eyes met, and it was him, Volodya N. We put our arms over each other's shoulders and from that time became friends. Then I came to know the heart of this intelligent, wonderfully sensitive, sincere child and also the terrible experience that had already crippled his soul and undermined his trust in other human beings.

I will not tell of that now. I have mentioned this genuine human encounter with Volodya to reinforce the principle: approach a child as one human being to another, find in their heart the part that responds to your call, and it will be easier for you to overcome the obstacles that impede education. I always tried to convince teachers that if you only see a student from behind your classroom desk, if they only come to you when summoned, if their whole conversation with you is just answering your questions, no knowledge of psychology will help you. You need to meet the student as a friend, as a like-minded person, and experience with them the joy of victory and the disappointment of loss.

Just as a doctor needs to know in detail what can strengthen and weaken the organism to prevent and cure disease, the school's main educator, the principal, needs to study and analyse the conditions in which a child's life unfolds during the years preceding his enrolment at school. In this respect, I was especially interested in the most difficult children. (If they do not change for the better at school, then the well-behaved children will change for the worse, learning bad attitudes and habits from the difficult children.) Each week I spend time with the families of these difficult children, trying to understand what has led to the formation of their values. I chat with the parents, neighbours and teachers who have already been involved in the children's upbringing. The staff come to know each child as a unique world of thoughts, feelings and desires, a world whose harmony has been destroyed by callous, egotistical people.

One such child was 11-year-old Kolya S. When he arrived at our school, we were all struck by his unsociable nature and bitterness. In a teacher's sincere kindness and affection, he saw some kind of trickery and subterfuge. He sought to isolate himself, avoided other students, and did not want to work. I went to the farmstead where Kolya's parents lived and learned some astonishing things. It turned out that he had grown up in a narrow little world, isolated from other people, in an atmosphere of dishonesty, deceit and crime. The moral concepts a previous teacher had tried to impart to her students in the small one-teacher school where Kolya had previously studied had been addressed to some abstract student, viewed by the children just as material to be memorised. The child was inquisitive, curious and often asked, in the teacher's words, 'strange' questions: 'Why does Uncle Fyodor say at the brigade meeting that they need to look after collective farm property, but then he brings home a whole load of maize from the field? Why has Uncle Grisha (who served in the fascist police force during the occupation and now works as a forester) built two houses for himself, while Aunty Galya, whose husband died at the front, cannot manage to get a pension? Why does the collective farm manager drive the car to the market in town every Sunday with his wife when he wouldn't let Grandpa Anton use the car to go to the hospital when he got sick, and Grandpa Anton died?'

The teacher brushed aside these questions, but the child's heart was confused. On the one hand, there were stories in books saying what a person should be like; on the other was his father's advice: without trickery you cannot survive, work loves a fool and the fool praises work, and so on, evil about which people always spoke under their breath. The child lost faith in everything bright, clean and fair. He suspected the heroic images of Pavlik Morozov and Zoya Kosmodemyanskaya were just fairy tales, like the tales about beautiful princesses, the elixir of life and epic heroes. Kolya became embittered, disobedient and irritable. He was rude to his teacher and his mother.

I travelled to the farmstead two more times, became acquainted with the people there and their little working group's life, and tried to understand the interests of the people surrounding the boy. The teaching staff devoted more than one conversation to Kolya's spiritual life. We came to the unanimous conclusion that there are still remote corners of our country where children are surrounded by a stifling atmosphere of petty smallholders' interests, acquisitiveness and the thirst for profit.

In such circumstances, if the educational work in schools is poorly arranged, a sensitive, impressionable child, thirsting for light, goodness and justice, but not finding support, experiences confused emotions. The little person does not want to accept injustice, and protests, but this protest is far from a conscious juxtaposition of good and evil. The child becomes bitter towards everyone and everything. The education of such a student is a very complex and difficult process. They have to be convinced that goodness, truth and beauty will triumph in our society, that a human being is not just a speck of dust in the whirlwind of fate but an active defender of goodness, truth and beauty.

Such conversations about the education of difficult children and the sources of their morality develop in us, as teachers, sensitivity, attentiveness, educational perception and observational skill.

In Pavlysh, we study and get to know the spiritual life in each family, but this is only the beginning of an education that brings family and school together. My deep conviction is that everyone must study pedagogy, both teachers and parents, and we try to give all parents some fundamental pedagogical knowledge. For this, we have a school for parents that parents enrol in two years before their children start school and attend until their children complete secondary school. The course in psychology and pedagogy in our school for parents encompasses 250 hours of classes. (Incidentally, this is significantly more than any college or university course.) Those attending the school for parents are divided into five groups according to the age of their children: preschool (aged 5–7), Grades 1 and 2, Grades 3 and 4, Grades 5–7, and Grades 8–10.[8] Each group attends classes twice a month. The classes are mainly lectures and discussions led by the principal, deputy principal and the most experienced teachers. Theoretical knowledge in psychology and pedagogy closely correlates with practical education in the family.

The program covers all sections of the institute course, but we give special attention to developmental psychology, the psychology of personality, and the theory of physical, intellectual, moral and aesthetic education. We try to ensure every mother and father relates the theoretical knowledge they acquire in our school for parents to the spiritual life of their own child. This requires great sensitivity and tact from us as teachers. We never 'expose a child's soul' or discuss sensitive, painful aspects of family relationships. Such issues may only be addressed in individual conversations.

We cannot imagine a complete education involving coordination between family and school without our school for parents.

Another constant area of concern for our principal is the children's health. Successful education is impossible without constant attention to strengthening children's health. Sometimes the only reason a child is not succeeding is that they are sick or ailing.

To have the best possible understanding of factors affecting children's health, I studied specialist medical literature. With every month, I became more convinced of the importance for educators to understand the inner physiological, psychological, developmental and sexual processes taking place in their students' organisms. A great deal depends on this understanding. Often children begin to fall behind in their studies because they are ailing, without being aware of it. An educator has no right to be ignorant of what is going on with a child, why they are unwell, and how their health is reflected in their intellectual development.

In our country, an atmosphere of love for knowledge, study and education is created by the very structure of our social life, and the education of a child's love for study depends greatly on the teacher. The acquisition of knowledge should give a child joy and a full spiritual life. The prime source nourishing a child's love for knowledge is the high level of teachers' intellectual culture, and first and foremost, of the school's principal. It is impossible to manage the instructional process in a school without the knowledge of all the subjects in the curriculum. From the very first days of work as a principal, I set about the study of physics, mathematics, chemistry, geography, biology and history. Over the course of three years, I independently studied all the school's textbooks and the basic methodological literature. I paid special attention to mathematics, solving all the problems in the textbooks and many of those in the supplementary textbooks. In my notebooks, I gradually organised these problems into sections and topics, and new problems are added to each notebook with each passing year.

However, this was only the beginning. I made it a rule to follow the latest developments and achievements in the sciences that are included in the school curriculum. It is especially important to keep abreast of developments in mathematics, physics, biology, biochemistry and electronics. In my 'laboratory', as I call my office, there are piles of exercise books (each devoted to a science or a scientific problem), containing thousands of notes from scientific journals or cuttings from newspapers. My interests and passions are sometimes communicated directly to students, but mainly via the teachers.

For example, I became very interested in research into biochemical processes taking place in the soil. Research in this area, both at home and abroad, is opening up particularly promising avenues for increasing crop yields. I had many interesting conversations about this research with teachers who loved agriculture and horticulture. The biology teacher and several of the primary school teachers became engrossed in this topic, and they presented the children with a fascinating picture of life in the soil and the wonderful microorganisms that help create plant nutrients. The children became enthused and began to conduct experiments in the nature room, the green laboratory, the experimental plot and the greenhouse. For the principal, this became yet another area of common interest with the students, another avenue for reaching the hearts of the most difficult children.

I take great interest in reading the scientific literature on genetics, automation, electronics and astronomy. The physics teachers know that no new development will escape our attention. Each conversation with a physics teacher gives rise to a new initiative and a new plan. I am drawn to the workshops and laboratories where various clubs gather for young people interested in automation and radio electronics, technology and astronomy. With the same enthusiasm as the children, I assemble my equipment and models as I set up a language laboratory. With the students, I equip a meteorological station and a children's astronomical observatory and excitedly gaze at planets and galaxies alongside them, dreaming of distant worlds.

With excitement, I look forward to the spring awakening of the soil, the movement of sap in the trees, the first leaves and flowers. In our school orchard and experimental plot, we conduct many experiments and grow dozens of varieties of crops and fruit trees. During spring, summer and autumn, our young botanists conduct several excursions into the fields to collect plants. We select drought-tolerant specimens of wheat and other grain crops for breeding purposes, collect soil samples and look for new (possibly as yet unknown to science) types of useful microorganisms capable of increasing soil fertility. During the winter months, you can smell the sweet scent of flowers and see golden lemons ripening in our greenhouses and lemonarium. These flowering areas attract those who need to be drawn into the beauty of work.

I am a teacher of literature, and I confess to being in love with my subject. My teaching methodology focuses on developing the ability to read, understand and relate emotionally to the primary source. At our school, we consider a necessary precondition for success in teaching literature to be a love of language, an appreciation of the beauty of words. As a staff, we constantly strive to refine our speech. We consider primitive, imprecise speech and poor diction signs of ignorance. 'Speak correctly. Every word has a precise meaning. An inability to choose the appropriate word is like drawing with a nail instead of with a sharpened pencil.' These words head a stand in the staff room where we post various materials concerning the development of oral language (descriptions of model lessons, cuttings from newspapers).

I have a rich personal library comprised of works of significant literary merit. I have strived to make this collection an exemplar of aesthetic culture. I lend my books to teachers, students and parents. Each encounter with such readers brings me great joy: we start chatting, I learn of others' interesting life experiences, and that widens my educational outlook.

I take great pleasure in tending to a grapevine and in reading poetry about nature and about humankind. I write for myself, not for publication, and to teach my students how to choose words carefully. During my teaching career, I have written over a thousand miniature compositions, each devoted to some natural phenomenon, feeling and experience. (A list of some of the topics of these compositions is contained in Appendix 3 at the end of this book.)

I sometimes read my miniature compositions and poems to students. I take joy in sharing my thoughts and impressions of the surrounding world, of nature and people. I see the children are particularly interested in the compositions and poems in which they recognise something they have experienced themselves. When one of my compositions or poems touches their hearts, they also take up their pens and try to express their feelings. It seems to me that sensitivity to language and an urge to express in words the subtlest movements of the human soul are an important source of genuine human refinement.

I cannot imagine teaching language without walks and excursions through our local area, contemplating natural scenes and expressing feelings in words. On the bank of a river, in a field, by an evening campfire, listening to the quiet sound of autumn rain in a shelter constructed from branches, I teach the children to express their thoughts about what surrounds them. I take joy in my love of language being transferred to the children, engaging their thoughts and feelings. They feel the beauty, flavour and subtlest nuances of words; they compose poems and miniature descriptions of nature. Sensitivity to the beauty of language is a powerful force, ennobling a child's spiritual world. This sensitivity is one of the sources of human refinement.

As principal, I try to ensure my main focus is on educational matters rather than business matters. Every day, early in the morning before classes start, I spend 10 or 15 minutes conversing with our business manager and do not devote any further attention to such matters for the rest of the day. All business matters I feel concerned about are recorded in a notebook (for the next meeting or discussion with teachers). A significant number of business matters are decided according to our educational principles, involving the whole school community, both teachers and students. Such matters are subordinated to our educational goals.

Whether a principal is managing the education process, participating in the life of student groups, or entering children's spiritual world, they need to pay close attention to intellectual development. Educational ideas must be incarnated in thousands of varied activities, always keeping in mind the development of the school community. In the life of a school, there are thousands of educational phenomena. The more you think about each of them—the lives of individual students and their actions—the more practical problems arise that need to be addressed by the whole school community. Logical analysis of the education process is best conducted at the end of the working day, more often than not in conversation with one of the teachers or parents, director of studies or students. Here are some of the issues addressed in such conversations or reflections:

How do we draw children into involvement with the school community? What inner, spiritual connections—thoughts, feelings, experiences—can form a healthy basis for strengthening the school community and children's friendships with each other? How can we ensure that personal happiness, the personal joys of each child, are harmonised with the community's and society's interests? Why do some children develop individualistic habits, and how can we prevent this? What has and is being done so children and their teachers may share common thoughts, interests and aspirations? By what means are the spiritual riches developed by humanity being passed on to the children? How can we educate honesty, honour and integrity, so children stand up to evil, injustice and deceit? How can we ensure every child, from a young age, feels their indebtedness to their homeland and previous generations for the material and spiritual benefits they enjoy, for their happy childhood? How do we develop an inner imperative to work? How do we bring moral, intellectual, vocational, physical and aesthetic development into harmony? How do we ensure morality informs every aspect of our students' lives? Does each student find happiness and personal satisfaction in what they do and what they give back to society? Is there a harmony between what a young person receives from older generations and what they give back to society, or what they are preparing to do in the future? What motivates those children who are of special interest and concern to us as teachers? How rich is the intellectual life of our school community? Are teachers doing everything they can to develop students' intellectual interests? What books are our students reading? What issues of science and technology are exciting our senior students? How is knowledge being applied in practice? Are students' individual needs and interests being satisfied? How are our school graduates performing in the workplace?

Reflection on these questions forms an important basis for practical planning to decide what to do tomorrow, in a month or a year's time, and to set goals for our school community. Each issue listed above from time to time becomes a subject for discussion among our school staff. We try to ensure all our staff, from the principal to the caretaker, is involved in realising educational ideas and that our community lives by these ideas.

Our teachers and educators

WHAT MAKES A GOOD TEACHER? First and foremost, a teacher must be a person who loves children, finds joy in their company, believes every child can become a good person, knows how to make friends with children, takes children's joys and sorrows to heart, knows a child's soul and never forgets that they were once a child themselves.

Second, a good teacher is a person who has a thorough knowledge of the discipline on which the subject they teach is based, loves their subject, and knows its horizons, keeping abreast of new discoveries, research and achievements. Additionally, a school can take great pride in teachers who are also enthused by the problems their subject grapples with and are capable of independent research. Good teachers know many times more than is required by the secondary school program. For them, a school subject is just the ABC of their discipline. Deep knowledge, broad horizons and interest in research are all necessary for a teacher to reveal to students the attractive power of knowledge, of the discipline, of scholarship and learning. Students should see in their teachers intelligent, knowledgeable, thinking people in love with learning. The deeper a teachers' knowledge, the wider their horizons, and the more erudite they are, the more they are not only teachers but educators. It is important for primary school teachers to have good general education and a special interest in a particular branch of knowledge.

Thirdly, a good teacher is a person with a good grasp of psychology and pedagogy, understanding and feeling that they cannot work with children without knowing educational theory.

Fourthly, a good teacher should have an excellent mastery of some work skill or another and be a master in their field. It is very important for a school to have a fine orchardist, a person who loves working with machinery, a master of electronics, a joiner, and a horticulturalist who loves digging in the school's experimental plot. In a good school, every teacher has some work passion.

Where are people with such multifaceted development to be found? There are good people all around us; we just need to be skilled at seeking them out. I always sought the right to appoint teachers independently and consider a school unthinkable without that right.

Without the moral support of all the teachers for my work as a principal, I would not stay in the school for a single day. At the beginning of each school year, we meet as a staff to determine each teacher's duties and workload, and together determine who will carry out the roles of principal, director of studies, senior Pioneer leader and class teachers. If the staff come to the conclusion that a teacher is not coping with their duties, that teacher leaves the school. These matters are decided with the participation of parents who are members of the school council. Their opinions are very important.

Good teachers do not always arrive at our school with all the above attributes in place. Often it is necessary to select a person who just has the potential to develop the comprehensive readiness outlined above. Then we begin meticulous work with that person, and they become a good teacher mainly because of the milieu of creative work undertaken by our staff and students.

Before formally appointing a new teacher through our national education department, I have always tried to get to know them as well as possible as a human being, to understand their interests, outlook and spiritual life. The best way of doing this is through relaxed and friendly conversations. We find topics that excite us, and express our views and convictions. During this process, it always becomes clear what a person lives for and what has led them to the idea of devoting their life to educational work. I place the highest value on teachers who combine a love for children with a creative interest in scholarship and research.

Quite often, the search for a future teacher begins with the fact that a person who has not yet undertaken teacher training shows the potential to be a talented educator. One of the enterprises in our district employed a demobilised soldier named Aleksandr Aleksandrovich Filippov, an electrician by trade who had completed secondary education. I was very interested to learn that this young worker had a whole workshop at home. During evenings and weekends, young people—students from our school and from a neighbouring school—came to his workshop and constructed working models and electrical equipment with him.

I got to know Mr Filippov and became convinced he would make a good teacher. I advised him to undertake external studies in education. Over the following year, Mr Filippov got to know our school and visited the lessons of experienced teachers. We helped him with his external studies, and he helped the school with extracurricular activities. Children, adolescents and senior students interested in technical innovation were drawn to him. We found a room for extracurricular work in technology, and the children referred to it with pride as their automation and telemechanics laboratory.

That was two years before Mr Filippov was officially appointed as our physics teacher. When he was appointed, the young teacher (still studying externally as a third-year student) presented me with a demand. Apart from a physics laboratory (which we had, although it was inadequately equipped), we needed to create an electronics laboratory and, in the future, a small technical workshop. I was very happy to agree, as I knew I could create this with the young teacher.

In the room for extracurricular work on technology, interesting work that engaged the children launched into full swing. The students began to construct working models of machinery and mechanical installations. With each year, this construction work became more refined and more complex. After constructing a working model of a thermal power station, they went a step further and constructed models with programmed operations, including a working model of an automatic lathe. Each year the supervisor of these technical clubs attracted new helpers, new clubs appeared, and new ideas were put into action. After some time had passed, the teacher became 'infected' with the idea of directly converting chemical energy into electrical energy and attempted to create installations that could function without an electrical generator. This dream took hold of the young technicians, and they began to conduct experiments and trials. Then the physics teacher presented me with a new request to open a laboratory with engaging science and technology activities. The realisation of this dream attracted the active involvement of myself and many other teachers. Soon this new laboratory was created and equipped with everything necessary for the work of our talented young people, for construction, modelling and the theoretical study of the achievements of science and technology.

In the editorial office of our district newspaper worked a man named Andrei Andreyevich Samkov, a passionate gardener and flower grower. Rumours of his passionate interests reached our school. I visited Mr Samkov at his home and was struck by his love of the soil and plant life and his deep faith in knowledge and science. On his tiny little plot, he was cultivating twenty varieties of grapes. I could not help thinking that this man was destined by his very nature to educate children.

Mr Samkov was studying part-time at an agricultural institute. On my advice, he began to visit the lessons of experienced teachers to acquire practical teaching skills. Then he was entrusted with teaching lessons in biology. The school's experimental plot and orchard became a genuine centre of research.

Nowadays, Mr Samkov runs biology and biochemistry clubs, as well as several clubs for young people interested in conducting experiments in nature. The young horticulturalist has become a talented teacher. He wins children's hearts through his love for his work and his deep knowledge of his subject. No matter how apparently simple agricultural work may be, he strives to always conduct it on a scientific basis. Into any task, he can breathe living ideas that make the work much more interesting. Mr Samkov teaches 150–170 senior students each year and additionally educates another 50 students from junior classes who attend his interest groups.

Among the members of these interest groups are several young people he refers to as 'mad keen'. These are children, adolescents, and young men and women who, while still at school, have uncovered outstanding talents as horticulturalists, orchardists, vegetable growers and stockbreeders. He conducts special work with these students.

Over a period of three years, Mr Samkov completed a course in pedagogy and the methodology of teaching the natural sciences. Under his direction, students cultivate grain and industrial crops on a section of the collective farm that is allocated to our school. They conduct experiments, trial new varieties, and study soil properties and local fertilisers. There is now a research centre based around our school experimental plot under the auspices of a local institute for postgraduate studies in education.

Teachers are the first and subsequently the main beacons in the intellectual lives of school students. They awaken in children a thirst for knowledge and respect for science, culture and education.

Many years' experience has convinced me that the most important precondition for children's all-round development is the rich, multifaceted intellectual life of the school staff—their variety of interests, breadth of outlook, curiosity and sensitivity to new developments in science.

This collective wealth is the product of individual personal wealth. The foundation on which a school stands, and upon which everything that happens in a school depends, is the multifaceted knowledge, rich intellectual life, breadth of outlook and constant intellectual growth of each teacher. Three to five years after graduating from higher educational institutions, teachers should know three, five, or ten times more than in their first year of work. If this does not happen, students will be condemned to boring rote learning and the blunting of their intellects. Teaching that is not stoked and illuminated by a teacher's thirst for knowledge becomes an arduous responsibility, a burden, and kills any thirst for knowledge that students may have, destroying their intellectual talents and abilities. Intellectual growth, constant enrichment, renewal, extending, deepening and perfecting knowledge—this is vital for a teacher, especially those who have been working for 10, 20 or 30 years. The danger of spiritual 'ossification' threatens such teachers no less than young teachers and sometimes more. Avoiding any such danger is a collective responsibility.

Each of our teachers is in charge of one, two or more groups, in which the rich and diverse spiritual life of the students is in full swing. For each group, the teacher is a source of knowledge and exemplifies a love for science. Through their character, work, interests and thirst for new knowledge, each teacher brings their own personal contribution to our collective multifaceted spiritual life. I cannot imagine a teacher who does not have the closest links with the spiritual life of the students—not only their own students but students in the school community generally. Among our staff are 35 teachers, a senior Pioneer leader and a librarian. Each of them is distinguished by something unique and personal.

I will describe our staff and what inspires them, and how they have become mentors and educators who inspire the spiritual lives of our students.

Of our 35 teachers, 25 have completed tertiary studies in education, one is in the process of doing so, seven have completed college training, and two have completed secondary education. Four have 25–35 years of experience, nine have 20–25 years, seven have 15–20 years, three have 10–15 years, six have 5–10 years, and four have less than five years of teaching experience. Two of our teachers have been working at our school for 25–30 years, six for 20–25 years, 12 for 15–20 years, and five for 10–15 years. In other words, 25 of our teachers have been working in our school for at least 10 years. The stability of our teaching staff is one of the most important reasons why the wealth of pedagogical skill, accumulated over many years, is carefully preserved and handed on to young teachers.

Despite the fact that so many of our teachers have been teaching for many years, only two of our teachers are over 50 years of age, and the average age of our teachers is 39.

In most cases, those teachers who have 20–30 years of experience began teaching when they were aged 17–20, and some as young as 16. All our teachers have committed themselves to working in a rural school for the rest of their lives. None have any desire to leave the village or to stop teaching. All our staff, with two exceptions, have families and children of their own. Our 30 teaching families have 69 children between them. Of those, 28 have graduated from school, 23 are currently studying at our school, and 18 are preschool-aged. Fifteen of our teachers are men, and 20 are women.

These figures are significant for the character and quality of our teaching staff. Currently, there are 276 children studying at our school whose parents have also been taught by us. Sometimes you look at a little child or an adolescent, observing their work during a lesson (how they think, how they solve problems, what they are interested in), and you cannot help comparing them with their mother or father, who once sat in that very same classroom, sometimes at the same desk. Now we are beginning to enrol the grandchildren of students taught by teachers who have been working in our school for more than 25 years. We know the family histories of all our students, we see how the spiritual worlds of our children are formed, and this helps us to educate them.

The balance of men and women among our staff is also significant. The staff at a school should not be composed only of women. We strive to achieve a balance, considering it important for the correct education of our boys and young men that they receive not only good advice and precepts but also fatherly male direction.

It has taken time to consolidate our staff group. Over a period of 20 years, five teachers who could not meet the collective requirements of our staff have left the school.

The question of whether a person is suited to the vocation of teacher, whether they should remain in our school or leave, is always decided collegially. And any such decision is only acted upon if it is unanimous, that is, if the colleague whose fate is being decided comes to the conclusion that educational work is not their vocation. It is important the person concerned chooses another avenue of work for which they have a genuine vocation. In fact, we have been able to achieve that in all five cases. A teacher's didactic and methodological inexperience is no cause for alarm, nor are gaps in knowledge if a person is industrious and has a thirst for knowledge. (Of the 25 teachers at our school with higher education, 12 graduated from their institute or university by studying externally while already teaching at our school. Of the 10 teachers who do not have a higher education, six are currently studying externally at tertiary institutions.) However, if a teacher has no faith in children, if they become depressed and disillusioned at the slightest failure and are convinced nothing will come of a child, they have no business being in a school—they will only torment the children and be tormented themselves throughout their life.

The intellectual resources of the staff derive primarily from each teacher's individual reading. A real teacher loves books: that is the golden rule governing the lives of our staff, which has become a tradition. This atmosphere of love for books, respect for books, reverence for books is the essence of a school and educational work. A school can have everything, but if it does not have the books necessary to support the holistic development of young people and enrich their spiritual lives, or if people do not love books and are indifferent to them, then it is not a school. A school can lack many things, it can be poor and modest in many respects, but if it has the books necessary to ensure there is always a window wide open to the world, then it is already a school.

In our school library, there are 18,000 books, while in the personal libraries of our teachers, there are more than 49,000. In the personal library of literature teacher Viktoriya Daragan, there are over a thousand books. The physics teacher Aleksandr Filippov has 1,200, the director of studies Akim Lysak has over 1,500, the language teachers Vera Skochko and Antonina Reznik have around 1,400–1,500 each, the work teacher Andrei Voroshilo has over 1,800, and in the library I share with my wife Anna Sukhomlinskaya, there are over 19,000 books: literature, historical works, educational literature, and books on the theory and history of art. Our school library is a resource for the self-education of the whole school community. Its collection contains all that is most valuable in Russian, Ukrainian, Belorussian, Bulgarian, Polish, Czech and German literature. It includes many works by Eastern writers, books for the preschool and early primary years, and all the works on our list of golden treasures of world literature that should be read during childhood, adolescence and youth.

All our teachers subscribe to several newspapers and journals, including one or two literary journals. These publications are exchanged and circulated among the teachers. In the staffroom, there is a stand displaying new books relating to science and literature. Teachers who are interested in a particular book acquire it for their personal library.

Some books are discussed among the staff, and it is not uncommon for lively exchanges to take place around important issues of communist education. During the past three years, our staff have discussed the following books: *Foundations of Communist Morality* by A. Shishkin, *Essays on Marxist-Leninist Ethics* by S. Utkin, *Polytechnical Education in Soviet Schools* by S.M. Shabalov, *Being and Consciousness* by S.L. Rubinstein, *The Psychology of Adolescence* by V.A. Krutetskii and N.S. Lukin, *Pedagogy and the Present* by A Levshin, *Nina Kosterina's Diary* and *The Tale of Boris Bekleshov* by L. Kabo, *Emergency* by V. Tendryakov, *Andromeda Nebula* by I. Efremov, *The Adventures of Werner Holt* by D. Noll and *Testament* by K. Roozbeh. We try to ensure our teachers take an interest in any social, political, ideological or scientific event of world significance, especially if it involves our own country.

Becoming familiar with issues in science, technology, art and culture has great significance for the all-round development of teachers and the deepening of their knowledge. Approximately twice a month, teachers present lectures to their colleagues on scientific issues. Between 1961 and 1965, lectures were delivered on the following topics:

> The brain and consciousness; Biochemical processes and thought; The physiological foundations of memory; Social life and moral education; Knowledge and morality; The moral ideal of a young person of our times; Combining intellectual and physical work, and the objectives of schooling; Scientific and technological progress, work, and the objectives of schooling; Classical genetics and school biology; Pathological deviations in the human psyche; Social causes of criminality among adolescents in our country; Theories about the origin of life on our planet; Cosmogonic theories; The power industry of the future; The theory of relativity; Cybernetics and programmed instruction; The electrical education of the masses (Lenin's words) and the objectives of the secondary school; Biochemical processes in cells; Beauty in life and in art; Aesthetic education and the objectives of schooling; Lenin's theory of reflection and the process of cognition; and Health and the all-round development of the personality.

For each lecture, a selection of literature is displayed on a stand in the staffroom or the library. We consider the goal of each lecture to have been achieved if familiarisation with the issue under discussion leads to a deeper reading of the corresponding scientific literature and journals.

Teachers have access to the following scholarly journals: *Issues in Philosophy, Nature, Knowledge is Strength* and *Technology for Young People*. We also have encyclopedias relating to various branches of knowledge (*Encyclopedia of Philosophy, Encyclopedia of Physics, Encyclopedia of History, Encyclopedia of Geography, The Art of Nations and Peoples, Encyclopedia of Theatre, A History of World Art, Encyclopedia* of *Philosophy*, *World History* and *A Brief Encyclopedia of Literature*), books from the series *Nations of the Earth*, *A Children's Encyclopedia*, and scientific journals in the fields of mathematics, biology, chemistry, automation and telemechanics.

The more a teacher knows, the easier it is for their students to master elementary knowledge, the more they are trusted and respected among students and parents, and the more children are drawn to them as a source of knowledge.

Our physics teacher Mr Filippov is in love with the science of elementary particles and has a deep knowledge of theories and hypotheses about the properties of matter, magnetic fields and gravity. Children listen to his explanations with bated breath. Knowledge, erudition and a broad outlook are the foundation of a teacher's authority. At every step, the students are convinced their physics teacher reads widely and knows far more than is included in the compulsory curriculum. His description of magnetic phenomena in plant organisms—a unique excursion to the frontiers of science—prompted several students to undertake new experiments. A teacher's ability to entice students with the attractive prospect of penetrating nature's secrets and to awaken feelings of amazement at science and knowledge is the spark that ignites children's hearts. Without this, a full intellectual life is inconceivable.

If we limit ourselves to the textbook and fail to show students the broader horizons of science; if we fail to show what remains to be studied and awaits the involvement of their curious minds and industrious hands, we will only awaken a distaste for the daily assimilation of the allotted 'portion' of knowledge. And to show these things, a teacher needs to know significantly more than the curriculum demands.

The biology teacher Olga Stepanova told her students about scientific conjecture that the capillaries in a plant are lined with something like muscles, contracting and expanding fine openings, and causing nutrients to move to the tops of the plant. Boys and girls interested in researching the life of plants were fired up to investigate this possibility. Interesting experimental work was undertaken in the experimental plot and the orchard, as the spark of Ms Stepanova's enthusiasm kindled a thirst for knowledge and an urge to understand nature's secrets.

Individual talents, abilities, interests and gifts will only shine when illuminated by the light of knowledge, science, culture and inquisitive, determined effort.

How could a lecture on the topic 'What is genetics?' be relevant to primary teachers working in Grades 1–4, except perhaps to broaden their horizons? While it is important to broaden horizons, that is not the only consideration. Any issue in science, technology or art has relevance to our educational work and can illuminate a child's mind with the light of knowledge. When a lecture was delivered on genetics, several primary school teachers and literature teachers who loved horticulture conducted some simple but very interesting experiments to investigate the action of various chemical substances upon the embryos, the chromosomes of grains, other crops and fruit trees. This was a deeply personal interest for the teachers, but what an influence it had on the education of their students! (Probably the brightest spark kindling the hearts and minds of children is the personal interest, passion and obsession of their teacher.) Several groups of children began to investigate the influence of chemical substances on plant chromosomes. This enthusiasm for research and urge to investigate led to the awakening of dormant talents and abilities.

The more a teacher knows, and the more frequently and effectively they reveal the horizons of science to their students, the more curiosity and interest their students will show, the more questions they will have, and the more interesting and difficult their questions will be. In turn, these questions stimulate us as teachers to think and to read: 'If inside a space capsule, in which astronauts are orbiting the Earth, all objects are experiencing a state of weightlessness due to inertia, how do the astronauts breathe? How does air make its way into their lungs? Would not the gas particles also be in a state of weightlessness?' To answer these questions, the physics teacher needed to read several articles.

Our staff consider it their duty to know everything that concerns each student: their thinking, emotions, talents, abilities, interests and hobbies. The staff only become a collective educational force when each student experiences the influence of many teachers, and each teacher invests some of their spiritual energy in them. Every one of our teachers knows every one of our 570 students. Without this, we cannot imagine a proper life for our school community. They know the environment in which the child's personality developed prior to school and continues to develop; they know the characteristics of their thinking, how they perceive their surrounding reality and their intellectual work; they know their individual character traits; and they know their strengths, abilities, interests, hobbies, difficulties, joys and sorrows. We strive to have a scientific basis for studying children in the family and at school. Twice a month on Mondays, we have a staff meeting or psychological seminar devoted to studying children. There is nothing more necessary, useful and interesting than talking about children.

During the first part of our 'pedagogical Monday', one of our educators (a class teacher or group leader) talks about the spiritual life of the group they supervise, the exchange of values and experience within it, and the group's collective aspirations, joys, disappointments and experiences. Then the educator focuses on one or two students, describing their personality, actions and behaviour, basing their account on actual facts. Other teachers who know the child well or have experienced difficulties relating to them express their opinions. It becomes evident what we still need to learn about the child and what we have neglected or failed to notice. Finally, the staff make suggestions for the teacher who already has some degree of responsibility for the child's education, and consider who else from the staff can become involved in the child's education, and how this should be done. The purpose of all this is to enrich the child's spiritual life, to help them find valuable interests, develop their good qualities and find their golden vein. With time and appropriate attention, this can contribute to their sense of worth and the richness of their personality.

Most of the time, we discuss children who pass unnoticed in their group, who do not display any particular qualities. A child who does not demonstrate their individuality in any way, who is not interested in anything, does not disturb anybody and does not cause any trouble is the most difficult child to educate. At one of our pedagogical Mondays, we discussed Kolya N., a boy in Grade 5. Everyone knew the boy and his family well but spoke about him with concern because nobody could say what Kolya was interested in, what his hobbies were, and what aptitudes he displayed. Quiet, unobtrusive, always trying not to be noticed—nobody could remember a single incident in which he stood up for himself or showed determination. He had never been involved in any mischief, and this concerned us just as much as his lack of interest in any particular subject or study generally. We concluded that we should expose Kolya to a situation in which he would need to demonstrate some determination, where he would feel responsible for something and experience a sense of personal duty. It should be something he felt enthusiastic about, something he would consider a deep personal involvement and in which he would take pride. We decided which of the teachers and parent volunteers would have daily contact with him, and which groups would suit him. Prolonged, meticulous work eventually succeeded in helping Kolya to achieve personal success, awakening his interests and pride in his creative abilities and achievements.

The second part of our pedagogical Monday is usually a theoretical presentation about instruction and the all-round development of the personality. These presentations are prepared by the principal, the director of studies and the most experienced teachers. Each presentation is based on the concrete facts of our collective educational work and is directed at improving our work. The presentation is usually followed by a lively discussion in which teachers express their views on important educational issues. Both the presentation and discussion are focused on children's lives and their spiritual worlds.

In each presentation, we analyse scientific research and experience relevant to the issue under discussion. Then we examine the successes and shortcomings in the work of our school, express our thoughts, and make suggestions for improving our approach to education and instruction. The presentation also draws on evidence from the practical experiences described in educational literature. It has become a rule at our school that such evidence, and the conclusions drawn from it, are systematically preserved in a staff library. Here, we keep books, brochures, annotations to books (written by teachers), folders with newspaper cuttings, and articles from journals. All of our teachers are interested in receiving information about what is happening in schools in our country and throughout the world. The presentations based on this information stimulate teachers to reflect on what has already been achieved in a practical sense, what needs to be done to embed proposed improvements, and whether we have all the prerequisites to adopt the most advanced innovations.

The discussion that unfolds following each presentation, which, as mentioned earlier, quite often develops into a heated debate, is not controlled by anybody. Each person can speak more than once, and their contributions may involve a generalisation from experience, a reflection of our attitude to the issue, or posing a new question. We collectively analyse emerging issues, such as acceleration: the accelerated physical development of children. Since the discussion always centres on children and their intellectual and moral development, such analyses refine the educational convictions of our staff.

At one of our pedagogical Mondays, I gave a presentation on the formation of students' abilities and interests. During the presentation, I analysed the educational and psychological aspects of abilities and interests. I cited examples showing that the most progressive teachers in our nation were striving to develop children's abilities through creative work. Considerable interest was aroused by the research of eminent Soviet psychologist Aleksei Leontiev into the development of musical abilities in children who were not especially gifted in that area.[9]

Analysing the experience of the most progressive teachers at our school and other schools led our staff to conclude that abilities are developed in the process of activity, and the term 'work' should be given a broader interpretation than is commonly the case. Work is not only a person's interaction with nature and coming to know the surrounding world as a result, but also a person's coming to know themselves. Any work a student undertakes should involve both the creation of things of material value and the development of personal values, based on deep moral satisfaction at one's spiritual growth, creativity and mastery. The organic need for work that we regularly speak of should flow mainly from a spiritual need for self-development and self-education. The challenge facing educators is to ensure students take a deep interest in work that creates things of value to society, and that work brings them true personal happiness. We try to ensure there is investigative, experimental, scientific and theoretical meaning to the work in which our students are engaged. However simple the work a child performs, that work involves an element of their own personal creativity. It thus behoves all teachers of natural sciences, all organisers of technical and agricultural clubs, all teachers who have a work hobby, to always consider the spiritual growth of their students when they are engaged in work activities.

I recounted the experiences of Petya Z., a boy in Grade 6 whose spiritual development I observed over a period of five years. Petya not only had no mathematical ability, he had great difficulty mastering even elementary arithmetic. In Grades 1 and 2 he could not solve the easiest problems as he could not understand their terms. His teacher thought he may never master the multiplication tables. But then Petya began to take an interest in the activities of the young mathematicians club. He became enthusiastic about constructing a 'mathematical box', a piece of arithmetical equipment that presents numerical relationships in a visual form. This interesting work awakened the child's intellectual powers. Petya developed a burning desire to know—his inquisitiveness and curiosity were aroused. The intellectual work he had previously found so burdensome became a requirement for him. I expressed my firm conviction that if a person develops an urge to think, if they see in intellectual work a goal that they wish to achieve, the inertia and constraint in their thought will inevitably disappear. Such was the case with Petya, who subsequently became the best mathematician in his class.

In conclusion, I suggested that many issues relating to finding harmony between abilities and interests are far from resolved and need reflection. These issues include: How do we combine the process of learning and study with creation and creativity? What are the laws that govern the development of diverse creative abilities, such as aptitude for several types of work activity or artistic creativity? Since happiness is found in creative work and creativity is impossible without constant intellectual growth, how do we give children a 'spiritual charge', instilling a lifelong thirst for knowledge? In a general education school, how do we structure our educational work so that creative work is akin to independent scientific and technical activity? (After all, this is what is required for science to flourish in our nation.) Finally, how do we ensure children feel they are creative, even when the methods applied in an intellectual task are monotonous?

The presentation stimulated a lively discussion. The core focus of our conversation was our conception of the essence of creativity, of the diversity of abilities and their spheres of application. During the discussion, we rejected the old-fashioned notion that some people have a capacity for creative activity and others do not. It was suggested that communism means finding happiness in creativity, and every person has a right to that happiness. How were we to lift all students without exception to the level of creativity in their work? Some teachers suggested the most important thing is uncovering individual talents—nurturing from early childhood any creative bent a child displays. Others, while not denying the role of individual talent for a particular form of creative work, maintained that talents and individual aptitudes are only be discovered through involvement in a variety of work. The staff as a whole concluded that genuine study is the individual creative construct of each child. A child will only feel themselves to be a creative personality when the intellectual work they undertake as part of their studies engages them emotionally, when the discovery of truth is perceived to be the result of their personal efforts. For an experienced teacher, a student is an active participant in the process of study, and not only from the teacher's perspective. In the process of coming to know the surrounding world, the student also comes to know themselves. Intellectual work is a multifaceted process of self-education. It is only when a person, in learning about the world, learns about themselves, that they experience the joy of discovery and develop their intellectual abilities.

* * *

Our staff is a creative association of like-minded people, in which each makes an individual contribution to our collective creativity. Each is spiritually enriched by our collective creativity, and at the same time enriches their colleagues.

Mariya Andreyevna Lysak has been working at our school for 27 years as a primary school teacher and mathematics teacher in Grades 5–8. She is a highly skilled and cultured person who knows and loves children deeply and has faith in them. In order not to be parted from the students she has taught in primary school, she 'progresses' with them into middle school, where she teaches mathematics. She is in love with her subject and with interesting and challenging problems that demand quick wits and good powers of observation. Her enthusiasm stimulates the mathematical talents and abilities of her students.

Ms Lysak supervises two mathematical clubs, one for junior classes and the other for middle school classes. Her mathematical games, evenings, competitions and organisation of a wall newspaper and a mathematical journal for junior and middle school students attract any students with a mathematical bent into her orbit. Ms Lysak also loves nature. She often takes children hiking into the forest or to the bank of a river. Here, in natural surroundings, she teaches children how to measure the distance to an inaccessible object, how to calculate the volume and weight of a stack of hay or straw, and so on. Her knowledge of the spiritual world of children permits her to make difficult topics accessible and understandable.

In addition, Ms Lysak is an artist who loves to draw landscapes, which also attracts children to her. When children go hiking with her, they take drawing pads and pencils. Ms Lysak tries to pass on her sensitive appreciation of beauty to children through other avenues as well: she supervises an embroidery club and a drama club.

Our literature teacher Viktoriya Trofimovna Daragan fosters kindly feelings and rich and varied spiritual interests. She teaches Grades 8–10 but mentors students in all classes from Grade 1 onwards.

Ms Daragan has a sensitive appreciation of beauty: in nature, relationships between community members, literature and visual arts. Alongside Raisa Zaza, Anna Sukhomlinskaya, Mariya Lysak and Mariya Verkhovynina, she is an indisputable authority on school decor. Ms Daragan plays an important role in promoting a love of reading and educating our young book lovers. She never reads from a book during literature lessons, as she knows all the required readings by heart. When she recites a poem or story at a literary evening or morning performance, students, teachers and parents listen to her clear, emotionally expressive interpretation with bated breath.

Ms Daragan supervises several clubs for literary recitation (for junior, middle school and senior students). Under her supervision—and that of the other literature and primary school teachers—children learn a love of language. Ms Daragan also supervises a drama club for middle school students and a creative writing group. Under the influence of her drama club and creative writing group, a fairy tale theatre group was formed, made up of our youngest school students and preschoolers.

In our creative writing groups, children learn to convey in words the beauty of whatever captivates them and brings them pleasure and joy. These groups are supervised by the five literature teachers (including myself) and seven primary school teachers.

The creative writing groups are joined by those who wish to test their creative abilities. At our school, no-one tells children which creative writing group to join, or indeed which group of any kind they should join. Each child joins the group with the supervisor they consider most likely to meet their needs.

Aleksandr Aleksandrovich Filippov has been working at our school for 19 years. He teaches physics and is a guide for those adolescents and young people who have a bent for technology or an aptitude for theoretical thought. He supervises the senior science and technology club, where adolescents and young men and women study problems of physics, telemechanics and radio electronics, where they discuss articles from scientific journals and dream of the future.

But Mr Filippov is also an excellent metal worker and lathe operator and can work with internal combustion engines, cars and tractors. He loves to construct and operate working models of machinery and equipment based on the principles of automation. He has his own corner in one of the workrooms, where he is always constructing something.

Fifteen years ago, Mr Filippov created our school's first club for young metal workers and modellers. Since that time, this club has been our most outstanding centre of skill and industry. The club attracts many small children who develop a love of technology from a young age. If a small child works for two or three years under the supervision of Mr Filippov, they will catch the 'technology bug' for life. When they reach the senior classes, these students become interested in automation and radio electronics. Mr Filippov is justifiably proud that during the 19 years he has worked at our school, 85 of his students have become engineers. He will not accept complacency, imprecision, sloppiness, laziness or negligence.

Mr Filippov is also a musician. He plays the bayan.[10] At school celebrations, when working with senior students on the collective farm, and on hikes and excursions, he directs the choir and plays the bayan.

Olga Iosifovna Stepanova, a biology teacher, has been working at our school for 21 years. She is a kind proponent of love for all living things, a campaigner for increasing our natural resources and maintaining the beauty of our environment. Our school has many clubs for young naturalists, young natural scientists and young plant breeders. All these clubs and all the children attracted to them 'pass through the hands' of Ms Stepanova. This teacher manages to ensure that every child creates something, beautifies the land in some way, and leaves behind a positive legacy, even in childhood. Her educational principle is to work from an appreciation of the beauty in nature to an appreciation of the beauty in work—from a sense of pride in a tree grown in childhood or a handful of grain grown from a tiny garden plot to a selfless love of work.

Ms Stepanova mentors the primary school teachers in educating a love of nature and a love of work. Her enthusiasm and ability to find a task within the powers of the smallest children has contributed to our staff's firm conviction that every little child who crosses the threshold of our school, from the first day of their school life, should become a toiler. Moreover, such tasks should not be just a way of occupying idle hands but should make a significant contribution and be challenging.

Andrei Andreyevich Samkov is a teacher of biology and agricultural technology who loves nature and the work of grain growers and orchardists. He consolidates and deepens what the small children have learned from Ms Stepanova and the primary school teachers. In the biological science and agricultural science clubs, his students conduct experiments in which work is carried out with a scientific purpose and an urge to discover nature's secrets. He finds young children in the junior classes who love the land, attracts them to the young soil scientists' section of the agricultural sciences club, and begins to train inquisitive young grain growers.

Mr Samkov is convinced that you have to know and understand the life of the soil to fall in love with the work of a farmer. The students working on his projects conduct experiments to ascertain how to influence the living processes in the soil.

Thanks to the work of Ms Stepanova and Mr Samkov, our staff have developed another conviction. No matter what profession a young person chooses after school, they will definitely love growing fruit trees and grapes. All our teachers love growing fruit trees and grapes. Every year the school produces hundreds of young apple trees, pear trees, peach trees and grapevines. We distribute these to the collective farmers and industrial workers. Our grape nursery is the pride of the school.

Mr Samkov is a true mentor to all the students interested in growing grain and other commercial crops, to young plant breeders and future masters of high yields. In our experimental plots, we grow hybrid varieties of grain crops. These trials are conducted not only by our students but also by young collective farm workers. They work with a spade and hoe while also conducting meticulous observations utilising a microscope and tweezers.

Mr Samkov and Ms Stepanova are joined by another advocate for integrating work and knowledge: the chemistry and biology teacher Evdokiya Evdokimovna Kolomyichenko. Students in the primary and middle school years who show an interest in how matter is constructed and who want to conduct experiments come together under her supervision in a club for young chemists and explorers of natural resources for research into organic matter. During spring and summer, the young chemists conduct geological expeditions and explore the natural resources of our local area. With Ms Kolomyichenko's help, the young chemists have created a mobile chemistry laboratory to take on excursions. In the chemical sciences club, young researchers conduct trials to create new organic fertilisers, chemical growth stimulants and antibiotics.

A year ago, Ekaterina Stepanovna Volik, a young chemistry teacher who had just graduated from the Poltava Pedagogical Institute, began to work in our school. Ms Kolomyichenko has already managed to infect the young teacher with her love of reading and ability to observe and investigate natural phenomena. She has also inspired the young teacher to create an experimental chemistry laboratory. Ms Volik has taken up this interesting challenge with great love.

Andrei Fedorovich Barvinsky has been teaching mathematics to the senior classes for 20 years. He is convinced that studying mathematics and developing mathematical ability requires constant mental gymnastics and tireless movement forward. If a student has fully mastered the material currently being studied, he provides opportunities for further progress individually. Students with a mathematical bent study higher mathematics under his supervision in a mathematics club and produce a mathematical journal.

Mr Barvinsky also teaches mechanics. He began his working life at the age of 15 and mastered the trades of tractor driver, mechanic, metal worker, electrician and lathe operator. He believes every student graduating from secondary school should be able to drive a tractor, a car and a combine harvester. These are not professions but basic work skills. With the staff's help, he demonstrates this in practice. Mr Barvinsky supervises one of the young mechanics clubs. He teaches young children who display a particular love for mechanics how to operate an internal combustion engine. He says, 'If a young child has learned to operate a small motor by the age of ten, they can be a fine machine operator when they grow up'. In this way, the teacher develops a valuable work characteristic in his students: a love for technology and a responsible attitude to machinery.

The young mathematics teacher Anna Grigorievna Arishchenko has been working with us for the four years since she graduated from the Poltava Pedagogical Institute. With an excellent knowledge of her subject and the psychology of adolescents, Ms Arishchenko is considered a master of the individual approach to students. She selects suitable tasks and examples for each student, and she is prepared to work with each individual to develop their abilities. Every student works thoughtfully, independently and with concentration in her lessons.

The young teacher is convinced that studying mathematics requires individual effort. During her lessons, each student completes work at the level of difficulty required to develop their abilities.

Ms Arishchenko supervises a mathematics club in which students create programmed learning aids. She is an excellent educator. Her talks about scientists and her excursions and hikes enrich the spiritual lives of the students.

Our director of studies, Akim Ivanovich Lysak, has been working at the school for 29 years. Over that time, he has educated at least half of the parents of our current students. He graduated from the philological faculty at the Poltava Pedagogical Institute, but since then, he has independently mastered higher mathematics. He teaches language and literature.

His considerable life experience and high level of culture give Mr Lysak great authority in matters of educational skill and morality. His discussions on moral themes always touch the hearts of our senior students.

Mr Lysak believes moral norms must be explained in vivid, convincing exhortations and rules that teach young people how to behave in difficult situations. This issue is currently the subject of heated discussions among our staff. The topic of a recent educational debate was 'How should we teach young people how to live?' Preliminary reflection and exchanges during the debate led to the conclusion that each teacher's most important task is to imprint on the minds and hearts of the students in their care the moral experience and spiritual inheritance of the finest people of the past and the older generation.

People from the older generation occupy a special place among our staff. Nearly all of them began their working lives at the age of 12 or 13 and invested great effort into getting an education. They are a living personification of the core ideals, views and convictions of our staff. Things do not always progress smoothly and easily for our staff group, and we have to overcome great difficulties. Whenever our staff are experiencing difficulties, teachers from the older generation are the ones who marshal efforts to overcome those difficulties. From time to time, we hold lively discussions on the topic, 'Let's talk about what is difficult'. These discussions are led by the senior teachers Andrei Barvinsky and Anna Sukhomlinskaya, and all teachers participate. Our greatest difficulty is finding a way to approach a student when it seems all means have been exhausted. The older teachers encourage the younger ones, telling them they should never despair, as education is a difficult but rewarding endeavour.

From their older colleagues, who have passed through the great living school of socialist construction, our young teachers assimilate respect for former generations who fought for our freedom and the opportunity to study and to live a rich spiritual life. The older teachers, who know the families very well, help the younger teachers understand the children's psychology, feelings and emotions. It was not by chance that I mentioned earlier how many of their own children our teachers have brought up and are bringing up. Those who are entrusted with the education of other people's children must make sure they educate their own sons and daughters to be decent human beings. The older teachers among our staff have reason to be proud in that respect. Their children have become good, honest, hard-working people.

The wisdom that comes with life experience, deepened by knowledge of educational theory, helps the older teachers to pass on to their younger colleagues educational skill as well as friendliness and humanity. The older female teachers have conversations with the senior girls about marriage and family life, bringing up children, and a woman's honour and self-respect. The male teachers from the older generation talk with the senior boys about a man's self-respect and honour, responsibility in his relationships with girls and women, a father's duty and the upbringing of children.

Anna Ivanovna Sukhomlinskaya has been working in schools for 30 years. She has higher educational degrees in philology and education and teaches Russian language and literature in Grades 5–10.

Ms Sukhomlinskaya is one of our teacher mentors for home reading. She takes an interest in what children are reading at home and helps the primary school teachers encourage children to read material that is of philosophical and aesthetic value. She supervises two creative writing groups, conducts creative writing evenings, and produces an annual handwritten compilation of student writing.

Vera Alekseyevna Skochko teaches literature and history and has been working at our school for 22 years. Her contribution to the spiritual life of our staff comes from her love of lyrical poetry and music. She knows hundreds of lyrical poems by heart. She is convinced that every teacher should try to instil in students a love of reading and an appreciation of the beauty of poetic language.

Ms Skochko and Ms Sukhomlinskaya have trained the primary school teachers to recite poetry. They also teach poetry recitation directly to all the young children in Grades 1 and 2, taking them to the forest, orchard and fields, and reciting poems that describe the beauty of nature and of human feelings. The school has created a sound library of musical works composed to the words of Pushkin, Lermontov, Nekrasov, Shevchenko, Franko and other poets. Children in the primary and middle school classes listen to these works in school and in natural settings. The simultaneous impact of the beauty of the music and the beauty of nature helps develop children's appreciation of the beauty of language.

Ms Skochko and Ms Sukhomlinskaya have organised evening and morning functions dedicated to lyrical poetry on themes such as 'The beauty of nature and lyrical poetry', 'Love for one's native land and lyrical poetry' and 'Russian poets writing about mothers'.

Ms Skochko, Ms Sukhomlinskaya, Ms Daragan and Ms Stepanova have also contributed to the school community through their love of flowers. In flower beds at their homes, they have grown roses, chrysanthemums, asters, carnations and nursery beds of lilies of the valley. Following their example, many students have also established flower beds at home.

In developing children's love of flowers, we seek to ensure that children's lives and work are accompanied by beauty. Through beauty, we show children human greatness, heroism, courage, steadfastness and humanity. Pioneer gatherings and Komsomol meetings dedicated to the life, work and achievements of eminent people are conducted in our 'nooks of beauty'—areas of our school grounds where flowers and greenery abound. Special days celebrating work, the harvest and tree planting serve to encourage a deep appreciation of beauty.

Antonina Ivanovna Reznik, a young literature teacher, has been working in our school for 10 years. Warmth, mutual trust and goodwill are characteristic features of her relationships with students. A child in her class cannot fail to learn a lesson or to complete their homework, mainly because it will cause Ms Reznik pain. If a student cannot cope with a task, they will speak openly about it with their teacher. Ms Reznik treasures children's trust as a precious gift. She says, 'As long as a child turns to me as to a mother or a friend, I am confident that a love of study burns in their soul'.

She talks to children about the most diverse areas of their spiritual lives, and this is the secret of her ability to find a way to a child's heart. Whether it is a sunny spring day, a clear summer morning, or a cold autumn day when the steppe is shrouded in white clouds of mist, Ms Reznik likes to take children on a literary excursion, as the children call these walks. She is accompanied by students from her class and also other little children and adolescents in whose hearts she has instilled a love of literature.

Spread out somewhere in the shade of a 100-year oak or in a grassy clearing by the river, Ms Reznik tells the children about heroes—strong, courageous people devoted to the lofty ideals of kindness, justice, humaneness and civic responsibility.

It has become a tradition at our school that every teacher spends several days each summer out in the fields with the children. The children especially enjoy the hay harvest. They impatiently look forward to the evenings when they will lie on the sweet-smelling hay under the twinkling stars and listen to tales about distant lands or distant stars, and then listen attentively to the rustling of the night. The twinkling stars, the tasty porridge, the dying embers of the campfire, the chill in the air just before sunrise, when you feel like burrowing into the hay, bathing in the river—all of these things leave an indelible impression on children's souls.

Communicating with children about all areas of their spiritual lives has become a principle of the educational work at our school. 'I would not be an educator, and the paths to children's hearts would be forever closed to me, if I only taught lessons.' This is what every one of our teachers thinks and feels.

Mathematics teacher Anna Yakovlevna Vovchenko has been working at our school for 12 years. In the clubs for young mathematicians that she supervises and in her lessons, students create interesting learning aids that help them study, think, and develop quick-wittedness and observational skills. Ms Vovchenko is convinced that completing creative tasks can develop the mathematical abilities of what might appear to be the most hopeless students. Her motto is: 'Each day a student should be more intelligent than the day before'. The class group she supervises lives a rich spiritual life. Ms Vovchenko loves art, conducts interesting discussions about painting and music, and teaches girls embroidery.

Even if they are not class coordinators, our teachers always maintain close communication with children. The language and literature teacher Mariya Vasilievna Limarenko supervises a club for young local historians. She loves our local area and knows dozens of places where significant historical events took place. In summer, she conducts local history excursions with the children. On one such excursion, the young local historians found the ruins of a gunpowder factory from the time of the Zaporizhian Sich.[11]

Our geography and history teachers Matrena Tikhonovna Syrovatko and Ekaterina Stepanovna Reznik also love our local area and supervise groups for young local historians. One of these groups keeps a 'Chronicle of our local area'. They record everything that is known about the history of our village and the surrounding area from historical documents, verbal accounts and legends. They have stored images of people who took part in the revolution, the civil war and the Great Patriotic War.

The young physics teacher Ivan Vasilievich Kompaneyets has been working at our school for eight years. Like many of our senior teachers, he began his working life as a 14-year-old adolescent and knows what work is and how to work hard. Mr Kompaneyets is in love with machinery and can operate a car, a tractor and any combine harvester. His educational influence is seen mostly among adolescents. He resurrected an old car that had outlived its normal lifespan and adapted it for use by adolescents. Looking after this car and repairing it is a true education in hard work, persistence and patience.

In Mr Kompaneyets' club, they literally recover spare parts and equipment from scrap and repair them. His experience demonstrates once again that you should not simply present students with everything ready-made. Overcoming difficulties is the high road in work education.

Our French teacher, Olga Ammosovna Pismennaya, has been working in our school for 20 years. She is fluent in French and reads German and English. She follows the principle that children can only appreciate the spirit of living speech when words and phrases are associated in their minds with vivid images, concepts and emotions. She begins by teaching her students to talk to each other in French about the surrounding world, their feelings and their needs. Only after the children master a certain range of phrases, expressions and concepts (that do not need to be translated into their native language because they are associated with objects, phenomena and feelings) will Ms Pismennaya begin teaching them to read and write French.

Living French speech is not only heard in Ms Pismennaya's lessons. Functions are conducted in the French language in the mornings and evenings, and students put on plays. For each student in the senior classes, there are several foreign language books in the school library for home reading. Children have pen pals in 17 countries, with 114 students in the middle school and senior classes conducting individual correspondence with peers abroad. This is an excellent way of deepening knowledge and fostering a love of the cultures of other nations.

Our staff devote a lot of attention to promoting intellectual growth and broadening the horizons of our primary school teachers. Someone who introduces little children to the world of nature and human society should be a knowledgeable, intelligent, holistically educated human being. A person's spiritual development depends greatly on how they learned to think, read, write, observe the surrounding world and express their thoughts in childhood. A crucial element in the spiritual development of young school children is the formation of moral convictions. The primary school teachers see their task as ensuring the first notions of good and evil, truth and untruth, honour and dishonour, are clearly reflected in the moral relationships between children. Through this, each primary school teacher contributes to the educational culture of the staff.

Vera Pavlovna Novitskaya has been working in our school for 20 years and has been a teacher for 32 years. She has mastered the precious art of inspiring her young pupils with work that is useful for society, and ensuring such work plays a major part in the children's spiritual lives. The many years of experience accumulated by

Ms Novitskaya and the other primary school teachers clearly demonstrate that a person's moral development and moral culture depends on the sources of their pleasures and joys during childhood and adolescence. The things of material and spiritual value provided by the older generation are an important source of childhood joys. But to achieve our educational goals, it is essential that a child finds joy in giving, in knowing they can also do something for their elders, and experiencing deep personal joy doing so. It is on the basis of such experience that Ms Novitskaya structures her work to give children a moral education. She shows children how the world is made up of things of material and spiritual value created by former generations and teaches them to preserve this wealth and add to it. She never tires of telling the children, 'The highest joy a person can experience, is to make the Earth more beautiful and richer than we received it from our parents and grandparents'. Ms Novitskaya develops the moral concepts of her youngsters through vivid, emotionally charged illustrations from the lives of people whose life and activity was driven by the welfare of the nation. The ability to introduce small children to the guiding light of an ideal in life is one of the most remarkable features of her educational skill.

Ms Novitskaya deftly imparts her deep love of nature to the children. In each child's soul, she fosters a caring attitude towards young trees and those great friends of people, birds. She also loves books and teaches children to view them as a miraculous achievement of human culture. On her initiative, we have seen the creation in the village of several family centres of culture, where the main activity is reading good books. For example, in one of these centres, for nine years in a row, there have been many readings of Pavel Zhurba's *Aleksandr Matrosov* and Anatoly Rybakov's *Dirk*, which have been attended by hundreds of children.

Raisa Karpovna Zaza has been working in our school for 14 years (six of these as a Pioneer leader). She completed an external course at a teachers' college and is now studying at a tertiary institute. A cultured person with diverse spiritual interests, Ms Zaza instils in her pupils a desire to serve others and bring them joy. Her educational skill is closely interwoven with her love of art and enthusiasm for music, painting and creative writing. Ms Zaza supervises a club for young painters and a drama group called the Fairy Tale Theatre, in which children prepare dramatic presentations of fairy tales.

During walks, excursions and hikes, Ms Zaza teaches children how to talk about what they see, feel and experience. On the first sunny spring day, she usually takes her students into the forest. She asks the children to describe in words what they can hear in the forest: birds singing, a woodpecker tapping, the murmur of a stream, the quiet rustling of leaves under a running animal's paws. It is difficult for the children at first, and she helps them find the necessary words. In this way, they collectively write a story about 'Life in the forest in spring', and create their first handwritten journal, illustrating their stories with drawings. The children develop an urge to describe the things in nature that make an impression on them and amaze them with their beauty. Later, the children who develop an interest in creative writing participate in a club for lovers of our native language. The members of this club include not only her current students but some who graduated from her Grade 4 class several years earlier.

Ms Zaza also supervises a folk embroidery club. Towards the end of their first year of studies, her girls always come to our end-of-year celebration dressed in traditional Ukrainian blouses they have sewn themselves. Following her example, other primary school teachers have begun teaching their children these skills.

Ekaterina Markovna Zhalenko has been educating children at our school for 11 years, and she was a Pioneer leader like Ms Zaza for five of these. Her work with parents is a model for all our staff. Almost every day, she talks with two or three mothers and fathers. She finds out how their child is feeling, their attitude to work, their hobbies and interests, what they are reading, and what difficulties they are encountering in their studies. If one of her students is upset by something, she does not rest until the child's sadness, anxiety or grief has been allayed. If a child is having problem with their studies or experiencing difficulties, she helps them immediately. The children feel her motherly concern and always tell her openly about their difficulties, grievances and failures. The children are honest with her. Before the beginning of a lesson, the children will tell her themselves if they have not completed their homework, could not understand it or found it too difficult to solve a problem or complete an exercise.

The class lives like a friendly family. The class group celebrates every student's birthday, and the child whose birthday it is receives a book as a present from the class. If someone is ill, their friends will visit them and help them make up any lessons they have missed.

The relationships between the children in Ms Zhalenko's class are a true school in sensitivity and humanity and a model for educating kindly feelings. With characteristic modesty, Ms Zhalenko describes this aspect of her educational skill thus: 'There are no special techniques or methods for educating kindness, sensitivity and warmth. You simply need to regard each child as you do your own child. You need to realise that a mother experiences pain when her child has a problem, and this in itself gives rise to kindly feelings. If a child feels that they are treated with kindness, they will be kind to their friends, elders and parents.'

Ms Zhalenko makes skilful use of work to inculcate warmth, sensitivity and empathy. She and her students do a lot of work in the garden and have created a nature corner in their class. She instils in the children the idea that a rose bush, an apple tree and a grapevine are all living creatures that give people joy. If you are indifferent or cruel to that creature, if you break its branches or pick green fruit, that indicates you are a heartless person and cannot expect love and respect from others.

The children transplant small, weak, sickly plants, and water them and defend them from the cold, doing their best to keep them alive. It is hard to say which teacher first had this idea, but it is most clearly expressed in the work of Ms Zhalenko. Ultimately, it became one of the most important educational convictions of our staff: if a child has nursed a weak plant with their own hands, warmed it with their breath and lived through concern, worry and suffering for its sake; if their inner resources have been spent ensuring a tender and defenceless shoot grows to become a strong and mighty tree, they will become a kind, sincere, warm and empathetic human being.

For Ms Zhalenko's students, the happiest day in their school life is when they present the seedlings they have raised to others. Twice they have presented young apple trees to the kindergarten group. The students who planted those trees are already adults, and the task of caring for them has been passed down to the little preschoolers.

Ms Zhalenko's other hobby, like Ms Zaza, is folk embroidery. (Nearly all our women are in love with this art.) Her little students also embroider.

Anna Anisimovna Nesterenko has been working at our school for 20 years. During that time, she has given a primary education to five cohorts of students, instilling in them a deep interest in intellectually challenging work.[12] She loves and understands nature and can talk to young children about various natural phenomena in an accessible and engaging way. In Grades 1 and 2, her students already know many things that are quite complex for their age group: how seeds germinate in spring, how the sun's rays form green leaves, and how a plant stores starch and sugar. The children would not understand these things without the insight they gained into the secrets of nature while working on our experimental plot. The teacher sets her little ones a goal: to grow two ears of grain where normally only one is grown, and to harvest twice as much grain as normal. She supervises a club for young natural scientists and plant breeders. Ms Nesterenko was the first among our staff to start celebrating harvest day, from which an excellent tradition has been born whereby work has become a source of rich aesthetic experiences.

Mariya Nikolaevna Verkhovynina has been working in our school for 22 years and is now educating her sixth cohort of primary students. A person with diverse cultural interests, she loves books and nature and educates her students to use language carefully and sensitively. She supervises a creative writing group, a drama group, and a children's section of the Society for Nature Conservation.

Ms Verkhovynina often conducts special lessons out in nature to teach children to observe and think. She supervises a methodology group for primary teachers that focuses on developing children's thought and language.

The experience of our primary teachers has firmly convinced our staff that a child's working life should begin as early as possible. Further, that children's work provides the most reliable foundation for forming children's first moral concepts.

The work of our primary school teachers has enriched our staff with another wise conviction: education is not some calm idyll. We encounter difficulties at every step. Educational skill consists in becoming aware of difficulties and overcoming them. Our primary school teachers unanimously agree that the greatest difficulty in education, presenting many pitfalls, is determining what a child is capable of, what you can expect of them and what you should not expect of them. Of particular concern for the primary school teachers and all our staff is the constant observation and development of the intellectual abilities of every child, and studying the level of moral development with which a child comes to school. The very fact that children are not all the same, that they do not all have the same level of intellectual and moral development, gives rise to the greatest difficulties in education. Only knowing the subtlest characteristics of each child's psychology can help a teacher overcome these difficulties.

Vasily Yakovlevich Taran, who teaches work studies in the metalworking and turning workshop, has been working in our school for eight years. He graduated from an engineering school, and our staff have assisted him in becoming one of our best educators.

He is a man with 'golden hands', an excellent metalworker, lathe operator, electrician, fitter and mechanic. He only has to look at a lathe or drilling machine to make one just like it and introduce some modifications to its construction to improve it.

Mr Taran is convinced that mastery of manual work is the foundation for technical skill. He believes a person needs to be taught from childhood to carry out delicate, meticulous work with a file, chisel and hammer, before gradually transitioning to the operation of machinery. 'A person's skill is on the ends of their fingers', he likes to say, and shows this is the case through his own example.

When we set up our workshop, we did not have any machine tools. Among the scrap metal at the automobile factory, Mr Taran found various discarded parts, from which he decided to make our first lathe. With the aid of a hammer, chisel and file, he made that lathe. Since that time, our workshop has been augmented with many items of equipment. Now we have more than 30 machine tools for working with wood or metal, and all were crafted by our students under the work teacher's supervision. Mr Taran supervises several clubs for young metalworkers, young mechanical engineers and young modellers. Both senior and junior students participate in his clubs, and the spark of creativity burns constantly. The students construct and assemble little drilling machines, lathes and milling machines for their younger friends. With his students, Mr Taran made a small reaping machine that is used to mechanically harvest grain crops on our experimental plot, and a threshing machine.

The work of this club has clearly demonstrated that students will develop a love for agricultural work if in childhood, adolescence and early youth they have designed, modelled and created small items of machinery and used them in their work on our experimental plot.

Andrei Antonovich Voroshilo has been supervising technology clubs for 14 years. He graduated from our school, and is another person with skilful, 'golden' hands, in love with technology and children. He is a lathe operator, metalworker, welder, electrician, fitter, milling machine operator and cabinetmaker. In all these trades, he is a true artist. The students say that metal 'sings' in his hands. His hobby is making machinery for working with wood and metal: milling machines, planing machines, universal machine tools. The milling machines he makes are on a par with factory machines in their processing accuracy and the beauty of their output.

While the students are still in Grades 5 and 6, Mr Voroshilo identifies future skilled craftspeople, who in the senior classes will assist him in supervising technical clubs for young metalworkers and modellers, young motor mechanics, young lathe operators and young electricians. Children with a technological bent start participating in these clubs as early as Grade 2 or 3.

In our school, we have created a miniature electricity generating station for the younger school students. In addition, the skilled youngsters learn to operate machinery. With his students, Mr Voroshilo designed and constructed a minicar for the youngsters, a winnowing machine, and a band saw. Under his direction, tool kits have been prepared for the collective farm mechanics to use when conducting field repairs.

Viktor Ivanovich Shengur is another of our school graduates. After completing his compulsory military service, he joined our school as a laboratory technician and electrical and radio technology teacher. His particular interests are radios, automation, electronics, television and equipment that requires great accuracy. He supervises clubs for young electrical engineers and young radio technicians, and an automation and radio electronics club. Each of these clubs has sections for junior, middle and senior school students, and the club members construct at least 50 radios each year, from simple valve sets to transistor sets. Every student who graduates from our school knows how to assemble a radio.

Under Mr Shengur's supervision, the students have created a radio centre and a television room. In the club for young electrical engineers, they construct and assemble model machinery with electric motors and working parts and make miniature generators. Each club member tries to introduce some innovation into their model to show ingenuity and inventiveness. In the automation and radio electronics club, the students construct and assemble models controlled via radio (car, aeroplane or tractor) and get involved in programming. They assemble demonstration lathes with programmed operations and simple electronic calculators.

The educational influence of our work teachers and technical club supervisors extends to all students in the junior, middle and senior school years.

Our music and singing teacher, Semyon Iosifovich Efremenko, has been working at our school for 19 years and has been a teacher for 24 years. His contribution to staff educational culture is a love of music and folk art and a desire to develop young talent. He teaches children how to listen to musical melodies and how to understand them, to experience pleasure from listening to music. He organises musical evenings and mornings, where children listen to folk melodies and compositions by eminent composers, and choirs from the junior, middle and senior school perform. (In the senior school choir, teachers also take part.) His favourite instrument is the bayan, and he directs a group of bayan players. Students who complete a seven-year course in this group read sheet music well, perform folk music and works by composers, and can direct a choir. Mr Efremenko has trained 76 young musicians. Among them are six talented young men and women who have become music and singing teachers in other schools.

Music occupies a major place in the spiritual life of our school community. It is heard at school celebrations, Pioneer gatherings, on hikes and during hours of rest at the field station.

Our art teacher, Grigorii Terentievich Zaitsev, has been working in our school for 17 years. A born artist, he mastered the secondary school curriculum independently and is now studying in the art faculty at the local pedagogical institute. He is a great admirer of the work of Taras Shevchenko, and for many years has been working on illustrations for lyric poems by the great Ukrainian poet.

Mr Zaitsev supervises several groups of young artists. On spring, summer and autumn days, the group members gather easels and sketch pads and set off for the forest, field, meadow or riverbank and learn to draw from nature. While teaching the students the secrets of his skill, Mr Zaitsev is also teaching them to understand, love and admire the beauty of nature. A love of painting has become part of the spiritual lives of many of our students. During moments of reflection, they often turn to their albums and notebooks, expressing their thoughts and feelings in their drawings. Several times a year we organise a school exhibition of children's artworks.

Mr Zaitsev also loves drama, and supervises the senior drama group.

Grigorii Ivanovich Reznik, our physical education teacher, has been working at the school for 10 years. Our staff view physical exercise as an important element of health and a source of joy in life. We discourage the pursuit of individual records or school sports success. For us, physical activity is a battle for health—strengthening our students' physical and mental powers is an integrated approach.

With our doctor, Mr Reznik works out a routine of physical exercises for each student and takes care to see it is practised. We all agree with his view that everyone should maintain the practice of gymnastics throughout their lives and that it is one of the noblest forms of sport. We have created everything necessary for the practice of gymnastics, and our gymnasium and sports areas have all the required equipment. Our school usually comes first at district sports competitions.

It has become a tradition that our senior Pioneer leader is chosen from students graduating from our school. We naturally choose someone who loves children, can sing and play musical instruments, and appreciates beauty in nature and art. Our previous senior Pioneer leader, Lidiya Mefodievna Kurilo, met those criteria, and so does our current senior Pioneer leader, Valentina Alekseyevna Gorbach.

In Pioneer work, the most important thing is to be able to kindle children's hearts with a spark of romanticism, to inspire them and lead them through personal example.

Projects inspire children when they feel the romanticism of struggling and overcoming difficulties. Lidiya Kurilo inspired the Pioneers with the idea of reviving an old, dying orchard. Because the leader put her heart and soul into achieving this goal, because the work was illuminated and inspired by friendship and a common desire to overcome significant obstacles, the goal also inspired the children. They achieved the goal they had set and revived the orchard.

The result they achieved convinced us yet again that you can only inspire a group of children when the group's leader—the senior Pioneer leader—sets an example through their own burning desire. It is impossible to inspire others when you remain cold and indifferent yourself. This is especially important in the independent activities of the Pioneers. At our school, every teacher participates in Pioneer work, working beside the children and inspiring them with their enthusiasm.

The leaders of our Pioneer troops and Little Octobrist[13] groups are our first assistants in educating the children. On the advice of the teachers, the Komsomol committee assigns as leaders those members who can enrich the children's spiritual life. The leader of one of the Pioneer troops, Valya Skripnik, created our puppet theatre. With the children, she creates little plays on the themes of children's folklore, and under her direction, the children present the plays to young students. During excursions and hikes, at stopping places and by campfires, the Pioneers read interesting books about courageous people and their journeys. Valya believes that each book should be read in a particular setting. In her opinion, there are some books that should only be read on a rainy autumn evening, when the wind is howling outside your shelter.

Another Pioneer leader, Yury Shvachko, is in love with technology and is one of our best machine operators. He passes on his enthusiasm to the Pioneers. The children assemble models in which there is an element of play and use them in children's games. Yury is also interested in our local area, studies its history and records folk songs and tales. On his initiative, Pioneers meet with old residents with rich life experience and listen to and record their accounts of events from the distant past.

One of the centres of the school's spiritual life is the school library. Here many children's interests are met, sparks are lit, and dreams take flight. Our librarian, Elena Emelianovna Malolitko, is a book lover and a good organiser. The school staff expect that she will be familiar with each child's life in the world of books and that she reads a lot herself. And she does read a lot. She knows all the works from world, Russian and Ukrainian literature that the staff consider the minimum for a rich spiritual life. Book lovers often gather to visit the library in the evenings. Attached to the library are several clubs for young book lovers, where the children read interesting books and rebind and repair books. With the teachers, our librarian manages to ensure that not a single book from our golden treasures of world literature remains unread by our students. Every single child has read the fairy tales of Hans Andersen and the Brothers Grimm, or the entertaining stories and tales of Arkady Gaidar. Every adolescent and senior student has read *A Journey from Petersburg to Moscow*, *Eugene Onegin*, *War and Peace*, *Quiet Flows the Don*, *Virgin Soil Upturned*, *The Young Guard*, *Mother*, *How the Steel was Tempered*, *Faust*, *Hamlet*, *Don Quixote*, *The Robbers*, *Intrigue and Love*, *The Divine Comedy*, *Jean-Christophe* and *Notes from the Gallows*. The library organises exhibitions and displays about each of these books. Through the school library, we organise educational work with those students who, due to various family circumstances, may have had little exposure to literature. We manage to ensure that each one of these students finds a life in the world of books.

Our school council

WE TRY TO COMBINE LEADERSHIP by the principal with collegiality in discussion and decision-making about important educational issues.

The effectiveness of collegiality depends on having common views on matters of principle that determine the direction and essence of education. These common educational views and convictions allow our teachers to make collective decisions at meetings of our school council on practical questions affecting the life and work of our school. (The school council meets seven or eight times each year.) Such collective decisions and recommendations on concrete issues are binding for all staff at the school.

Our school council consists of the teachers, the senior Pioneer leader, the librarian, educators from the after-school program, a doctor, club supervisors, the school principal, the director of studies, the deputy principal responsible for the school site, five to seven members of the parent committee (chosen each year by a general meeting of parents), and representatives of the Komsomol. Each year we elect a chairperson, deputy chairperson and secretary of the school council. The school principal is usually elected as chairperson, with one of the teachers as deputy chairperson.

Each year the school council elects the principal and the director of studies, allocates subjects and classes to the teachers, and appoints the class coordinators and club supervisors. For each subject, a senior teacher is appointed to chair a methodology group. The Pioneer leaders (senior students recommended by the Komsomol committee) are also appointed.

The school council approves the school report that is submitted each year to the education department. Each year the staff recommends outstanding teachers for awards: a monetary prize awarded by the Ministry of Education, a certificate of honour, a badge for exceptional services to education, and the honorary title of distinguished teacher. Corresponding references are compiled by members of the school council.

In allocating lessons and extracurricular work, the school council is governed primarily by what is in the best interests of the work. Each teacher must ensure a high standard in teaching their subject and in character education. We consider not only the opinions of the teachers but also those of the parent community. We had one instance when the parent representatives on the school council demanded that a history teacher not be allowed to continue in his role since he did not approach his work conscientiously, adequately prepare for lessons or upgrade his knowledge.

When allocating lessons and extracurricular work, we also consider the teacher's interests, including their salary. If it is not possible to allocate a teacher a sufficient number of lessons to guarantee an adequate salary, they are allocated paid extracurricular work. We try to ensure a teacher's total earnings are one and a half times the basic salary so that they approach the earnings of the principal and director of studies. This rule is strictly observed. The school council will not approve the allocation of lessons and classes if the interests of a single teacher are harmed.

The school council takes care to ensure children are prepared for entering school. We monitor all children in the village from the age of four. These children's families are visited by the teachers who will educate them and by our doctor. They get to know the parents and help them establish routines to guarantee the health and normal psychological development of their child. From time to time, the doctor reports on the health of these children to the school council.

We take measures to ensure that sick children receive treatment and the health of weak children is strengthened. Responding to representations from the school council over the past 12 years (1955–1967), the collective farm and trade unions at local enterprises where our parents work (a railway carriage factory, a hydroelectric station, an automobile factory and a creamery) have allocated funds for supplementary diets for 45 children and medical treatment for 63 children. In this way, we have been able to avoid lengthy absences due to illness.

The school council also decides which students should be issued with free supplementary food products and milk in our dining room (paid for with state, collective farm and trade union funds).

The school council is concerned about children's and teachers' routines of work, rest and recreation. They approve daily routines recommended for students in the junior, middle school and senior classes. Guidelines about these routines are explained at the sessions of our parenting program. Special routines of work and rest are established for some children who have experienced illness or are weak and prone to respiratory illness. Teachers, the doctor and members of the parent committee monitor children's level of tiredness at our school and their homework load, and the doctor determines the state of health of individual children at the beginning and end of each quarter. Periodically the doctor reports on the condition of our students' circulatory systems, breathing passages, sight and hearing. Thanks to these measures, during the past 18 years (1948–1965), we have been able to prevent the development of serious heart, lung and eye conditions in 28 cases. Once a year the doctor, and a teacher to whom this important task is assigned, report to the school council on the condition of the school furniture and make sure every student has a desk of an appropriate size.

The school council examines and approves safety rules for our school workshops, workrooms and laboratories, the children's electricity generating station, and our experimental plots. We consider the duration and level of difficulty of socially useful work undertaken by each age group. If one of the local managers expects work beyond children's capacity (which unfortunately does sometimes happen), they will have to contend not just with the school principal but the whole school staff. Decisions by the school council on whether to permit students' involvement in any particular work project are final and cannot be overturned by anybody.

The school council approves the timetables for lessons and extracurricular work. We pay particular attention to plans for educational work during the holidays. The combination of work and rest must be such that summer work does not come at the cost of adequate rest. Plans for educational work during the autumn, winter, spring and summer holidays are made with a view to ensuring every teacher, apart from two months annual leave, has at least 20 days rest during holidays. Teachers' work demands an enormous expenditure of energy, and without periodical rest, their spiritual growth is impossible.

The school council is involved in the creation, replenishing and improvement of our educational infrastructure and with easing the burden of physical work through mechanisation. Teachers introduce proposals for group discussion regarding the preparation of visual aids, tools and equipment. In such discussions, we focus on educational and methodological considerations. School council decisions on these matters are carried out by the whole school community. (For example, children's tools for use by the junior students and equipment for watering trees have been prepared by teachers and senior students.)

At the end of the year, the school council discusses the quality of our book collection and decides what books to purchase for the library and reading rooms.

Each year before classes begin, the school council discusses curriculum content and compiles lists of practical skills and abilities that are not detailed in the curriculum. For instance, it has become a tradition to approve a list of spelling words that all students should master during their primary school years. Based on the observation of their students, the teachers augment and refine a list of spelling words that has been developed over the course of several years. We also consider recommendations from the teachers of mathematics, physics, chemistry and biology, about what assignments students should complete during the year; what working models of machinery and equipment students will have to complete as practical assignments for assessment; and what botanical samples they will have to collect during the summer holidays. Every year we discuss and refine the creative writing topics, composition topics for each class, and essay topics for senior students.

The school council discusses reports by the principal and director of studies about lessons they have visited over a period of time. These reports include analysis of key instructional and educational issues: student engagement with intellectual tasks, the development and deepening of knowledge in the process of instruction, the application of knowledge in practice, ensuring students do not fall behind, the formation of moral convictions, etc. One of the forms that teacher participation in collective management takes is the presentation of short reports on their work experience. The teachers put forward proposals that often have a major influence on the practical work of the whole staff. For instance, during the 1959/60 school year, Ms Verkhovynina gave a presentation on the topic, 'The role of feelings in the moral education of students in the early years'. Her presentation contained vivid, convincing facts, showing the enormous importance of emotional and behavioural training. Ms Verkhovynina's experience was taken on board by all our staff. The emotional side of children's spiritual life became a special focus of our daily work.

The school council also discusses the aesthetic environment at our school, its creation and preservation, the language used at our school, and the observance of school hygiene rules.

Leadership roles

THE DIRECTOR OF STUDIES and I carry out the same work. We help teachers perfect their skills, visit and analyse their lessons, organise students' extracurricular work, study educational experience, monitor the observance of routines of work and rest, and participate in the work of the Pioneer organisation and the Komsomol. In the course of our joint work, we discuss successes and shortcomings and take advice from each other. We coordinate our efforts by meeting at the beginning of each year, quarter and working week to discuss our progress and allocate concrete tasks. For instance, we allocated our tasks for one school year as follows. During the year, I visited and analysed a series of lessons for seven teachers, and the director of studies visited eight teachers. (For each teacher, we visited several lessons, during which a complete topic or section of the curriculum was studied.) I assisted teachers with creative writing in Grades 1–7, and the director of studies assisted teachers in Grades 8–10. I individually mentored two young, inexperienced teachers, and the director of studies also mentored two teachers.

When preparing for the new school year, I went through the curriculum with the primary teachers and the teachers of mathematics, physics, history, drawing, draftsmanship and singing. The director of studies worked with the teachers of language, literature, chemistry, biology, geography and work studies. I participated in the methodology groups for primary teachers, physics and mathematics, and the director of studies was involved with methodology groups in chemistry and biology, history and geography, and language and literature. I presented three open lessons, and the director of studies presented five open lessons. I monitored the work of 17 students who required constant, individual supervision, while the director of studies supervised 14 students. I conducted discussions on extracurricular reading and homework with students in Grades 4–7, and the director of studies did the same with students in Grades 8–10. I monitored the assessment (the texts of tests, maintenance of exercise books, completion of technical drawings, class assessment records) of students in Grades 1–7, and the director of studies monitored assessment in Grades 8–10.

At the beginning of each quarter, we arranged which Pioneer gatherings each of us would participate in.

After analysing lessons I had visited, I gave presentations at staff meetings on the following topics: 'The intellectual work of students when studying new material in class', 'The development, deepening, and application of knowledge following its initial introduction in class' and 'The ability to study'. Similarly, the director of studies gave presentations on the themes: 'Taking an individual approach to students in the process of instruction', 'A teacher's preparation for a sequence of lessons', 'Visual aids in teaching' and 'Didactic adaptation of textbook material when preparing for lessons'.

Apart from visiting and analysing a sequence of lessons (which is the most valuable way of studying the work of a teacher and their students), the director of studies and I periodically visit the lessons of all teachers, with a view to observing 8–12 lessons for each teacher. (Each week, we visit and analyse a total of 10–12 lessons.) We come to an arrangement regarding these periodic visits about twice a month.

Each week the director of studies and I set aside two or three hours for discussion. We share any thoughts that have arisen in the process of analysing lessons and monitoring students' work. Often a small detail will lead us to reflect on an important issue and may lead to addressing a significant problem. As we share our thoughts, we refine our educational views and deepen our didactic knowledge. These discussions give rise to ideas that are then developed in the creative work of our staff.

Analysing the lessons of experienced primary teachers and mathematics teachers, I focused on a detail that seemed to me to be very important. An experienced teacher sometimes revises material studied earlier—not through simple repetition but by introducing the old material in a new problem or throwing fresh light on it with new information, concepts or laws. I shared my observation with the director of studies. Reflecting on many facts, analysing the experience of many teachers, including our own experience, we concluded that we were dealing with the development of students' knowledge. Conducting further observations and talking with teachers, we became more and more convinced that the development of knowledge is a major didactic issue that can only be addressed with special techniques, and requires a special analysis of the material by the teacher. Discussion of this issue occupied a major place in the work of our staff. The teachers shared their experience in developing knowledge. Preparing for work at the beginning of the school year, each teacher considered what concepts, facts, laws and rules it was important to develop knowledge about.

We also came to an agreement about the allocation of work between the school principal and the coordinator of extracurricular work. The coordinator of extracurricular work is the young mathematics teacher Anna Grigorievna Arishchenko. She supervises technical and agricultural clubs, helps teachers prepare and conduct elective activities, and organises social and political activities conducted by the Komsomol. I organise the parenting program, plan and supervise the socially useful work on the collective farm, and oversee the work of the Pioneer troops. When allocating work over a year, the principal, director of studies and extracurricular coordinator come to an agreement about who among us will take responsibility for areas of work we encountered significant difficulties in during the previous year. For example, in the 1967/68 school year, it fell to me to supervise work to ensure theoretical knowledge was integrated with practical skills, the director of studies took on individual work with children with mental processing difficulties, and the extracurricular coordinator took on the development of supportive peer groups[14] in the Grade 1 classes.

Professional development

IT IS THE PRINCIPAL'S JOB to help every teacher establish their own creative laboratory. Individual work with teachers encompasses both examining the educational methods they use and rendering practical assistance. The content, methods and character of this work depend on the level of a teachers' pedagogical expertise, their outlook, interests and motivation. At the beginning of the school year, we come to an agreement on who I will work with and with whom the director of studies will work. As a rule, such work is conducted throughout the year in parallel with the analysis of a sequence of lessons. Each of us passes on to teachers both our own experience, pedagogical views and convictions, and the experience of other teachers. Each of us is mentoring particular teachers. The most important element of this work is to show teachers how the results of their work depend on their knowledge and culture, what they are reading and studying, and how they are enriching their knowledge.

An example of this work is provided in the following description of how I worked with the physics teacher Mr Filippov. Mr Filippov became acquainted with the pedagogical views and convictions of our staff even before he was appointed to our school, through involvement in our extracurricular programs. I had several conversations with this future teacher about instructional methods and types of lessons, children's independent work and taking an individual approach to students. I was convinced the young teacher could only become a master of his craft if he developed common spiritual interests with his students—intellectual, vocational and creative interests—as this is the only way to get to know a child.

I helped the teacher to study several books on pedagogy devoted to lesson formats. Then, he began a didactic analysis of the textbooks used in the subjects he intended to teach: physics in Grades 6 and 7 and mathematics in Grade 8. He visited experienced teachers' lessons, sometimes accompanied by me. On these occasions, particular attention was given to the didactic analysis of curriculum planning and textbooks.

When analysing planning, we formulated the following important questions:

1. When studying physics in Grades 6 and 7, what role did the observation of natural phenomena play in preparing students to understand theoretical principles taught in this subject in the senior classes?

2. What concepts from the elementary course in physics was it essential for students to understand deeply for them to successfully study and fully comprehend the laws of physics in subsequent years?

3   What rules, laws, formulas and numerical data were essential for students to commit to long-term memory to facilitate active thought processes?

4   What relationship should there be between theoretical knowledge and practical skills? What skills enable children to study well: to analyse, understand and make sense of the phenomena of the surrounding world?

5   What sorts of tasks should be assigned for homework, and how can such tasks activate intellectual processes and develop curiosity and a thirst for knowledge?

6   What practical work should students carry out with their own hands?

7   What popular scientific literature should children read, and how can this contribute to the broadening of their outlook? How can we assist them in developing their individual interests and talents during extracurricular activities?

Then we went through the textbooks paragraph by paragraph, paying particular attention to those important sections that were most challenging for the students.

Every teacher in the school studies the curriculum and the textbooks in this way, with assistance from me or from the director of studies. During this process, teachers in the primary school pay particular attention to ensuring they give students a tool without which further study will be impossible: the ability to study. This tool has five 'blades', which means being able to do five things: 1) read, 2) write, 3) think, 4) observe the phenomena of the surrounding world, and 5) express in words what the student sees, does, thinks and observes. Teachers compile lists of the spelling words that children must master during the primary classes. When training teachers to work in the primary classes we analyse how to prepare children for further study in Grades 5–10.

The next stage in this individual work with teachers is assistance in preparing their first lessons. It is counter-productive to visit the first lessons of a beginning teacher: you need to give them time to get to know the class and find their feet. But at the same time, it is important to help prevent possible errors. When discussing the content of the first lessons with Mr Filippov, I posed the following questions:

1. What facts from the surrounding world will you use to develop concepts relating to physical phenomena, motion and the relativity of motion?
2. How will you structure the study of new material so students can draw their own conclusions and make generalisations—analysing, finding meaning, juxtaposing phenomena they encounter in life?
3. What prior knowledge should be developed and deepened during the process of studying new material?
4. What phenomena from surrounding life and workplaces will you direct the children's attention to when setting homework?

Reflecting on these questions should lead the teacher deeper and deeper into the lesson content.

During the first two weeks of classes, Mr Filippov told me about his lessons at the end of each working day. Discussing lessons I had not yet visited helped me clarify the extent to which he was able to analyse the dependence of students' knowledge on his preparation for the lesson. I was pleased that Mr Filippov spoke openly about both the positive and negative aspects of his lessons and tried to understand the reasons for any failures. From our conversations, it became clear that most of his difficulties arose during the study of new material. In only their second lesson, students in the Grade 7 physics class had already forgotten the material studied during the first lesson.

I explained how to gather information about the work of the whole class and individual students when studying new material; how to observe and analyse the effectiveness of the students' intellectual work. The first and most important stage of instruction—the deep understanding of the essence of the phenomenon, rule, or cause-and-effect relationship that has just been explained—should be clearly observable by the teacher during the lesson. Homework is only for deepening, developing and applying knowledge acquired during the lesson.

Later conversations showed that Mr Filippov was now trying simultaneously to instruct and to get students to demonstrate their knowledge, to avoid gaps in knowledge or understanding and observe how individual students worked. But obtaining feedback was proving most difficult for the teacher. It was now clear to me what I needed to focus my attention on at his lessons and in what areas he needed more help. The time had come to begin visiting and analysing his lessons.

The very first lesson I visited showed me that Mr Filippov had difficulty combining exposition, discussion and practical activities with the assessment of students' knowledge and observation of the process of students' intellectual work. He had to simultaneously think about the content and what unforeseen variations he needed to introduce into the lesson plan to avoid students' lack of comprehension and overcome their inability to reflect upon and analyse the facts.

In analysing the first lesson, I directed most attention to the way students were taking steps on the path to knowledge. The analysis involved comparing what the teacher had done with what he should have done. But in such cases, even the most thorough analysis is not enough. The teacher needs a demonstration of what you are talking about and recommending. We agreed that Mr Filippov would visit my grammar lesson and then I would visit his physics lesson, and we would continue visiting each other's lessons in turn.

I spent a long time preparing the lesson the young teacher was to visit. It was very important for him to see and understand how to observe and analyse the process of acquiring knowledge.

In my lesson, students were studying the classification of simple sentences and revising some spelling rules. Each student worked independently on an individual card with sentences and spelling words. The children's responses took the form of reflections that led them to go deeper into the facts. Through reflection, each student arrived independently, based on their own data set, at an understanding of a grammatical rule. The assessment was not a separate part of the lesson but took place during the course of the lesson.

Our conversation after the lesson showed that the young teacher had understood the main point. To observe the process of intellectual work, it is necessary to skilfully organise independent work (in the broad sense of the word) in which the children make sense of facts and phenomena. I discussed my lesson in detail, directing particular attention to the fact that deep knowledge is only possible if a student is conscious of many facts and discovers the truth by analysing those facts.

We visited each other's lessons for a year, and also the lessons of other teachers. The young teacher was always set the task of analysing how students were stimulated to work actively when studying new material, how they independently made sense of facts, and how memorisation and learning takes place on the basis of deep understanding. Simultaneously with visiting lessons, the young teacher studied a section in a pedagogy textbook devoted to the process of active and conscious learning, and a section on 'thought and language' in a psychology textbook.

It is impossible to learn from others' experience and develop pedagogical mastery without theoretical understanding. At our school, regardless of their previous education, every beginning teacher studies didactics and psychology in close connection with an analysis of their practical work and the experience of other teachers. Mastery comes to teachers only when they have theoretical insight into each pedagogical phenomenon.

Mr Filippov experienced significant difficulty in revising previously studied material. He could only understand how revision takes place during the study of new material by clarifying the psychological, pedagogical and logical connections between the objects and phenomena of the surrounding world. The study of pedagogical and psychological literature helped the young teacher understand what he observed during the lessons of experienced teachers. He understood that revision is not an end in itself but a means of developing and deepening knowledge. The skilful selection of material for revision comes about through determining the logical connections between topics, concepts, laws, rules and formulas.

At the end of the first school year, Mr Filippov and I had a discussion that included other teachers whose lessons he had visited. The young teacher had learned to engage children in intellectual work and had developed a strong connection with them. He had mastered the logical, step-by-step exposition of new material and the heuristic discussion method.[15] He had taken the first steps towards combining the study of new material with incidental assessment of prior knowledge. But there were still many areas for improvement in his work: an inability to plan revision over a sequence of lessons; a separation between the application of knowledge and the acquisition of new knowledge; and insufficient use of individual students' enthusiasm for technical innovation, construction and modelling to broaden their outlook and deepen their theoretical knowledge.

We decided to continue working together for another year. The other experienced teachers and I would visit 8–10 of his lessons. The aim was to further develop his methods of instruction, especially setting students independent work to analyse facts and phenomena. Mr Filippov would visit three or four of my lessons to study methods used in discussion and exposition, techniques for revising previously studied material, and the application of knowledge with a view to deepening it. We would both visit a sequence of Grade 6 algebra lessons conducted by Mr Panchenko, to familiarise ourselves with his lesson preparation and study the processes he utilised for revising, developing and deepening knowledge. After that, we would cooperatively prepare a single physics lesson plan (with a verbatim exposition script). Mr Filippov would study this lesson plan and conduct the lesson. The aim was to perfect the exposition of new material. We would also continue to study the curriculum and textbooks, and texts on pedagogy and the methodology for teaching physics and mathematics.

The second year of Mr Filippov's work began. Analysing his lessons, I delved deeper and deeper into the students' intellectual work. We became aware of an interesting rule of thumb: the more students utilise material that has been studied earlier to understand new material, the more their intellectual activity will be stimulated, the deeper their understanding of the new material will be, and the more they will consolidate the material studied earlier. Students' intellectual activity is stimulated most when material studied earlier is used as a key to understanding new material. The more I reflected on what was happening during these lessons, the more new pedagogical ideas, creativity and conviction I developed.

My educational experience owes a great deal to the intelligent, thoughtful teachers whose lessons I have visited and analysed. When

I became aware of some new facet of educational work but was having difficulty understanding its essence, I would visit half a dozen lessons in a row, trying to find an answer to the question that was bothering me.

Studying the dependence of students' active intellectual work on the application of prior knowledge at Mr Filippov's lessons, I discerned another rule of thumb: the more difficult it is to grasp some abstract truth (which has to be memorised and is required as a key to the explanation of some new fact or phenomenon), the more the memorisation of this abstraction (rule, formula, law) depends on the body of facts a student has analysed and made sense of independently. Going through the young teacher's lessons, we concluded that deep memorisation of a rule (law, formula) takes place when students focus on the relevant facts, analyse them, and work out their own theoretical generalisations based on the relationships they see. This is the creative thinking that leads to the development of intellectual ability.

During our final conversation at the end of the second year, Mr Filippov and I planned our further work together, this time for the next three years. I was to visit and analyse 10–12 of the young teacher's lessons each year, paying particular attention to lessons in which knowledge was systematised. Now I would analyse whole systems of lessons, including laboratory and practical lessons, excursions, observation of natural phenomena and of work processes, and independent work with textbooks and popular scientific literature. We also compiled a list of pedagogical and methodological literature he would study independently during the coming three years. Towards the end of his fourth year of work, he prepared a presentation on the topic, 'The interpretation of facts and memorisation of generalisations'.

When I visited Mr Filippov's lessons, I now focused on the path to knowledge, from observation and the analysis of facts to the formation of generalisations and their application in further study. We kept discovering new principles governing the education process. We became convinced that generalisations can be memorised without any special effort if they are applied multiple times as keys to understanding more and more new facts. In this way, time is gained for practical work, training and developing good study habits. The study of new material now incorporated the development, deepening and consolidation of prior knowledge.

We often reflected together on detailed aspects of individual lessons. (Such reflection is also a form of educational creativity.) For example, we were once planning a lesson on magnetic fields. The teacher's idea was that the students would observe an experiment and then independently draw conclusions from it. But as we talked about it, it became clear that this observation would be largely passive. The students would memorise an explanation and then reproduce it. We thought about how to use observation as a means of actively acquiring knowledge. We came to the conclusion that the concepts the students would come to understand during the lesson (space, force, line, field, etc.) needed to be included in their active work to acquire knowledge. Let each student make independent observations and mentally explain what they see. They would arrange small compasses around the magnet and describe the phenomenon taking place before their eyes. They would explain how the compasses and magnet interact, and the role lines of force played in the magnetic field. I advised the teacher to prepare questions beginning with the word 'why' to stimulate students' thoughts while they were working independently. In answering these questions, the students would actively use their observations to investigate cause-and-effect relationships and consequently acquire knowledge.

Mr Filippov became very skilful in using visual aids to promote active intellectual work. Posing questions beginning with 'why' gradually transformed into thought-provoking problems that combined the observation of phenomena with the analysis of theoretical principles. He read a number of articles on the psychology of thought processes. The idea of combining observations and laboratory and practical sessions with thoughtful analysis of theoretical principles was developed and deepened by our staff. We conducted our first theoretical seminar devoted to the intellectual work of students during lessons. Since that time, we have conducted 19 annual seminars on that topic: I deliver a presentation in which I analyse lessons and student responses; the teachers share their creative experiences and discoveries.

At one of the seminars, Mr Filippov raised an interesting question: how can a teacher be aware of what is going on in a student's head when apprehending new knowledge? 'I should know,' he said, 'even before I finish my exposition, how students are making connections between the new material I am presenting and their prior knowledge.' He was touching once again on the problem of feedback that had concerned him for so long. He had already gained some experience relevant to this issue.

Subsequently, the teacher and I discussed methodological techniques for obtaining feedback, and we have now been working on this issue for over 10 years. He is able to explain the essence of facts and phenomena to students in such a way that questions arise in their minds that are emotionally charged with feelings of wonder at why things happen in that way. The feeling of wonder is a powerful motivator of the desire to know. During his introduction, Mr Filippov skilfully organises independent intellectual work: the students, while following their teacher's train of thought, record it in a drawing or diagram. Consequently, even during the course of his exposition, the teacher can see how individual students are understanding the material and what difficulties they are experiencing.

Other valuable techniques Mr Filippov uses to obtain feedback include students' preparatory observations of natural phenomena, work and technological processes; compiling reports based on these observations; talks and essays; and the completely independent study of sections of the curriculum (without explanations during the lesson) using visual aids. Now the issue of feedback is being studied by all our teachers. Mr Filippov tries to ensure that every student who takes an interest in the theoretical aspect of their work in the workshop or laboratory reads scientific literature, does experiments and conducts research. Supervising several creative technology groups, he has trained some of his senior students as supervisors of children's groups. He has never had a student fail his subject.

Now Mr Filippov gives presentations, shares his work experience with other teachers, and participates in district methodology groups. During the past five years, he has given presentations to other teachers in the district on the following topics: 'The application of knowledge as a vital element in study', 'Conceptual frameworks in the physics course', 'Types of independent work carried out by students when learning new material', 'Educating aptitudes and a vocation', 'How to observe and analyse the intellectual work of students', 'Educating focused attention during lessons' and 'Developing individual abilities and the motivation to learn'.

If a teacher analyses their work thoughtfully, they will inevitably develop an interest in theoretically interpreting their experience, and an urge to explain the cause-and-effect relationship between their educational skill and their students' knowledge. The logical consequence of a teacher analysing their own work is they will focus their attention on some aspect that they believe is crucial in the current educational context. They will conduct research, study the facts, and read educational and methodological literature. This is the beginning of the highest stage of educational creativity: combining practice with elements of research. The result is that after one, two, or three years of work, the teacher delivers a theoretical seminar or a presentation at a staff meeting.

At our school, we publish a collection of manuscripts under the title 'Educational thought'. Twenty-six teachers at our school have published articles in educational journals and newspapers.

We do not allow our teachers' independent work to be mired in record keeping. We keep plans and outlines to a minimum and do not require any written reports from teachers. That is a rule at our school. Teachers need free time to reflect on the latest achievements of science, increase their knowledge and enrich their experience. Our staff strictly observe the rule that they should only be involved in work on a theoretical seminar, staff meeting or methodological group for one day per week. All remaining days are used by teachers for independent work, rest and those spiritual exchanges with students that give them moral and aesthetic satisfaction. The most important thing a teacher needs time for is reading. Without reading, without having a spiritual life immersed in books, all professional development activities lose their meaning.

I would like to give some advice to school principals. However pressing the issues facing a teacher, they cannot be addressed instantly. Whether a teacher is a novice to education or already has experience, the person in charge of a school must understand their capabilities, level of educational and general culture, horizons and erudition. It is important to be meticulous in avoiding shortcomings or mistakes during lessons. After the very first lesson observations, it is essential to draw conclusions about what is required to improve the work of the teacher you are assisting.

The success of this individual work depends mainly on the extent to which, following the advice and recommendations of the principal, the teacher masters the technique of independently analysing their successes, weaknesses and omissions. At our school, the character and even the tone of advice and recommendations serve this end: they flow from a joint analysis of the process of instruction conducted with the teacher. We discover something new at each lesson, and our thought delves into details we had not noticed before. It is important that the principal's thoughts enthuse the teacher, that the principal and teacher are inspired by a common quest and become joint researchers into the educational process. Even the most experienced teacher should not rest on their laurels. If they are not moving forward, they will inevitably begin to fall behind.

In individual work with an experienced teacher, a principal's job after discussion with the teacher (often more due to the abilities of the teacher than to those of the principal) is to find an area of creativity in which they can further perfect their educational skills. And in our work, there is no limit to how much one can improve.

If you are working with an inexperienced teacher, begin by showing them something small they can work on. However, just as a grafted bud will not start growing until the living sap starts rising vigorously in the rootstock, someone else's good experience cannot be adopted until certain conditions are met in the person who wants to adopt it: a level of general culture, a broad outlook, knowledge of pedagogy and methodology, and an ability to understand a child's psychology. It is harder to help someone meet these prerequisites than it is to show them someone else's experience and get them to understand the essence of that experience.

In this connection, it is worth repeating: never forget to take an interest in what a teacher is reading and how they relate to books and learning. A teacher can only learn from someone else's experience if reading has become a psychological imperative for them and they have the necessary books and time to read them. Time is a teacher's spiritual wealth, and we need to protect it through skilful organisation of the educational process.

A true educator is an embodiment of all our best achievements in educating the next generation. A teacher sets an example for the younger generation through their inspired work, service to high ideals, and rich and diverse spiritual life.

Collective research

WHEN EACH TEACHER DELVES EVER DEEPER into the details and intricacies of the education process, analysing their work and the mental work of their students, there is a kindling of living thought among the staff who seek answers to questions posed by life itself. An educational idea provides the wings upon which collective innovation can soar. An idea inspires the staff, and there begins the most interesting and necessary thing in the life of a school—collective research.

Twenty years ago, while analysing one of the lessons I had visited, I began thinking about why students' answers were so dismal, so colourless and inexpressive. Why were children's words not expressing their own living thoughts? I began to record these answers to analyse students' vocabulary and the logical and stylistic elements of their speech. I realised many of the words and phrases students used were not connected in their minds with clear concepts or the objects and phenomena of the surrounding world.

Analysing observations in my own lessons and those of my colleagues, I tried to find answers to the following questions. How does a word find its way into a child's consciousness? How does it become an instrument of thought? How does a child learn to think with the help of words? How does thought, in its turn, develop speech? What were the weaknesses afflicting our educational management of that most complex and subtle thing in the spiritual life of a school—a child's thought?

My research focused mainly on my own work, my own lessons and the answers of my students. For example, one child was describing the journey of a drop of water. I was looking for an account of the awakening of the first spring streams, spring rains, a rainbow, the quiet lapping of a sleeping lake. These are things a child should speak about, describing the world that surrounds them and feeling themselves a part of living nature. But what did I hear? Tortured, clumsy phrases learned by rote: word combinations, the meaning of which was hazy to the children. I listened carefully and reflected on the children's speech and gradually realised that we, as teachers, do not teach a child how to think. From the very beginning of their school lives, we close a door on the captivating world of the children's natural surroundings, so they stop listening to the babbling streams, the sound of spring raindrops and the song of the lark. They just rote learn dry, colourless sentences about all these wonderful things.

I took my Grade 5 class to the school orchard. Half the sky was covered with a dove-grey rain cloud. The sun lit up a rainbow. The apple trees were in bloom—milk-white, pink and red—and the air was filled with the quiet humming of bees.

'What do you see, children? What excites you, delights you or amazes you?' I asked my companions. Their eyes sparkled joyfully, but they struggled to express their thoughts, to find suitable words. My heart ached for the children: words had entered their consciousness unaccompanied by vivid images. Instead of being exposed to sweet-scented, living flowers, they had been presented with dried flowers, pressed between the pages of a book, a mere reminder of their vibrant life.

No, we should not continue like that. Forgetting about the most important source of knowledge—the surrounding world of nature—we push children towards a world of rote learning, and in so doing, blunt their thought. We forget the lessons learned by classic educators such as Comenius, Pestalozzi, Ushinsky and Diesterweg.

Lesson after lesson, I began to take the children into that inexhaustible and ever-new source of knowledge—into nature—to the orchard, forest, riverbank and fields, and we began to study the art of conveying in words the subtlest observations of objects and phenomena.[16]

A lark sings in the sky while the wind drives a billowing wave through a field of wheat, all the way to the horizon… Through a dark blue haze, far, far in the distance, ancient Scythian burial mounds reach up to the sky... Amidst 100-year-old oaks, in a forest thicket, babbles a transparent stream, while above it an oriole sings its artless song... All of these things should be described precisely and beautifully.

More and more new books appeared on my desk: educational essays about object lessons, dictionaries, books on botany, ornithology, astronomy and flower growing. On quiet spring mornings I would walk to the riverbank, into the forest or orchard, and study the surrounding world, trying to convey as accurately as possible in words its forms, colours, sounds and movement. I started an exercise book to record my miniature compositions about a rose bush, a lark, a crimson sky, a rainbow. I began to call my excursions into nature 'journeys to the source of living thought'. Gradually they became richer and richer in their purpose and in the forms of intellectual work undertaken by the children.

Sometimes I recite my miniature compositions and poems to my students. It gives me joy to share with them my thoughts and impressions of the surrounding world, nature and people. I notice the children are especially moved by any compositions and poems which reflect their own experiences. When one of my compositions or poems touches their hearts and souls, the children themselves take up their pens and try to express their feelings. It seems to me that sensitivity to language and the urge to express in words the subtlest movements of the human soul are among the most important sources of genuine human culture.

Here are two examples of such miniature compositions:

Autumn

The warm, golden days of autumn have arrived. The air has become transparent and pure. Now we can see deep into the steppe. The distant Scythian burial mounds appear ash-grey in the gentle light of the distant sun. By the road is a bright chamomile flower. Drops of morning dew sparkle on its petals like emeralds—the melting remnants of the first frosts. Yet, the flower lives on and does not shed its petals.

In the evening, the sky turns greyish pink. Ravens, their dark shapes silhouetted against an orange-ashen sunset, seem like creatures from a fairy tale as they fly with wings outspread towards their nests. The forest stands quiet and thoughtful, only a few distant leaves rustling from the troubled stirrings of a cold autumn breeze. With each minute the field grows darker. It is as if the dusk is flowing in waves from the gullies and ravines, covering the earth and spreading a blanket over the forest. In the grey sky a lonely star loses its grip and falls to Earth.

Sunrise

The sky blazes with the dawn. I am standing next to a field of clover. Its gigantic, multi-coloured carpet trembles as it is flooded each minute with waves of changing hue. It is as if it is being deluged with thousands of multi-coloured pebbles: sky-blue, lilac, pink, orange, crimson and gold. Now it is being sprinkled with sky-blue pebbles, but as soon as the eye manages to capture this hue, it turns to lilac, which then is transformed into pink. Then the pink disperses, and the whole field appears engulfed in flame. In the distance, where the earth meets the firmament, shines the blinding light of a golden rim. Soon the sun will rise.

A lark bursts from the clover and soars upwards, then halts. This trembling little ball of grey turns golden in the rays of the sun. Soon sparks of sunlight play in the drops of dew on the clover flowers, and bees hum over their opening petals. It is as if the whole field is singing, the whole world is singing, as spellbinding music floods the earth.

Then I turned my attention to my school lessons. The lessons I conducted were primarily lessons in thought. At one lesson, the children and I began to discuss the concepts of phenomenon, cause and effect. At my suggestion, the children began to seek cause-and-effect relationships in the surrounding world and describe them.

Before my very eyes the children's thinking gradually became more and more clear, rich and expressive. Their words took on emotional colouring and came to life. I became aware of an amazingly rich area for developing pedagogical skill, inexhaustible in its beauty: the ability to teach children how to think. This discovery inspired me, and I experienced the exceptional happiness that comes with creativity.

I told my colleagues about my thoughts and observations, and they began to accompany me on lessons out in nature. I read them my miniature compositions. One day in early autumn, the teachers and I walked to an oak grove to admire the trees' many shades of colour and attempted to describe this beauty as clearly and expressively as possible.

The teachers became interested in these journeys to the source of living thought, and began to take the children on similar excursions themselves. During spring and autumn, we began conducting nearly a third of our lessons outdoors, and nobody complained of a lack of time. The primary school teachers began to compete with me to see who could write the best miniature compositions.

Gradually our staff became focused on the idea of the unity of language and thought. We began to come together to discuss this interesting idea, and gradually our discussions gave birth to the understanding that every teacher, regardless of the subject they teach, must be a teacher of language. Language is our main pedagogical tool, and nothing can replace it. Nature, with its inexhaustible richness and diversity, is the main source of thought and the main school for developing intellectual ability.

These truths gradually became educational convictions shared by all our staff. The primary school teachers acquired exercise books for their miniature compositions. Ms Novitskaya began to analyse the vocabulary that children could learn during an excursion to the source of living thought during different seasons of the year, for example, by visiting an orchard in autumn, spring, summer and winter. She wrote down the nouns, adjectives, adverbs and verbs that could be introduced to children's active vocabulary during observations. She told the staff about her interesting experiences in a presentation on 'Vocabulary and a child's thought processes'.

Mr Filippov began to take children to natural settings to teach them how to think and how to express their thoughts in a logical sequence. 'We need to teach logical thought in natural surroundings', he told us subsequently in a presentation on his observations about this interesting aspect of intellectual work. 'We forget that physics is a science about nature. I have now planned nature excursions for the first three years of physics lessons. I will show the students causal, temporal, and functional dependencies and relationships as illustrated by natural phenomena, and in doing so, I will teach them how to think. My senior students will write reports on their continuous observations of natural phenomena.'

As we uncovered the secrets of children's thought processes, this collective research work brought us all together. The primary school teachers and I began to work on a book describing our lessons during excursions to the source of living thought. Each excursion was dedicated to some natural phenomenon or season of the year (e.g., 'The living and the non-living in nature', 'Everything in nature changes', 'The sun is the source of life', 'Nature wakes from its winter slumbers' and 'Birds in the forest in winter'). Our descriptions were passed from hand to hand, discussed and criticised. It was interesting that these excursions turned out to be necessary for the physics teacher, mathematics teacher and chemistry teacher. This intensive, collective work has now been going on for 15 years. We have compiled a book entitled *Three Hundred Pages from the Book of Nature*, containing descriptions of 300 lessons. We are still collectively researching this issue and teaching children how to think.

Currently, our teachers are interested in a new aspect of this issue. We are conducting research into the emotional colouring of words that arise in the process of observing nature. We are excitedly considering the unity of thought and feeling. We are delving ever deeper into the didactic details of our lessons and researching thought processes at different stages of instruction.

The creativity of our staff involves scientific research into our own work and a deep study of each child.

Our traditions

FOR THE REST OF THEIR LIVES, our students will undoubtedly have the warmest memories of their childhood, adolescence and youth. Some school customs are already being passed on from one generation to the next and becoming traditions.

I will describe our most important traditions:

The meeting between the Pioneers and the five-year-old children who will enrol in Grade 1 in two years' time. This is conducted in the middle of August. The children meet with the Pioneers who, in two years' time, will be organising their Little Octobrist groups and supervising their games, excursions and other interesting activities. The Pioneers lead their little friends into the garden. On the green grass by the grapevines, the little ones watch a performance by the children's puppet theatre and listen to songs and poetry recitations. Then the Pioneers bring their guests several baskets of grapes as a treat.

Greeting the seven-year-old children who are soon to enter Grade 1. This is conducted at the beginning of June. The children are met by their old friends, the Pioneers, who are now studying in Grades 6 and 7. Each child is presented with a book for home reading: a collection of poems by Pushkin or a little edition of Taras Shevchenko's *Kobzar*.[17] The young children are treated with fruit from the school orchard. From this time on, they come to our school every day and are considered our students.

The 'first bell' celebration for Grade 1 students is conducted on the first day of the school year. Students graduating from the school congratulate the new students on becoming part of the school family and present each child with a book inscribed with the greeting and signature of the presenter. They lead them into the school grounds and entrust them with the care of a tree that they had planted on their first day at school, 10 years earlier. Then they perform a traditional ritual: the planting of a tree of eternal school friendship, with the graduating class and the new students planting an apple tree together. We are trying to develop the romantic thought someone had that as long as green trees of school friendship grow in our school grounds, our friendships will continue to develop and strengthen.

The 'final bell' celebration for graduates. This is conducted on the final school day that graduates attend. The graduates and Grade 1 students line up facing each other. Each Grade 1 student presents each graduating student with flowers and a book with an inscription and signature. (As gifts on this occasion, it has become a tradition to present collections of poems by Pushkin, Taras Shevchenko's *Kobzar*, Goethe's

Faust, Servantes' *Don Quixote*, Homer's *Illiad* or *Odyssey*, collections of poems by Adam Mickiewicz, Sándor Petőfi, and Hristo Botev, Byron's *Childe Harold's Pilgrimage*, Hugo's *Les Miserables*, Dante's *Divine Comedy*, Jirásek's *Ancient Bohemian Legends*, Rustaveli's *The Knight in the Panther's Skin*, *David of Sassoun* [an Armenian epic poem], Japanese and Arabian folk tales.) This celebration is attended by parents who have graduated from our school many years earlier, and even elderly members of our community. The youngsters' gifts (books inscribed in large childish letters with touching good wishes) symbolise the eternal, undying nature of the school community. One of the youngsters steps up to a table draped in a white cloth (part of the tradition) and takes a bell tied with a light blue ribbon (also traditional). Responding to the sound of the bell, one of the senior students steps forward and gives a short vote of thanks to the teachers on behalf of their cohort. Much time is spent preparing this address, but its content remains a secret until the day of the celebration.

The graduation ceremony for the senior secondary school students, at which their graduation certificates are presented. The most senior teacher addresses the graduates with a farewell address. This address is prepared in good time by all the teaching staff and expresses our educational ideals and collective educational convictions. We attach great significance to both the form and content of the farewell speech. The impression made by the farewell address is intensified by the solemnity of the occasion and the emotions the young men and women are experiencing on that day. The farewell address from the staff remains in the memories of those to whom it is addressed for the rest of their lives, as shown by the recollections of people who graduated from our school long ago. The educational power of language is enormous.

It has become a tradition for graduates from past years to meet annually at the school on 30 January. This gathering is attended by students from the graduating class, tertiary students, industrial and agricultural workers. These gatherings foster respect for the school. The results of work over the past year are reviewed, and the fruits of the graduates' work are shown to the teaching staff.

Mothers' Day. Every student spends a long time preparing for this day. On the eve of the celebration (the evening of 7 March), mothers are presented with gifts: albums with drawings and poems or simple handcrafted gifts, always made by the children. On this day, many children give their mothers a flower or the flowering branch of an apricot tree grown in the school greenhouse. The value of the present is measured by the love a child has invested in their work. On the actual day of the celebration, 8 March, each child brings their mother some joyful news about their work or their studies at school. For example, they could show a composition that has been awarded the highest possible mark by their teacher or tell their mother about a success they have had in their extracurricular work. This tradition helps children develop a correct view of the sources of joy that one human being brings to another: joy comes primarily from good deeds, from upholding a family's honour.

Girls' Day. This is held on the first Sunday of the winter holidays. On this day, the boys give presents to the girls: flowers or drawings.

The ceremonial handover of red scarves from the Grade 8 students (15-year-old adolescents) to the children who are joining the Pioneers. This event takes place on 22 April, the anniversary of Lenin's birth. On this day, the Grade 8 students who are graduating from the Pioneers conduct their final meet. One of the Pioneers addresses the Grade 3 students on behalf of the Grade 8 students. Telling them about the life of their troop, they urge the new troop to uphold the honour of the red scarf. When the Grade 3 students have spoken the final words of their solemn pledge as young Leninists, the Grade 8 students approach them, and each one ties a scarf on a young comrade. The gathering ends with the singing of the Pioneer song. Many adults come to the school on this day. The ceremonial handover of the red scarves is gradually becoming an important event in the lives of families. The parents experience it as a significant step that their son or daughter takes in life. Thanks to this tradition, we have been able to overcome an attitude of indifference to Pioneer work on the part of adolescents moving on to their next stage in life.

Spring festivals: the song festival, the flower festival and the bird festival. At the song festival, the school choir, small groups of singers, and individual students sing new songs. This is their gift to the community.

The flower festival is conducted at the end of May. Each student brings several flowers they have grown in special beds in their parents' gardens or gathered in the fields or forest and demonstrates their ability to make a small but beautiful bouquet. After lessons, the children visit their friends' homes to see their flower beds and indoor flowers. On this day, the young flower growers club organises an inspection of their rose bushes and flower beds. Parents come to the school, and each may take some flower seedlings from the greenhouse or seedling beds. We also have a flower festival in autumn, at the end of September, which is a sort of competition in the art of growing autumn flowers. The bird festival is held when the swallows arrive. This is a festival for the junior primary children. They release birds that have been rescued half-frozen during the winter and cared for in our bird hospital. On this day, children also give each other pigeons. This festival educates kindly feelings of a moral and aesthetic nature, deepens friendships, and educates love and care for nature.

The day of remembrance for Zoya Kosmodemyanskaya, whose name is born by our Pioneer group. On the anniversary of her heroic death,[18] there is a gathering of the Pioneer group. In the centre of our hall is a large portrait of the heroine framed by a garland of autumn flowers. Pioneers read poems about her heroic feat. By tradition, the ceremony ends with a speech by a Komsomol member who was born in November, the month when Zoya died.

A report to our sister school. Our school community has a long-standing friendship with school students from the Kormyansky District of Gomel Region in the Belarus republic. Once a year, usually in September when lessons begin, we compile a collective letter to our friends, in which each Pioneer troop reports on all the good things they have done and experienced. This tradition is a good way of educating feelings of international friendship.

The day of the unknown hero. In a square in the centre of the village, next to the memorial cemetery for heroes who fell during the Great Patriotic War, is the grave of the unknown hero. On the anniversary of the liberation of our village from Nazi occupation, one of the Pioneer troops (usually the oldest Pioneers) comes to this grave. Flowers are laid on the grave. Observing a minute of silence, the young

Leninists honour the memory of those who gave their lives for the freedom and independence of our Soviet homeland.

The New Year fir tree for our youngest children. The youngest citizens in our community, who have just learned to walk and talk, are invited to the school to see our New Year fir tree. They are brought by their mothers. The children are given presents, then watch a performance of the puppet theatre and a performance by their older friends, the Grade 1 students. (The most valuable and interesting aspect of this tradition is that the Grade 1 students take on the role of mentors. They help their little friends prepare for this celebration by teaching them to recite poems. Each little guest recites a poem here for the first time.)

The winter festival of the snow town. It is not just the junior and middle school students who participate in this festival, but the senior students as well. In a meadow at the edge of the forest, the children construct Grandpa Frost's town from snow, with little houses and towers. It has become a tradition on this day to dine in the snow town, next to the constructed snow houses. A meal in the cold always seems very tasty. Then the preschoolers play in the snow town until the sun melts it.

An important educational goal for our school community is to educate our students to be mutually supportive, always ready to come to each other's aid. Even in small children, we try to arouse feelings of concern for their friends, to teach them to treat one person's misfortune as a misfortune for the whole group. Developing a collective feeling of solidarity and readiness to help is an important way of preventing egoism. Every child suffers some misfortune while at school. One may fall ill themselves, another's mother may fall ill, a third child may have their nest of pigeons destroyed in a storm, and a fourth may lose their dog. All of these cases require friendly interest and sympathy. From a young age, we teach children to show kindness to anyone who experiences misfortune. One girl's grandmother was seriously ill for two weeks and then died. Her classmates asked her teacher not to assess the girl's knowledge or ask her to come out to the blackboard until she felt herself again. Throughout that time, her classmates, both boys and girls, helped her with her work so she would not fall behind.

'If you know how to do something, but your classmate does not yet know how, teach your classmate.' We instil this thought in children from their first days at school. In our workrooms, workshops and laboratories, there are special benches for peer tutoring.

Work traditions occupy a special place in the life of our school community. Thanks to them, work acquires a romantic aura and is associated with bright feelings and emotions. The spiritual uplift that children experience while working brings them joy. Work and happiness merge, and this is of great moral significance.

Before the summer holidays, children prepare gifts for the school in the form of visual aids and decorations for the classrooms and the Pioneer room. For instance, the children completing their studies in Ms Nesterenko's Grade 1 class presented the school with 'An album of stories in pictures about what we like most'. On each page is a story by one of the students. When the same children completed their studies in Grade 2, they gave us an inlaid picture made of pieces of straw from various cereal crops, showing a boy next to a flowering rose bush. At the end of Grade 3, they built a small model house, 'a real one, just like grown-ups build'. A year later, they presented us with a collection of samples of grains and other commercial crops in a beautifully constructed box laminated with fine sheets of wood to look like mother-of-pearl.

The older the children, the more significant the value of the gifts they present to the school. In the middle and senior school years, the work process itself takes on the atmosphere of a celebration due to the sense of expectation leading up to that proud moment when the work will be completed and the gift will be revealed to the school community. The work of the middle and senior school students reflects the interests of their age group and their aptitude for certain types of work. The following are the gifts presented to the school by students in various grades at the end of the 1963/64 school year. The Grade 5 students presented frames for the portraits of Zoya Kosmodemyanskaya and Oleg Koshevoy together with embroidered portraits. The Grade 6 students made a working model of a steam engine for the physics laboratory and embroidered a picture inspired by a folk tale. The Grade 7 students made a working model of a seed drill. The Grade 8 students made a working model of a thermal power station and embroidered a portrait of Vladimir Lenin. The Grade 9 students constructed a working model of an electrified railway with overhead power lines and presented the school with several lemon trees they had raised over a period of three years. The Grade 10 students made a radio-controlled model car and a valve radio.

Feelings of attachment to the school especially move the Grade 10 students. They feel an urge to show gratitude for their education and are sad at the prospect of parting with their teachers. They want to leave behind a significant record of their presence at the school that will remind future generations of students of the work of their older comrades. The graduates of the 1964/65 school year laboured to produce two presents for the school: an automated model of a blooming mill and an embroidered picture inspired by Ukrainian folk tales.

A second work tradition is to prepare visual aids for the biology laboratory during the summer holidays: samples of soil, seeds, insects, plant collections, flowers dried in sand to retain their form and colour, botanical presses and other items. Children bring their gifts to school on the first day of lessons.

A third work tradition is to decorate and beautify the classrooms and schoolyard before the start of the school year and before exams. On the last day of the holidays, 31 August, the students and their teacher come to school and each class group decorates their classroom. They weave garlands of fresh flowers to decorate portraits and place a bouquet of flowers on the teacher's desk. The Grade 1 classroom is decorated by senior students. Then the students work outside, levelling the pathways in the school grounds, loosening the soil in the flowerbeds and watering the flowers. Within three or four hours, the school takes on a smart, festive appearance and, in the evening, everyone gathers for a Pioneer campfire. People who have graduated from the school many years earlier come with their children. The first day of the school year is a significant event in the children's lives, giving them many joyful experiences.

A fourth tradition is work during the spring and autumn orchard weeks. On the Sunday that marks the beginning of an orchard week, all the students come to school. Each class digs up the cuttings in the school nursery and prepares holes, fertiliser and water. All the students plant trees, beginning with Grade 1. The Grade 1 students are helped by the Grade 4 students, which is also a tradition. Each year the Grade 1 students plant one or two trees in the school grounds, the middle school students plant three or four trees per class, and the senior students seven or eight. Each class records the varieties planted and the date of planting in a special 'Orchard Week Book'. The students in the senior classes read the entries they made several years earlier. Their apple trees, cherry trees and pear trees are already bearing fruit. This thought gives rise to a feeling of pride in their work.

Thanks to the fact that the execution of normal agricultural work is framed by a number of solemn rituals, the children feel uplifted, and the beauty of work enriches moral relationships in the school community.

Then the children work in groups and individually to plant trees in community areas or their parents' gardens. Each student plants a tree where it will bring joy and will benefit both their family and others (e.g., by the side of the road). It has become a tradition for each Grade 1 student to plant an apple tree for their mother, one for their father, one for their grandmother and one for their grandfather during the first spring of their school lives, and to subsequently take responsibility for the care of these trees. Several years later, the trees begin to bear fruit. Each child presents the first apples, and the first grapes planted the same spring, to their mother, father, grandmother and grandfather. This is a good way of educating feelings of warmth for others. This tradition includes the students' collective work in a communal vineyard and communal orchard planted several years ago. The children experience joy in creating something of value that belongs to everyone.

During orchard week the students exchange fruit tree cuttings and plant them in memory of each other. For instance, one student may bring a nut tree seedling, while others bring cherry trees, plum trees, apple trees or pear trees. Once they have exchanged trees, they plant them at home or in the school grounds. A tree planted during their school years provides a living reminder of their strong friendship.

A fifth tradition is the day of the first grain harvest. All the students come to school early in the morning on the first day of the harvest. The teachers congratulate them on the harvest. The senior students and adolescents travel out into the fields and work with the machine operators and animal breeders. The younger students gather the largest heads of wheat and other crops for sowing in our experimental plots. In the evening, they all come to school. On a table covered with an embroidered tablecloth, we place a harvested sheaf as a symbol of abundance, and next to the sheaf, a loaf of bread baked by the senior students. The senior students sing and dance.

A sixth tradition is the day of the first bread. This is a celebration for the junior students. After harvesting wheat from their small plots and separating the grain in a small threshing machine, the children give their grain to the flour mill to make into flour, and their mothers help them bake bread. The children invite their mothers to school and treat them to their first bread. This festival expresses very clearly the beauty of work. The days spent preparing for this festival are full of deep emotion.

A seventh tradition is the summer hay cutting. At the beginning of June, the senior students travel at dawn to the flood meadows. They work for a week, cutting hay with mechanical mowers and scythes, raking up the hay and stacking it in haystacks. On separate days the Pioneers also work, preparing vitamin hay for the calves. The attractive aspects of this work are the friendly collective life, sleeping under the open sky, catching fish, cooking on a campfire, the sunrise, the summer twilight and the twinkling stars.

An eighth tradition is conducting community projects in the village. Every year the school community does something to add greenery to the village. This work began during the first spring after the war when the students planted poplars along one of the village streets. Since then, our community projects have involved collective work that benefits all the inhabitants of our village. We established a new park, planted trees around the cemetery, set up a sports ground for the young people in the village, planted greenery in the grounds around the creche, and planted two community orchards and two community vineyards.

A ninth tradition has been for classes to provide practical assistance to the parents of their classmates. This tradition also arose during the difficult years of the war and the post-war years, when many were in need of material and practical assistance. The father of one of our students began to build a house and then fell seriously ill. The mother could not manage the building project on her own. Senior students came to the aid of their classmate's family. For several days, all the students in Grade 9 helped with the construction until all the basic work was completed. Then other class groups provided similar assistance to their friends, helping to establish vegetable gardens, prepare fuel, harvest crops, and so on. In providing this aid, the students invest noble feelings and thoughts in their work. Two Grade 9 students, 16-year-old boys, set off at night during a severe winter frost and travelled ten kilometres through a blizzard to take an elderly and seriously ill neighbour to hospital. Thanks to their timely assistance, his life was saved. There have been many similar incidents. The most important thing about these actions is that they are performed in response to the voice of conscience, completely unselfishly.

In associating work with joyful, lofty thoughts and feelings, we ennoble the souls of our students.

Students planting trees in the school grounds

CHAPTER TWO

Our School Environment

Caring for the environment

THE SCHOOL'S MATERIAL BASE (including the environment that surrounds the children) is both a prerequisite for a proper education and a means for influencing the students' spiritual worlds—their attitudes, convictions and good habits. Everything that surrounds a child contributes to their physical, intellectual, moral and aesthetic education.

Our Soviet state provides significant material and spiritual resources for the education of young people.

The art of education involves educating people not only through human relationships, the examples and words of elders, and traditions carefully preserved by the community, but also through objects of material and spiritual value. In our view, education through an environment that is created by the students themselves, through things that enrich the spiritual life of the community, is one of the most subtle aspects of the education process.

We see the material base of the school as being inextricably connected with the environment, which includes nature and the work and social activities of the surrounding people. The objects in this environment—many of which have been created by the students themselves or their older friends and imbued with their loving attitudes—become dear to each of them, and are linked in their emotional memories with events, human relationships, feelings and experiences. I have dozens of letters from former students whose childhood, adolescence and youth were spent in an environment very dear to their hearts—the hospitable and comfortable environment of their school, a second home. Our former students want to hear what is new at our school, what is driving the life of our community. In every letter, there are moving lines that awaken memories: 'How is the apple tree I planted the day before my final exams? How is the rose that dried out after we transplanted it but then recovered? Have the rowan trees sent by our Belorussian friends taken root?'

Thanks to the life with which these objects are imbued, and the loving bond children have to them, our material assets, the objects in the environment, become part of each child's spiritual life and strengthen our community.

In the school orchard grew an apple tree planted in distant times. The oldest people in our village said it was 100 years old. Under this luxurious tree, the most heartfelt conversations took place, and the first confessions of young love were spoken. But then this old tree began to die. The children decided to graft a cutting from the old tree to some young stock so it could grow to be just as big one day. Now former students often ask in their letters how 'our apple tree' is feeling. This is not just an expression of a love for nature but an expression of extreme care for something that was formerly part of their spiritual lives.

The things children create in their environment, which at present may only be of practical use or meet an essential need, will in the future be dear to them as reminders of their previous life in our community.

Our school is located on the outskirts of a large village, about 15 kilometres from the city of Kremenchuk. The school grounds occupy an area of about five hectares, bordered by forest, the fertile fields of the collective farm, and to the south the Omel'nyk River, a small tributary of the Dnieper. There is a dam across the river at this point, which has created a large reservoir.

The village is surrounded by gardens and orchards. Between the school and the fields of the collective farm, we have planted several oak groves and thickets to protect the fields from erosion. Next to the school is a sports ground, around which we have planted apple trees. On the school's north-western boundary was a dark ravine, which we planted with young oaks, and lilac bushes on its slopes. An oak grove sprang up and a wonderful lilac thicket. The land on which our school is built is slightly hilly. If you climb one of the hills you can see wonderful views of the distant banks of the Dnieper. From the heights of an ancient burial mound in the steppe, on a fine day, you can see the fields around Poltava beyond the Dnieper, the dark blue waters of the Kremenchuk Reservoir, the outline of the hydroelectric power station on the horizon, and in a misty haze the buildings of the railway construction and car factories. To the west and south spread wide open fields scattered with ancient Scythian burial mounds.

The school is located on the quiet outskirts of the village amid nature and near large expanses of water. This has a beneficial influence on the children's physical development and health. The fields surrounding the school are planted with wheat, clover, buckwheat and meadow grasses. Science has shown that about 500 tonnes of dust constantly hovers over each square kilometre of land that lacks vegetation, while above the same area of greenery is no more than 40 tonnes. In a cubic metre of city air there are more than 5,000 microbes, but in the same volume of air in a locality dominated by vegetation there are only 400–500.[19]

Metabolism is activated in the organism of a child who breathes air saturated with the oxygen of forests and fields, preventing illness. For our part, we do everything we can to ensure the air is enriched with the phytoncides that kill microorganisms. The school grounds are luxuriant with plantings of nut, cherry, apricot, chestnut and fir trees, all particularly good sources of phytoncides.[20] For instance, there are never any flies in a hazelnut grove. All of this has been created by our children's hands and can be created in any school.

The phytoncides of many agricultural plants (especially grains) cleanse the breathing passages and blood vessels of pathogens that can give rise to colds, rheumatism or tuberculosis. Someone who has spent two months harvesting wheat near a reservoir will not fall ill with influenza or tonsillitis during the following six months. With correct routines and a good diet, children who have breathed air saturated with the phytoncides of trees, grain crops and meadow grasses throughout spring and summer will never fall ill with tuberculosis.

The abundance of greenery in and around the school grounds creates a forest microclimate. During the hottest months, our temperatures are three or four degrees cooler than in the neighbouring open spaces, and during the strongest frosts they are two or three degrees warmer. In both summer and winter we have higher precipitation than in surrounding localities, especially in the form of dew, which cleanses vegetation of microscopic dust. Our own research[21] has shown that dew, falling plentifully on vegetation near a water catchment on an area of one hectare, washes 70 kilograms of dust from plants into the soil in a single night. It is thus clear how significant it is not to allow a single square metre of the school grounds to remain without greenery. For many years the doctor and I have been systematically observing children who enter school with symptoms of nascent tuberculosis or joint tuberculosis. Air saturated with phytoncides, in combination with a good diet and correct routines, performs miracles. The children are literally transformed, becoming rosy-cheeked and full of joy. Life amid nature is as important a factor as fresh food, rich in vitamins and phytoncides. Peace and quiet, cool air during evening and night, and fresh early mornings are all part of our routines for work and rest.

One cannot help thinking that the school of the future should promote the harmonious development of human beings by fully utilising all of nature's gifts and all means of ensuring that nature serves human interests. If for no other reason than this, we should preserve and enhance all our natural resources. Our children's efforts to increase our natural resources have, over a comparatively short time (two decades), significantly transformed the surrounding environment. During those 20 years, we have converted 40 hectares of barren clay soil into lush meadows and flowering orchards.

At the same time, a school should not be too far from industrial centres. Our school's proximity to major industrial enterprises (railway carriage construction and car factories), a hydroelectric station and an established agricultural station—cradles of science, knowledge and skilled labour—is a major factor in determining the work skills and interests of our students, and the content and character of their extracurricular work, which includes technical construction and modelling.

Our facilities

LESSONS AT OUR SCHOOL ARE CONDUCTED in four buildings. The main building, with ten classrooms, is allocated to Grades 5–10 (Grades 4–7 on the ground floor and Grades 8–10 on the upper floor). In the three adjacent buildings are classrooms for Grades 1, 2, 3 and 4, and there is a staff room in each building.

Each of the smaller buildings is like a home in which a family lives, where all the children know each other. Gradually each of these families also joins the life of the greater school community. There is none of the hustle and bustle or pushing and shoving from which little children tire so quickly. From their home building, children run straight out into a garden with green lawns. There are concrete paths that allow them to access the other buildings in any weather without getting their shoes wet so that they can visit their older or younger friends.

When they arrive at school, the children leave their coats on coat hooks and do not put them on again until it is time to walk home. However often they need to walk from one building to another (and this happens several times a day), they do not put their coats on.

In each of the buildings for younger children, and on each floor of the main building, there is a reading room: a place that supports children's intellectual, moral and aesthetic development. In these rooms, they will find a collection of literature that is continually updated: popular science books, magazines and brochures, children's anthologies on science and technology, a children's encyclopedia and works of fiction. There are also stands with age-appropriate literature in the corridors. These books are arranged and tidied by the students themselves as part of their Pioneer and Komsomol duties. Anyone can read a book at school or take it home to read. Everything that is on offer in the reading rooms is designed to gradually draw students beyond the framework of the standard curriculum so that reading can become a favourite pastime. The allocation of a special room for reading, and systematic attention to the development of individual interests, is a very important aspect of intellectual education.

Taking into consideration the children's particular interests at any given time, and what is needed for their intellectual development, our teachers select books and place them in bookshelves, with each shelf allocated to a particular branch of knowledge. Each reading room also houses the following magazines: *Knowledge is Power, Technology for Young People, The Young Technician, The Young Naturalist, Knowledge and Work* (in Ukrainian), *Nature, Around the World, New World, October, Problems of Physics, Art, Youth, Young People and Technology* (in German), *Friendship* (in French) and *Aesthetic Education* (in Czech).

Without this extracurricular reading, our class lessons would be reduced to rote learning.

Books for each section are purchased using a special book fund. Failing to supplement the literature in our reading rooms would dig up the roots that feed the intellectual work taking place in lessons.

In the main school building, apart from the classrooms, there is a mathematics laboratory, a language and literature room, a language laboratory with an audio library, a radio laboratory (with a school radio studio), a music room, a Pioneer room, a Komsomol room, a school museum, a teaching methodology room, a parent room, a photography darkroom, a visual arts area, a gymnasium, a quiet place (where students can withdraw to reflect, dream, talk with a friend or read a book or newspaper) and a storeroom where students can access cleaning equipment for their regular cleaning duties.

Students in Grades 5–10 have all their lessons in the main building, apart from physics, chemistry, biology and vocational studies, which are taken in laboratories and workshops located in other buildings. In warm weather, physical education lessons are conducted on our sports ground in the open air.

Many students of all ages come to the mathematics laboratory for extracurricular activities. This is where the clubs for young mathematicians gather. Here you can find mathematics games for younger and middle school children, while for older students there are books on the history of mathematics, collections of mathematics problems, calculators and other mathematics equipment. There is also a collection of all the school's past mathematics exam papers.

In the language and literature room, there are copies of 200 works of fiction that every student is expected to read during their school years to be well-educated in the field of literature. That is significantly less than a person normally reads by the time they reach adulthood, but ensuring students read these particular books (some of them several times) is quite a complex educational task. In this room we have lists of literature recommended for reading at each year level, and separate lists of books that children are expected to read several times. Without this, we cannot imagine a complete moral and aesthetic education. We also have commentaries on classical works of fiction (compiled by the students), advice for young students, exercise books containing exemplary essays written by past students, issues of our own literary wall display newspaper, and the archive for our handwritten literary journal, 'Our Creative Writing'.

The list of works we recommend students read several times is prefaced by the following words: 'Young men and women, here are the titles of books that are among the literary treasures of humanity. You should read them several times. These books will teach you how to live and will reveal to you the beauty of art.' (A list of recommended literature is included in Appendix 1 of this book.)

We sometimes conduct discussions of books that have been read, and in this way encourage students to renew their interest in these books.

In our foreign language room, there is extracurricular reading material in French and German (the two languages taught at our school) and English (which any student can study in a study group as an elective). There is also a sound library containing tape recordings of lessons, artistic recitations of poems and prose, and recorded presentations by teachers, writers, engineers and public figures. A separate section of our sound library contains recordings of student responses during foreign language lessons and subsequent phonetic analysis of their pronunciation. Folders contain our collective correspondence with students in foreign countries (in the foreign language) and a map showing the locations of cities and countries where our students' pen-friends live.

The radio laboratory has the equipment necessary for practical work in radio electronics: parts for assembling new radio sets, a radio transmitter, and radio control equipment for operating working models of machinery. There is also a radio set for listening to broadcasts and recording them on tape, a radio on a stand and a television set. (A second television set is in the physics laboratory, where students watch broadcasts.) The radio laboratory also houses a school radio studio for broadcasting a daily radio bulletin—there are speakers in all the classrooms and workshops—and equipment for tape recording student performances and guest presentations to students and parents. The students have set up two radio stations: one in the radio laboratory and one in the physics laboratory.

The music room is where we conduct extracurricular work in music and singing. It contains equipment and visual aids for learning to read music, and a sound library of recordings of works of classical and contemporary music. We encourage students to develop an interest in listening to these musical works and to come here in their free time. Folk instruments are also kept here.

The Pioneer room contains all the equipment and regalia of a Pioneer group (the group banner, the troop flags, scarves presented to our children by Cuban, German and Czech Pioneers, a bugle and drum), and folders containing written pledges made by our children when they joined the Pioneers. Sometimes a father, attending the ceremony when his son joins the Pioneers, shows his son the pledge he wrote 20 or 30 years earlier. The father's words to his son, and to all the other children, touch the children's hearts and excite their emotions. In the Pioneer library in this room are biographies of eminent people and, on a separate shelf, books about the lives and deeds of child heroes of our own and other nations. There are also books about friendship and brotherhood between nations, the struggle for peace, and the lives of children in other countries. Our children understand very well that the children of workers in all countries have the same thoughts and aspirations.

In our Pioneer room, next to the portraits of Pioneer heroes, is a portrait of the Japanese girl Sadako Sasaki from Hiroshima, who fell seriously ill as a result of the detonation of the American atomic bomb. Like other children throughout the world, when our Pioneers learned that the little girl was critically ill, they sent her paper cranes, which, according to Japanese belief, bring people good fortune. Cranes that were not sent (some remained when we received news of the girl's death) lie under the portrait, alongside a poster with the angry words: 'An eternal curse upon those who used and plan to use nuclear weapons against peaceful towns and villages. We, as Soviet children, wish that there will always be a peaceful, blue sky above.'

In the Pioneer room, there are portraits of our former Pioneers who have distinguished themselves as workers in industry or agriculture, and their presents: books and drawings. Here there is also a sound library with recordings of children's music. We strive to ensure there are as many places as possible where a child can listen to their favourite music, dream, spend time with a friend, or enjoy some solitude.

In the Komsomol room, you can have a heart-to-heart conversation with a friend, read, or, as in the Pioneer room, listen to music. For reading, there is a selection of books from the series *The Lives of Remarkable People*, books on the history of the Komsomol and, on a special shelf, books about deeds done in the name of lofty ideals—fiery, burning pages about the lives of people with mighty souls and high ideals. These books have the same symbolic meaning as the fresh flowers in front of a red banner inscribed with words about the meaning of life from courageous fighters for social progress such as Giordano Bruno and Campanella, Jan Hus and Garibaldi, Kościuszko and Kossuth, Ernst Thälmann and Hristo Botev, Sen Katayama and Patrice Lumumba, Julius Fučík and Nikolai Ostrovsky, Chernyshevsky and Aleksandr Ulyanov, Marx and Lenin. In moments of solitude, senior boys and girls read here and think about life.

The musical works in the Komsomol room have been selected considering the feelings and emotions common to young adults.

In the school museum, we are gradually collecting everything that the school community is proud of, and that brings us together as a family. There are objects that demonstrate our students' work skills (working models, equipment, drawings, etc.), portraits of former students who have performed deeds that bring honour to our homeland, portraits of teachers who have retired, and their speeches to the school community recorded on tape. The museum keeps records of good deeds done by classes of students, the best literature compositions, and exercise books of students who graduated from our school many years ago. The museum also keeps newspaper cuttings of reports in which someone from our village says kind words about our school or individual students or teachers.

The methodology room is a place where teachers can work, read and think. In the pedagogical library, there are books on the theory of instruction and education, psychology, ethics and aesthetics, an encyclopedic dictionary and other reference books. There are also newspaper cuttings and journal articles on educational topics, stored in folders under the following headings:

> The theory and practice of moral education; intellectual education; physical education; aesthetic education; polytechnical education and instruction; educating a love of work; the spiritual life of students; the psychology of learning; psychological characteristics of children in the junior, middle school and senior school years; choosing a profession; boys and girls in the school community; methodology of teaching the foundation subjects (a separate folder for each subject); educational work in the primary classes; students' creative writing; innovations in science and technology (with separate folders for 'humanities subjects' and 'natural sciences').

Some of the material stored in the folders is stuck to large sheets of paper so it can be used in displays. A display entitled 'Use this in your educational work' offers teachers notes, essays and articles about human morality and deeds that can serve as examples to the younger generation. A 'new books' display exhibits new educational literature.

In the parent room is everything that characterises the work, study and creativity of our children. Every mother and father will find something good here that relates to their child: an exemplary piece of writing, a tool or working model they made in the workshop, an exercise book, diagram or drawing. Here teachers can talk with a student's mother or father (privacy is very important at such times).

In the staff room, apart from a timetable of lessons, there is nothing to remind teachers that they are in a school. There is an aquarium on a table, and an area with plants that freshen the air (lemon trees and a laurel). Around the table are soft chairs, and on the table are magazines and a chess board.

The visual arts area consists of a classroom and part of the corridor on the second floor. Here we organise exhibitions of drawings by our young artists. On a bookshelf there are books and albums about art, conveying some idea of the treasures held in the major museums of the world. There is an 'Art news' display for cuttings from newspapers and magazines.

Our 'quiet place' is a small, cosy room. Reproductions of paintings by eminent artists hang on the walls. (There are two reproductions hung on a rotating basis. In recent years we have used Levitan's *Golden Autumn*, Kuindzhi's *A Birch Grove*, Vasnetsov's *Alyonushka*, Vasilyev's *Before the Rain*, Trutkovsky's *On a Moonlit Night* and Pokhitonov's *Winter Dusk in Ukraine*. There are albums with reproductions of paintings on a table and a sound library with recordings of works that predispose one to reflection, reminiscence and dreams.

The 'girls' area' is a small room with a display of books and brochures (the supply is continually topped up) on anatomy and physiology, female hygiene and motherhood. The girls willingly take these books and brochures and usually do not return them. We consider this normal. Girls are often shy about discussing such matters or asking their teachers. They can take a book discretely without being noticed.

Every building used for classes has a supply of cleaning and maintenance equipment used by students. Every class has a bucket, watering can for flowers, brushes for cleaning dust from walls, and rags. Every floor has a vacuum cleaner. Every item has its own place.

Before entering the school, every student cleans their footwear twice. The first time is at the school boundary, in a trough for washing shoes. Then, after walking along concrete paths, their shoes are completely cleaned in another trough at the entrance to the school building. Students on duty check the cleanliness of the shoes. Each student stands on a piece of white cloth and wipes the souls of their shoes. If they leave no trace on the cloth, the shoes are clean, and the student can enter the school building. If they soil the cloth, they return to clean their shoes again, taking the soiled cloth for cleaning as well. All of this (washing the shoes and checking their cleanliness) takes no more than two minutes a day for each student, but those two minutes make it much quicker and easier for the students and cleaners to keep the buildings clean.

The paths that students walk on to move from one building to another are kept spotlessly clean, and if they do get wet in the rain, students only bring moisture with them into buildings and no mud or dust.

Every classroom has a housekeeping area, where there are needles, thread, buttons, rags and pieces of material.

In the building for Grades 1 and 2, there is a playroom and a story room. The playroom houses a collection of toys that encourage the development of attention, quick-wittedness, practical skills and, most importantly, a happy relationship with the surrounding world. Children play here during cold weather. A significant number of toys are operated by electricity, and some built by the senior students are automated. In selecting and using toys, we follow the principle that play should be a means of all-round development.

In the story room, props and models create a fairy tale atmosphere. In one corner is a forest, a hut on chicken's legs and a hollow tree where an eagle owl lives, providing a setting for a story about the witch Baba Yaga. In another corner, there are plywood models that set the scene for the Ukrainian folk tale about the boy who was carried away on the wings of a goose. A third corner has the setting for one of Hans Andersen's fairy tales, and the fourth corner has the setting for a Japanese folk tale. All of this is created to make an emotional and aesthetic impact on children. Lessons are conducted here to develop reading and oral language. Reading and telling stories in this environment during extra-curricular activities leaves an indelible impression on children's souls.

In every classroom building there are nature areas where you can see flowers grown by the children and where children conduct experiments with agricultural plants and soil.

Some primary school lessons are conducted out in nature, in the greenhouse or on the experimental plots. On warm autumn and spring days, lessons in Grades 1 and 2 are conducted in the green classroom. In winter, some senior school lessons are held in a winter classroom that is set up especially for the purpose.

Each class has its own property: one or two flowering potted plants, a cupboard (with exercise books, pencils, visual aids and equipment for manual work), a blackboard ruler, a pair of compasses, a pointer, a box of coloured chalk, and an arithmetic or logarithmic ruler. Class valuables (money, class library books, etc.) are stored in the teacher's desk.

The laboratories and workrooms are located in a separate building 30 or 40 metres from the main building. These include the physics, chemistry, biology and soil science laboratories, as well as workrooms for studying mechanics, electrical engineering (for the senior classes), junior electrical engineering (for junior and middle school classes), radio technology, a design, automation and radio electronics workroom, and a room for manual work in Grades 1–4. A separate entrance (at the other end of the building) leads to the school electricity generating station and a small 'foundry'. Toxic chemicals are stored in a safe in the basement. There are special preparation rooms where the physics and chemistry teachers can prepare for lessons.

The physics and chemistry laboratories each have 20 benches for pair work, screens for showing educational films (the projectors are stored in neighbouring rooms), blackboards and an electrified periodic table. Each bench has a sink for disposing of water and residual chemicals when conducting laboratory work. Each workplace is supplied with electricity and water. In the cupboards are sets of equipment and materials for individual laboratory work, and for assembling radios and electronic devices. Each workplace is furnished with a 'pocket laboratory': a small individual set of dry chemicals, crucibles, a burner, pincers, mortars, glass rods, funnels, a pipette, filter paper, hydrochloric acid, a blowpipe, and a supply of dry alcohol and urotropine. The pocket laboratories, which the students assemble themselves, play a major role in their independent work, especially when the young geologists go on expeditions.

In the biology laboratory, there is a screen for showing educational films and slides. Each workplace is equipped with a microscope, a set of magnifying glasses, and preparations and botanical samples collected by the students.

In the physics, chemistry and biology laboratories, there are folders for 'Innovations in science and technology', with cuttings from newspapers and journals, and translations from foreign language popular science magazines prepared by teachers and students.

During the past three years, the physics laboratory has acquired three sets of equipment for programmed learning, assembled by the radio technology teacher Mr Shengur and students in the senior classes. There is a management console on the teacher's desk, connected electronically to each workplace. And at each workplace, there is a device for receiving assignments from the management console. The teacher is able to set 36 different variations of an assignment simultaneously, with each student set individual work. When they have completed the assigned work, each student communicates their result to the management console and receives a mark and a new assignment. This equipment is used during lessons in physics and mathematics. Similar equipment is set up in the mathematics room and the foreign language room.

These laboratories and workrooms are intended not only for students studying the curriculum, but also for extension work by the most capable students, who begin studying some topics a year or two before they encounter them in their lessons. When some students extend their knowledge beyond the curriculum, it enriches the intellectual life of the school community, raises the level of intellectual development of the less capable, and reduces the risk of falling behind and failure.

In these working rooms, there are also displays (which can be set up for collective reading) on the themes 'Physics wherever you look', 'Chemistry wherever you look', 'Biology and biochemistry wherever you look' and 'Mathematics wherever you look'. Some of these displays have accompanying equipment that demonstrates the laws of nature in an engaging way.

In the room for senior mechanics and electrical engineering, there are working models of electric motors, a battery charger, transformers, a working model of an electrified railway, models of vehicles and machinery, and other scale models and plans. There are workplaces for 15 people (half a class) and others for group work. Students in the senior classes assemble working models here, as well as machinery and electrical equipment.

The workroom for junior and middle school electrical engineering is used by clubs for young electrical engineers and electricians. There are workplaces for 15 students. On some benches, there are models of machinery operated by electricity. At each workplace, there is a supply of parts and materials needed to design and assemble electrical equipment, and electrical tools for metalworking. The models of machinery in this workroom are selected with a view to demonstrating the conversion of energy through mechanical, thermal and chemical processes. As well as machinery and equipment explaining the foundations of electrical engineering, there is machinery and equipment that points to the future (thermo-electrical equipment using semiconductors, a model illustrating how electricity may be derived without a generator). There is also a bench and several workplaces with special sets of tools and parts for the youngest students interested in electrical engineering. These children make little models of generators and assemble models from kits.

In the workroom for radio technology, there are 12 workplaces for the primary and middle school students who show an aptitude for radio electronics. Nearly all the apparatus and equipment here has been made by club members under the direction of the most capable students in Grades 8–10. Each workplace is equipped with the tools and materials needed to complete tasks of varying complexity (assembling radios, making radio control equipment). The projects undertaken here are long-term and require the combined efforts of a group of participants.

In the workroom for design, automation and radio electronics, there are tools and machinery for working with metal and wood (vices, two lathes, drilling, milling and planing machines), an electric arc oven, soldering irons and electric fretsaws. There is an area for the smallest children with miniature machines: two drilling machines, two lathes and two milling machines. The world of machinery that surrounds children here develops their interest in technological creativity.

Another part of this workroom is set aside for the automation and radio electronics club. Here there are five workplaces for completing delicate metalwork, equipped with measuring instruments, soldering irons and a selection of materials for assembling various circuits and making automated models of machinery. There are small lathes and drilling machines for the younger children. In the centre, there is an automated lathe for manufacturing parts from plastic and soft metals. The very environment of this room reminds you of the work conducted here. The lights, the fume hood used when smelting and the clocks recording the hours that club members work automatically switch on and off.

In the manual workroom for Grades 1–4 there are workplaces for a whole class, a cupboard with materials and tools, electric fretsaws and two wood lathes. By the time they complete Grade 4, all the children can turn wood on a lathe. This is just as basic a work skill as using scissors. It is no accident that this room is located next to the workrooms where clubs operate. Each time they come here, the younger children visit the young designers or young masters of automation and radio electronics and see what their older friends are doing. They see that if they want to participate in one of these interesting activities, they have to be able to saw, plane, glue and use a lathe. As a general principle, young children should observe older children working as much as possible.

The school electricity generating station consists of two sections and has an educational function.

In the first section is a power plant with a 16 kilowatt AC generator, a power plant with a 4.5 kilowatt AC generator, a power plant with a 2 kilowatt DC generator, a thermoelectric generator, a battery charger, a galvanising tank, an electric arc oven, electric welding equipment, a milling machine, a grinding machine and a circular saw. They are located here so that when the electricity generating station is started up for educational purposes, its energy is put to use.

In the second section is the children's electricity generating station, which has a low voltage AC generator with a low output. The generator can power working models. The senior students have made several safety devices that automatically control a small internal combustion engine to prevent any accidents.

Next to the electricity generating station is a 'foundry' and a blacksmith's forge.

Nearly everything in the laboratories, workrooms and workshops is made by our students and teachers. Every year our workrooms and laboratories are upgraded with new machine tools, working models and equipment, displays and benches. For instance, during the 1963/64 academic year, the students and teachers made a milling machine for metalwork, a universal machine tool for woodwork, a circular saw, two automated lathes, six small metal lathes for students in the junior and middle school years, 15 working models of an AC generator and 45 radio sets. We make metalworking machine tools for neighbouring schools as well as for ourselves. During the past 10 years, we have supplied eight-year schools with 18 machine tools and 45 visual aids for teaching physics, mathematics and chemistry.

Next to the main block is the building housing our workshops. When entering the workshops, a student puts on a lab coat or overalls, depending on the work they are carrying out. The workshops are in three sections: carpentry, metalworking and electrical engineering. There are 20 workplaces in each of the first two sections, and 18 workplaces and an assembly bench in the third section.

In the carpentry section, there are five woodworking lathes, one planing machine, one milling machine, one universal machine tool, a circular saw and three small lathes. Next to each carpentry bench is a well-organised toolbox. An exhaust fan clears the air of dust. There is also some equipment made by the students that converts wood shavings and sawdust into compressed blocks for use as thermal insulation material for piping.

In the metalworking section, there are four lathes, one drilling machine and one milling machine, two small lathes and one small drilling machine, small vices and five soldering irons. Each workplace has a vice and a set of tools.

In the electrical engineering section, each workplace has parts and materials for assembling generators and making electrical measuring equipment and other electrical devices.

There are a few more workplaces in each section than required for lessons. This is because students in the middle and senior years have younger friends with the same interests, talents and aptitudes. Wherever senior students are working, we always consider the work of the younger students, which is why each section also has smaller versions of machine tools.

When you enter the workshops, there is a metal grid over a small chamber connected to the exhaust fan. Stepping on the grid automatically turns on the exhaust fan, and the suction cleans the person's footwear of dust.

The same building that houses the workshops also contains the library, which has a separate entrance. The library houses the books children read, including those read in the reading rooms, the language and literature room, and the Pioneer and Komsomol rooms. The library collection includes all the books that are studied as part of the curriculum. The library club keeps a record of the books that are read. This record includes a list of the students and headings for each book the children are expected to read. As each book is read, the student records that.

Several bookshelves are allocated to 'Immortal works of world literature'. Here we keep an adequate stock of the treasures of world literature. A list of these books is displayed in the vestibules of each class building, and students are expected to read them. If, for one reason or another, a student shows little interest in them, this will be discussed by staff.

The academic literature for the senior classes is organised in the library according to subject: literature, history, mathematics, physics and chemistry.

We are constantly adding to the parent section.

Our school grounds

THE SOUTHERN, WESTERN AND NORTHERN areas of the school grounds are occupied by a two-hectare orchard, in which we grow all the fruits cultivated in Ukraine: apples, pears, plums, apricots, peaches, cherries and nuts. Planted by students 20 years ago, the orchard expands every year. Next to the main building is a grape plantation 0.2 hectares in area, a favourite project for both students and staff. From May to November the children admire a sea of greenery and then the ripening grapes.

All our school buildings are surrounded by the lush greenery of cherry, apricot, apple, pear and nut plantations. There are many peach trees and catalpas, as well as trees and shrubs that are rare for our area: rowan trees, weeping willows, pine trees, birch trees, fir trees, cedars, almond trees and others.

Thanks to this abundance of greenery, on hot spring and autumn days the air in our school grounds is always clear and cool.

Between the orchard and the grapevines are greenhouse No. 1 and the green laboratory. In the greenhouse we grow flowers and vegetables and conduct experiments. There is a rack in the centre of the greenhouse with folding benches around it for class seating. The greenhouse was built by students, and they also laid the pipes to it for water and central heating. On the coldest winter day, the temperature in the greenhouse is maintained at not less than 27 degrees.

Along the path to the greenhouse is a row of metal arches with wires supporting a frost-resistant variety of grape. One end of this path ends at the school dining room, which is located in the main building.

The green laboratory is a centre for young naturalists and the natural science clubs. There is a well-lit room for activities and experiments and a small storeroom for supplies. The main room houses racks of drawers with soil samples. In the storeroom, there are containers, samples of soil mixtures and tools (spades, hoes, rakes, watering cans, spraying equipment and secateurs). On the south side is a glassed-in veranda. In winter, experiments are conducted here that require lower temperatures for hardening plants. In spring, this is an extra greenhouse for raising flower seedlings. From the veranda, there is an entrance into the cellar, where there is an icehouse for biological and biochemical experiments. It is also where we store the seeds and seedlings of plants that require lengthy periods at cold temperatures for their development.

In the green laboratory there is a drying cabinet for drying seeds, fruit and plant parts (leaves, stems, roots). Two cupboards contain collections of plants, soils and fertilisers. Like all the other school buildings, the green laboratory is supplied with water from a central pressure tank into which water is pumped. In the pressure tank, there is a floating sensor for regulating the water level that automatically turns the pump on and off. This mechanism was made by the senior students under the direction of the physics teacher. The students also built the green laboratory with their own hands.

Next to greenhouse No. 1 are cold frames, with soil warmed by biofuel.

Next to the building housing the laboratories is greenhouse No. 2. It was also built by the students and is used for growing citrus.

Beyond the cold frames, amid the orchard greenery, is the home of our experimental rabbit farm. The building of this structure gave students valuable work experience. They learned to lay bricks, mix mortar and prepare reinforced concrete panels. In this building, there are cages for rabbits, feeders and a storeroom. The floor in this building is constructed so the liquid draining from the cages is discharged through an underground pipe to the experimental plot and used for feeding plants.

Our school infrastructure includes a small section at the collective dairy farm located close to the school, where members of the young animal breeders club look after cows and calves. This farm operates very efficiently. Mechanisation lightens the workload and makes it more interesting. For instance, liquid manure is mechanically transferred to a vegetable garden, where the students obtain high yields of vegetables and learn to operate a tractor and irrigation equipment.

Between the rabbit farm and the laboratory building is a peach grove. When these trees flower in spring, it is as if part of the orchard is covered in a pink cloud. The senior students come here to admire the beauty of nature. Work becomes more interesting and attractive when such beauty is at hand.

Next to the grapevines in the shade of the trees is our apiary. This is one of the quietest parts of the school, where students can withdraw to chat or dream.

Not far from the apiary are the chestnut and fir alleys. The little fir trees were a present brought by our Belarussian friends from the Kormyansky boarding school in Gomel Region. They planted the fir tree alley together with our students as an alley of friendship. On the northern side of the school grounds is a building housing our children's theatre and cinema. It also houses a room for the activities of our drama circle, where we put on plays, hold amateur performances and screen films. Films are chosen by the staff. Students should view only the best films, and cinema should not occupy the main place in the children's spiritual lives.

Next to the children's theatre is an oak grove that gradually gives way to shrubbery. This is a wonderful place for the youngest students to rest and play. Beyond the grove is a sports area, with running tracks and areas for playing volleyball, basketball, tennis and hockey.

Our school pumping station is located at the nearby reservoir, beyond which are flood meadows—an excellent place for summer recreation and nature excursions.

On the western side of the school grounds is a hut for the young builders' club. From spring to autumn, the club members prepare reinforced concrete slabs, blocks, pipes and other parts used in maintaining the school. Next to this structure is a geography area and a meteorological station with the necessary equipment for monitoring air pressure, wind force and direction, air temperature and rainfall. Next to the geography area is a small wind generator, providing a low voltage current for small working models.

Next to the orchard is our experimental plot, which is two hectares in area. The plot incorporates a field for crop rotations of grains and other crops, a fruit tree nursery and the children's fertiliser factory. We use the experimental plot to conduct trials and research the optimum conditions for plant life. Harvested grain is used for seed and given to the collective farm and other schools. The harvests from the orchard and grapevines are distributed to the children at our school and to children from other schools who frequently visit us.

We prepare rooted cuttings in the fruit tree nursery. There are also nurseries for raising grape seedlings and the seedlings of valuable decorative trees (chestnut, walnut, catalpa). Approximately half of the seedlings we grow each year are distributed free of charge to neighbouring schools, parents, and other people who love nature and want to get involved in gardening. During the orchard weeks we hold in spring and autumn, our biology teacher conducts discussions with our villagers about how to care for trees. The other half of the trees we raise are sold. These funds are used to upgrade our school infrastructure (including the purchase of electric motors for the metalworking and woodworking machine tools we make at school).

The fertiliser factory is a plot 300 square metres in area, where students prepare various mixtures of organic and mineral fertilisers and study their influence on soil structure and the activity of beneficial microorganisms. At the factory, there is a concrete chamber in which organic refuse is converted to fertiliser.

At our experimental plot there is also a machinery workshop and a garage housing two vehicles used for instruction, two tractors and agricultural machinery (seed drills, ploughs, a cultivator, spraying equipment for the fruit trees, etc.). The workshop and garages (apart from the main garage, there is a small garage for two minicars constructed by club members) were built by senior students. Attached to the small garage is a working area for the young mechanics, where they store tools for repairing engines and materials for modelling. Interesting work is conducted in this area—small-scale mechanisation involving the construction of electrical machinery to replace manual work.

The principal's residence is in the main building. The principal should be as close as possible to the children and keep their finger on the pulse of the school community. The principal's residence exits onto an alley. By unspoken agreement, the students never disturb the privacy of this area, just as the principal and teachers do not disturb the privacy of those isolated areas that are essential for the students.

The school grounds are a kingdom of greenery. A school does not need a vast, open yard from which clouds of dust blow in the windows. We have many green glades, secluded areas covered in grass. We have so much greenery that, although the students walk and sit on the grass, they never wear it out.

Within the grounds there are many flowers, flowering alleys and groves. The path from the main building to the laboratory building, workrooms and toilets is planted with rose bushes. This rose alley is a favourite spot for walking. In the orchard, peach grove and oak grove, there are at least 30 secluded areas where flowers spread their sweet scent, and you can talk or just daydream. Everything that is connected with human life should be beautiful. That is why we pay so much attention to the beauty of our environment.

In those secluded spots intended for solitude, rest and conversation, the flowers and trees are not planted haphazardly but with consideration for the aesthetic and emotional impact each flower will have on people's spiritual lives. Planting new rose beds, looking after them, grafting a rose to a dog rose is the work of the whole school community. We even involve young preschool children in such work (they collect dog rose seeds for growing rootstock).

There are several mallow plantings. Mallow is the flower of joy, and people visit it in moments of reflection and disappointment. In one such area there is a large grapevine winding around the trunk of a cherry tree. Combined with the bright purple flowers of the mallow, the bunches of grapes create an especially life-affirming picture, reminding the person trying to disperse their sorrow of the eternal renewal in nature. Stocks, carnations, asters, gladioli and poppies each dominates its own secluded area. In one of the most remote areas, there is a planting of lilies of the valley. They were planted by adolescents, who come here to admire the beauty of the emerald-green grass and the white bell-shaped flowers. Flowers are rarely picked for bouquets. Indeed, we rarely present large bouquets of flowers and only use them for decoration when they are at the end of their flowering period. People create living beauty so they can admire it. In spring, the students take pleasure in a flowering tree; in summer and autumn, in the fruits of cherries, plums, apples, pears and peaches.

In one secluded area we have retained the original forest. Students come here to greet the onset of spring and admire the first snowdrops. In two other areas the branches of a weeping willow form a pergola. (One of these has become the favourite haunt of a nightingale.) Senior students come here when they feel sad or happy. Each age group's thoughts and feelings are characterised by certain emotional and aesthetic overtones. The little ones are attracted to noisy, lively clearings and well-lit 'transparent' groves. We have allocated several such areas to the care of young children. Here they have organised 'dining rooms' for the birds, hanging feeders for tits and other feathered friends. There are also some 'secret' areas where the little ones play and hide their treasures. There is even an old, half-ruined shelter where no-one but the little ones are allowed to go. Here they pretend to be Indians or astronauts and play other games.

The adolescents seek striking, unusual, romantic settings and play games that involve a test of strength or overcoming difficulties. They have created several areas in the lilac grove, a gulley overgrown with trees, and the forest. These areas are difficult to reach. There are several secret caves and an old run-down structure once used for storing bricks. A stove has been laid in one cave where adolescents come on cold autumn evenings and weekends to tell stories and undertake imaginary journeys. We pretend we do not know about these secluded spots, but we help the adolescents in whatever way we can. One day a group of adolescents approached me hesitantly and asked where they could get an iron chimney pipe. I did not ask them why they needed it, as they would not have told me in any case. The other teachers have the same approach in similar circumstances. Any teacher who is invited to one of these 'caves' considers it their lucky day, as not every teacher is so favoured.

In another remote area is a home for animals—a little hut with several cages. This is where the children's little friends live: a fox with a broken paw, two baby hares (one with an injured eye and one with a torn ear) rescued by the children, a grass snake, a hedgehog, a stray cat with kittens, and a puppy discarded by some heartless person and adopted by the children. In autumn, you may find a wild duck with a broken wing. There is a 'creche' for the chicks of swallows and sparrows that have fallen out of their nests, who receive constant care.

Sometimes the little children manage to adopt a lamb from the collective farm—one the animal breeders believe to be hopelessly ill. Then a host of nature lovers frequents this secluded little hut. This modest little shack is one of our centres of moral education. The act of rescuing a sparrow that has fallen from its nest, raising it and then releasing it embeds kindly feelings in a child's soul.

In the middle of the orchard is a dovecote. This skilfully made little house, decorated with carvings, sits on a tall post in the middle of the trees. There is also a swallow nursery in the school grounds—many swallows have built their nests under a wooden awning erected by the children. Places for swallows' nests have also been created on the school buildings, and nesting boxes for the tits have been hung from the trees. Caring for swallows and tits is an education in humanity.

With the first days of autumn, the leaves on the trees in the orchard and the neighbouring forest take on the most varied colours: orange, yellow, crimson and violet. Each week the display of colours changes. The leaves on many of the trees last until winter, and one of the oak groves stands covered in crimson and orange leaves right through the winter.

Each area of the school grounds belongs by tradition to a particular age group. The youngest children frequent the grape bower; the Grade 8 students love the roses and hollyhocks; among the weeping willows is the alley of youth. The teachers carefully protect adolescents and young people's right to privacy and all that is deeply personal, intimate and untouchable. A teacher considers it tactless to go to an area that has become a traditional place of retreat for senior pupils. In gratitude for this, the senior pupils also guard our right to peaceful rest and solitude. There are a few areas in the school grounds that pupils never visit, and one secluded area is just for the young teachers. This has not come about by some special agreement but of its own accord. The basis for relationships between our teachers and students is mutual respect, especially respect for each other's feelings.

For the environment the children create and live in to have a formative influence on their moral and aesthetic views and deepen their moral relationships, it requires creative 'housekeeping', so to speak. For example, an abundance of greenery and flowers requires a lot of water. We have created a network of equipment to ensure not a single drop of precipitation falling on or near the school grounds is wasted. Near the buildings are rainwater tanks that are used for watering plants. There is a network of anti-erosion and water retention banks on the school grounds to ensure all rain is fully absorbed into the soil. During downpours, the flow of water from the roads and area surrounding the school is directed via channels to the orchard and the experimental plot. Excess water is stored in pools lined with concrete. The school grounds receive a supply of water each year approximately five times greater than our rainfall. A great deal of moisture comes from storing snow. All winter, the children collect snow from the roads and create enormous piles of snow on the school grounds. This labour ennobles the children because its aim is to create human joy.

Inside our school buildings

IN THE DEVELOPMENT OF A CHILD'S PERSONALITY, a major role is played by what they see around them—in the school corridor, classroom or workshop. Nothing here should be left to chance. The environment surrounding a child should challenge them in some way and teach them something. We try to ensure every picture, every word a child reads, prompts them to think about themselves and their friends.

The environment in each school building and on each floor corresponds to the age and interests of the children using that area.

In the corridor of the building where the Grades 1 and 2 classes study, the children's attention is captured by a display of drawings that change from time to time and whose meaning is clear without captions. They are intended for children who have only just started school.

At the beginning of the school year, the children see drawings telling them about the interesting things even the smallest children can do at school. It is a sort of 'world in pictures' that acquaints the children with their immediate environment. With great interest, the little ones study pictures showing other children just like them in the games room, in the nature area, in the green laboratory, in the greenhouse, in the workrooms, by a small drilling machine or lathe, or by a little vice with miniature saws and fretsaws. Then there are pictures showing the recreational activities and work of the Pioneers—students in the primary school. Here they can see how children not much older than themselves are driving a mini car, which is even more interesting. In this way, the world shown in the pictures begins to open up the real world to the children.

In the next display are pictures on the theme, 'If every Grade 1 student in our country…'. These pictures show work that children can cope with and the results that it could achieve on a national scale. For example, if every Grade 1 student picked up one ear of grain, our nation would gain five railway wagons full of grain. If they all planted one little tree and looked after it, they could grow a forest 200 hectares in area. This sequence of pictures concludes with the words: 'That is how great your work is. Work, and create riches for your homeland.'

As soon as children begin to master reading, they try to read every caption under these pictures. In deciphering these captions, many children learn to read.

For the young children, we also display pictures that help them make sense of the surrounding world. For example, there are pictures under the heading, 'Why does this happen?' These pictures show familiar things to the children relating to nature and work, but in each picture, there is something unusual, something unexpected that makes them think. A sprig from a willow tree, thrust into moist soil, produces shoots and turns into a tree, but a sprig from an oak tree dries up. Why? On a cold spring night, when a wave of cold air descends from the north, burning the blossom on trees, bonfires are lit in the orchards, and the trees are not harmed. Why?

Another series of pictures answers the question, 'Why do they do this?' In winter they cut holes in the thick ice on ponds. Why? In very hot weather, the dry soil around vegetables is sprinkled with compost. Why? On summer days, jugs of milk are wrapped in wet towels. Why? When people want to make an axe or hammer from a piece of iron, it is first heated until it is red hot. Why?

The next series of pictures has the heading, 'What is wrong with these pictures?' In these pictures, deliberate errors have been made. For example, in the dense shade of an oak tree, red tomatoes are ripening. Collective farmers are carrying watermelons past a flowering apple tree. The shadow from a poplar is pointing towards the sun. Beehives have been placed in the middle of a field sown with wheat. These drawings lead children to think about natural phenomena and work.

The next series is called, 'Where does this happen?' The pictures show phenomena the children have learned about secondhand: from books read to them by older people, the accounts of older people or films. For example, a plane is landing on a small landing strip surrounded by ice hummocks. Where does this happen? Peasants are planting rice in a field flooded with water. Where does this happen? A herdsman is catching a horse with a lasso. Where does this happen? Surrounded by stars, a space capsule is flying through space. In the window of the space capsule, the familiar face of the first Soviet astronaut smiles at the children. Where is this happening?

The younger children are, the more interest they take in the pictures and in opportunities to widen their understanding of the surrounding world. Wonder and amazement prompt thought. Our pictures arouse children's interest in the surrounding world, awakening curiosity and inquiry.

In the corridor where students in Grades 1 and 2 spend part of their leisure time, cuttings from children's newspapers and magazines are displayed. The teachers and Young Octobrist group leaders help the children select material that familiarises them with the life of workers in our country and abroad, especially material about the lives of children. Sometimes a collection of cuttings is used for creating an area dedicated to children, such as the son of the Greek hero and freedom fighter Nikos Beloyannis (who was shot on orders of a fascist government) or Sadako Sasaki, the young Japanese girl from Hiroshima.

A separate stand and little table are used for a permanent display of children's work (handicrafts, constructed models, items made from paper or papier-mache). A stand in the middle of the corridor is used for displaying children's drawings.

In the cosiest part of the corridor is the Lenin area. Here there is a bust of Volodya Ulyanov[22] and an attractively arranged display with the sections 'How Volodya Ulyanov studied', 'What Vladimir Ilyich Lenin bequeathed to us', and 'The Young Octobrists'. Next to the Lenin area is a picture drawn on canvas with the words, 'Have you read these books?' A little girl points at a list of books that Grade 2 students are expected to read. From time to time, the list is updated.

There is a 'work board' in every classroom, showing a list of duty monitors and a list of books for home reading. Every class has a display of student exercise books, with the heading 'Write beautifully and correctly'.

In the buildings where students in Grades 3 and 4 study, a significant amount of space is once again devoted to pictures that help children understand the world and develop their interest in nature and work. As in the previous grades, the presented material is arranged from things that are close to those more distant and from the simple to the complex.

For example, one display is called, 'Pay attention to how this happens, and think about why.' The pictures show how a bee approaches a clover flower, touches it, and then flies up high before settling on the flower and gathering nectar. Why? A sunflower turns towards the sun. Why? Perhaps you can find the part of the flower that 'follows' the movement of the sun? Sometimes drops of moisture appear on the lowest leaves of a weeping willow. What is happening to the plant at such times, and why? These questions make children think about the phenomena of the surrounding world and stimulate curiosity and inquiry.

On a stand with the heading 'Why do people do this?' there are pictures with the captions 'Why are the metal parts of machinery coated in oil for the winter?', 'Why are fields harrowed two days after rain?', 'Why are seed potatoes warmed in the sun before planting?' and 'Why is coal wet before being burned?'

Another sequence of pictures is grouped under the heading, 'How can you find out…?' How old is a fruit tree? How can you find out without cutting a single branch? Will an apple tree flower in spring? How can you tell in winter? What sort of aeroplane is flying overhead? Does it have a propeller engine or a jet engine?

Under pictures showing parts from a broad selection of agricultural machinery (a combine harvester, a threshing machine, a cultivator and others) are the questions: 'Think, what machine does this part come from? What function does this part perform? Why will the machine not work properly without this part? If you do not know, observe and think!'

A series of portraits of famous people (defenders of the freedom and independence of our homeland, writers, artists, scientists, explorers) are grouped under the heading, 'Who is depicted in these portraits? What do you know about the lives and activities of these people?'

From time to time, on a stand with the heading, 'Think how to solve this problem', we display problems (with pictures) that require sharp wits and deep thought about the relationships between the phenomena of nature or of work. Another stand displays puzzles relating to technical creativity, construction and modelling. For example, a picture of several disassembled parts has the caption, 'What working model can be assembled from these parts?'

In pictures grouped under the heading, 'What country do these children live in?' are shown children from various nations. They are playing or working, and their activities are characteristic of the origin nation. 'Our friends around the world' is the heading of a display of postcards, photos, drawings, stamps and books that our children have received from penfriends abroad.

In the Pioneer areas in the Grade 3 and 4 classrooms, there are sometimes displays of new books about Lenin or Pioneer heroes.

On the work boards in these classrooms, in addition to material relevant to all students in the primary school, there is sometimes material displayed under the headings, 'Advice for young engineers' or 'Advice for young naturalists', with cuttings from children's newspapers, plans or descriptions of experiments. Class displays of children's work in Grades 3 and 4 are significantly more varied than those in Grades 1 and 2. The most capable young designers are already displaying working models made from wood or metal.

In the main building where Grades 5–10 study, the decorations and displays take into consideration the psychology of adolescents and senior students, their intellectual interests and requirements.

The displays in the corridor on the ground floor, which are directed at students aged 12–14, are also seen by visitors to the school. They reflect the educational philosophy of the staff, their way of working, their views, and the hard work of both teachers and students.

Opposite the main entrance is a colourful panel. Against a light blue background, the following words addressed to the students stand out: 'The most important thing that you must find in our school is an aim in life. Think about the words of these famous people.' Under this exhortation are the portraits of eminent people and, next to each portrait, the words attributed to them:

'No matter what the obstacles, I will continue on to my goal.' (Karl Marx)

'When I am no longer able to fight, may it be granted that I die.' (Friedrich Engels)

'In order to achieve something great, you have to begin with something small.' (Vladimir Lenin)

'Whoever is not moving forwards, is moving backwards: there is no stationary position.' (Vissarion Belinsky)

'Pitiable is the one who lives without an ideal.' (Ivan Turgenev)

'A person's highest calling is not only to explain the world, but to change it, to make it better.' (Ivan Michurin)

'The dearest thing in life is to be always a fighter, and not to trudge along in the rear as a third-class soldier.' (Nikolai Ostrovsky)

'Tell me what you dream of, and I will tell you who you are.' (Vladimir Nemirovich-Dachenko)

'Be passionate in your work and in your strivings.' (Ivan Pavlov)

'What has always been important and will always be important is what is necessary for the good of not just one person, but for the good of all people.' (Lev Tolstoy)

'A rational life without a philosophy is not a life, but a burden, something horrible.' (Anton Chekhov)

'All human skill is nothing more than a mixture of patience and time.' (Honoré de Balzac)

'There are no great deeds without great obstacles.' (Voltaire)

'A useless life is equivalent to an early death.' (Goethe)

'A person who makes others happy cannot be unhappy themself.' (Helvétius)

'Any person, great or small, is a poet if they see an ideal behind their actions.' (Henrik Ibsen)

'The most terrible thing possible is to die while still alive.' (Martin Andersen Nexø)

'There is nothing more shameful than to be no use to society or to oneself, while being sufficiently intelligent to do nothing.' (Blaise Pascal)

'All the joys in life are in creativity. To create, means to defeat death.' (Romain Rolland)

Our adolescents and young men and women read and re-read these words, thinking about them and writing them in their diaries. Questions that are addressed to them also prompt them to reflect on their short lives and dream about the future: 'Have you thought about your aim in life? What goals have you set yourself, and what have you achieved? What difficulties have you overcome? Have you tested your will and strengthened your character in some endeavour that meets the needs of others? What will you remember your young years for? Make sure that in the future, when you review the path travelled, you do not feel pangs of conscience for years lived aimlessly.'

Another colourful panel is dedicated to the theme of work. The portraits and words of eminent people are framed by ears of wheat, bunches of grapes and oak leaves:

'You need to love what you do. Then work, even the crudest, is raised to the level of creativity.' (Maksim Gorky)

'Getting rid of freeloaders and glorifying work: that is the constant trend of history.' (Nikolai Dobrolyubov)

'Without an intense love of work there is no talent and no genius.' (Dmitry Mendeleyev)

'If you choose your work wisely and invest your whole soul in it, happiness will seek you out of its own accord.' (Konstantin Ushinsky)

'An idle life cannot be pure.' (Anton Chekhov)

'Lazy people are always mediocre, whatever they undertake.' (Voltaire)

'Someone who knows from childhood that work is the law of life, and that bread is only obtained from sweat, is capable of doing something great, because at the necessary hour they will find the will and strength to see it through.' (Jules Verne)

'Genius is 5% inspiration and 95% perspiration.' (Thomas Alva Edison)

'The most fortunate gifts are spoilt by idleness.' (Michel Montaigne)

'Every person who does not work is a scoundrel.' (Jean-Jacques Rousseau)

'The lazy and idle people in a state are like the drones in a beehive, eating the honey made by the workers.' (Miguel de Cervantes Saavedra)

'Work is the best medicine, moral and aesthetic.' (Anatole France)

Each thought expresses the moral significance of the relationships between members of our school community that we work so hard to establish. Eminent people's thoughts about work prompt the students to critically evaluate their own behaviour and educate themselves.

There is great educational significance in the panel, 'Great deeds performed by young people'. On this panel are the portraits of scientists, social activists and writers who achieved outstanding success at an early age, making a significant contribution to the spiritual life of humanity:

> 'Mikhail Sholokhov was not yet 23 when he completed the first volume of his world-famous *Quiet Flows the Don*.'
>
> 'Maksym Rylsky published his first book of poetry at the age of 15.'
>
> 'Nikolai Lobachevsky became an assistant professor at the age of 21, and a professor of mathematics at the age of 23.'
>
> 'Lesya Ukrainka was 13 when she published her first poem in a journal.'
>
> 'Arkady Gaidar was a regimental commander in the Red Army at the age of 17.'
>
> 'Sofia Kovalevskaya was awarded the degree of Doctor of Philosophy at the age of 24 for outstanding works in mathematics.'
>
> 'Alexander Lodygin invented the electric light bulb at the age of 25.'
>
> 'Miklouho-Maclay completed his first voyage to the Canary Islands when he was 22. At the age of 25 he landed in New Guinea, where he lived for more than a year with the Papuans.'
>
> 'Petr Semenov-Tian-Shansky completed a journey to Tian Shan and Lake Issyk Kul at the age of 29. This journey paved the way for a number of expeditions to Central Asia.'
>
> 'Giuseppe Verdi wrote his first musical work when he was 10 years old.'
>
> 'Thomas Alva Edison, the great American inventor, published a newspaper as a 15-year-old. He wrote the editorials and did the typesetting, page make-up and printing.'
>
> 'Nikolai Dobrolyubov, the great Russian critic and revolutionary democrat, lived for 25 years. His works will live forever.'
>
> 'Sergei Mergelyan, the Soviet mathematician, graduated from university at the age of 18 and became an academician at the age of 25.'

Below this panel is written: 'Work, dare, give happiness to others. In this you will find your own happiness. Know that it is possible to become a poet, an artist, an explorer in any work. Do not be afraid to dream of excellence in science or art. Here, within the walls of our school, there may be a Raphael or a Tchaikovsky, a Sholokhov or an Edison. Work, work and more work, that is what will help you to uncover your talents and abilities. Great people are great toilers. Make a life of work your ideal.'

Next to this panel is a quiet corner (a couch, a few chairs, some flowers, a chessboard), where it is intended that a young man or woman can stop and reflect on their aim in life.

At the end of the corridor is the Pioneer room. Above a bust of Lenin hang the portraits of Pioneer heroes who gave their lives for their homeland. On a little table is a porcelain vase, where children's careful hands place fresh flowers. A poster displays words with a direct message from the fallen heroes to those who are preparing to embark on life:

'Pioneer, Komsomol member, spare a moment! Honour our memory with a minute of silence. We gave our lives for your happiness. We were just as happy and full of life as you are, and just like you we loved to run, play, swim and get up to mischief. When our homeland was in peril, each of us found the courage in our hearts to perform a heroic deed. We died for our homeland. During this minute, think about your own life. Remember at what dear cost your happiness has been won. Do you value it? What are you doing with your life? Are you preparing to perform great deeds in work? Are you prepared to give all your energy, and if needed, even your life, for your homeland?'

The whole atmosphere of this area prompts one to forget the mundane for a minute and absorb a sense of the heroic, the exceptional. Next to Lenin's bust is a portrait of Zoya Kosmodemyanskaya, and then posters on the themes, 'What Lenin bequeathed to us' and 'Rules for young Leninists'.

On the ground floor there is a colourful poster with the words, 'Knowledge is great wealth. Be determined in your quest for knowledge, so you can make the world a better place, find happiness, and bring happiness to others.' Underneath this exhortation are the portraits and words of eminent scientists, writers, and public figures:

'In science there is no main road, and the only people to reach its shining summit are those who, disregarding their fatigue, clamber up its stony tracks.' (Karl Marx)

'If I know that I know little, I will manage to know more.' (Vladimir Lenin)

'If I was told, "Go and study, but for that we will beat you with sticks every Sunday on Nicholas Square", I would probably accept those conditions.' (Maksim Gorky)

'Never think that you already know everything. And however highly others value you, always have the courage to tell yourself, "I am ignorant."' (Ivan Pavlov)

'Knowledge is only genuine when it is acquired by applying all your thought, and not just by memorising.' (Lev Tolstoy)

'Pity the student who does not excel their teacher.' (Leonardo da Vinci)

'It is not enough to know; you must apply. It is not enough to wish; you must do.' (Goethe)

'Of all nations, the greatest will always be the one that excels the others in the fields of thought and intellectual activity.' (Pasteur)

We try to make sure that in our school even the walls speak.

The deep thoughts displayed on these posters and panels are absorbed by our students and prompt an emotional response because they are a part of our system of moral, intellectual and aesthetic education. If these quotations were not connected meaningfully with our school community's current life, all these words would be just empty sounds and would not affect our students' hearts and minds. Our displays are updated from time to time, depending on our educational priorities.

In the vestibule of the ground floor, we also have poster displays aimed specifically at children in the middle school to develop curiosity and a thirst for knowledge. One such poster contains the following message for adolescents: 'Think about whether it is possible for people to harness natural forces that have never been harnessed before.' Under these words are a series of pictures: huge ocean waves crash on the shore, lightning pierces a storm cloud, expanses of the desert are lit by the blazing sun, and in the depths of the Earth are hot springs. Under the heading 'Read books about these natural forces' is a list of recommended literature.

Another poster display on the theme, 'Do you know mechanics?' contains a series of pictures showing machinery operated by internal combustion engines or electric motors (a threshing machine, a stone-crusher, a chaff cutter, a separator, a groat cutter, a pump, etc.). Under each item of machinery there is a problem: 'Think about what changes would need to be made to the mechanism if the shaft rotation speed of the engine were increased by a certain number of rotations per minute. Think about what the diameter of the flywheel on the mechanism must be if the diameter of the flywheel on the engine is a certain size.' There are similar problems for each machine.

A third display is called, 'Mathematics wherever you look', with the upper part of the display devoted to depictions of manual and mechanical work processes that require some knowledge of mathematics. Students are asked to think about what formula they need to know to make calculations for some work process or to choose a tool. The rest of the display is made up of puzzles that require sharp wits and concentration. (This material is changed from time to time.)

Another display is called 'Questions wherever you look'. This display has pictures showing common natural phenomena and work processes that, on closer inspection, reveal something that requires explanation. For each picture there is a question. 'Why, on a clear day, can you see stars at the bottom of a deep well? Why are thunderstorms so rare in winter? Why, in damp, foggy weather, is there no echo in a forest? Why does a driver reduce speed on a sharp bend?'

Another display is called 'Have you read these books?' Next to the names of books students in Grades 5–7 are expected to read are some guidelines for young readers (advice on how to read a book, how to keep a reader's diary, how to collect quotations from what is read).

Another display is called 'How to work on compositions'. It contains advice on selecting material for creative writing assignments and developing intellectual work skills, together with samples of outstanding compositions, poems and essays.

Next to a small map of the world is a stand with the heading, 'The world this week'. Here the students display cuttings from newspapers and magazines about major world events that have taken place during the past week. Each news item is connected by a thread to the location on the map associated with that event. Above these news reports is a message for students: 'Think about the causes of these events. What could they lead to?' With this display, we are trying to prompt adolescents and senior students to reflect on the fate of humanity.

Another display is called 'Love your native language. Speak correctly, expressively and clearly.' Examples are given of how to speak and how not to speak. From time to time, these examples are changed by members of the creative writing group.

One area of the vestibule is devoted to a display of new publications of popular science literature about mechanics, electrical engineering, radio technology, biology, astronomy, chemistry and geology. Here students can also find fresh issues of literary and scientific journals.

In an area for young local historians is a map of our district showing the locations of significant historical events. This map is gradually updated with new discoveries made by our local historians. This work both enriches our knowledge and deepens our love of our homeland.

On the ground floor, there is also an exhibition of children's art from throughout the school.

Another part of the vestibule on the ground floor houses a display headed by Gorky's words: 'Without a mother, there can be no poet and no hero.' This display includes the portraits of mothers who have given humanity exceptional people: Vladimir Lenin, Nadezhda Krupskaya, Nikolai Gogol, Vladimir Mayakovsky, Ilya Repin, Petr Tchaikovsky, Zoya Kosmodemyanskaya and Yury Gagarin. Under the portraits is a message: 'Your mother gave you life, showed you the world, and taught you your native language. She cares about your health and wants you to be happy, honest and courageous. Look after your mother. Guard her health and hold her hopes dear. Do not do anything to darken her life. Be the sort of person that your mother can be proud of.'

On the wall next to the stairs that lead to the second floor is a panel showing the life and work of the Pioneers, with images such as a Grade 5 girl planting a tree and a Grade 8 boy driving a tractor.

At the entrance to the second floor, where the senior classes study, is a panel with the following message: 'Senior boys and girls! You stand on the threshold of an independent life. To become a good person, you must educate yourself. Think about these thoughts on self-education.' The panel presents the thoughts of eminent people:

'Nothing will bring you under control if you are unbridled on the inside.' (Maksim Gorky)

'If you cannot take directions, do not give them.' (David Guramishvili)

'All victories begin with victory over oneself.' (Leonid Leonov)

'Long live stubbornness! Only the strong in spirit are victorious. To hell with people who do not know how to live usefully, joyfully and beautifully! To hell with snivelling whiners!' (Nikolai Ostrovsky)

'We do not reason in order know what virtue is, but in order to become good people.' (Aristotle)

'Behaviour is a mirror in which each shows their face.' (Goethe)

'It is worth constantly refreshing young people's memories of the golden rule "nothing in excess", so as to avoid overindulgence and revulsion.' (Jan Amos Komenský / John Amos Comenius)

'Someone who finds it necessary to close their eyes to something will soon find themselves compelled to close their eyes to everything.' (Jean-Jacques Rousseau)

'Truth will triumph, but we definitely need to help it.' (Julius Fučík)

'Someone who harshly expresses their thoughts about the actions of others, in so doing obliges themselves to act better than others.' (Vissarion Belinsky)

'Avoid people who, when they see your vices and shortcomings, justify them or even approve of them. Such people are either flatterers, or cowards, or simply fools. Do not expect any help from them in trouble or misfortune.' (Grigorii Skovoroda)

'It is not a problem if people praise you for your deeds. It is a problem if you do deeds to be praised by people.' (Lev Tolstoy)

'Egoism is the greatest poverty that can afflict a living creature.' (Friedrich Schiller)

These thoughts of eminent people reflect our staff's ideas about the education of our students, ideas that are debated and that students read in books and argue heatedly about. From time to time, new quotations appear in this display, reflecting new ideas inspiring our educational work.

Another display is called 'Learn to live from those who find personal happiness in seeking the happiness of the nation.' This display incorporates the portraits of famous freedom fighters and truth seekers with short descriptions of their deeds and activities. In a cosy area where you can think, chat or simply find solitude is a display with the heading, 'Friendship and love are noble feelings that are only accessible to honest people.'

Next to portraits of famous people are their thoughts about friendship and love:

'To love, means to wish good fortune for others, and to wish it not for your own sake, but for the sake of the one you love, and to make every effort to secure that good fortune for them.' (Aristotle)

'A faithful love helps one to bear all trials.' (Friedrich Schiller)

'Love is only truly known when it is tested.' (Romain Rolland)

'The most intelligent thing man has learned to do is to love a woman, to bow down before her beauty. Everything beautiful on Earth has been born from love of a woman.' (Maksim Gorky)

'Friendship is above all sincerity, which entails criticising a friend's mistakes.' (Nikolai Ostrovsky)

'Someone who is capable of relating to a woman with crude, shameless cynicism, does not deserve to be trusted as a citizen. His attitude to the common cause will be just as cynical, and he cannot be completely trusted. (Anton Makarenko)

'It is terrible to grow old, having squandered your love, like small change, not knowing yourself to whom you gave it.' (Stepan Shchipachev)

These wise words are closely connected to the spiritual lives, thoughts and emotions of our senior boys and girls.

One display is devoted to science and learning, and has the following heading: 'In nature there is still much to be discovered and studied. Investigative human thought is now directed at problems whose solution will bring nations great benefits. Think about at least one of them and read the scientific literature! Here are some of the problems that scientists are working on at the present time.'

There follows a list of such problems:

Managing thermonuclear reactions with the aim of securing a new source of energy.

Obtaining electricity without generators.

The direct conversion of chemical energy into electricity.

The practical application of superconductivity, a property of some metals at temperatures close to absolute zero.

The creation of substances that can withstand temperatures greater than 5,000 to 7,000 degrees Celsius; the creation of substances harder than diamond.

Explaining the laws governing matter in fields: electromagnetic, gravitational, nuclear.

The conversion of elementary particles into energy and the materialisation of energy: the formation of elementary particles.

Studying the properties of matter in a plasma state.

Explaining the essence of biochemical processes taking place in living organisms. The artificial reproduction of these biochemical processes with the aim of converting substances and obtaining energy.

The artificial creation of protein molecules.

Managing the processes that lie at the basis of heredity.

Researching the living conditions of microorganisms capable of producing proteins from nitrogen, air and carbohydrates.

Using polymers to improve soil structure and fertility.

This list is followed by a second message to the readers: 'Prepare for creative work from an early age. Prepare to make your small contribution to solving these problems. Now science is becoming a productive force in society. Work and reason walk side by side, and the more skilfully you can work with your hands, the wider the door to science will open for you.'

One of the displays shows work processes the children are familiar with from their lessons in productive work, from activities in the workshops and excursions to enterprises. The students are challenged to think about elements of the work processes, where manual work could be replaced by automation.

A special display stand is devoted to developing study skills in the senior classes. The senior boys and girls are given tips on how to observe and how to use their observations in study; how to choose literature and how to read books; how to work on a literature essay; and how to alternate work and rest.

In a visible place in the vestibule on the second floor is a display with a list of literary works that will forever be part of the treasures of world culture. The list is prefaced with the following message to students: 'Senior boys and girls! Below are the names of books that humanity will read for eternity. You should not only read them but re-read them, seeking wisdom and beauty in them, finding joy and satisfaction. Acquire these books for your personal library. When you are adults and have your own families, give these books to your children.'

One of the displays is devoted to choosing a profession. Here, from time to time, we display material describing various types of work activity, work skills, machine technology and opportunities for gaining further qualifications. There is literature about various professions and specialisations on a small table.

In a central part of the vestibule is the Komsomol area, with posters on 'Lenin's ideas on communist morality', 'Deeds of Komsomol heroes' and 'The finest people in our village'. Framed in red is a list of books to read about Lenin.

In one of the most visible places is a display stand with the heading 'What all of humanity is concerned about'. Here we display information (reports and images) about significant events in our country and abroad.

In the vestibule on the second floor is our school art gallery, where reproductions of outstanding works of art are periodically rotated. Portable exhibitions are also organised from time to time in the buildings housing junior classes.

Next to the picture gallery is the foreign language area. Here students can read foreign newspapers and cuttings from foreign magazines.

The senior students maintain a colourfully decorated stand for 'News about culture and the arts'. They display cuttings from newspapers and magazines with information about theatre, painting, music, sculpture and architecture. In April each year, they display correspondence, reviews and other material about works that have been awarded the Lenin Prize.

In the vestibule on the second floor are wall newspapers maintained by various clubs about science and technology, literature, history, geography and other areas ('Young mathematician', 'Technical creativity', 'Literary creations of young people', 'Sputnik', 'The past and present of our local area').

In our workshops and workrooms, there are special display stands acquainting students visually with the safety rules. Other stands show plans and descriptions for working models that students are currently making.

In our workrooms and workshops, we also have displays about the work of famous people in our country—masters with 'golden hands'. From time to time, we set up special displays to challenge our students to take part in competitions to create working models of machinery.

Everything that I have just described has been created by our students and teachers. They draw the posters and set up the displays.

The immediate setting in which our students find themselves is a part of the overall educational environment. This environment has to be created, trying to ensure the moral experience of humanity, expressed in striking images, drawings and the wise thoughts of eminent people, becomes a part of our students' spiritual life. We believe deeply in the power of language, in the power of directly addressing a person's spiritual world. At the same time, we do not forget that such messages will only touch hearts and minds when the one the message is addressed to is already seeking answers to questions that agitate them—when they want to learn how to live, and strive to know the truth. This quest and these aspirations depend on what motivates the school community and the ideals that inspire people in that community.

Good health makes a child feel as if they have an endless supply of energy, and is a source of joy, optimism, and a readiness to overcome any difficulties.

Physical work plays just as important a role in the development of physical perfection as sport. Without healthy tiredness a person cannot fully experience the pleasure of rest.

CHAPTER THREE

Health and Physical Education

Physical and mental health

GOOD HEALTH MAKES A CHILD feel as if they have an endless supply of energy, and is a source of joy, optimism and a readiness to overcome any difficulties. A weak, sickly child predisposed to infections faces continual adversity.

For 20 years, we have been trying to understand why some students fall behind in their studies. Research into the physical and intellectual development of children who fall behind has led me to the conclusion that in 85% of cases, the reason for falling behind or repeating a year is a poor state of health: some sort of illness or indisposition, more often than not imperceptible to a doctor and able to be diagnosed only as a result of the combined efforts of mother, father, doctor and teacher. We began to uncover conditions that were imperceptible at first glance, masked by the child's lively and active nature—conditions affecting the circulatory, respiratory and digestive systems. With each year, we saw more and more clearly the dependence of a child's inner life—of their intellectual development, thought, attention, memory and application—on the 'play' of their physical energy. For example, observation convinced us that in the vast majority of cases, so-called 'slowed thinking'[23] is not the result of any physiological or functional impairment of the brain cells in the cerebral cortex, but rather the result of a general malaise of which the children themselves are unaware. Children with such an indisposition work hard at the start of the lesson, but after 10 or 15 minutes, their eyes glaze over, they stare into space and they cannot focus their thoughts or listen attentively to the teacher. These hidden ailments and indispositions are particularly evident when the teacher attempts to fill every minute of the lesson with intense intellectual work to ensure not a single moment is wasted. This accelerated tempo, this gallop (e.g., when a teacher asks students in a maths lesson to solve five or six difficult problems in succession), brings some students to a state of complete exhaustion. Their eyes become dull and their movements apathetic. We need to warn proponents of so-called effective, accelerated instruction not to play games with children's health. Our staff are seriously concerned that the forced introduction of a three-year program for primary schools—without significantly raising the pedagogical skills of all teachers, enriching the children's whole intellectual life, or giving sufficient thought and planning to intellectual education in general—will be detrimental to children's health.[24]

When it became clear to us how much the intellectual work and whole inner life of a child are dependent on their health, our staff decided to begin our study of each child by looking at their health. Following a thorough medical examination, a doctor reports to our staff on the health of each child enrolling in Grade 1. Any children who are found to have weaknesses of the circulatory, respiratory or metabolic systems are constantly monitored by our teachers.

We try to halt the development of any illness and to strengthen the children's immune systems. We cooperate with parents to develop routines governing work, rest and diet. Children whose slow thought processes are due to general weakness, leading to sluggishness and depressed activity in cerebral cortex cells, are encouraged to sleep outside in spring, summer and autumn, and receive a diet rich in vitamins and phytoncides (honey, milk, butter, eggs, meat and fruit). This has a truly miraculous effect on their health and intellectual development.

With each year, we become more convinced that the most important prerequisite for effective study and general psychological wellbeing is the prevention of illness and susceptibility to illness by strengthening the organism. If we still have two or three students repeating a year, that means we have not been able to improve those children's health due to deep pathological anomalies that are mostly inherited (e.g., mental processing disorders in the children of alcoholics).

This issue has a reverse side to it. Health depends to a huge extent on the inner life, which includes a child's approach to study. We do not permit the implementation of methods of 'effective', 'accelerated' instruction that view a child's brain as an electronic mechanism capable of limitlessly absorbing information. Children are living creatures, and their brains are delicate, tender organs that must be treated with care and concern. It is possible to give primary education in three years, but only on the condition that there is a constant concern for the children's health and the normal development of a child's organism. The basis for effective intellectual work is not found in its tempo and intensity but in giving due attention to its organisation and carrying out multifaceted physical, intellectual and aesthetic education. Educators need to give particular attention to the spiritual lives and health of students during the adolescent years.

The psychological resilience of adolescents and senior students flows from a sense of joy in life, vitality and abundant energy. I use the word 'sense' advisedly because at this age, students do not think about their health or appreciate it. Our teachers' concern for their students' health is tactful and subtle and does not discourage their noble scorn for children who are overprotected by their parents and afraid of catching a cold or getting tired. The fact that our adolescent and senior students consider it a form of valour to stretch their physical energies and even risk their health is not recklessness, as some members of the older generation may imagine. It is an expression of the deep moral processes involved in affirming one's identity and developing moral maturity. We try to maximise our contact with students through shared interests, so our concern for their health is expressed subtly and in a friendly way.

Young men and women protect the intimacy and inviolability of everything connected with the physical and physiological spheres. Any tactless comment in which they perceive disrespect, criticism or mockery of any aspect of their physical development is keenly felt as an encroachment on their inner worth. It is particularly unacceptable to comment on any physical imperfection a young man or woman is trying to conceal.

Sensitivity to any encroachment on a person's deeply personal, intimate life is one of the attributes of human spiritual beauty. We try in whatever way we can to encourage physical independence and comradely relations between our adolescents and young men and women, and especially encourage a sense of self-worth. This is particularly important for the girls. The more self-respect a girl shows in her conduct, the more noble and chaste a boy's feelings of love towards her will be, and the greater the educational influence the girl will exert on the boy's moral character.

We also need to bear in mind that adolescents and young men and women seek to strengthen their willpower by testing their physical strength. Following the examples of their favourite heroes—the Gadfly, Pavel Korchagin, Julius Fučík, Musa Cälil, Zoya Kosmodemyanskaya—they constantly seek to test their physical and mental powers in some endeavour. This sometimes gives rise to a silent competition between friends of both sexes.

Adolescents and young men and women also react very sensitively to the aesthetic side of their physical development. They take to heart the opinions of others about their physical appearance. Looking after their appearance is just as important to them as looking after their health. Each generation of students looks at themselves ever more critically. Consequently, we focus on ensuring students' concern about their appearance is balanced by involvement in work and creativity. We do not want people to care solely about their physical appearance, as that leads to an empty soul.

Rapid physical development during adolescence and young adulthood requires educators to pay significant attention to balancing their students' physical and intellectual work. Many years of observation has convinced our staff of the significant danger of excessive, crippling intellectual work during adolescence. We will not tolerate young people aged 12–15 doing four or five hours of homework daily in addition to attending classes for five or six hours a day. This will cripple them, affecting their health for life, as well as their physical appearance. They will become round-shouldered, narrow-chested and possibly short-sighted. In this book, I will explain how we manage intellectual work in a way that takes care of a person's health and beauty.

We do not allow girls to carry heavy weights or participate in excessively strenuous physical work. One of our traditions is that our female teachers are also excused from such work. This tradition provides a good example for our young men.

Hygiene and student routines

ROUTINES GOVERNING WORK AND REST are a very important factor in maintaining good health and good spirits. The conscious maintenance of routines is also a significant factor in the development of a strong will. I will show how the observance of hygiene expectations and routines governing work and rest facilitates a student's integrated physical and spiritual development.

There are more than ten trees per student in our school grounds, and this 'oxygen factory' expands each year. During the spring and autumn months, some Grade 1 and 2 lessons are conducted in 'green classrooms' in the open air, on green lawns surrounded on all sides by trellised grapevines. These are also used for conducting extracurricular activities after school.

We do not allow students in junior classes to spend more than three hours a day doing intellectual work in closed classrooms. The parents in every family in our village construct outdoor pergolas in which young children can read, write, draw and do manual work. We have a special nursery that produces wild grape cuttings and seedlings for this purpose, and we freely supply them to anyone who needs them.

At our staff meetings, we often discuss what more we can do to ensure our students breathe fresh, clean, oxygen-rich air, free of microbes. We decided to create green barriers around our workshops. We planted grapevines along the walls, which have covered them up to the rooves. The windows of our workshops now open onto a sea of green foliage that diffuses the sun's bright light and permits only clean air to enter the workshops. As we have many citrus trees, the air in the school grounds is enriched with oxygen and cleansed of carbon dioxide even during the winter months.

All our lessons are conducted in a single shift, so all are conducted in natural light.[25] Further, our children's eyesight is checked medically on a regular basis. If we observe the slightest abnormality in vision, we take measures to strengthen the whole organism to prevent any deterioration in eyesight. The children concerned are given augmented diets rich in plant and animal vitamins. Children with weak eyesight are given special reading routines, incorporating more frequent breaks and greater variation. Some children are excused from lessons for a few minutes to have a walk.

As well as periodically checking that desks are an appropriate size for each child, some individual modifications are made to desks used by round-shouldered children. Neither the child nor the class is aware of these modifications. Routines governing desk work affect the harmonious development of the body and posture. Teachers and parents cooperate to ensure there are daily limits to the total time students spend sitting at desks at school and at home: two hours in Grade 1, two and a half hours in Grade 2, three hours in Grade 3, three and a half hours in Grade 4, four and a half hours in Grades 5 and 6, and five and a half hours in Grades 7–10.

The key feature of healthy routines is the judicious alternation of work and rest, waking and sleeping. Studying children's work patterns showed us that this area is fraught with hazards that can adversely affect children's health and state of mind. Irregular work patterns—where periods of idleness alternate with periods of extreme, unacceptably stressful work—are a serious threat to both health and moral development. At our parenting classes and in conversations, we have spent a great deal of time convincing parents that it is unacceptable for children to go to bed late. Lack of sleep, leading to sluggishness and eventually chronic indisposition, negatively impacts how a child feels and their intellectual development.

The restorative role of sleep depends not only on its duration but also on which part of the night is spent sleeping and how a child works during the day. Children feel best when they go to bed early, sleep sufficiently, rise early, and complete any intense intellectual work during the first 5–10 ten hours after waking (depending on their age). The intensity of any intellectual work should be lowered during the waking hours that follow. It is quite unacceptable to carry out intense intellectual work, especially memorisation, during the 5–7 hours before sleep (and for those who are weakened or recovering from illness, 8–9 hours before sleep). Using the hours before sleep for intense intellectual work leads to a sharp drop in productivity and unhealthy sleep, making it impossible to engage in intense intellectual work upon waking. We were convinced by many cases that if children sit studying their lessons for several hours before sleep, they begin to fall behind in their studies. A lack of engagement in intellectual work during lessons is most often attributable to children sitting over their books when they should be out in the fresh air, in the garden or throwing snowballs.

For example, if a young child rises at six, intense intellectual work should not be expected after 12 noon or one in the afternoon. During the middle and senior years of school, given the same hour of rising, the duration of intensive intellectual work may be extended by another two, three or sometimes four hours.[26]

We have come to these conclusions after 30 years of observations. Observing the effectiveness of intellectual work during various times after waking, we became convinced that intense intellectual work has a detrimental effect on the health and intellectual development of children if undertaken after these times. Students studying at night leads to poorer memory, less clear perception, impaired cognitive functioning, poorer appetite and reduced sleep quality. We have observation notes on the intellectual work of 32 students, showing they lagged behind in their studies for the simple reason that despite weak health, they sat over their textbooks until late in the evening. Removing this abnormality, establishing a healthy diet and increasing the time spent in the open air resulted in these children being able to cope with their studies. (Eight of them completed the seven- and eight-year school programs with excellent marks, and 12 with a combination of excellent and good marks. All of them successfully completed their secondary schooling. Of 19 who completed the full secondary program, four were awarded medals for excellent marks, and five received a combination of excellent and good marks.)

We try to ensure that young children (aged 7–12) sleep for 10 hours, that children in the middle and senior years sleep for eight and a half hours, and that 40%–45% of that time is before midnight.

Such an allocation of rest, combined with intensive intellectual work during the first 7–11 hours after waking (as long as that intellectual work is conducted properly—we will come to that question later), is an important precondition for healthy sleep the following night and the complete restoration of strength. Going to bed early and rising early, and starting work straight after completing one's physical exercise routine, without sitting idle, is one of the main requirements of our system of character education. We consider it very significant that sleep, which plays such an enormous defensive role for the nervous system and the whole organism, has been assigned to the hours of darkness by nature itself throughout the history of human development. To interfere with this adaptation is to do great harm to a child's organism.

Two years before a child begins studies, we recommend to parents at our parenting program that they establish a routine for their child of going to bed early and rising early. In this way, children enrolling at our school are already prepared to some extent for our routines. Once children are attending school, our work with their parents continues. We encourage them to make the children independent in going to bed and rising. Little children find it interesting to get up at the sound of an alarm clock. This is not difficult if sleep has been of sufficient duration and 40%–45% has taken place before midnight. Then early rising becomes a habit. We have observed the intellectual work and health of many students who have risen early, at the same time every day, throughout their eight or 10 years studying at our school. They feel bright and cheerful and actively engage with material during lessons.

Our junior students usually go to bed at eight in the evening and rise at six in the morning. (During school holidays these hours are advanced to an hour later.) Students in the middle and senior years go to bed at nine and rise at half past five. (During holidays this routine may vary depending on circumstances and involvement in work and recreation, but the principle of early rising remains.) After morning ablutions, exercise and breakfast (which take no more than 20 minutes), students commence work. For the one and a half to two hours before setting off for school (two and a half hours for those who live close to the school), they do their homework. In this way, their working day begins with the most challenging task. In completing homework tasks, the emphasis is not on memorisation but on reading, reflection and analysis. The overwhelming majority of homework assignments involve creative work. Morning is the optimum time for this. The intensity of intellectual work over the ensuing hours of the working day gradually diminishes. This is a most important requirement that facilitates the maintenance of good spirits. Periods of intense work alternate with periods of rest. The first significant break is the walk from home to school, which takes 5–30 minutes. Those who live close to the school are encouraged to take a walk for 10–15 minutes before classes begin.

Varying the nature of intellectual work and alternating work and rest are especially significant for the health and intellectual development of students in the early years. The length of a lesson in Grade 1 is the same as in other classes—45 minutes—but during a lesson, children are involved in a variety of activities such as writing, counting and reading. In the middle of the lesson, the teacher sets an activity that requires children to get up from their desks and come to the front of the classroom or go outside to observe something. In Grade 1, there are initially no lessons devoted completely to writing or completely to arithmetic. The transition to 'pure' lessons in arithmetic, writing or reading is made gradually at the end of the first semester. Periods devoted to acquiring knowledge, requiring memorisation, alternate with periods of actively applying knowledge. After solving a problem, students will measure something, count, calculate or define. After several hours of intense intellectual work during lessons, students do not pick up a textbook for the rest of the day. Homework is only completed in the morning before school. Experience has convinced us that if lessons are conducted properly (especially the introduction of new material during lessons), children can complete twice as much work in one and a half to two hours (sometimes two and a half hours) in the morning as they would complete during the same time after lessons. Students in Grades 1 and 2 complete all their homework in 20–25 minutes, while students in Grades 3 and 4 take 40–45 minutes. Experience has shown that we cannot manage without some homework. Several days are allowed for work that requires considerable time, such as essays or complex drawings. Teachers advise students on how to do this. A child's intellectual work in the morning begins with reviewing material that has to be memorised and consolidated in long-term memory.

It is very important to timetable lessons according to the level of difficulty and the nature of the intellectual work. Lessons late in the day are generally reserved for drawing, singing, physical education, manual work and work in our workshops or agricultural plots. Work skills lessons are held at the end of the week. Lessons in reading comprehension and literature, which differ significantly from lessons in other subjects, are held in the middle of the day. Lessons early in the day are allocated to subjects in the natural sciences (mathematics, physics, chemistry, biology) and grammar.

Students have lunch and spend time in the open air during a 30-minute break in the middle of lessons.

In the second half of the day, after lessons, the children spend most of their time in the open air taking part in interesting, intellectually stimulating creative work that satisfies their individual needs. Workshop benches and equipment are often taken outside. The children all have an outdoor working area at home. During holidays and weekends the routine does not change significantly. The main difference is the children spend the whole day (and in summer even the nights) in the open air.

Just as excessive intellectual work is inadmissible during the term, a complete absence of intellectual life is inadmissible during the holidays. The intellectual work of our pupils during the holidays is connected with experimentation in nature (in the plots, collective farm fields, orchard, apiary or animal farm), construction and modelling, operating machines and driving vehicles.

The more time spent in focused physical and intellectual work in the open air, the more harmoniously all the organs function and develop, the healthier tiredness is, and the greater the restorative role of sleep. Students sleep with their windows slightly open, and during summer they sleep outside on hay near grain crops and meadows. The phytoncides produced by grains and meadow grasses kill harmful microbes that cause respiratory infections. If a student has spent the whole summer breathing air saturated with the phytoncides from grains and pastures, they will never catch colds (sore throats, bronchitis, inflammation of mucous membranes in the respiratory passages).

During summer our students generally holiday in their village, without travelling anywhere special. They bathe several times a day, in the lake or river, or taking a shower. Most students have a shower at home that they use from spring through to late autumn. The boys wear just singlets in summer, and until the age of 12, they wear shorts. From preschool through to the age of 13 or 14, the children go barefoot from spring to autumn in any weather. Conditioning the feet in this way is an important way of developing the body's defences against illness. I have medical records for 980 children who, from the age of seven to 14, went barefoot all summer, fearing neither rain nor heat. Not one of them fell ill even once. Some of our children are not afraid of walking barefoot in the snow and walk outside for 5–10 minutes daily in winter. They are distinguished by exceptional endurance.

Completing homework before school and freeing the second half of the day from intense intellectual work are decisive factors conducive to strengthening health, but they also provide the opportunity for a rich spiritual life and all-round development. They are the source of a priceless benefit that a full human existence is impossible without: free time.

However, freeing the second half of the day from intense intellectual work does not mean freeing it from any intellectual work at all. Rather, it provides students with the opportunity for a genuinely rich and diverse intellectual life. The education of intelligent, fully developed human beings is only possible when students have 5–7 hours of free time at their disposal each day, to use as they choose according to their own interests. Without this, any discussion of all-round development, of developing talents, abilities and a vocation, will remain empty words.

We do not allow our students to sit pouring over their textbooks after several hours of intense work in classrooms because this exhausts the brain, dulls intellectual abilities and undermines the will to study. After classes, our students are engaged in creative work in clubs and societies, according to their interests and choices, participating in games, excursions, walks, hikes, reading fiction and popular scientific literature (again according to their own choice), and engaging in artistic pursuits. Moreover, no less than 90% of this time is spent outdoors in the fresh air.

Students do not do homework in after-school care either. They do it early in the mornings. After-school care assists families, but it does not take their place. Indeed, nothing can take the place of a family. An education in which children are deprived of consistent, daily, meaningful communication with their parents is an abnormal, unnatural education, just as parents' life is abnormal and unnatural if they do not consistently care for their children.

Having observed the physical and intellectual development of many children over the years, we have concluded that an adult's health depends greatly on having had a healthy diet and daily routines during childhood, adolescence and youth. It is crucial to combine a complete, healthy diet with work, adequate sleep, fresh air and the constant, rational strengthening of the body. Diet must be adequate in calories but also rich in easily digested foods (milk, butter, sugar) and dietary elements that play an important role in the growth of the organism (especially proteins and vitamins). Our experience suggests the calorific intake should be 25%–30% greater than the norms generally recommended in children's institutions. These norms do not allow for the fact that children should spend most of their time in outdoor activities, and this increases their metabolic rate.

Milk and sugar (including sugar from fruits) are especially important in a child's diet. In the morning, after waking, children drink a glass of cold milk and eat some bread and butter. We ensure this happens through regular discussions with parents. Every family has written guidelines for a normal, healthy diet that take into account their child's individual needs. The parents prepare some foods especially for their children, including a supply of dried fruits to ensure a supply of fructose over the winter months.

After completing their homework, the children have a hearty breakfast before setting off for school. After two lessons, during a 30-minute break, every child receives a glass of milk in the school dining room, and after school every child receives bread and butter with tea or milk (for those that require an enhanced diet). Children should never feel 'a hole in their stomach'. After returning from school, the children have dinner at home. After dinner, they go for a walk or do some light outdoor work.

Gymnastic exercises and swimming play an important role in strengthening health. Apart from exercises done at home upon waking, gymnastic exercises are conducted at school before lessons with the specific aim of developing good posture. Before the 30-minute break, the teachers conduct a minute of physical education (with a specific routine for each age group). There are several platforms for swimming set up at the lake near the school.

We do our best to ensure children take personal responsibility for observing healthy routines, making sure they alternate work and rest, intellectual and physical work, and do their individual exercises upon waking. When discussing self-education with students, we draw attention to the moral significance of fully adhering to the requirements of a routine. The students develop the attitude that self-discipline is a moral virtue. This is facilitated by a number of rules that govern work routines throughout the whole school community. For instance, all extracurricular activities must end at least an hour before sleep. We try to ensure children spend the evenings with their families.

Work as a means of strengthening health

PHYSICAL WORK PLAYS AN EQUALLY IMPORTANT ROLE in the development of physical perfection as sport. Without healthy tiredness, a person cannot fully experience the pleasure of rest.

There are many work procedures in which the harmonious, graceful, coordinated movements of the human body may be compared to gymnastic exercises. For example, work such as cutting hay by hand or laying brick walls is on a par with gymnastics in its dynamism and aesthetic expression of movement. Young people perform such physical work with great pleasure, especially in a group. Work like this even has some advantages over sport as it has more layers of significance and involves various combinations of physical strength and skill. Our young men and women prepare for such work as if for a holiday. During the summer holidays, our senior students spend several days cutting hay by hand. It is difficult to exaggerate the value and charm of this work in the fields, camping out and preparing food together. The students love the collective manual work of tree planting, grafting fruit trees and covering grapevines for the winter. Every year our senior students take part in laying brick walls for structures around the school.

Having participated in such work throughout their time at our school, our students are distinguished by their attractive physical development, harmoniously proportioned bodies, plasticity of movement and ability to apply physical strength in proportion to a task's demands. A characteristic feature of their physical development is the combination of harmonious proportions, graceful posture and physical strength. They seek to express beauty in any physical work and strive for aesthetic perfection in any work process.

When we speak of the joy of work, the source of that joy is first and foremost the beauty of the work and the fact that in doing the work, a person becomes beautiful themselves.

From their very first days at our school, our students do physical work in the nature room, workshops or experimental horticultural plots. We can even find work of appropriate difficulty for our seven-year-olds: maintaining fruit trees and grapevines, growing seedlings, collecting seeds from ornamental plants and fruit trees, and selecting seeds for grain and other industrial crops.

During the middle school and senior years, outdoor work can amount to two or three hours per day.

During the summer, our Pioneers live for two or three weeks in a Pioneer camp, where work is combined with recreation. (The children work for two or three hours per day). The children maintain defensive belts of trees that protect the banks of our water reservoirs from erosion. They work in the mornings and evenings when the air is cool and fresh, and they eat and sleep in the open air.

Our senior students spend at least three or four weeks living and working in the fields. They gather and dry the hay and harvest grain crops.

In winter during moderate frosts (down to minus 15 degrees), our senior students work in the open air for 10–12 days. During this time they work, eat, rest and spend their leisure time outdoors in the fresh air. They are only indoors at night. We begin to involve children in this sort of work when they are still young. It plays a significant role in developing the respiratory and circulatory systems and strengthening metabolism. When combined with a healthy diet, such work stimulates all the body's functions and strengthens the nervous system. The nutrition of all the nerve cells, especially those of the brain, is intensified, and the restorative role of sleep is heightened. It is a wonderful way of tempering the body. In spring when the days grow longer, many senior students do their homework in the garden under pergolas. Even in winter they read outside if the weather is fine.

Coughs and colds have become very rare among our students. We have records of the physical development of 26 students who often caught colds during the first two or three years of their studies. Four of them had a latent form of tuberculosis. Thanks to a special regime that included spending all day outdoors near densely vegetated areas, sunbathing and swimming, and diets high in calorific content, the state of their lungs improved significantly and all traces of tuberculosis disappeared.

We currently have our own system of treatment for children who are prone to respiratory infections and those with weak health generally. The most important thing for these children (mainly young children, as by the time they reach their teens we do not have any sick children) is to establish a healthy diet rich in animal vitamins. They must avoid sleeping with completely closed windows in winter or sleeping indoors in summer. For three months, from June to September, they live outdoors in the fields, eat well, get suntanned and swim. Consequently, these children become strong and full of life without any medicines whatsoever.

To strengthen health in childhood and not permit children to enter their teens sickly and lethargic is to give them full access to all life's joys.

Outdoor work has a beneficial effect on children with heightened nervous reactions who are irritable and unsettled. Some children enter school with functional disorders of the nervous system caused by incorrect upbringing at home, mostly through excessive supervision and overprotection. Overcoming these disorders and weaknesses is an important task facing the school. We have records for 27 children who entered the school with obvious symptoms of neurosis. Most of these children were unable to study normally. An important ingredient in treating these children was outdoor work in a quiet environment—work that demanded more concentration and attention than physical effort (e.g., weaving handicrafts from willow twigs and other materials). Grafting fruit trees had a particularly beneficial effect. We make a point of teaching nervous, irritable children how to graft fruit trees. During this work, the children completely forget everything that surrounds them and their nervous systems stop reacting unhealthily.

Physical education during lessons and sport

PHYSICAL EDUCATION AND SPORTS ACTIVITIES only play a significant role in the all-round development of pupils when all scholastic and educational work is permeated with a concern for health.

We seek to ensure that gymnastics exercises are a source of pleasure and become an organic requirement. People should participate in sport not only for competitive success but to develop physical strength, grace and endurance.

Our physical education lessons take place on our sports ground, and during bad weather in the gymnasium. The gymnasium and sports ground have all the necessary equipment for athletics, games, climbing and other forms of exercise. Our school has chosen athletics and gymnastics as the main physical education activities, with the addition of exercises on apparatus for students in Grades 8–10. The aim of such exercise is to develop a sense of beauty in movement, strength, harmony, dexterity and endurance. During physical education lessons we give a lot of attention to aesthetic refinement, to beauty in movement. Self-directed efforts to develop graceful posture is a prime motive for students to do daily morning exercises.

Following medical examinations, all students are allocated to one of three groups: basic, preparatory or special. Each group follows its own program, with most attention given to those with poor health (the special group) rather than the students capable of breaking records in competitions. We regularly review the gymnastics routines for this special group, considering their age and whether they are boys or girls. We try to ensure that by adolescence, as many of these children as possible move from the special group to the preparatory group and then to the basic group. We have achieved this for all students whose poor health has been connected with functional weaknesses of particular organs or past illnesses.

We give particular attention to children with organic weaknesses of the heart and circulatory system or the central or peripheral nervous systems. Together with a doctor, we compile a special routine of exercises for these children to assist in the gradual strengthening of their health. These exercises are changed from time to time according to the children's state of health.

We try to instil in our pupils the conviction that by exercising regularly they will not only develop beautiful bodies, but also strong character and strength of will.

When running, skiing and swimming, we attach great significance to aesthetic satisfaction. In these and other sports it has become our custom to conduct competitions on the criteria of beauty, elegance and harmony of movement, with speed considered secondary. We are working towards creating beauty and physical perfection, which are the main goals of physical education. In general, we consider it unacceptable to conduct competitions where the only criterion for success is speed of movement. That encourages unhealthy excitement and egotism. In such competitions there is often no beauty, no aesthetic requirement and, most importantly, no mass involvement or consideration of individual capabilities. One must not turn sport from a means of physical education for all children into a means of battling for individual success. We must not divide children into those who are good at sport and those who are not good at sport, and we must not stir up unhealthy passions by encouraging students to battle for the supposed honour of their school.

Sport becomes a means of education when it is a favourite pastime for all.

Leisure activities

LEISURE MAY BE IDLE OR ACTIVE. Idleness, in the best sense of the word, is essential as a means of relaxing following intense work—intellectual or physical. But there should not be a single moment in a person's life when they are not acquiring spiritual wealth. For those who know how to use leisure, even the contemplation of nature or works of art is a form of creativity. Leisure is only truly leisure when apparent idleness is the active play of spiritual and physical energies. It is concerning that at many Pioneer summer camps children are treated like resort patrons—their leisure consists of having others meet nearly all the needs they would normally meet for themselves.

A student should see leisure as a means of improving their physical and psychological health. Teaching children how to make active and purposeful use of leisure time is one of the main elements of our system of education. We consider that recreation involves the rational variation of activity, work that satisfies aesthetic requirements and creative appreciation of the beauty of nature. With such an approach, children enjoy leisure every day, which has great significance for their normal physical and psychological development. The way to find free time for such leisure is to organise work during, before and after lessons correctly, and this includes scheduling the most important and intense intellectual effort during the first half of the day. (Idleness during lessons—the absence of intellectual work at a time when it should take place—is the main reason for lack of free time. People only appreciate free time and take pleasure in leisure when they know what hard work is and when work is experienced as a vital need. With such an attitude to work, pupils seek out active leisure—reading literature and working in the open air.)

Our summer Pioneer camps are designed to foster independence, so there are no adults working to 'service' the students' leisure. The young Pioneer campers look after their own needs. Leisure is combined with moderate, age-appropriate work. For example, one of the Pioneer troops sets up camp in an orchard. While holidaying, the children manage the trees and harvest the crop. Other troops camp in the forest. The children protect the trees, collect plants as specimens, collect seeds and prepare them for planting.

Hikes are a wonderful way to spend leisure time as they develop physical strength and encourage the formation of moral convictions and aesthetic appreciation. Students see nature in all its variety, and such leisure is easily combined with other activities.

Our children take part in hikes from the age of eight or nine. Initially, they complete one- or two-day hikes through local fields and forests and along the banks of the Dnieper under the supervision of teachers and senior students. As they get older, the children's hikes take them further afield. Our senior students complete three- or four-day hikes covering distances of 100–150 kilometres. On these hikes, the children cook their own food and pitch tents for the night.

We have developed a list of skills essential for participating in hikes. These include being able to find points of the compass without reference to the sun or stars, lighting a fire without matches, lighting a fire in wet weather, and constructing a shelter from branches and leaves. Before each hike, educational goals are set—we must learn something. Each hike serves to stimulate some new interest that enriches the students' spiritual worlds. This may be an intellectual, vocational, social or aesthetic interest. The children may learn something interesting about the history of their local region. On one hike, Grade 4 students met with veterans from the Great Patriotic War—heroes of the battle for the Dnieper. This led to exchanging letters with workers and farmers from Russia, Belarus, Georgia, Uzbekistan and Armenia, who had participated in the liberation of Ukraine from the fascists. The children created a local history display, putting together a rich collection of material: photographs from the war years and unique editions of underground newspapers circulated in occupied areas. All of this is cherished and studied.

On one of our hikes dedicated to searching for natural resources, the children discovered iron ore deposits. After this, we began to study our local natural resources in depth.

Hours of leisure are the most problematic time in our spiritual lives, when we use cultural resources created by others. We consider it essential for a true education that the hours free from study or physical work should be filled with exciting ideas and deep feelings. The richer their spiritual interests during leisure hours, the more children are attracted to study and intellectual work during lessons, and the more they appreciate the beauty in works of art.

The depth of thought and feeling during leisure hours depends on the nature of the activity undertaken. Intellectual life at these times should be different from study. When reading a book, presenting a talk to friends, learning a role in a play, or taking part in an amateur art group, students feel they are creating something valuable for the community. The active satisfaction of varied spiritual interests during leisure time provides a vital source of spiritual energy, optimism and confidence. Even intellectual work can be a form of leisure if freely chosen, and if in the process of that work a student discovers new strength and abilities in themselves. For example, we have a chemistry club for senior students. The young chemists conduct interesting experiments that open new horizons for discovering more and more of the secrets of nature. (Experiments exploring the action of chemical substances on chromosomes aroused particular interest.) This often involves quite intense work, but it does not make the students tired, as it feels like a break from lessons.

As they enrich their spiritual worlds during leisure time and develop their talents, the students are educating themselves.

We educate children in the spirit of heartfelt care and concern for all that is living and beautiful, for plants, flowers, birds and animals.

At our school students aged nine or ten have already had the emotional and moral experience of socially useful activity.

CHAPTER 4

Moral Education

Basic values

MORAL EDUCATION BEGINS WITH CHILDREN'S first conscious steps in life. At this early age, when the soul is very susceptible to emotional influences, we reveal to children the universal ethical norms of humanity, the ABC of morality. We strive to bring these universal norms to life through civic activities and independent actions. It is important not only to know what is good and what is bad, but to act in a good way.

We consider young people's acquisition of universal moral norms a very important stage of moral development. Teaching children to observe basic moral norms, we provide every child with the opportunity to live and work happily, cultivating in them their first civic impulses, their first concerns for the welfare of their community and society. In this connection, it is very important that explanations and exhortations lead to conviction and motivation. The universal norms of morality will only become a person's own voice of conscience when their actions have social significance. To teach children to live among others in society is to teach them to carry out socially meaningful actions and express their relationship to others in their actions.

What universal human norms do we teach children as the ABC of moral culture, as a first school in civic-mindedness?

1 *You live among other people. Do not forget that your every action, your every desire, has a consequence for the people around you. Remember that there is a difference between what you want and what is acceptable.*

Check your actions by asking yourself: am I doing any harm or causing any inconvenience to others? Act in such a way that the people around you benefit.

In explaining this moral principle, we provide examples showing how we should behave among others. You may want something, but first think about whether you are causing others unpleasantness in doing what you want. For example, there are roses growing in this alley, and you want to pick a flower. Think what would happen if every child in the school were to satisfy such a desire. Nothing would be left of the flowering bushes but a few bare stalks.

Children's hearts are very receptive to such thoughts. A child's soul experiences deep joy in doing good for others. If such moral homilies are accompanied by judicious exhortations, prompting children to do good deeds for others, they develop an inner spiritual strength from a young age and learn to limit their desires and whims. This is very important for the formation of civic-mindedness. If during childhood a person considers only their own interests and not those of others, governed only by their own desires and not recognising the interests of the community, they will grow up as self-centred egoists. To control one's desires is an elementary rule, the first stroke of the first letter in the ABC of moral behaviour. Loud, sentential statements about morality are not understood by children. Instead of spouting flowery language, we need to carefully refine human conduct, to hone developing habits.

2 *You enjoy good things created by other people. People give you the happiness of childhood. Repay them with kindness.*

Before children comprehend that they are citizens of a society and this entails major responsibilities, they must learn to repay kindness with kindness. Their consciences should not allow them to be mere consumers of gifts and pleasures. We tell our children: 'During the quiet pre-dawn hours when you are still asleep, milkmaids are working at the dairy farm. They are preparing fresh, nourishing milk for you. The cook is heating the oven in the school kitchen so you can have a tasty breakfast. Miners are descending mineshafts to work at the coalface so it will be warm in your classrooms. During severe frosts tractor drivers go into the fields to get feed for the cows whose milk you drink. Your mothers and fathers leave early for work so you can have clothes and shoes so that you can play under the sun and the blue sky. You are generously given many blessings, but people also expect good things from you.'

We teach our children how to do good to others. We say: 'Here is a place where the workers on our dairy farm rest. Let us plant some rose bushes and lilacs here so that it can be a place of beauty and joy for our mothers and sisters.' When our children begin planting and then take on the plants' care, this work brings them great joy because it is motivated by noble feelings.

The children progress from one good deed to a second and a third as we lead them step-by-step up the ladder of moral refinement. And the children experience sincere feelings of joy at the opportunity to do good things for others. I repeat, such feelings are only established in a person's heart when they are experienced many times during childhood.

3 *All the good things and joys of life are created by work. Without work, it is not possible to live honourably. There is a folk saying that those who do not work do not eat. Remember this precept till the day you die. A lazy person, a sponger, is like a drone bee eating the honey made by the worker bees. The first work you must do is to study. When you go to school, you are going to work.*

To accustom children to work and teach them a genuine love of work as their first civic duty, we have created an atmosphere of work at school and intolerance of laziness, negligence, idleness and sloppiness. A little idler is the living root of parasitism. We should not accept little idlers in our society. A child can only understand that life is impossible without work when they experience the joy of work in their community, and such joy is incomparable. Applying all their strength, young people do not just do what they feel like, but what is necessary. In the end, experiencing joy at what they have accomplished for others, they want to do whatever is necessary for the common good. At the age of seven or eight, our children plant small orchards and vineyards and turn barren land into flourishing gardens. Our aim is that by the age of 12 or 13, children will be able to see mature orchards created with their own hands. This is how they will find true joy in work. In this way, they see themselves as hard-working people even in childhood. During adolescence and early youth, each sees themselves in their work as in a mirror—their skill, strength of will, thoughtfulness and persistence. And the conviction grows in each one's heart that they cannot live without working. Giving oneself to others, establishing a love of work in one's consciousness is a deeply individual process. That is why we ensure that in childhood, each student invests their strength of soul in work and takes pride in what they have achieved, whether planting a tree or constructing a working model of a car for our workshop. To begin such education in adolescence or early youth is a thousand times more difficult if it is not done in childhood. The ABC of morality is best absorbed in childhood.

4 *Be kind and sensitive to others. Help the weak and defenceless. Help a friend in trouble. Do not cause people harm. Respect and honour your mother and father—they have given you life. They want you to become an honest citizen, a person with a kind heart and a pure soul.*

To foster kindness, warmth, empathy, a willingness to come to the aid of others, sensitivity to all things living and beautiful—this is an elementary principle of school education. Indeed, this principle is the foundation of school life. Heartlessness gives rise to indifference, indifference gives rise to self-centredness, and self-centredness is the source of cruelty. To prevent heartlessness, we educate children in the spirit of heartfelt care and concern for all that is living and beautiful, for plants, flowers, birds and animals. A child who takes to heart the plight of a blue tit defenceless against a winter frost and saves it from perishing in the cold, or who takes care of a young tree, will never become heartless and cruel towards people. Conversely, if a little person breaks or heartlessly destroys something that is living and beautiful, they may become a little tyrant, mocking those close to them. And how many such tyrants we come across in life. Consider a little seven-year-old getting ready for school: they cannot lace up their boots and they angrily break the lace and throw their shoes across the room. They want their mother to get upset and even to make her cry, and when they do drive their mother to tears, they feel some relief. This is the sort of 'harmless' tyranny against which we must tactfully, sensitively, but relentlessly fight. The child must feel that every person has a heart that should be spared pain, and to cause it pain is a great evil. May each child's heart feel concern for the fate of all that is living and beautiful. Then it will never know the spiteful feeling of sweet pleasure at the thought that someone's heart is suffering because of them.

We ensure each child is responsible for the care of flowers and plants, birds and animals, fish in an aquarium. This work refines heartfelt sensitivity and awakens a desire to do good. We encourage children to care for other people, primarily for mothers and grandmothers, fathers and grandfathers. On their very first day at school, we explain to the Grade 1 students how hard it is for their parents and what a hard life's journey their grandfathers and grandmothers have had to traverse. That very day, in their gardens at home, the children plant an apple tree for their mother, an apple tree for their grandmother, another for their father and another for their grandfather. They take on responsibility for the care of these trees (of course, they have to be reminded and literally led by the hand). Eventually, the day arrives when fruit ripens on these trees and the children offer the fruit to their parents and grandparents. (This too has to be taught, and the child reminded a thousand times.) If you manage to make these the most joyful moments in a child's life, you have entrenched moral values in the child's heart. We do not believe that moral vices are due exclusively to the remnants of capitalism in people's consciousness. Moral vices can arise wherever there is a lack of genuine education, where a little person is treated like a little god for whom anything is permitted or, conversely, like a neglected weed that is taught nothing good or evil. For there to be no evil, we must teach only goodness.

5 *Do not be indifferent to evil. Fight against evil, deceit and injustice. Do not accept the ways of those who would live at others' expense, cause harm to others, or steal from society.*

We consider it important to educate high civic expectations and an active approach to fighting evil and untruth. It is unacceptable for children to silently witness the squandering of resources, laziness, carelessness or inhumanity. But since those who do evil are often adults, educational work in this area demands great thoughtfulness and tact.

In our school, we have a Pioneer observation post for the preservation of green plantings. This is one of our cradles of civic education. If the children see that an adult has destroyed or harmed trees, then the fight against this evil must not be limited to words alone. A child's heart experiences pain if evil goes unpunished. For this reason, we are at pains to ensure the community makes the person who has committed the crime carry out work to repair the damage done. When they see that good triumphs over evil, children are more enthusiastic about participating in work that benefits society. If children are outraged at the evil they witness in life and express their indignation, that is good. But they must also know how to do good, to entrench goodness in life through their own actions. Otherwise, they may become empty windbags, demagogues, 'protesters' who do nothing to ensure that goodness and truth triumph.

Such is the ABC of moral culture through which our children grasp the essence of good and evil, honour and dishonour, justice and injustice. At the same time as teaching these elementary truths, we gradually explain moral values such as love for our homeland and the need to show heroism, resilience and courage in defending its honour, independence, greatness and power. The skill and art of education lies in presenting these moral values to young hearts through vivid images that engage the mind and excite the soul, awakening idealistic moral aspirations. According to a wise Latin proverb, *verba docent, exempla trahunt* (words instruct, examples lead). We try to ensure children are inspired by the world's moral inheritance. In our moral discussions, we cite the most shining examples of spiritual beauty, greatness, courage and loyalty to one's people and their ideals.

The task of a school is to build genuinely moral, highly idealistic civic relations within its own community based on the moral values created, attained and fought for by older generations. Moral values must become part of the personal spiritual wealth of each pupil. This is achieved when the moral concept revealed to the student's mind and heart through a vivid image awakens deep moral and aesthetic feelings. When we wish to impress the hearts and minds of our students with the moral values of our society and humanity at large, we select historical examples that fill our children with wonder and amazement at the greatness and beauty of what someone has done to serve the common good.

We have created a unique anthology of moral values: descriptions of thousands of deeds carried out by people loyal to their homeland, to the ideals of working people, to their convictions. The fruit of many years' work, this anthology includes moral values created by humanity from ancient times to the present. But its main pages are devoted to the heroic battle of our people for freedom from exploitation, for the freedom and independence of our homeland during the years of the revolution, the civil war and the Great Patriotic War. Some pages of the anthology are devoted to working people, whose heroic achievements are especially important to share with young people so they realise that a person does not need exceptional circumstances to attain greatness. Through examples of the lives and battles of our homeland's best sons and daughters, we teach our students to be true citizens.

We encourage our students to make their lives like the lives of those who consider it an honour to work for our nation. We show each generation of adolescents and young men and women the pages of our anthology devoted to the eminent builder and welder Aleksei Ulesov, who has twice been awarded the medal of a Hero of Socialist Labour. During his lifetime, Ulesov has built several towns. We read our students his letter to our school: 'It is worth experiencing at least once in your life the happiness of being a creator on this Earth. It is worth seeing how your buildings grow and are inhabited by people, how your electricity generating station, your first unit, delivers current. Or how your canal runs through the countryside, or children start attending your kindergarten. For me, this is such a satisfying feeling that no prizes or fame can match it.'

One of the pages of our anthology is devoted to the eminent animal breeder Stanislav Ivanovich Shteiman. Our students are full of wonder at the life of this man. During the early years of the Soviet state he was a shepherd and farm labourer in the village of Karavaevo. He had a very difficult childhood and did not go to school, but he became a Doctor of Sciences and developed a new breed of cattle. We share the words of this great scientist who emerged from such humble origins in the hope that his moral significance will find a place in our students' hearts: 'I have spent the greater part of my life in animal yards and cowsheds. But when I look back at the life I have lived and the work I have done, I feel like a traveller who has explored unfamiliar pathways, or a mountaineer who has climbed mighty peaks.'

Dozens of pages in our anthology have been devoted to people who, like Aleksei Maresyev, overcame great hardship, showing true spiritual courage, and achieving success in work, in intellectual or artistic creativity. The lives and deeds of these people provide an extremely powerful means for instilling the conviction that morality and strength of spirit are at the core of citizenship. They can also provide a spiritual shock to jolt the weak, indecisive, weak-willed or simply lazy, a way of awakening the voice of conscience and prompting a student to take their first steps on the path of self-education.

We encourage our adolescents and young men and women to reflect on these people's lives, to compare their own willpower and decisiveness in overcoming difficulties with theirs. There is a page about our Ukrainian equivalent to Maresyev: Ivan Moldavsky. He lost both hands and his left leg during the war, but he did not become despondent. He completed high school and then graduated from an institute and became an agricultural scientist. He works in the Odessa Region.[27]

Grigorii Zmienko lost both his legs. He found the courage to return to work as a tractor driver in the village of Petropavlovka in the Kharkiv Region.[28]

Dmitry Kruzhilin, a tractor driver with the Karginskii Tractor Station in the Rostov Region, lost both hands while saving a child's life. He found the strength of spirit to return to work and is once again working with tractors, repairing them, as he explained in a letter to our children.[29]

Vasily Voropaev, an engineer with the Azov Steel Factory, lost his sight while saving a young worker from a crippling injury. The blind engineer remained in the workforce. He successfully completed a research degree.[30]

'I cannot imagine life without work, without overcoming difficulty.' We wrote these words from a letter written by Voropaev under his portrait and hung it next to the desk of Grade 7 student Victor S., who was 'hopelessly lazy' according to several of his teachers. A change came over Victor's life, one that we have come to expect when we expose weak-willed (often spoilt) children to the moral value of spiritual strength and courage. The boy took himself in hand and developed a strict work routine, not allowing himself to get up from his desk until he had completed the work allocated for that day.

When talking to a class about the strength of spirit of such people, we arouse feelings of collective admiration and of being inspired by others' deeds, and any lazy person feels disgraced. They burn with shame, even though the teacher does not mention them directly, as the whole account is essentially directed at them. It is best to avoid as far as possible any direct accusations of laziness, carelessness or any form of immorality, since such reproaches have little use compared to the impact of a positive example.

Moral understanding and moral conviction

THE ACQUISITION OF KNOWLEDGE about nature and society is only the beginning of education. Beyond that is the long, complex process of forming personal moral convictions. Personal moral convictions are the ultimate result of moral education, the main indicator of a person's moral character, their ability to match thought and action, words and deeds.

We may speak of moral conviction when knowledge of a truth or concept permeates a person's psychology at a deep level. It becomes their personal view, arouses deep feelings, merges with their will, and manifests in their actions, conduct and relationships with others and themselves. A moral conviction is an active expression of one's personality, involving a zealous urge to defend the correctness and prove the truth of one's point of view and a preparedness to accept any privations to do so. Convictions are revealed not so much in what a person knows but how that knowledge is transformed into action.

We seek to ensure that a child forms personal views from their first day at school and that these views become sacred to them, as dear as their honour. We strive to ensure the whole life of our school community, the many-faceted relationships and interests of our students, should all have a philosophical and civic meaning, should awaken a deeply personal attitude to what each person sees, learns and does. Any event, however little it appears to relate to them personally, is experienced by students as affecting them. The violation of a moral principle causes them personal concern and is experienced as an assault on their honour.

A moral conviction is an ideal, a high point in one's moral development. The path that leads to it is through a combination of moral habit and moral consciousness. Practical experience has convinced us that a firm foundation for moral conviction is laid in childhood and early adolescence, when good and evil, honour and dishonour, justice and injustice, are only accessible to a child's understanding if the moral significance of what they see and do is visible and obvious. We try to ensure that goodness, honour and justice bring children personal joy, and that evil, dishonour and injustice bring disappointment, concern and even personal grief.

Feelings are the flesh and blood, the very heart of moral conviction, principled behaviour and strength of spirit. Without feeling, morality becomes just dry, colourless words, capable of educating hypocrites. That is why the path from moral understanding to moral conviction begins with actions—habits accompanied by deep feelings and a personal attitude to what the child does and sees around them. If an evil deed someone does brings no harm to me personally, it will only prompt a personal reaction from me if I have often experienced the joy of doing good to someone else with no expectation of reward, just the satisfaction from knowing I have done good. This is the principle that governs our practical educational work as we seek to bring behaviour in line with awareness.

The life of our students is conducted in an atmosphere generated by moral conduct that becomes habitual. (This is especially important for small children.) We teach little children to perform moral actions that develop a personal attitude towards civic duty—an aspiration to act in the interests of society and oppose evil.

In our school grounds are hundreds of fruit trees. From their first days at school we teach the children: if you see that the branch of a fruit tree is broken, carefully tie it up and put some dressing on the wound. If it is done skilfully and in time, the branch will mend and the tree will heal itself. We teach them how to do this, but that is only one part of the lesson. The main thing is that the child's heart should feel pain when they see an injured tree. We achieve this by instilling in children a burning desire to affirm beauty in life and fight against destruction and passivity. When children notice a broken branch and run to the classroom or their home to get some string, or, if they are not confident to do it themselves, run with concern to tell an adult or older friend that the wind has broken a branch on a tree, we consider our goal has been achieved. The important thing is that the children view the tree as a living creature that needs care.

Gradually these actions become habitual. An adolescent or senior student no longer thinks about whether it is necessary to bind a broken branch, cover the exposed roots of a tree with soil after heavy rain or help an old woman carrying a heavy suitcase. They are incapable of ignoring these things. They cannot help making an effort when it concerns another human being or society at large. The repeated experience of joy accompanying good deeds in childhood is transformed over time into a voice of conscience that bears witness to a high level of moral consciousness. They cannot help doing good, not because they want to hear praise (giving encouragement in moral education is a very subtle thing and not without some danger), but because if they walked past and ignored the situation it would make them feel ill at heart.

The first actions we teach to provide a foundation for forming moral habits frequently relate to material objects, but human labour is personified in these objects. They are incarnations of skill, hard work and consequently of human virtue. An emotional response to the work inherent in material objects, and consequently to people and society, is exceptionally important for forming moral habits. From their first days at school, we teach children how to behave in the following situations:

> *If you see dry, cracked soil around a rose bush, peach tree or recently planted apple tree or grapevine, rake the soil and in the evening water the bush or tree.*

Pick up any bit of metal that has been thrown away or accidentally dropped on the road. Bring it to the school grounds and put it in the special place reserved for that. Every bit of metal is a small part of a machine.

If you see some paper dropped outside, in the corridor, or in the classroom, pick it up and put it in the rubbish bin.

When you are returning a tool to the workshop (a cutting tool, a chisel, a knife, a plane), have a look and see if it needs sharpening. If it does, sharpen it. Remember that any tool you return (or equipment like a spade, rake or watering can) should be in a better condition than it was when you received it.

A book that you return to the library should be in better condition than when you borrowed it. Remember that it takes the work of many people to make a book.

If you notice that any machine entrusted to you or that you are working on is not working properly, immediately seek help from someone older and ask them to fix it. If you can, fix it yourself.

The moral significance of these actions is they express respect for work and, in turn, for the creative people who carried out the work. These are not simply routine expectations but lessons in life, giving rise to the conviction that it is immoral to expect others to carry out your work and take on your responsibilities. This thought is acknowledged by the child every time they act in line with societal expectations. But it is not the frequent repetition of such actions that leads from knowledge to moral conviction. Human consciousness is not the same as the memory of an electronic machine. Knowledge only becomes conviction when such actions are accompanied by a feeling that one is doing the right thing, when they excite children, when they feel joy, energy and spiritual upliftment in their souls.

The process of forming convictions presupposes a child's conscious attitude towards their desires and managing those desires. It is no coincidence that we have many flowering rose bushes in our school grounds. Children sometimes want to pick a flower but are restrained by the thought that they will harm others by doing so. Gradually they forget this thought, but they retain the aversion to evil. The children no longer wonder whether or not they should pick a flower. The thought does not enter their head. This is the essence of moral habits. A person's conduct is governed by the voice of conscience, and the main note in that voice belongs to feeling. I read some words written by the famous French politician Édouard Herriot that are engraved forever in my memory: 'That which remains after all else is forgotten is culture.' Indeed, moral culture is not an accumulation of knowledge preserved in one's memory but that which is distilled in the human soul from knowledge that has been deeply processed and experienced.

Many years of educational work have convinced us that by the time young people reach late adolescence and young adulthood, it is already too late to teach them to look after trees and flowers and that this brings joy to people. Similarly, to teach them to rake the soil under rose bushes without anyone telling them to or repair the cover of a book before returning it to the library. They will understand the social requirement for these and other analogous actions, but they will not act in this way if they have not formed deep moral habits in childhood and early adolescence—if the thought prompting them to act morally has not been deeply experienced, leaving a trace in their soul. The moral habits that reflect the attitudes of our adolescents and young men and women towards objects, and through the objects towards people, continue to strengthen in late adolescence and early adulthood. This is a very important prerequisite for successful moral education. Attaining the more complex objectives of moral education in late adolescence and early adulthood (forming convictions about an ideal in life, understanding significant elements of a scientific world view, etc.) is only possible because more elementary moral habits were acquired in childhood and adolescence.

In the process of forming moral habits that reflect their attitudes towards material objects and (via those objects) towards people, children acquire their first notions of good and evil, honour and dishonour, justice and injustice, duty, happiness and dignity. But this is just the beginning of moral development. A higher level of development is attained when children are motivated to perform actions that involve a direct relationship to people, to themselves, and to society's interests. The goal of such actions is to awaken the thought that my actions must harmonise with the interests of the people surrounding me, that my happiness must not bring them disappointment or unhappiness. Actions that teach us how to live among other people provide a foundation for moral culture upon which all future development depends. To appreciate the moral concepts or principles that underlie these actions on an emotional level, the school community must live a rich spiritual life. Let me illustrate how, as a result of engaging in certain actions, moral convictions may be formed that demand respect for the interests of others. We teach our children:

> *When you speak about a person, action or something that has happened, say what you think. Never try to guess what people are expecting you to say. Trying to say what you think others want to hear can make you a hypocrite, a toady, and ultimately a worthless person.*
>
> *You have witnessed an act of injustice, deceit, humiliation or some other wrong action. Your heart burns with indignation and you want to intervene, to stand up for the truth. But the calculating part of you says you should not intervene, that it is none of your business. You must realise that this is the voice of cowardice. Follow your first impulse, your feeling, the voice of conscience. Your first impulse is usually your noblest. A cold, calculating attitude towards evil, injustice or dishonour can turn you into an indifferent, heartless person.*
>
> *Do not criticise your friend's failings in public if you have not first spoken to them in private and have not tried to convince them of their error. If you have succeeded in convincing them, criticism is unnecessary. It will be no more than empty chatter.*
>
> *If you have heard something said about a person, action or event, do not repeat the words like a parrot, but think about what you have heard. Have your own opinion, your own view about everything. But if you are convinced that what others are saying is true, support them and defend their point of view.*
>
> *Do not forget what you need to do today (a lesson, work in the workshop or the horticultural plot, participation in a club and the like). When you wake up, your first thought should be about the work you need to*

complete today. Putting things off until tomorrow leads to laziness and disorganisation. At least a small part of what you need to do tomorrow should be done today so you can have a clear conscience. Let this be a rule that governs your life.

Acquire knowledge through your own efforts. It is dishonourable to rely on your friend's work. Failing to do your homework independently is the first step towards becoming a parasite.

At the end of the day, think about what you have done to bring joy and happiness to others, and to become more intelligent yourself. (That also brings joy to others.) If you cannot think of anything you have done, you have lived a day in vain, and tomorrow you need to redouble your efforts to make up for lost time.

In a workshop or classroom, you see a sample of what you have to produce: a part, a model, an instrument or whatever. However perfect or beautiful the sample is, try to make something better. Know that there is no limit to the skill and mastery that can be attained in work.

If your friend is falling behind in their studies or work, show them how to overcome their obstacles. If you are not concerned about your friend's difficulties, you are an indifferent person. The more you bestow heartfelt warmth, kindness, care and concern on your friend, the more joy will come into your life.

Do not expect your mother and father to do your work for you. In your actions, show respect for their work and their need for rest. You will bring your parents joy by studying well and working hard. Do not disappoint them. Do not let them always give the best things to you.

Men should respect women. Their attitude towards women is a mirror reflecting their moral development. To love a girl means first and foremost to bring her joy, to create joy. If you witness someone insulting a woman, stop them and rebuke them.

How do we practically encourage students to follow these precepts? Where do they find an experience of justice and moral concepts? How are their convictions formed and strengthened?

We show students pages from the moral history of humanity devoted to people who fought courageously for truth and the freedom of their people. Images of these people kindle a burning ambition in the hearts of our students to be just as courageous. This experience, this feeling, is the embryo of conviction. But an idea really takes hold of a person's soul when they feel their own greatness and beauty. A child is standing at the crossroads of philosophical influences. Circumstances arise in their life where they see and hear evil. What they see is illuminated by the shining examples of great people from the past. The young person standing on the threshold of life takes up the battle against evil. In many cases this results in conflict, but this is as it should be since conviction is born in a battle of ideas. It is very important that a young person can recognise and respond emotionally to evil, battle with it and emerge the victor, gaining the conviction that goodness and justice triumph in our society.

Our young Pioneers were helping some adults load corn cobs collected for seed into the tray of a truck. They were choosing the biggest cobs. Suddenly the team leader suggested, 'Children, throw any old cobs into the bottom of the tray and put the best cobs on top. We need to complete our quota as quickly as possible.' The children had just been listening with bated breath to an account of Alexander Ulyanov's courage. 'How can we follow such advice? Why should we deceive anyone?' they thought. And with indignation, they told their teacher all about it. This was their first battle for justice, and it left a deep impression on their young hearts.

Members of our children's committee for the defence of nature go out in groups to patrol our fields, forests, meadows, and reservoir banks to see if anyone is raising a hand against our green friends, attacking our forests and fields, or if a poacher is stealthily approaching our waters to catch fish during the spawning season. Sometimes these patrols are crowned with success, and the Pioneers succeed in preventing something bad from happening, or at least in establishing the truth.

We do not think it acceptable for children to merely recognise evil and evaluate it from the perspective of moral norms. If a child understands very well that evil is being committed in front of them and just takes note of who is guilty and tells their elders, leaving them to sort it out, they will grow up indifferent to everyone and everything. Everything will be subordinated to dispassionate rationalism and then cold calculation. When they witness evil, they will consider whether to protest or not to protest and become hypocrites.

Such people are frightening. During their lives, they commit thousands of betrayals. These betrayals are terrible because they seem insignificant at first glance. If they see a hooligan insulting a young woman they will not always ignore it. They may stop and look and complain about the lack of a response from the police or volunteers, but they will not step in themselves. This is a vile betrayal that has its roots in an inoffensive, indifferent childhood.

The spiritual life of a child is distinguished by a great sensitivity to those phenomena that affect our feelings. Foremost among these is the grief and suffering one person causes another. Every teacher is often obliged to listen to little children's complaints about the misdeeds of their friends or older students. Usually, this involves someone hurting someone else's feelings. The child is expressing their indignation to the teacher because that is all they are capable of at that time. It is so important to listen attentively to these little children's complaints! The child is not asking the teacher to punish the guilty party, even if they are the injured party. They want the teacher to share their grief and indignation. The offence is usually very small from an adult point of view, but children have their own perspective and perception of good and evil. We need to bring ourselves down to the level of the child's interests, to deeply empathise with the child's thoughts, experience their feelings and be agitated by their concerns. We should not encourage children to complain, but when a child brings their grief to you, they are hardly aware they are complaining. They want their feelings to find a response in the heart of another human being.

It is important not to cool the passions in a child's soul, wound their sensitivities or make them indifferent. In sharing a child's indignation and experiencing their grief, we are developing their moral sensitivity. We are teaching them to find an effective outlet for their feelings: not only to feel indignation at evil, but to fight against it; not only to go to someone to seek justice, but to affirm justice themselves. It is important to give the child concrete advice, indicating how to deal with the concrete situation.

Children's uneducated emotions can lead to egoism. A child feels helpless in the face of an evil that seems insurmountable, and when they feel helpless, a sense of loneliness arises. If a young child bares their soul to other people, they no longer feel they must battle evil alone.

We try to gradually bring a child to the conviction that doing something good, useful or necessary for society displays moral valour, while thinking only of oneself is dishonourable. It is very important that the actions illustrating the essence of these ideas are accompanied by moral feelings, and the child feels a personal aversion for dishonour.

At our school, students aged nine or ten have already had the emotional and moral experience of socially useful activity. They have seen the results of their work for society—growing grape seedlings, for example—and have experienced joy in this. The early experience of this feeling is exceptionally important for the formation of moral convictions. Such feelings lead a child to be concerned if they have not done anything for others. By the time they reach adolescence, students see the results of their consistent, socially useful work: an orchard cultivated in a previously barren area or a field with a rich crop, where previously the soil was poor. By their late teens, students have moral wealth: the joy of knowing they have graced the earth with their work. This feeling gives rise to true patriotism and a sense of civic duty.

We give a lot of weight to the moral significance of independent work to acquire knowledge. We try to ensure all students experience feelings of self-worth when studying. From their first days at school, we awaken feelings of joy in the acquisition of knowledge. An emotional appreciation of success becomes an important feature of intellectual work. The teacher and students become enthused by a common intellectual goal: to know, discover the truth and overcome difficulties. When students see that the teacher takes joy in their successes and is disappointed by their failures, these feelings are transferred to them. In this way, they are convinced by experience that the work they do to acquire knowledge through their own efforts brings satisfaction. That is why we seek to ensure that of two ways to acquire knowledge—one that is easy and carefree but does not bring the satisfaction of overcoming obstacles, and one that is difficult and thorny, accompanied by the joy of creativity—children consciously choose the second path. This choice depends on how clearly an educator has managed to show children the purpose of work: not only to achieve an end but also to affirm one's moral worth and show one's capability. The more often children make the correct choice, the more deeply they realise that choosing whether to complete work, see it through to the end or abandon it half-way through is a matter of personal honour and worth. To reveal to children the significance of study is a whole area of educational creativity. We have many types of assignments with the clearly expressed goal of giving children the experience of pride in their work.

During our arithmetic lessons, we normally give the children several variants of a problem or example for independent work, with varying levels of difficulty. Students are given the option of choosing any variant. The children are very sensitive to this freedom of choice and see the opportunity to affirm their honour. This intellectual work takes on the character of a keen and interesting competition.

Many assignments set for students consist of two parts: one that is compulsory and another that is supplementary and voluntary, intended for those wanting to complete more than is demanded. The supplementary task is closely connected to the compulsory one. Such independent work takes on a moral significance. Students choose of their own free will to do something they find attractive because of the opportunity it affords to test their strength of will. The inclination to choose the more difficult path gradually becomes a moral habit. Moral refinement consists of moral habits that lead to keeping an emotional watch over behaviour. The voice of conscience of an educated person does not permit them to even consider copying a friend's work. For them, this is just as unacceptable as appearing naked in public.

In this way, a certain line of conduct is formed, characterised by an ingrained aversion to deception, dishonour or taking the easy path to success. It is only possible for each person to develop such a line of conduct when moral convictions are built on the firm foundation of moral habits.

Moral habits are associated with an ideal that inspires good conduct—this is the ABC of moral refinement. Just as a literate person reads a word without thinking about each letter, a morally educated person does not need to find a logical basis for noble action. Just as reading words is impossible without letters, moral conviction is impossible without actions and moral habits.

A person's moral refinement is characterised by their moral convictions having become an independent spiritual force, prompting new moral actions. The establishment of this independence depends on how the community's and individual's lives are spent. A single day, an hour during which a person displays strength of spirit may play a greater role in their life than years of not really expressing themselves. A school should try to ensure its students develop independent convictions as early as possible. We may refer to this stage in a person's spiritual life as moral maturity. Most of our students enter this stage during adolescence and early youth. Let us examine in detail how the moral development of students occurs during this stage.

How convictions grow and strengthen

IDEAS BECOME FIRM CONVICTIONS when they are not only understood but hard-won; when a person has invested their inner resources in the triumph of those ideas. The formation of philosophical and moral convictions is an active process. Students are not passive objects of education but actively seek the truth. A person's moral character during adolescence and youth depends on the philosophical direction that guides their actions and behaviour. We seek to ensure the spiritual efforts of our adolescents and young men and women are directed towards achieving goals of great social significance. People should do as much as possible in the name of an idea. The work or task that fills their lives should be a means of achieving a lofty goal and not an end in itself.

Young people are very sensitive to the moral significance of each task proposed for them and each action they perform. If you tell senior students they have to harvest beetroot in cold autumn weather without explaining why they should take on such a difficult task, you will be met with indifference and a reluctance to work. Young men and women are always interested in the moral significance of the work they are asked to do. If they see that they have to make a great effort to compensate for someone else's negligence or laziness, that work loses its educational value. Work that has resulted from someone else's laziness should only be given to groups that already have a high level of moral resilience. In such cases, the goal is not only to complete a certain amount of work but to fight against evil, laziness, indifference and egoism. Only then will the consciousness of overcoming difficulty elevate the students in their own eyes. If the young people do not feel they are battling with evil and emerging as victors in that battle, they should not in any circumstances be asked to complete work to make up for someone else's inactivity.

It is especially important to show students the moral significance of work that is monotonous, of little interest in itself and very difficult. We always try to impress on our students' hearts and minds the significance of their work so that participation does not shake their convictions but strengthens them.

We lead our students from noble actions associated with positive feelings to a conviction that people, through their own work, can transform the face of the Earth and transform themselves; that simple daily work in the nation's interests is indeed the patriotic and heroic achievement to which young people aspire. We seek to ensure this conviction becomes a source of inner strength for every student, inspiring noble actions and a strict code of personal conduct.

During adolescence and youth, our students are inspired by work that has symbolic significance. It provides a material manifestation of a great social idea and proof such an idea can be realised in practice.

Several years ago, we planted grapevines on the bare slope of a gully. When they began this work, the young people saw that the soil on this bare slope was wonderful black soil. The slope faced south in full sun, and the possibility of retaining water from spring snowmelt and rain convinced us that nature assigned this spot as ideal for growing grapes. We planted vines over an area of 3,000 square metres. We worked there for four or five days each year. In return for this modest investment of labour, nature rewarded us with a rich harvest: every 100 square metres yielded at least 400 kilograms of fruit.

When the amber bunches of grapes ripen in autumn, it is particularly galling to see the several hectares of neighbouring land baking in the sun and producing nothing but weeds. If we were to plant grapes over all these extra hectares, every inhabitant of our village could receive 100 kilograms of grapes each year, and grapes are a source of health, beauty and joy. A person who eats three handfuls of grapes each day lives 20–30 years longer than average. And really, we would not need to spend any money to create a vineyard on this slope. All that is required is for each able-bodied person aged 16–60 to work four days per year. It sounds easy, but for now, it is impossible. Our hands are capable, but many of our people are not yet ready to discover the wealth of nature. It pains us. We are deeply concerned by this lack of readiness for happiness (in the words of our young people). Our little vineyard, our 12 tonnes of grapes, show that our dream is achievable. At the end of August and beginning of September, we give grapes to mothers with young children and to the elderly and sick. We tell each person who comes to us of our dream, explaining what the earth can give us in return for our labour. We keep repeating, 'These nine hectares should become a collective vineyard for our village. We could harvest 300 tonnes of grapes each year. That would give us health and life!'

We believe that such a vineyard will be created one day when all the inhabitants of the village are mentally prepared for it. But for now, it sometimes happens that young lads passing by who do not know us come into our vineyard and pick grapes that are not even ripe. Many people think we are strange and obsessed and ask us cynically what we gain from our efforts, what benefit we accrue. These questions do not so much offend us as concern us. Those who see everything only from the perspective of personal gain are not yet ready for the collective work of which we dream. We try to convince such people of their error.

Why are we making such an effort? For people's happiness. For us, communism means happiness and joy for all people. We are making such an effort because we do not want each person to drag happiness into their own little corner, to surround it with a high fence and guard it with chained dogs. We want to create it together with others, seek it among our comrades and find it in common work. Next to our vineyard is a nursery where we cultivate hundreds of seedlings. We are pleased that many collective farm workers request seedlings, and people admire the grapes. But it is very concerning that some collective farm workers set up vineyards just to make some extra money. We might become despondent if not for other, joyful facts. Three families have planted a collective vineyard, pulling down the fences between their allotments, caring for the plants together and creating a common joy. Two families have planted pear and apple trees on the boundary between their yards. We are happy to see that the trees that belong to 'nobody' bring the greatest joy. Soon we will begin planting grapes over the whole nine hectares of slope and will realise our dream.

Communist morality and communist convictions do not mean self-abnegation and asceticism. The flow of material wealth Marx wrote about[31] is created by us for our happiness. But the fullness of happiness is comprised not only of the material wealth created for people to serve their needs but also derives from the spiritual creativity that allows a person to affirm their moral worth and good name as a citizen. Our main educational goal is that our adolescents and young men and women develop a conviction that the meaning of life can be found in such spiritual creativity.

How can we realise this goal in practice? In our view, this is one of the most complex and subtle spheres of the education process. This is because every person lives in a unique concrete situation, and each is subject to different, sometimes contradictory, philosophical influences. Education is most effective when a person aspires to be creative so they can have a rich spiritual life, and expresses this aspiration in their activities, actions, behaviour, relations with others and in conflict situations. And where does this aspiration come from? It comes from experiencing joy in creating something for others, which leads to work inspired by a lofty ideal. During adolescence and youth, it is exceptionally important that people draw renewed strength every day from this well of experience. If this well exists, your student is not a passive object of education but someone who actively develops conviction. Convictions are not abstract truths, existing independently of concrete, living people. Convictions involve a beating heart and a mind illuminated by a realisation, and they only become a reality through self-affirmation.

Gennady S. loved technology from childhood. The family he lived in with his mother, grandmother and younger sister was very poor. His mother, still a young woman, could not read a single letter. His grandmother took him to church and told him interesting stories about a mighty god in heaven, witches and house sprites. We never say to children, 'Don't believe your grandmother's stories, she is tricking you.' This is one of the most sensitive areas of family life, and you need to approach it with exceptional care. We directed the boy along a path whereby as he acquired knowledge at school, he brought the light of knowledge, science and culture into his family. Gradually this idea inspired him, and educating people became his aim in life.

By the time he was in Grade 2, he had taught his mother to read. His grandmother learned to read as well. When Gennady was in Grade 4, we helped him set up a small wind generator at home, and an electric lamp lit up their peasant hut on the outskirts of the village. Then Gennady assembled a radio set. (All of this was long before the electrification of our village, 12 years before the launch of the first satellite, so you can imagine how interested neighbours were to visit the hut where Gennady's mother lived to see the electric light and hear the wonderful singing coming from the little box of the radio set.)

A passion awoke in the boy's soul to promote the light of knowledge, science and reason. As he grew up, the boy became a young educator. His mother's hut became a unique centre of enlightenment, a club for learning about natural science. Collective farm workers gathered there in the evenings. Gennady told them about the achievements of science, showing them working models of machinery and equipment (many of which had been specially created for that purpose at school). He was always proving something or convincing visitors of something. The young man could not remain calm when he saw ignorance and superstition. Once, on a frosty winter's day, a second, false sun appeared in the sky. Gennady's neighbour, an old man of 90 years, began to persuade Gennady: 'You see this sign from God? It is to show you that no matter how much a person believes in the power of reason, whatever he says, it is not granted to him to know everything. Prove otherwise.'

The young man invested all the passion of his heart in shaking this conviction in people's powerlessness. To the amazement of the old people, he demonstrated that he could reproduce in miniature the optical 'miracles'. Soon the first television appeared in the village, assembled by Gennady.

When he graduated from school, the young man became an electrician at one of the industrial enterprises established nearby. His club for learning about the natural sciences is still operating. Now it has several sections: for old people, middle-aged people and young people. The young people study radio technology and electrical engineering, and assemble radio sets. The old people are interested in everything, from life in the depths of the oceans to spaceships. Gennady tells them about the achievements of science and technology and shows them slides with drawings, pictures and diagrams. For the middle-aged collective farm workers, he has organised a group to study electrical engineering. It bothers him that there are still people in the village who do not know how to operate an electric motor or how to connect machinery to it. His mother, who used to be completely illiterate, has passed an exam as a qualified worker and operates a shift at an electrical substation.

Lunacharsky said that a communist personality is a strong personality.[32] These words anticipated the deep processes that characterise personality development in our times. To educate a strong personality means to ensure each person's moral convictions are expressed in living human passions, in individual aspirations, interests and impulses. There is no person in whom, given skilled educational work, a unique talent will not unfold. There is no sphere of activity in which the individual will not flourish if we, the educators, can entice a person with the noblest creative endeavour—the creation of joy for other people. It is especially important to awaken the aspiration to live for an ideal, for principles and convictions. A person will not find their vocation without the inspiration of an ideal, without understanding and experiencing the meaning of life. Yet, a vocation is not something a person finds or encounters; it is something a person gradually develops as a result of their activity and convictions.

Several years ago, Vasily B. graduated from our school. He was one of those students who did not appear to be interested in anything. But then we noticed that he related with great love, warmth and kindness to little children. He liked to play with the little ones and made toys for them, and he liked it when children turned to him for help. We helped him build a playground for little children in his parents' yard. Vasily planted an orchard and grapevines for them, and the little children on his street gathered there. They listened with interest to Vasily's fairy tales and stories. Vasily began to teach the children how to look after the trees, and it turned out he had a real talent as a gardener.

The children found a good word to name their group and their orchard: 'Joy'. The little ones could not wait for him to come home from school and come out to see them in the orchard. Then, when he was in Grade 9, the young man created a fairy tale corner for his little friends in an old barn.

With the onset of autumn, days spent in the Orchard of Joy were a real celebration. Each evening the children took home presents for their mothers or little brothers or sisters who could not come to the orchard.

Vasily has been an adult for some time now. He has a family with two children and works as a tractor driver. But the Orchard of Joy still brings happiness to new generations of little children, just as it did when Vasily was at school. From early spring to late autumn, happy children's voices ring out just as they used to. Vasily has set up a shower and sports area for the children. On his days off, he takes the children to the forest, where the fairy tale corner is now located in a cave they have fitted out together.

People only express their natures fully when convictions are at the heart of their actions and behaviour.

As the blade of a plough is cleaned of rust and becomes mirror clean when it daily turns the soil, so a human soul shines when it labours and overcomes difficulties, courageously meets failure and is not seduced by success. Difficulties, obstacles and hard times are a touchstone for our convictions. How a person relates to difficulties during adolescence and youth determines their strength of spirit and loyalty to their principles.

The socialist way of life has spared the younger generation many difficulties and hardships that were the fate of people living under an exploitative social order. But this does not mean that life under socialism or communism will be without difficulties, conflicts and privations. Difficulties, which are so essential for tempering the spirit, are inherent in creative work, in harnessing the forces of nature for the good of the nation. Someone who gives the warmth of their soul to warm others and finds personal happiness in struggling for the happiness of society is attracted by the prospect of doing something exceptional. In such work, a person climbs to a higher level of moral development. To show young men and women the refinement of such spiritual growth is an important factor in developing convictions.

Whatever work our students are doing, we suggest to them that it provides an opportunity for their creative abilities to bloom. No person can ever say they have reached a ceiling. For example, we may have cultivated ears of wheat with 55 or 60 grains, but it is possible to cultivate an ear with 100 grains. In practice, we never grow pears and apples from cuttings. But if you apply thought and skill, it is possible to plant a cutting directly in the ground and grow a tree from it, and it will be distinguished by some interesting features. Usually, arable land with the best fertilisation and crop management gives no more than four tonnes of wheat per hectare, but if you fully develop the plant's potential, yields equivalent to nine, 10 or even 15 tonnes per hectare are possible. (So far, we have only conducted trials on a small area of land.) In our locality, we usually only harvest one crop of grain per year, but it is possible to harvest two crops, and so on.

Young people are attracted by the romanticism of a difficult challenge that demands ingenuity and creativity. Our students try to follow a work path that has never been trodden before. There are work tasks in our system of education that aim to form and develop convictions. These tasks require consistent application over a significant period. Time tests the strength of young people's convictions. We choose work tasks that are calculated to begin in early adolescence and be completed in early adulthood.

In 1960 we inspired a group of students with the prospect of growing a wheat crop yielding the equivalent of nine or ten tonnes per hectare. To make the task more challenging, we chose an area of infertile clay soil that first had to be made highly fertile. The prospect of difficult work was made attractive because we were challenging the forces of nature. The elements had destroyed the soil, but we were going to restore it. That was just as wonderful as building a hydroelectric power station in the taiga or inventing a new machine.

We set to work, digging fertile silt that had been deposited in a gully and transporting it to our plot of clay soil. To encourage life to develop more quickly in the clay soil, we also introduced organic matter, providing a medium for the activity of beneficial microorganisms. All of this was difficult, but you cannot achieve anything significant without effort! We drew inspiration from the thought that we were creating something new. It was as if we were creating a window into the future: if it is possible to create 1,000 square metres of fertile soil, it is possible to create many thousands of hectares.

Half a year later, we sowed our plot with plants that add nitrogen to the soil. Then we ploughed the earth again and brought more silt. We repeated this process for three years, analysing the composition of the soil each autumn to see if it was ready for sowing winter wheat. However, each time we tested the soil we found it was deficient in some nutrient. On each occasion we were determined to find some fertiliser that would eliminate the deficiency. The more we achieved, the more we were determined to overcome each new difficulty because experience taught us: if today is difficult, tomorrow will be joyful. The joy we each experienced in this purposeful work grew drop by drop into a wellspring that fed the conviction that we would achieve our goal. If you want to see difficulties lead to strength of spirit and reinforce convictions, connect these difficulties with invisible threads to some significant work that demands time, effort and a group united by shared ideals.

When our next analysis showed that the soil was ready, we spent several days going into the fields. From millions of ears of wheat, we chose only the biggest, those that showed the greatest resilience to drought (it was a dry year). Then we sorted the grains from those ears, discarding any that were small or poorly developed.

Before sowing, we again incorporated organic matter into the soil, activating beneficial microorganisms. We sowed the seed not in narrow rows, but in nests, with a greater distance between the rows, giving each plant maximum room to grow and absorb nutrients. In winter, we mounded snow on our plot.

The wheat plants grew big and strong. We fed them, and after each rain, we raked between the rows. Each plant yielded five or six times more ears than usual, each ear had twice as many grains as usual, and each grain was twice the normal weight. Our hearts were filled with joy. The harvest was a real celebration. One thousand square metres yielded 1.05 tonnes (equivalent to 10.5 tonnes per hectare). No-one had ever seen a harvest like that.

In 1965 we grew the equivalent of 13.7 tonnes per hectare. But our students are still not satisfied and have set themselves the goal of growing the equivalent of 15 tonnes per hectare. All of us, adults and children alike, speak with enthusiasm of the upcoming day when the boundless fields of all our collective and state farms will harvest crops just as bountiful as those on our little plot. The grains of wheat will be as large and heavy as rice.

The education of convictions is impossible without work, without people expressing their values through exercising willpower. Work is a powerful means of developing philosophical convictions, but only if a person uses their work to prove something—to affirm an idea that has become an inseparable part of their soul. People must see in the results of their work a living incarnation of truths and values they hold dear.

Work is a concept with many facets. A person may invest their spiritual and physical energy in another person or in the things of material value they create. As they understand the moral significance of such work, they attain a high level of moral culture. In educating another person, they truly educate themselves.

Our staff are very concerned with creating moral relationships in which this sort of work facilitates the formation of strong personalities. We seek to ensure every adolescent, every young man and woman, mentors some little friend in the school community, shows concern for them and takes to heart their successes and failures. Here the skill in education consists in being able to help the older child to find interests in common with the younger child.

We encouraged Grade 6 student Olya N. to take an interest in the life of Valya K., a little six-year-old girl whose father had committed a serious crime in front of his daughter and was sentenced to a lengthy period in prison. The little girl experienced a spiritual crisis. She did not believe in goodness, did not love her mother and did not have anyone to whom she felt close. Then 12-year-old Olya became Valya's friend.

The establishment of this friendship was not easy: for a long time, Valya did not trust Olya. Olya often visited the little girl, who lived next door to her, and brought her toys. Then, when Valya began school, Olya created a story corner at her home. She cut out and decorated cardboard story characters and gave her several interesting children's books for her bookshelf. Her sympathy and sensitivity restored the little girl's faith in other people. For several years, until she graduated from school, Olya taught Valya a love of books. Our staff used to refer to this friendship as an education through books. With the money she earned on the collective farm, Olya bought many books that became their shared treasure.

When a person educates themselves through their work, when they feel all the goodness and moral beauty in themselves imbibed by another person, and that person becomes close and dear to them, these things lead to the formation of moral convictions.

Educating sensitivity and empathy

IN MORAL EDUCATION, AN IMPORTANT ROLE is played by the development of subtle moral feelings: a sense of duty, sensitivity, empathy. To put into practice the principle that 'each human being is a friend, comrade and brother or sister', requires that each child from an early age is sensitive and attentive to the spiritual world of each person they meet. Further, that the source of each person's happiness is found in the moral purity, beauty and refinement of deeply personal, intimate relationships.

The ABC of educating humaneness is that a child finds personal joy in giving the warmth of their soul to others. In our experience, the most important thing in this subtle area of educational work is that the child should feel the sorrows, cares and suffering of another human being and personally respond to the one who needs help or sympathy.

The early childhood years are especially favourable for this sort of educational work, as little children react particularly sensitively to others' suffering. Since grief, worries and suffering are always present in our social environment, a thoughtful and sensitive teacher who can talk about such things expressively, will always be able to conjure up vivid images in a child's imagination and influence the feelings of the little ones listening to them.

We tell children about people who need help, sympathy and heartfelt consideration. Once I told our little Grade 1 students about a seven-year-old boy named Misha who had been bed-ridden due to illness for two years and could not come to school. Straight away the children wanted to visit the boy. The first visit to the sick child left a deep impression on the children's souls. They told him about school and brought him toys and drawings. The next day they brought him a box of alphabet blocks. After that, visiting the sick boy was not something they had to do, but something they deeply wanted to do, an inner imperative. Each one visited Misha whenever they wanted. Misha memorised the alphabet and learned to read. In the school workshop, some of the students made a little table on which he could write. All the students in the older classes, as well as in Grade 1, wanted to be part of Misha's success. For his part, the boy wanted to do something to express his thanks to his friends. It turned out he had an exceptional gift for drawing, and he drew pictures and gave them to his friends.

Summer came and Misha spent whole days in the open air. His bed was put in the shade of some trees and the children helped him to undergo a course of sunbaking. They played on the grass near his bed, told him stories, and acted out dramatised versions of folk tales. Misha could read aloud very expressively, and he began to read poetry and stories to his friends.

Another year passed, and again the children spent the summer with Misha. He kept up with them in his studies and transitioned successfully to Grade 3. The boy grew stronger. In the words of the children, his sick legs 'woke up'. When Misha stood on his own two legs and walked several steps, each of his friends experienced this as their own personal good fortune. For several months the children brought Misha to school in a little wheelchair. During the spring Misha's walking improved significantly, and when lessons started he walked to school himself. Each year his health improved. He graduated from secondary school and works as a metalworker at a car factory. He has become a sportsman.

Caring for their friend played a major role in the spiritual life of the children. Each one felt they had invested their strength and energy in a person who had been brought back to life. Each child who had befriended and helped Misha developed a trait that could be called gentleness or tenderness.

Human grief has many faces and is unique in each case. The important thing is that children are able to bring joy to others. Then they will feel others' grief naturally and will themselves find a way to engage in that most joyful creative labour that is humaneness.

I told those same Grade 1 students about the life of former partisan Andrei Stepanovich N. During the Great Patriotic War, fascists killed his wife and took his two little sons, aged two and four, to Germany. They published a note in the local newspaper stating that the partisan's sons would be educated in the Aryan spirit and would become enemies of communism. When the war ended, Andrei Stepanovich went to search for his sons but his efforts were fruitless. He could not forget his terrible grief. He worked as an electrician on the state farm but kept to himself and avoided contact with people. In such cases a special kind of help is needed: a sensitive, tactful awareness of the feelings of the grief-stricken person. The person who needs such help is sensitive to the slightest insincerity or artificiality. I tried to awaken feelings in the hearts of the little children that would allow them to offer help and sympathy in a way that did not rub salt into painful wounds but gave warmth through their kindness. They simply needed to bring joy to the man. In the remote lane where Andrei Stepanovich lived, we pulled out the weeds and planted apple trees. Andrei Stepanovich did not pay any attention to us for a long time, and we were disappointed. But then he began to come out of his house to see us. We saw how he was drawn to the sound of the children's voices. Then he asked us to bring him some grapevines. This request brought us great joy.

Andrei Stepanovich planted the grapevines, invited us into his house, and gave us apples to eat. A lively conversation followed. Andrei Stepanovich asked the children about school. The children told him about their games and their walks in the forest and shared their secrets. They had a little cave in the forest in which they hid their toy weapons. They knew of a secret place on the bank of the lake where pike swam.

The following Sunday, Andrei Stepanovich went with the children to the forest. It was an unforgettable day. Andrei Stepanovich could talk very engagingly about nature. He showed the children a hare's burrow and a fox's den, a squirrel, and a muskrat by the dam wall.

It was as if the man had been waiting for years to meet people who really felt his grief but would never mention it. Andrei Stepanovich stopped being a loner. The long extinguished need for human company awoke in him again. Each Sunday, the children went with him to the forest, riverbanks, lakes and steppe, and everywhere they discovered something new and previously unknown. During the spring and summer holidays, they rowed to an island, chose a remote spot, cooked dinner, and collected natural specimens and botanical samples. During ten years of friendship, no-one broke the promise they had given. Not a single word was spoken about Andrei Stepanovich's past as a partisan; no-one asked him to tell them anything about the cruel years of the war. The students became adults, and their friendship with him became even stronger.

The years of friendship, filled with the mutual creation of joy for each other, educated a sensitivity in the children to a person's inner world, an urge for human fellowship. One who has this urge is led by some sixth sense to people in need of kindness. My pupils found such people when they were studying in Grade 4. Returning home from the forest one day, they saw an old man. It was a hot day and the old man was also making his way home. The children helped him to carry some clothes. The children's heartfelt sensitivity allowed them to see that the old man was sad about something. 'He is grieving about something big,' said the girls. They learned from their parents that their new friend was a 70-year-old retired doctor who had recently moved from a neighbouring village. Several months ago, he had buried his wife of nearly 50 years and moved away from there so that nothing would remind him of the loss of such a dear person. Now he went every Sunday to his wife's grave with flowers he grew in a little greenhouse.

The children sensed that the old man needed sympathy and friendship. On the eve of the following Sunday they took the doctor a bunch of roses. The old man was moved. They asked his permission to accompany him to the neighbouring village, but he declined. They accompanied him only as far as the forest and waited for his return. They kept doing that every Sunday. The children were not deterred by rain or cold.

The children began to help their new friend look after his flowers, and he taught them the secrets of floriculture. He was delighted that the children were so interested in flowers. He passed on to the children his love of beauty, teaching them to appreciate its subtlest shades.

The children wanted to bring Petr Afanasievich (that was the old doctor's name) some joy. They found out when his former wife's birthday was celebrated and placed a bouquet of flowers on her grave the day before. Petr Afanasievich was deeply moved, and from that time, he did everything in his power to show his appreciation. In spring he helped the children establish a nursery of gladioli and a new grove of lilac bushes. Looking after the flowers brought the children new joys. Each of them created a flower bed at home, and some built greenhouses. Flowers became part of the spiritual life of their families. Vera T.'s parents had been quarrelling a lot. Vera planted some ornamental flowers in the shape of their initials in front of their window. This had an amazing effect on her parents. The arguments stopped, and peace reigned.

Two years later, the old doctor died. His death was a great loss for us. He was buried next to his wife. From time to time bouquets of flowers appear on their graves. The young people do not forget the one who showed them another facet of human beauty and kindness.

We consider such lessons in humanity an important component of moral education. Here we are dealing with the education of positive emotions. Many years of experience have convinced us that the education of emotions is not an isolated, narrow task but the very essence of the whole process of establishing a person's moral character.

For 20 years, I have been observing our students' perception, interpretation and reinterpretation of the concepts, truths and norms that make up the values of our society. These observations confirm that a child's sensitivity, thoughtfulness and personal attitude to the words of a teacher who is explaining the essence of moral values, depends on the extent to which they have developed positive emotions. A student who has not developed positive emotions remains indifferent to the teacher's words. If a student takes the misfortunes and suffering of others to heart, if they have frequently experienced a burning desire to come to another person's aid and have expressed that desire in action, they take a teacher's words as a challenge directed to them personally, even when the teacher has not directly addressed them.

We have become deeply convinced that emotional sensitivity and emotional refinement stimulate thought and reflection on the essence of moral exhortations and advice. Soviet research proved long ago that activity in the cortex of the brain is stimulated by the emotional centres of the sub-cortex. 'The main impulse for the activity of the cortex comes from the sub-cortex', wrote I.P. Pavlov. 'If these emotions are excluded, the cortex will lose its main source of energy.'[33] Neurological science relating to the higher functions of the human nervous system helps explain what goes on in the hidden recesses of a child's psyche. It also helps us find a pathway to educate children properly.

The most significant of all the complex processes taking place in the spiritual worlds of our students is the formation of personal convictions and personal views—the process of transforming truths into the flesh and blood of actions and behaviour. There can be no doubt that this process depends hugely on emotional education and the formation of positive feelings. Educating humane feelings is one of the most important aspects of developing moral refinement.

Humaneness is impossible without sensitivity to other human beings. It is simpler to love humanity at large than to love a single person. It is more difficult to help a single human being than to affirm that 'I love my nation'.

Each person embarking on life must be not only a skilful worker able to produce material goods but also a warm, responsive, sensitive human being. Belinsky's words, spoken over 100 years ago, will never lose their significance: 'We may be carpenters, metalworkers, or factory workers; but will we be true human beings—that is the question!'[34] The most important and most difficult challenge is ensuring our students embark on life as genuine human beings. A person living at a time when we are building communism in our country cannot live without doing good for others.

Educating in a spirit of honesty and integrity

SOME EDUCATORS CONSIDER IT INAPPROPRIATE to speak with children about loafers, parasites or embezzlers of public property. We fundamentally disagree with this point of view. We consider any effort to create an ideologically sterile environment around a child can only deform their soul.

We should not gloss over or embroider reality. We should not create a situation where a child says one thing when speaking openly at home or among their friends and something else when at a meeting or in an official situation. We should not accept children learning to be two-faced hypocrites. It is unacceptable to suggest to children that such insincerity is required, that it is inappropriate to suggest some of our frontline communist workers fall short of the ideal or write in an essay that people are living in poverty because of some collective farm managers' negligence and incompetence. Glossing over life gives rise to dogmatic judgements and restricts thought. It leads to scepticism and a lack of faith in communist goals and principles, leaving people defenceless in the battle for communism.

We advise our educators: above all, avoid insincerity, the 'splitting' of the soul, the existence of two 'truths'—one for everyday life and another for speaking at meetings or writing editorials in school newspapers. Avoid hypocrisy, deception, indifference or falsehood justified in the name of some imagined lofty goals. If someone makes a flowery speech at a Pioneer meeting about 'experimentation' just because something manages to grow in the school's experimental plot, and that does not embarrass the children, then there is something wrong with that school's educational work.

For young people to believe in communist ideas, for communist convictions to become as dear to them as personal honour, we must tell them the whole truth honestly and directly and teach them to speak only the truth. We try to permeate our school's whole life with a spirit of honesty, integrity and intolerance for evil, untruthfulness, deception or insincerity. We instil in our students the conviction that in the eyes of communism all are equal, from the collective farm watchman to the minister. We seek to ensure this truth is the only prism through which all the phenomena of life, including the moral character of people, are viewed. The more clearly and deeply each student sees the link between the high principles of communist ethics and the affairs of people's daily lives, the more attentively and perceptively they will gaze within themselves, and the more they will expect of themselves. If each living fact, each event in their lives is fanned and enlivened by the breath of communist ideals, this leads to the formation of a pure and sensitive conscience.

We need to begin with the smallest and simplest things that children encounter every day. We do not allow the rough edges of life to be glossed over, euphemised or hidden from public sight. For example, if the children witness the squandering of resources or learn of the theft of public property when working with adults, we expect the children's active participation in groups will have educated an intolerance for such things.

Our school life is structured so students encounter resources that belong to the community at every step. The use of these commonly owned resources becomes habitual. If a child needs a new exercise book, they take it from a cupboard containing our collective supplies. They take any book of interest from a stand in the classroom or corridor and read it on the spot or take it home. When reading the book, the student is aware that others wish to read it and will be waiting for it. Among the smaller children, interesting books literally pass from hand to hand, and you only see them back on the stand when everyone has read them.

In a situation where everyone uses the same resources to meet the community's spiritual needs, any dishonest, reprehensible action is met with general condemnation. If someone steals or damages a book that everyone needs, the children find the culprit themselves, and they feel the weight of their collective anger and indignation. Only when there is such an emotional consensus is punishment effective: the community limits the culprit's access to some cultural resources.

The collective use of cultural resources that meet student needs also plays a major role in the middle and senior school years. An individual's integrity and honesty are tested in the way they relate to the school community's interests. We allow any student to borrow recordings of musical works to listen to in their spare time, or books from the reading room, without asking anyone for permission. In our physics laboratory, there is equipment on the benches that anyone can use at any time. Our students' responsible attitude to our material resources and respect for community interests is the result of moral habits they have developed from their first days at school.

A spirit of honesty and integrity, and intolerance of insincerity or deception, permeates our students' work. From an early age, we teach them that the results of work, especially agricultural work, depend not only on human effort but also on the elemental forces of nature. They should take credit only for what they have accomplished with their own hands, for their intelligence and creativity, and not for what nature has given them. The observation of this rule entrenches an intolerance for everything illusory or false. To objectively assess effort, industry and diligence, we choose work tasks that require students to overcome difficulties. It is no great feat to harvest a good crop grown in good soil. But if a student turns infertile soil into highly fertile soil, the fruit of their labour embodies a spiritual struggle, a quest, and they value it. In this context, it is not uncommon for students with a relatively small harvest to receive more praise and encouragement than students who collected a significantly larger harvest.

In the primary school classes, we strictly observe the following rule. Until the results of a student's work (a dictation, composition, problem or exercise) deserve a positive assessment, they are not awarded any mark. Marks are earned by the sweat of one's brow—that is the conclusion children gradually come to. If a child has not yet received a mark, that means either that they cannot cope with the work (this problem can be overcome with persistence) or they do not want to work (this is also a problem, but of quite another kind.) In the vast majority of cases, we are dealing with the first problem. Nobody wants to work in vain, so students strive to overcome their difficulties. They feel the moral significance of a mark and value it. Children who have learned from an early age to attain knowledge through their own efforts never attempt to take the easy way out.

The honest assessment of behaviour has great educational

significance, especially in the senior classes. Using a five-point scale for assessing behaviour, we never award 'excellent' ('5') to a student who just sits silently through their lessons without drawing attention to themselves through any expression of their inner life. Such faceless behaviour is highly undesirable. When assessing behaviour, we rely on the following criteria: the ability to educate oneself, conscientious work (both study and community service), protecting and increasing public wealth, honesty, respect for working people, parents and elders in general, respect for women, steadfast resistance to evil, assisting with the education of young school children and preschoolers, and the ability to serve others.

It is very important that, at every age, children understand how these expectations should be met in practice. Such understanding is facilitated by the participation of each class group in assessing behaviour for each term and for the year. The class arrives at a conclusion regarding what mark each child has earned by discussing their work, study and social activity. The mark is awarded by the class teacher at a class meeting, and there is hardly ever any divergence between the teacher's and class group's opinions. If there is a divergence, the issue is examined at a staff meeting. In this case, a mark is only awarded when a class representative and the student in question agree with it.

Our students are particularly strict when it comes to laziness and lack of effort. From an early age we instil in students the idea that using the results of someone else's work (a cheat sheet, copying) is shameful. No allowance is made for any weaknesses. If you are sitting at a desk, you are a worker. You are responsible for your work to your family, your class and society at large.

If the staff are convinced a student graduating from our school is capable of studying successfully at tertiary level, we send a letter of recommendation to the tertiary institution, signed by the school council chairperson and the parents' committee chairperson. In such letters, we outline the interests, talents, abilities and favourite pursuits of the student. Such letters are recorded in the minutes of our staff council meetings. We re-read these letters each year to check how accurately we assessed the strengths, abilities and talents of those we recommend for tertiary studies.

In a place of honour in our parent room is an attractively formatted display entitled, 'They are the pride of their families and our school'. Here we display the portraits of teachers, engineers, doctors, agricultural scientists and animal specialists: our former students. We also display the numbers of students (they change every year) entering and graduating from tertiary educational institutions (organised by areas of specialisation). This is our way of showing accountability to our parents.

A very important precondition for educating in a spirit of honesty and integrity is giving students the right to say what they think without worrying they will be shouted at instead of receiving patient explanations and assistance.

Young people pay close attention to everything that happens in the surrounding world. They have a heightened sensitivity to the correspondence between lived experience and communist ideas and principles. The slightest disparity between word and deed prompts many questions, which cannot be ignored or dismissed on the grounds they are misguided or excessively critical. These questions are born of the best motives—a desire to be convinced of the correctness of those lofty communist ideals that we, as educators, have presented to our students as something sacred. The posing of such questions is a search for proof that 'our ideals are not some fairy tale, not just a beautiful idea that someone dreamed up, but a living truth'. In posing such questions young men and women frequently cite evidence that starkly contrasts with communist principles. The more serious this evidence, the more pressing the need to provide an answer that can dispel the doubts about the validity of the communist ideal.

Young men and women bring issues that trouble them to the Komsomol discussion group. Not a single question troubling them is left 'hanging in the air' unanswered. We try to ensure that young men and women who turn to the community, to their older comrades, with their doubts and thoughts, leave deeply convinced of the validity of communist ideas. They are not always able to dispel their doubts through their own efforts, so older comrades with significant life experience always participate. We of the older generation try to respond to young people's questions and engage in discussion with them in ways that allow them to find clear living evidence themselves, convincing them that communism's validity is incontrovertible. Further, that the mission of a true human being is not to be a passive observer, but to struggle, to overcome difficulties in the name of truth and justice.

Discussions are held whenever questions that trouble our young people arise. The Komsomol committee invites senior students, teachers and communist elders: veterans of the October Revolution and the Great Patriotic War. The secretary of the Komsomol committee usually begins the discussion. They formulate the question troubling the young people at that time. Young people present their points of view and express their thoughts and concerns. Then the older comrades respond, helping them to find answers and dispel their doubts.

Young people listen with deep emotion to the tales of communists who preferred death to renouncing their convictions. The young people express the view that steadfastness and courage, the ability to defend the truth whatever the threat, are important characteristics of a true communist.

Respectful relationships

WE CONSIDER THE EDUCATION of pure, refined, ethical relationships, of friendship, comradeship and love, to be one of the school's most important tasks.

The coarseness, vulgarity and cynicism of some young people is rooted in unrefined feelings, indifference, heartless relationships between people, first in the family, then at school, in the Pioneer and Young Communist organisations. Cynics, vulgar people, Don Juans grow up in families where love is defiled by betrayal of duty, the cynical flaunting of animal instincts or the calculated seeking of material gain. One of the sources of crime among young people is that many of them enter life devastated by the indifference and heartlessness of their parents. Our staff are aware of two 'unwanted' children, Olya and Aleksandr D., who grew up without a father, and without the affection and love of their mother, who reminded them every day that they were her punishment. From the time they could understand anything, they knew only that there were two people in the world who had given them life but no happiness, that they were worthless scoundrels, like so many others, that there is no such thing as love, only cunning and the ability to deceive. Such 'life wisdom' was developed by Olya and Aleksandr from early childhood. Suspicion, wariness, a lack of faith in other people: these were the traits we encountered in them when they entered school.

These negative traits must be overcome long before a person becomes capable of creating new life. One of our subtlest educational challenges is to see that young people relate to the creation of a new human life strictly and chastely. The birth of a new person should be anticipated as a happy occasion for celebration. The first thought entering every child's head should be that I bring joy to my parents, that they cannot live without me, in their joy is my own happiness, and I should be eternally grateful for the happiness my mother and father have given me. Love is, figuratively speaking, the flower that crowns all that is noble in a human being, and one must think about the beauty of this flower long before a person spontaneously experiences sexual attraction; their feelings must be refined.

The preparation of students to become good husbands and wives, mothers and fathers, is not to be found in explaining the relationship between the sexes, initiating them into knowledge prematurely. A child's whole life—everything they see, do and feel—should instil the conviction that the dearest thing in life is a human being. The highest honour, the greatest moral distinction is to bring happiness to another person, create beauty for them and at the same time be kind and beautiful yourself. The source of misfortune and sometimes genuine tragedy in moral and aesthetic relationships, is that some young people only see what they can take in love and not the responsibility of giving the other person happiness and joy. True love, especially the love of a man for a woman, of a boy for a girl, is an enormous expenditure of one's inner resources, a creative act giving rise to happiness.

Long before a young people experience sexual attraction, they must be taught to give more than they take—to give another person all the warmth of their soul and find satisfaction just in that. To give joy to another person is much more complicated than bringing a vase of flowers to the classroom or making a cage for rabbits. A highly moral act that touches the heart is a very subtle thing. It is the physical manifestation of the real movements of the soul, of an aspiration. The very worst thing is when good deeds are done only to attract praise. If a child learns from an early age to 'release portions' of goodness just because they are praised for it, they will grow up to be cold, calculating, heartless egoists. We remember one 12-year-old boy who was often praised by his Pioneer leader for helping a lonely old woman. We later learned, having reported to his Pioneer leader that he had carried water to the old lady, the boy went home, threw his muddy boots and coat on the floor, and his sick grandmother spent the whole evening scraping and washing the mud off them. We had to make quite an effort to explain to that boy the unseemliness of his conduct. It helped that he was only 12 and the community was united in supporting him.

The moral preparation for pure and beautiful love begins with establishing kindly feelings in a child's soul: warmth, empathy, sensitivity to those who are near and dear. The younger the child, the easier it is to awaken kindly feelings in them and inspire them to do good deeds. Little children try to bare their souls in their actions. Their feelings live in actions that express their relationship with other people.

To every generation of young children enrolling in Grade 1 for the past 20 years, we have told the same moving story of one person's tremendous loyalty to another. Two young people got married. After three months, the wife fell seriously ill and was paralysed in both legs. For 23 years the husband cared for his sick wife and took her to see doctors. He believed his wife would get better. Eventually she walked again, and they had a son.

We also tell children about our friend, the old doctor Petr Afanasievich, who walked to a neighbouring village every week to lay flowers on his wife's grave. These stories touch the sensitive corners of children's hearts. The children feel that the dearest thing in the world is another human being. I repeat, the main thing here is feeling. A child cannot yet reflect deeply. The important thing is that they feel the beauty of humaneness. If we manage through clear, emotionally laden words, to bring tears to a little boy's eyes when he learns that the little girl who sits next to him is sick and cannot come to school, when he grows up that boy will become a loving, caring husband and father. His conscience will never permit him to harm a girl, wife or mother. Kindly feelings are the first guardian of our conscience.

When we talk about humaneness, we awaken sensitivity to the suffering of others and safeguard against self-pity, one of the sources of egoism. Kindly feelings prompt kindly deeds: a child shares the suffering and misfortune of a friend, or even a complete stranger. They develop an urge to bring joy to others and willingly give the warmth of their soul to those who they feel need moral support (to adults, this support often goes unnoticed).

Seven-year-old Kolya and Galya were enthusiastically preparing for the New Year celebrations: learning songs and making costumes. Galya's mother sewed her a beautiful headdress and starched it. The little girl brought it to the New Year party carefully packed in a cardboard box. Just before the dancing began, someone sat on the box and squashed it. We adults would consider it a minor episode not worthy of attention, but for the child it was a grievous matter. Kolya noticed that Galya was standing to one side with her head lowered, the squashed box beside her, and before we had time to intervene, he approached her. Without saying a word—he did not know how to express his sympathy in words, but tears appeared in his eyes—he took Galya by the hand and took up position. A second later, the pair were dancing as if nothing had happened.

No words are necessary when there is a living, palpitating feeling.

Incidentally, we should not train children to express feelings in words that are not their own. We should not ask them to learn by heart lofty greetings for various ceremonial occasions attended by adults. We should not ask them to march in military formation to the beat of a drum. As adults, we should not be moved to tears by their ringing voices, repeating words we have asked them to learn by heart. We will only educate chatterboxes in this way—lively orators prepared to spout on any subject—and will cripple the children's souls. In the incident I just described, the boy's sympathy was a bright ray, shedding light on the little girl's soul: so there is a person in the world who experiences my grief as his own. And now, instead of tears, Galia's eyes sparkle with joy. The little girl plays and dances, and nobody notices that she is without her beautiful headdress.

There are so many such events in a child's life when sincere feeling turns out to be that fabulous water of life that drives away sorrow, lightens grief and returns joy. To give another person the warmth of one's feeling, to take their troubles to heart is the beginning of that refined experience of love that leads a youth to become a man and a faithful husband, and a girl to become affectionate, devoted, and at the same time firm, strict and chaste.

How important it is that in the lives of our children, teenagers, young men and women, nobody should suffer alone. How essential it is for the moral refinement of human nature that boys and young men should give more of the warmth of their souls to girls and young women. Pure, refined feelings: these, figuratively speaking, provide the spiritual energy for morality. Everything we create is in the name of human beings and for human beings. And no material or cultural wealth will bring happiness if people do not bring happiness to each other.

In a society where the roots of economic and political suppression have been eliminated, humaneness and respect for others begins with respect for women. We inspire the thought in our children that human beauty is expressed most fully in girls and women, because they are the creators of new life. The warmth of soul that a future man gives to a future woman refines his spiritual beauty. And again, the most important thing is feeling. It is important for boys and young men to experience joy from having brought joy to girls and young women.

On the first Sunday in January, our students celebrate Girls' Day. Life during this time is full of moving emotions. Every boy prepares a present for his sister or female friend. All presents are created by hand, through the boy's work. The boys cut with fretsaws, glue and sew. Often, their presents are fairy tale characters cut from plywood, animals, birds and also dolls, caskets and drawings. Many boys grow flowers or tree blossoms for the occasion. To grow snowdrops or lilies, or to get lilac to flower in January, is more difficult than cutting the most elaborate figure from plywood. The boys work, carefully cultivating chrysanthemums, lilies and snowdrops in greenhouses, calculating when they need to stimulate flower formation to have blooms at the right time. All of this is done to bring the girls joy.

In educating boys and young men, we consider relations in the family to be of great significance. We encourage sons to relate to their mothers as the dearest person in the world. Caring for their mother's apple tree is one of the most important concerns of each boy. Many boys also have a grapevine planted in honour of their mother. Sons are excited when they bring the fruits of their apple trees and grapevines to their mothers. On Mother's Day, sons give their mothers lilies and bring them drawings and embroidery. Older boys bring their mothers essays and poems, written in exercise books and illustrated with drawings. (Expensive albums are not necessary.)

In educating young men, it is very important to direct the spiritual energies of future husbands towards seeing the spiritual beauty in girls. Appreciation of this beauty—beauty to which they have also contributed through their creativity—gives rise to common interests, a need for companionship that is true love. Boys and girls must be brought together by common interests and feelings. In all fields of activity that engage, excite and inspire them, there is a girl next to each boy and a boy next to each girl. Before falling in love with the woman in a girl, a boy experiences a feeling of reverence for the beauty of the girl as a human being.

The life of teenagers and young men and women at our school is characterised by competition in showing creative ability, spiritual beauty, strength of will and persistence. (Of course, this competition is not supported by any organised activities. It takes place in hidden and secret ways.) This competition may take place in work, socially useful activity or artistic pursuits. In this competition, girls affirm their sense of pride regarding their place in society and their work. Just like the boys, the girls learn advanced skills in technical clubs and try to outdo the boys in creative work.

In choirs and music and drama groups, the boys and girls are brought together by common feelings and common interests. In such creative activities, the girls tend to set the tone, but the boys try not to be outdone by them. Such aspirations encourage the boys and girls to progress even more, refining their mutual attraction and surrounding the years of youth with a romantic aura.

Competition in creative work, artistic activities and the development of intellectual interests enriches the girls intellectually, and creates a spiritual wealth, without which there can be no beauty. Girls should be intelligent with rounded development; they should not be outdone by the boys but should excel them. This is the foundation of their pride and self-worth. The heartfelt love between two people remains pure for many years only when they are able to share throughout their life the inner beauty that was created in youth. We strive to impart to each student in their youth a multifaceted inner wealth sufficient to last a lifetime of giving. Each one is proud of something and manifests their individuality. Before creating a new human being, love must learn to create those things that elevate the human race: wisdom, beauty, creativity, skill.

Before the awakening of a mutual sexual attraction, each finds life's happiness in their favourite work and is not seeking love merely to fill an emptiness of soul. In the flowering of abilities, talents, and gifts, in the fact that each one feels a poet in some endeavour, we see preparation for a morally pure family life. When the fire of creativity is kindled in a person, its light illuminates from within the face, eyes and movements. The beauty of the external features is animated and ennobled by inner beauty. Where such beauty is, there will also be pride. How important it is to create such beauty in each girl! It gives rise to self-respect and the distance, chastity, pride and strict femininity that refines the relationship between a man and a woman.

Philosophical refinement at a major, national level is impossible without refinement at a personal level. Each person must be a friend, comrade and brother or sister to others. Not only in fighting for the nation's happiness, the greatness and might of our homeland, but also in the creation of personal happiness, in educating our children and in the joys of life. Each boy, each girl, who is sitting at a desk and learning to write their letters, is not only a future creator of material and cultural wealth, but a future mother or father. All the best things achieved by humanity should fill their hearts.

A love of reading begins at an early age.

Sukhomlynsky with guests in the school greenhouse.

CHAPTER 5

Intellectual Education

Intellectual education and its objectives

INTELLECTUAL EDUCATION IS ONE of the most important elements of communist education. It includes the acquisition of knowledge and construction of a scientific philosophy of life, the development of cognitive and creative abilities, the establishment of a culture of intellectual work, and the fostering of a compelling urge to engage in intellectual activity, to constantly enrich our scientific knowledge and apply knowledge in practice.

Intellectual education takes place during the process of acquiring scientific knowledge but is not to be identified with the mere accumulation of a certain volume of knowledge. The process of acquiring knowledge and enhancing its quality will only result in true intellectual education when knowledge is transformed into personal convictions, into a spiritual wealth that is reflected in philosophical life goals, work, social activity and personal interests. At the heart of intellectual education is the development of a philosophy of life.

'The actual spiritual wealth of an individual is entirely dependent on the wealth of their actual relationships', wrote Marx and Engels.[35] Intellectual education requires us to constantly enrich the lives of our students with all the spiritual wealth of our society. Such enrichment harmoniously integrates the education process with the life of society.

Marx wrote that people's minds are always connected by invisible threads to the body of the nation.[36] The mind of a developing person imbibes the nation's ideology and psyche, its convictions, traditions, and intellectual, moral and aesthetic culture.

Instruction is an essential form of intellectual education. The success of intellectual education during the process of instruction is determined by factors such as the richness of the school's whole spiritual life; the teacher's spiritual wealth, breadth of vision, erudition and culture; the curriculum content; instruction methods; and the organisation of students' intellectual work in class and at home.

During the process of instruction, the main aim of intellectual education is intellectual development. 'We should strive for the education of flexible, living thought, thought that reflects the movement of nature itself', wrote Albert Pinkevich.[37] Just as a person cannot read without knowledge of the alphabet, intellectual education is impossible without intellectual development, without flexible, living thought.

How do we practically carry out intellectual education? We must never forget the wealth of actual relationships about which Marx wrote. A person receives an intellectual education only when surrounded by an atmosphere of diverse intellectual interests, when their intercourse with the people around them is characterised by investigative thought and enquiry. A concern for the intellectual richness of school life as a whole is a decisive factor in providing genuine intellectual education.

Every teacher needs to be a skilful, thoughtful educator of students' minds. Intellectual education only takes place during the instruction process when the teacher sees the accumulation of knowledge—an increase in the volume of knowledge—as only one means of developing cognitive and creative powers, of developing flexible, investigative thought, and not the ultimate aim of instruction. In such teachers' lessons, the knowledge acquired by pupils is used as an instrument that allows them to consciously take new steps in discovering the world around them. The transfer of acquired methods of cognition to new objects then becomes a regular feature of the pupils' thinking activity: they continue in future to independently investigate the cause-and-effect relationships of new phenomena, processes and events. Productive work, research and experimentation become important elements in intellectual education when studying subjects in the natural science cycle. The independent study of life phenomena and literary sources, and creative writing attempts become important when studying humanities subjects.

Intellectual education is necessary so a person can apply knowledge in their work, but also for the fullness of their spiritual life, so they can appreciate the riches of culture and art. We need to give people the happiness of appreciating things of cultural and aesthetic value. We should not view the curriculum only from the viewpoint of the practical application of knowledge in work. In recent years some articles have expressed the view that school instruction and education has become too 'intellectual'. Some have even been reluctant to use the expression 'intellectual education'. This is, figuratively speaking, just foam on the wave of the ill-considered 'restructuring' that has unfortunately taken over national education as well. Intellectual education has always been and will always be one of the most important elements in the education process.

Developing a philosophy of life

A PHILOSOPHY OF LIFE is not just a system of views of the world that predominates in a given society, or the ideology of a given class, but also a subjective frame of mind that is manifested in thoughts, feelings, will and activity. A philosophy of life integrates consciousness, views, convictions and activity.

The development of a scientific view of the world depends on how deeply students comprehend the key ideas on which science is founded: the material basis of reality and knowability of the world; the interdependence of phenomena; the possibility and natural necessity of human transformation of the surrounding world; the possibility of understanding the essence and causes of social phenomena, especially war, revolution, and other social and economic upheavals and transformations; the irreconcilability of the interests of oppressors and the oppressed in all exploitative societies; the nobility of the struggle for liberation from exploitation, from social and national enslavement; the historical inevitability of the transition from capitalism to socialism; the influence of class and social position on views of good and evil, justice and injustice; the struggle for the freedom and independence of the homeland, for freedom from exploitation of one human being by another, as the highest moral virtue; and the transformation of work in a communist society into an organic human requirement. We consider it an important educational goal to ensure that a worldview is expressed in the ability to explain the essence of phenomena and in practical activity, in work. When investigating the facts and phenomena of the surrounding world and discovering the laws of nature, when becoming convinced of the truth and validity of scientific views, students simultaneously strive to prove something, to affirm and defend something. Only when intellectual work touches students' personal interests does their thinking during the study process lead to the independent development of a scientific philosophy of life. A scientific philosophy of life is a blend of thought, feeling and will. A philosophy of life is developed when the quest for knowledge is also a quest to harness nature's forces and to make sense of the surrounding life of society. In our system of intellectual education, there are work assignments with the principal aim of developing a philosophy of life. For example, when working on an experimental plot, a pupil may demonstrate that soil is a medium for the activity of microorganisms. The demonstration of this truth is only the first step towards autonomous activity that leads to developing a philosophy of life. The next step is creating soil that will yield a rich harvest. It is in this work that the wealth of actual relationships of which Marx wrote unfolds. The development of a philosophy of life, a personal attitude towards the phenomena of the surrounding world, touches all areas of a student's spiritual life: their thought, feelings, will and activity. During the early childhood years, acquired knowledge is closely associated with subjective experience. This association—this unity of thought and subjective experience—is largely retained during the middle school and even the senior school years.

It is very important for the development of a philosophy of life that thought processes are reflected in a student's practical activity. Experienced teachers do not assign any particular idea associated with a scientific philosophy of life to any particular section or sections of the curriculum. They strive to ensure the idea is expressed many times in the students' personal activities. A materialist philosophy of life will only become a child's personal view when their thought is enlivened by emotion—when accompanied by a feeling of wonder and the joy of discovery. A personal attitude to a scientific philosophy of life or materialism is only possible when a child has a personal attitude towards work that expresses the essence of such a philosophy of life.

We attach great significance to the investigative nature of intellectual work. As they observe, think, study and compare, children discover the truth, or they see they need to undertake new observations, reading and experimentation to discover the truth. For example, before studying the structure of the seeds of grains and legumes, our students germinate seeds, paying attention to the peculiarities of each variety, making initial observations of their common and specific characteristics. Before studying the internal combustion engine, each student disassembles and reassembles a miniature aviation compression engine and starts it, observing its operation's dependence on its construction. The students have many questions. This search for answers stimulates positive emotions that provide a psychological foundation for a child's personal attitude towards the truth.

The investigative nature of intellectual work is important not only when students are dealing with the observable aspects of subjects and phenomena. When engaged in the process of thought, students apply all the generalisations (conclusions, laws, formulas, etc.) they have learned about objects and phenomena. For example, the scientific concept of power is explained in a physics lesson. The teacher asks the students to think about the characteristics of work carried out by machines and animals. The object of thought is not only what can be immediately observed but also a generalised conclusion about the capacity to carry out a greater or lesser amount of work during a unit of time. This conclusion is formed in the students' consciousness as a result of living experience. Based on this conclusion, they investigate phenomena they have not observed directly.

Any experiment, any laboratory or practical work, aims to reveal a cause-and-effect relationship, a link, and also prompt students to exercise their minds and wills as they attempt to take a small step on the path of harnessing natural forces. To grow a tree when thousands of the same tree are already growing in your locality is just to see the world as it already is. But to grow grapes in the north, or to cultivate two crops of wheat, means to understand nature and harness its forces in new ways. In conducting such experiments, people understand reality more deeply, but they also come to know themselves and gain the conviction that they are not mere toys at the mercy of nature's blind forces. Experimentation and work, during which an idea becomes a personal conviction, is the very essence of a student's wealth of actual relationships. During their years at our school, every student carries out several work assignments in which they harness the forces of nature (e.g., growing two grain crops, accelerating plants' maturation with special fertilisers, developing a frost-tolerant variety of wheat through plant selection, transforming several dozen square metres of barren soil into a fertile medium, or increasing the sugar percentage in sugar beet). The value of this work is not only that it stimulates an interest in science, inquisitiveness and curiosity. The most important thing is the philosophical impulse that makes a student think hard. In this work, a student feels a deeply personal attitude towards the truth.

People who have carried out work tasks with a philosophical orientation in adolescence and youth are distinguished in their mature years by their independent attitude towards the important laws governing nature and work. These people work creatively; they are always proving something or testing something in their work. For example, one former student, a young agronomist named Victor Shch., demonstrated in his experiments that the viability of wheat seeds is affected by the addition of micro-fertilisers to the soil. At his suggestion, others have begun adding micro-fertilisers to the soil at seeding sites to increase the seed germination rate.

These people are inquisitive and curious. They strive to understand the complex interweaving of cause-and-effect relationships in natural phenomena. They love physical work and try to introduce an intellectual basis for it (keeping diaries of observations, comparing results of work activity over several years). They convince their work colleagues that not a single phenomenon should remain unknown, unstudied.

To teach children to have an active vision of the world and to be governed in their work by convictions is one of the main prerequisites for ensuring that knowledge truly educates. We believe one of our most important educational tasks is to ensure philosophical convictions are formed through practical activity. An important conviction giving rise to an active vision of the world is that people not only come to know the surrounding world, but they can also harness the forces of nature and transform life through their reason, creative ability and work.

There are many ways to show the validity of this idea. Children listen with interest to accounts of the lives of eminent scientists, who demonstrated through their research and discoveries the enormous power of reason, thought and will. They see a flourishing meadow created by their older schoolmates where before there was a barren wasteland. The teacher shows them how to grow vegetables in a laboratory without soil, using a solution of mineral fertilisers. But finding out about all these things is not yet a conviction. An active vision of the world requires that a child attains knowledge through their own efforts, interprets that knowledge and experiences the joy of discovery and overcoming difficulties. Then the truth becomes something precious.

The younger a child, the more brightly and spontaneously their feelings colour their thoughts when working. That is why we attach such significance to early childhood in the development of philosophical convictions. The active development of philosophical convictions begins simultaneously with discovering the first laws of nature. Developing a philosophy of life becomes an integral part of intellectual education when a child, learning about the laws of plant growth and the creation of organic matter, simultaneously becomes convinced that people can influence living processes in the soil and the living organism of a plant. They become convinced of this because of their own work and investigation.

Our students prove through their work that it is possible to harvest high yields of grain and commercial crops, achieve yields several times what is normal on a collective farm, and harvest mature maize 20 days earlier than normal. They prove it is possible to grow wheat with a protein content 2%–3% greater than the best existing varieties, get an apple tree to bear fruit in the third year rather than the typical sixth or seventh year, grow sunflowers with an oil content 5% greater than the best varieties in our area, and enable a winter wheat crop to survive a 30 degree frost.

To prove something while learning, and to learn while proving something: the integration of intellectual education with the development of a philosophy of life is found in this assimilation of thought and work. As a result of their work, children do not just see material results. They see themselves at work, their persistence and their strength of will. It is very important that an active vision of the world begins at an early age, and children enter young adulthood having already established a strong foundation of philosophical convictions.

The older the students and the more significant their strengths and abilities, the more necessary it is for their moral development that they be engaged in activity that affirms their philosophical convictions. We attach great significance to the activities of young men and women that test and strengthen their inner resources. It is very important to direct their young energy so it is not squandered.

'On these three hectares of land we have never harvested more than 1.2 tonnes of grain', we tell our senior students. 'But it is possible to make this poor soil fertile, just as a skilful tradesman can make a fine tool from a scrap of rusty metal. Let's take on that challenge.' The young men and women take on the challenge and are victorious. They grow a crop with a yield of 3.6 tonnes per hectare. In meeting this challenge, they are inspired by a lofty goal: to show that human beings are not just grains of sand in the universe. They create fertile soil. We manage to ensure that every student in young adulthood passes through a school of fighting for the common good, for an ideal.

Developing a scientific world view

HAVING A SCIENTIFIC PHILOSOPHY of life means a person has an active relationship to what they see, know and do. Knowledge contributes to a philosophy of life only when a person takes a personal stance regarding that knowledge, when acquired knowledge is reflected in their practical living and determines how they behave. A person's conviction reflects their personal attitude to the knowledge they have acquired.

One of the main tasks of an instruction process that truly educates is guarding against the student's apathy and indifference towards knowledge acquired, when they feel the content has nothing to do with them. The development of a scientific philosophy of life involves the educator's reflective insight into the soul of the child and skilful pedagogic management of their thinking, of the process of getting to know the surrounding world and of their work activity. Knowledge only contributes to the development of a philosophy of life when the process of study is a part of a student's multifaceted intellectual life—when the 'play' of their intellect and will is initiated, when study opens a window on the world, when they discover many interesting and engaging things in that world, when they seek answers to questions that excite them in books, nature and the surrounding world. The thirst for knowledge is not just a by-product of skilful teaching; it is the very essence of developing a philosophy of life.

The mastery of scientific knowledge begins from the first days a child attends school. Although the knowledge mastered by children in primary school seems extremely elementary to adults, it is this stage in education that experienced teachers regard as especially important in developing a scientific philosophy of life. It is in early childhood that students first discover many aspects and phenomena of the surrounding world. They learn about many things for the first time, and the attitude to the surrounding world, with its mysteries and natural laws, that the teacher manages to equip them with determines each child's attitude to knowledge.

Experienced primary teachers encourage students to become active participants in the quest for knowledge from their first days at school, so the process of discovering the world brings children deep feelings of joy, excitement and emotional uplift. This state is important for developing a desire to know, a thirst for knowledge.

Children arrive at school. The teacher acquaints them with the surrounding world and the phenomena of nature, living and non-living. The teacher takes the children to the forest, a field, a meadow and the riverbank. The children see lush meadows and then the lifeless clay on the slope of a gully. In one place grapevines are growing and 'sunny grapes' are ripening, while a short distance away is a barren patch of clay soil, full of stones, on which nothing is growing. 'Why is nothing growing there?' the children ask. The teacher explains it to them, and the children understand the cause-and-effect relationship between the phenomena they observe, but this has not yet led to the development of a conviction. It only provides a basis, a foundation. One warm autumn day, the children return with their teacher to that same patch of infertile soil. The children clear several square metres of wasteland, bring baskets of fertile soil and fertiliser, dig a hole, make the site fertile and plant their first grapevine. This is how we make a connection between theoretical knowledge and practical activity, and we consider it our most important educational task to ensure this connection is never broken, not for a single day. Learning from their own experience the transformative power of knowledge, seeing the grapevine flourish in a lifeless wasteland, the children adopt an active position in relation to knowledge. They want to learn more about how to prepare the soil for cultivating useful plants, how to increase its fertility and protect plants from harm. It is more interesting to work when you are armed with knowledge. Children feel pride in the fact that, having acquired knowledge, they are doing something necessary and beautiful for others.

This feeling is like a fertile soil on which the seeds of knowledge fall. The seeds germinate, and the children become more engaged in their work and their learning. They experience the excitement and joy of work, they want to learn more about it, and they become more inquisitive. That is why it is very important this feeling of joy in creativity should never wane. On the contrary, it should become ever stronger, supported and fed by continual new success in work. The process that begins during a child's first days at school when they learn about living nature, plants and animals, about the environment in which the processes of life unfold, is always accompanied by the application of knowledge. This is very important for the development of a scientific philosophy of life. And this work is not simply an illustration of what the child is learning. While working, the children discover more and more secrets of nature and establish themselves as active investigators.

While studying natural sciences (botany, zoology, human anatomy and physiology, the foundations of Darwinism), students gradually deepen their understanding of an important idea upon which they can base their philosophical convictions. In the surrounding world there is an eternal, ceaseless interaction between the living and the non-living.

The forces of nature create the living from the non-living, fashioning organic substances, the source of life. Living things take the primary material for creating organic substances from inanimate nature, and metabolism takes place. Human beings, themselves part of nature, do not simply observe, study and learn about this complex process. They boldly intervene in it, creating conditions favourable for enhancing living phenomena, modifying and creating environments for organisms.

To deepen and strengthen students' urge to understand the mysteries of the surrounding world, we structure the teaching of the natural sciences so that day after day, students discover more and more new details, broadening their understanding of the material essence of the world. In planting a grapevine in an environment created by human hands, the students gain their first concepts of fertile and infertile soil, which initiates a new stage in their understanding of the interaction between the living and the non-living.

In the primary classes, children learn about plants and soil, living processes, mineral and organic fertilisers, and the role of work in creating conditions favourable for living processes. But acquiring understanding is only one aspect of children's intellectual education. Children should think while working with their hands, and work with their hands while thinking. Only then will knowledge be transformed into conviction, and a child's very nature demands a 'hands-on' approach. Their intellectual operations are clearest and most vivid when they are at work. When their understanding is corroborated in their own work, it arouses deep emotions that provide a powerful stimulus for human behaviour.

In the primary classes, our students are already creating soil blends in the greenhouse and on our experimental plots, selecting the various components and testing the influence of various mineral and organic substances on soil fertility. Students in Grades 2–4 grow masses of green barley and oats in hydroponic solutions and are soon convinced it is possible to create conditions favourable for living processes even without soil. As their theoretical knowledge grows, their work becomes more complex, revealing the secrets of the interaction between the living and the non-living. In Grades 5–7, students create conditions in the soil favourable for developing beneficial microorganisms. In Grades

9–10, they find various ways to influence the biochemical processes taking place in microorganisms. They now see the soil as a medium in which complex living phenomena take place, and once they have this knowledge, they act as human beings to bring these phenomena under the influence of their reason and will.

In the process of acquiring knowledge about the vital activity of organisms, students create the conditions for developing and improving plant varieties in ways desirable for humans. At biology lessons, they learn about scientific research to develop new varieties of grain and commercial crops through selection. This knowledge is applied in their work. Students experiment with various ways of cultivating the soil and growing agricultural crops on the school's experimental plot and the collective farm. For instance, the children are growing a crop of winter wheat using a bush cultivation method: each seed planted in the ground is allocated an adequate area from which to draw nutrients. The ground between the rows is tilled as it would be for some horticultural crops. The wheat plants bush out, and each bush yields many more large ears than would be the case with the normal method of sowing. With this method of planting, the yield at harvest is three or four times greater than for normal sowing in rows. This work is a little research project for the students. They are studying the soil composition and creating favourable biochemical conditions for developing beneficial microorganisms.

In the senior classes, students acquire knowledge that provides a philosophical basis for creative work when studying the basics of agrotechnology and biochemistry. They learn about mineral fertilisers for plants, photosynthesis, respiration, the qualitative characteristics of plant metabolism at various stages of development, the physiology of growth and development and methods for managing these processes, the biological foundations of crop rotation and the physiological foundations of seed production, plant selection methods, inherited characteristics, and chromosomes and genes. The acquisition of this knowledge is closely connected with work on our experimental plot and in the collective farm fields.

This integration of knowledge and work teaches our students about the material basis of organic living processes that play a major role in lifting work productivity. It is possible to manage these phenomena, but extensive knowledge is required to do so. Our senior students have their own experimental plot, where they conduct research that significantly influences the development of a scientific philosophy of life. For the past 15 years, there has been constant research conducted here into the following areas: chemical and biological means for accelerating the growth and development of wheat and sunflowers; increasing the oil content in sunflower seeds; stimulating the vital activity of beneficial microorganisms that enrich the soil with humus; and increasing the protein content in wheat. We refer to this work as research because it is included in the local agricultural research station's planning.

Teaching physics, chemistry, astronomy and mathematics provides many opportunities to develop a scientific philosophy of life. In the process of observing and studying physical and chemical phenomena, even during the first stage of study (up to Grade 8), students discover some important scientific truths about the eternity, non-creation and indestructibility of matter; the limitlessness of the universe; the material nature of movement, time and space; and human consciousness as the highest stage in the development of matter. Students take their first steps on the path of knowledge in scientific fields where much remains to be studied and learned, such as elementary particles, matter and energy, cosmic rays, the origin of the universe, electromagnetic oscillations and waves, the wave and particle characteristics of light, and the biochemical foundations of living processes.

Our experienced teachers of physics, chemistry, mathematics and astronomy strive to structure the learning process so the knowledge of scientific truths and the laws of nature may become a tool, an instrument or key to solving creative work tasks, unlocking the secrets of nature, and developing further knowledge of the surrounding world. This is achieved because research and experimentation turn the learning process into a thoughtful, inquisitive, emotionally engaging search for the truth. In coming to know the truth in this way, students also come to know themselves. They feel and experience the creative power of being human, which provides the emotional and intellectual foundation for a philosophy of life.

By the time they complete Grade 8, students have some conception of various forms of energy: mechanical, thermal and electrical. Deepening this theoretical knowledge, they construct working models that convert one form of energy into another. Every student tries to incorporate some unique feature into the construction of their model that will distinguish their design and work from those of other students. Students who become enthused by this work develop a heightened interest in learning and a personal understanding of how knowledge and work are integrated. In electronics, automation and radio electronics clubs, they construct models, equipment and installations in which the most complex processes are based on converting one form of energy into another. This is a way of putting philosophical conviction into practice. Those who have passed through this remarkable school of work are distinguished by a strong urge to be creative. They strive to find new opportunities for the application of electricity in their work.

Children enter the world of social activity through collective work. We seek to ensure that collective work of social significance is experienced at a young age as a deeply personal pursuit that engages hearts and minds. Each generation of our students, at a young age, plants an orchard for the benefit of others. By the age of 11 or 12, children see the fruits of the work they began in early childhood. In their minds, they look back on the short journey they have made in life and take pride in what they have done for others. The deeper the joy they find in creating something for others and the richer a child's actual relationships, the more closely they take to heart the interests of society. At the age of 14 or 15, each Pioneer looks with pride at their fertile meadow and the plot where they have worked for several years to convert dead, infertile soil into highly fertile soil. They take joy in knowing the grapevine they planted with their own hands is already bearing fruit to feed people. They want to work for the good of society because they have already invested a great deal of energy in their native land.

The integration of knowledge and work creates an environment that educates character, deepens intellectual, vocational and creative interests, and awakens an urge to acquire more scientific knowledge. We use the word 'environment' in a broad sense to encompass the rich intellectual life of the teaching staff, the exchange of spiritual wealth (knowledge, skills and experience) within the student body, and the encouragement of children's interests and hobbies. We strive to ensure that during the school years, 'science really becomes part of our flesh and blood'.[38] Our experimental plot is a laboratory for scientific work. The more our teaching staff take an interest in current scientific and technological issues, the more they read, think and exchange ideas, the wider and deeper the horizons of scientific knowledge open up before our students. Our teaching staff strive to keep abreast of contemporary scientific developments. During the past four years, teachers have given lectures to staff on the following topics:

> 'New developments in the science of elementary particles', 'Quantum generators', 'The problem of direct conversion of thermal and chemical energy into electrical energy', 'The material nature of an electromagnetic field', 'New developments in the science of cosmic rays', 'The theory of relativity and its further development in our times', 'Cosmogonic theories of the origin of the solar system', 'Matter and energy', 'Biochemical processes in the soil', 'Organic synthesis', 'Intracellular processes', 'Achievements of genetics', 'Life in the universe', 'Vitamins and phytoncides', 'Electronics in the national economy', 'What is bionics?' and 'New scientific data about prehistoric cultures and Friedrich Engels work *The Dialectics of Nature*'.

The constant enrichment of teachers' scientific knowledge is an essential precondition for developing a rich intellectual life in the student body and a high level of instruction in science foundations.

In our scientific clubs, senior students study scientific literature and acquaint themselves with issues in the natural sciences. Our club members have created small specialist libraries and give lectures to each other on scientific issues. These lectures encompass philosophical problems. During the past two years, students have given lectures on the following themes:

> 'The creation of organic substances from inorganic matter in nature', 'Materialistic biology on the origins of life', 'The brain as the highest level of development of matter', 'Contemporary conceptions of the structure of the atom', 'Electromagnetic vibrations and waves', 'Wave and quantum characteristics of light', 'The materialistic essence of the theory of relativity', 'The issue of superconductivity', 'The plasma state of matter', 'Synthetic

materials in the national economy', 'The origins of petroleum', 'The nature of cosmic space', 'The solar system' and 'Matter and antimatter'.

Our senior student members of the science clubs assist the teachers in helping middle school students develop a scientific philosophy of life. They read articles, stories and essays from popular science journals to the Pioneers and conduct science and technology presentations. The Komsomol committee and the school Pioneer council organise meetings between students and agricultural scientists, engineers, doctors and livestock specialists. These people working in intellectual fields tell the students about current issues in science and technology. Such meetings broaden students' outlook and help them in their vocational orientation.

When inculcating a scientific philosophy of life, we attach considerable significance to elucidating the historical pathway of scientific development, the battle of materialism against idealism, ignorance and superstition, leading to the triumph of reason. The students come to realise that humanity's path to knowledge has been difficult and thorny, and many scientists on this path have displayed genuine heroism and made enormous sacrifices in the service of progress. In our lessons, we accord a significant place to the biographies of such heroic scientists. These shining participants in the philosophical battles within science illustrate the truth and humanistic nature of dialectical materialism and awaken an emotional response to knowledge and culture. We conduct a series of evening and morning presentations devoted to the theme of 'heroic scientists'. One idea running throughout these presentations is that the battle for the triumph of reason is also a battle for a better future for all workers. During the past five years, we have had presentations on Giordano Bruno, Galileo, Copernicus, Charles Darwin, Robert Koch, Pierre and Marie Curie, Nikolai Lobachevsky, Ivan Michurin, Ivan Pavlov, Kliment Timiryazev, Ivan Sechenov, Konstantin Tsiolkovsky, Nikolai Zelinsky, Nikolai Gamaleya, Igor Kurchatov, Ivan Bardin and Sergei Korolev.

One of the main aims of studying humanities subjects in school is to educate responsible citizens. Students learn about great events that have influenced human development, and at the same time, they learn about the souls, thoughts, feelings and experiences of individual personalities. Students assimilate knowledge about society as young people who are vitally interested in their Soviet homeland flourishing, preserving peace, strengthening friendship between nations, affirming the beauty of human relationships, and eliminating all that is ugly and vulgar and still debases human dignity in our times. The individual's personal attitude towards the knowledge they acquire plays a crucial role here.

Our primary school teachers and teachers of humanities subjects present their material in such a way that children are concerned for the fate of humanity, and their souls are engaged with the fate of their nation in the past, present and future. The ability to arouse personal feelings—a personal engagement—is especially important in the primary school. At this age, the feelings are a vantage point from which a child views the surrounding world.

For example, a teacher may be giving an account to Grade 2 students of events from the distant past: of an uprising of serfs against landowners. Vivid images are conjured up before the children's eyes: enraged by the arbitrary rule of those exploiting them, the serfs set fire to a landowner's estate and overpower their merciless overseers. The teacher addresses the minds of their students: 'Children, your ancestors rose up against their oppressors. You can take pride in the heroic past of your nation.'

The children experience even deeper emotions when the teacher tells them about the struggle for their homeland's independence and freedom, for liberation from exploitation during the civil war and the Great Patriotic War. The teacher takes the children to the edge of the village and shows them the place where a tragedy played out during the civil war: the White Guard shot a group of peasants, Red partisans, who had been wounded and fallen into the hands of their enemies. The students walk to the bank of a river and see a pile of stones: silent witnesses of the heroic deeds of Soviet soldiers, who had crossed the river and defended this plot of land to their last breath.

'Every corner of our land has been washed in the blood of those who fought for the freedom and independence of our homeland during the Great Patriotic War,' the teacher says. 'People gave their lives so you could live freely, so the sun could shine down on us, so future generations would not know grief, poverty and injustice. Hold dearly, children, the things your parents and grandparents won for you. The best memorial to those heroes will be a rich, fertile meadow, golden wheat and a flowering orchard. Don't forget, children, those to whom you owe your life and happiness.'

These words touch the children's hearts and awaken a feeling of gratitude to those who defended the freedom and independence of our homeland, the happiness of families. And gratitude is the root of a sense of duty.

The idea of duty to one's homeland, to one's people, who have created all the conditions of a happy, carefree childhood, runs through all the lessons in which we discuss our past, and especially our present and future. The teachers devote some lessons to the work of Soviet people. A picture emerges of the heroic work of millions of people, and the child is not a mere spectator of this work, but an active participant in the life of society, with close ties to those who work. The clearer the conceptions a child forms about the creative activity of the older generation, the greater is their readiness to repay the homeland for all that it gives them, especially if study is accompanied by work that gives children a feeling of civic pride. Even in their childhood and adolescence, they have partially repaid the homeland for what the older generations have given them.

Whatever they study in history, literature or social studies lessons, however distant from the present the events the teacher describes may be, students' thoughts are always directed to the present, to problems that concern the whole nation. This is one of the rules of our system of character education. This direct appeal to each student's inner world, their thoughts and feelings, is aimed at provoking reflection about their own destiny and the destiny of their family.

But how do we connect the personal and the civic in children's minds? How do we appeal to hearts and minds when studying events in the distant past, studying issues that determined the fate of humanity?

The laws of history do not depend on people's wills, but living people create history, a knowledge of which is so important in the development of a person's philosophy of life. Teachers of this subject always remember the need to reveal the historical process to young minds and hearts, not just as the operation of objective laws, but as a battle between good and evil, a battle in which people love and hate and experience joy and suffering. We strive to ensure that the historical process is presented to students as a colourful contest between living people, full of human passions, thoughts and feelings. If students are shown the image of a living human being at history lessons, if an idea is clothed in flesh and blood, if the teacher speaks little of the idea but it is appreciated and experienced as a living human being's passionate battle for happiness, students will not be just dispassionate 'consumers of knowledge'. They will not be indifferent to the outcome of this or that historical event. They will sympathise with goodness and hate evil.

The *humanisation* of history is especially important when the topic for analysis and interpretation involves critical contemporary issues. When showing the contradictions in the capitalist world, experienced teachers try to make sure students do not just learn social truths by heart but come to their own conclusions. In humanising the concept of exploitation in a capitalist society, they create in students' minds a vivid image of living human beings who are not enslaved by work itself, but by the inhumanity of a system in which the main aim of production is not the population's welfare but the capitalists' profit. An experienced history teacher concentrates on giving students an understanding of the enslavement of human labour in a capitalist society.

We try to reveal the historical process as a passionate battle between living people. This is impossible without a teacher's vivid, engaging stories about famous people. During their studies in Grades 7–10, every student listens to talks about the founders of Marxism-Leninism, the famous revolutionaries Dzerzhinsky, Babushkin, Sverdlov, Thälmann, Dimitrov, Kamo (Ter-Petrosian), Fučík, Nikos Beloyannis, Garibaldi, Aleksandr Ulyanov, Stepan Khalturin, Sophia Perovskaya, Zhelyabov, and others. Each of these lessons is a page from the history of the heroic fight for a new, just world. The lives and struggles of these people are torches, kindling young hearts, awakening an urge to devote one's life to the great ideals of humanity.

One of the most important means for forming a communist philosophy of life is literature. Setting themselves the goal of making literature a 'textbook for life' (Nikolai Chernyshevsky), our teachers direct their main attention to the aesthetic, philosophical, political and moral ideals expressed in literary images. The ideals of kindness, honour and truth, expressed through literary images, are seen by students also to constitute an ideal of beauty, and awaken an aspiration to live honestly, honourably and beautifully. During their secondary school years, every student reads works that embody the moral inheritance of humanity in literary images. Over the years, our staff have compiled a list of literary works that make up a golden collection of world literature, Russian literature and literature of the peoples of the USSR. These books constitute our program of intellectual, moral and aesthetic education. All of the books in this collection are held in the school library in sufficient quantities to meet demand, and each family incorporates them into their own library.

A literature lesson is only the beginning of work to develop a communist philosophy of life. Having awoken in students' hearts feelings of admiration for the ideals of kindness, honour, truth, and beauty, and feelings of hatred towards evil, injustice and ugliness, the literature teacher seeks to ensure each student reads literature independently, reflects on social, moral and aesthetic issues, and thinks about the future of their nation and their own personal future. Works of literature, which because of their philosophical and artistic value may be considered teachers of life, become our students' constant companions.

The curriculum

A PROPER INTELLECTUAL EDUCATION can only be realised when the most valuable intellectual achievements of humanity are passed on to students. A school's practical task is to allocate appropriate time to fundamental studies about nature and work, the human organism and thought, society and people's spiritual lives, and art. Although geology and minerology, biochemistry, cosmogony, psychology, stylistics and ethnography are not included in the school curriculum, a proper intellectual education is unthinkable without some knowledge of these subjects.

Mathematics takes pride of place among the foundations of science.

It is the only subject studied from the beginning of primary school to the end of secondary school. From the very first steps taken at school, concepts and laws from the field of mathematics are an important means for studying and understanding the world, for developing consciousness. Mathematics plays an exceptional role in intellectual development. Mathematics is a subject that affects one's outlook on life. It pervades both the natural and social sciences. Mathematical thought is not only understanding quantitative, spatial and functional relationships between numbers, measurements and geometrical shapes, but also a special approach to understanding reality, a method for investigating the facts and phenomena of nature, social life, work and economics, a way of analysing causal links between phenomena.

From Grade 1, our teachers teach children to see the relationship between numbers and reality. In the primary school, children solve problems they have set themselves in the process of observation, in the process of investigating spatial, functional and causal relationships between objects and phenomena. Until students understand the source, the origin of a mathematical problem, they are not given textbook problems. In the middle and senior classes, students prepare geometrical problems based on figures they have created themselves. Algebraic equations are constructed on the basis of relationships established in the process of work. It is not possible to plan this in detail in the curriculum. Here a decisive role is played by a teacher's creativity.

Mathematical thought is essential for successful study in all subjects. Mathematical ability is a clear manifestation of qualities of mind that play a major role in investigative and creative work. A school needs to take care to develop every student's mathematical abilities. Mathematics teachers teach students how to express thought scientifically and how to draw conclusions from data. The thinking skills children develop in the process of studying mathematics leave an impression on all their intellectual work, on the way they observe natural phenomena when studying biology, physics, chemistry and astronomy. The ideas of functional dependence and variables that play such an important role in mathematics develop dialectical thought, facilitating the understanding of causal relationships in other subjects.

Our students apply mathematical methods of proof when analysing natural phenomena and when making observations during the study of mechanics. The application of mathematical thought when investigating the world, and in work, is a primary way of linking theory and practice when studying mathematics. Mathematical methods of proof are applied during laboratory experiments when studying chemistry. Some laboratory work involves problem-solving. We have developed a system of creative written work in mathematics, physics and chemistry. A student needs to be able to apply theoretical knowledge when completing work in modelling, horticulture, soil science and agrometeorology. We attach considerable significance to applying mathematical methods when selecting the best way to achieve a work goal by comparing the advantages and disadvantages of alternative approaches. For example, students compile tables and graphs to determine the best fertiliser for various soils.

We attach great significance to mathematics in fostering initiative, a love of work, precision and critical thinking. For example, every mathematics teacher has a collection of problems that may be solved in multiple ways. The choice of method is the educational stimulus.

Evenings of mathematical creativity, competitions and quizzes are conducted from Grade 3 onwards. Students in senior classes give presentations to the mathematics clubs that are attended by junior and middle school students, and publish a mathematical journal. Students with a natural gift for mathematical thought are given extension work through consultations and lessons. Over the past 18 years, 59 of our students have received a higher mathematical education. Of these, eight have become designers, six are enrolled in post-graduate studies, five have post-graduate degrees, 26 are working in research institutes, and 14 are teaching mathematics in secondary schools.

The educational significance of knowledge in physics, chemistry and astronomy depends on how much teachers emphasise the creative, transformative power of the intellect when studying the properties and laws of matter, energy and motion. The assimilation of these ideas arouses students' thirst for knowledge, especially when studying issues such as the structure of matter, radioactivity, atomic energy, elementary particles, thermonuclear reactions, polymers, the artificial synthesis of protein, the origins of stars and planetary systems, and the relationship between the microcosm and the macrocosm. The more a person strives to penetrate the ultimate source of knowledge—the structure of matter, the origin of life, biochemical processes in living organisms—the deeper their interest in knowledge becomes. Experience has convinced us that if, when studying physics, astronomy, and chemistry, the powers of the mind are directed to understanding the mysteries of matter, students will leave the walls of our school curious and inquisitive, their self-education will never cease, and they will strive to elevate the intellectual level of their work and at the same time enrich their spiritual life.

Our experienced teachers of physics, astronomy and chemistry—Mr Filippov, Ms Kolomyichenko and Ms Stepanova—keep two programs in mind: one made up of the compulsory curriculum, the other directed at students' gradual familiarisation with broader issues of science and technology. This is especially important when considering the natural sciences. Here knowledge is essential not just to understand the surrounding world. It is an instrument to be applied in creative work, and in creative work, the knowledge acquired in school comes in contact with knowledge not yet studied at every step.

For every topic in the compulsory curriculum, we create an intellectual background made up of material that is not compulsory. For example, before, during and after studying the laws governing electrical currents, we conduct evening activities at the school that involve practical electronics activities and competitions that expose the students as much as possible to the achievements of science in utilising the electrical properties of matter. While studying the chemical and physical properties of the elements, we conduct a series of discussions entitled 'Stories about the elements', in which we explain the structure of matter to students in an entertaining way. Since geology and minerology are not covered in the curriculum, we organise evenings, discussions and readings devoted to these branches of science. Students in the senior and middle years learn about hypotheses and theories concerning the origin of minerals, and how we make use of natural resources. The more facts, phenomena and laws a student assimilates, the keener their interest in acquiring new knowledge. Material that engages a student because it is intrinsically interesting facilitates the involuntary memorisation of compulsory material. Experienced teachers strive to take students beyond the curriculum to facilitate the mastery of the curriculum. When they go beyond the curriculum, students gain a deeper understanding of the world. For example, the more they are exposed to modern cosmogonic theories, the more clearly they understand the idea of relativity.

The role of botany, zoology, anatomy and physiology in intellectual education depends on how deeply students acquire scientific convictions concerning the essence of life as the highest form of development of matter, the material nature of living processes, and, most importantly, the possibility for humans to actively influence these processes. Such convictions prompt adolescents and young men and women to have a deeply personal attitude towards scientific truth, knowledge and creative work, and stimulate curiosity, inquisitiveness and faith in the power of reason. We are convinced that a person's attitude to work, including agricultural production, depends greatly on their attitude towards the material basis of life processes formed during the school years.

Each student who falls in love with biology conducts a biological experiment during their school years, not just to convince themselves of what is already well known to science but also to take at least one small step on a path at the frontiers of science. Each student who takes a special interest in biology is allocated an area in our school plot for experimentation. Young biologists investigate the dependence of living processes in the soil and in plants on the physical and chemical conditions in an environment created and regulated by humans. Understanding this idea is a stimulus that arouses interest in problems that go beyond the limits of the curriculum. Many students conduct experiments to intensify living processes at various stages in a plant's development (e.g., to hasten the maturation of fruit or vegetables). These experiments require a deep study of the essence of biochemical processes taking place in seeds, leaves and roots.

Experiments at school are an indispensable means for enriching work intellectually, for combining work with thought and analysis. We consider it a significant achievement of our educational work that many of our young men and women aspire to discover the secrets of the life of plants, animals and the soil. Problems that our senior students are working on include: increasing the protein content of grains, creating favourable conditions for the development of micro-organisms that retain moisture in the soil, and biochemical methods for preparing stock food. Our young men and women are especially interested in trials to increase the protein content in wheat. The plot where these trials have been conducted has become one of our cradles of rich, intellectual life.

The history curriculum should offer as much opportunity as possible for a teacher to directly address the personal spiritual world of each pupil. Intellectual development in the process of studying history depends, more than in any other subject, on interpreting a broad range of facts and phenomena. To interpret a large volume of material does not mean that it all has to be memorised. The success of intellectual education when studying history, compared with other subjects, depends less on the volume of knowledge retained. The important thing is students develop scientific, materialist views of the historical process. A broad intellectual background is required for such views to become convictions. Students must consider and interpret a large volume of material. Only then can they distil the essential principles and develop a personal, emotional and ethically informed attitude towards the past, present and future—to problems that concern humanity. All of this requires that students are exposed to a far greater volume of factual material than the history curriculum contains.

If we compare history with other subjects, then the second, extra-curricular program creating a background for intellectual and moral development is far wider than any other subject. We acquaint children in the lower school with a wide spectrum of historical events. We conduct historical readings for the little children: short stories about humanity's past, the battle against social evil in the past and present, popular uprisings and wars against oppressors. These stories are intended to provoke an emotional response and express the idea that working people will never accept social injustice. Workers' liberation movements have always given rise to noble people devoted to their nations.

We devote special cycles of discussions and readings to the battle between progressive social forces and the forces of reaction. One such series, entitled 'The great humanists: fighters for human happiness', is conducted over a period of five or six years. Each student, from the age of 10 or 11 until aged 16 or 17, learns about the lives of leading humanists: Petrarch, Dante, Boccaccio, Leonardo da Vinci, Michelangelo, Bruno, Galileo, Rabelais, Montaigne, Müntzer, Dürer, Huska, Copernicus, John Ball, Thomas More, Shakespeare, Bacon, Winstanley, Vives, Cervantes, Erasmus of Rotterdam, Radishchev, Herzen, Belinsky, Dobrolyubov, Chernyshevsky, Gorky, Shevchenko and others. Evenings are devoted to the lives and struggles of these people, and extracts are read from their works. Particular emphasis is given to the existence of socialist ideas in germinal form long before the development of Marxism as a social science.

Evenings and readings on the following themes are of considerable educational significance: 'The forerunners of scientific communism', 'Popular uprisings from ancient times to the 20th century', 'The first communists' and 'A life devoted to freedom'.

The study of humanity's material and spiritual culture occupies a significant place in our extracurricular work. We conduct evenings devoted to the civilisations of Ancient Greece, Egypt, China and India, and indigenous cultures in Africa, America, Latin America and Siberia.

Mastery of one's native language determines the richness and breadth of a person's intellectual and aesthetic interests. We seek to ensure that teachers of all subjects enrich children's active vocabularies, teach them how to think, make use of inner speech, and express their thoughts orally and in writing. We direct children's thoughts to what they see, do and observe. The quest for clarity and precision of thought facilitates the more accurate reflection of reality: students strive to better understand the links between facts and phenomena and understand their role in the life that surrounds them. Teaching children how to speak properly is a whole area of educational work that is vital for the community's spiritual life.

In our society, speech culture is ever more closely linked with work culture and human culture generally, so we attach great significance to mastering the practical stylistics of literary language and developing an individual style. With this in mind, we encourage extension work on the style of compositions on both literary and free (abstract) topics. Students read their compositions, stories, essays and poems at creative literary evenings. As we attach exceptional significance to the ability to express thought and precisely and vividly describe one's surroundings, we give students the opportunity to write examination compositions on topics that require them to express their own thoughts, views and judgements (e.g. 'My thoughts on the threshold of independent life', 'My conception of happiness', 'The social and the personal in an individual's life', 'Our generation's duty to the homeland and to humanity' and 'Is an ideal person possible?').

To use Gorky's expression, literature clothes ideas with flesh and blood.[39] The subjective factor in literature is of great importance, as social and moral ideas and aesthetic principles are incarnated in artistic form and make a deep impression on one's personal spiritual world, convictions and actions. A knowledge of literature is closely connected with a person's moral development. For those who truly know literature, literary works become textbooks for life and a benchmark for morality. Thus, it is extremely important that works are judiciously selected for reading and study, and that a teacher of literature should be an educator of character who understands and senses a pathway for students' moral development. A rigorous selection of works for reading is a significant prerequisite for the development of a moral ideal. Thanks to such a selection, students develop an understanding of the most important stages in the spiritual life of humanity.

We have already described how a list of books that have entered the treasure house of human culture have been presented in an attractive wall display: two pages, framed with the portraits of great writers (Homer, Shakespeare, Pushkin, Shevchenko, Goethe, Hugo, Dreiser, Jirásek, Mickiewicz, Nexø and Rustaveli). The list is preceded by the following exhortation: 'Students! Here is a list of books that have become immortal and earned a place as treasures of world culture. Humanity will read them forever. You should not just read these books, but re-read them, seeking wisdom and beauty, and finding joy and aesthetic pleasure. "Books gather pearls of human thought and pass them on to our descendants. We will return to dust, but books, like monuments of iron and stone, survive forever." (Oybek)'.

As we attach such significance to the selection of literature for reading during adolescence and youth, a complete list of recommended literature is included in Appendix 1 at the end of this book. The vast majority of our students read the listed books during adolescence and youth.

The power of an artistic image depends not only on how we teach but also on what motivates community life. If the community's spiritual life is rich and diverse and students really know how to read, then the creative work of teachers bears fruit. As they prepare for their lessons, they reflect on what thoughts and feelings should excite the students, on what they should direct their attention to. The study of a work of literature begins with the independent reading of the primary source. The most striking passages from major works are read aloud during lessons.

Literature teaches us how to live and becomes a textbook of life because artistic images awaken aesthetic and moral feelings in close association. Reading or listening to a work of literature is a creative process. While reading a work of literature, students colour the words with the passion of their hearts—either with delight at beauty, refinement and moral strength or with indignation and outrage. That is why we attach such exceptional significance to reading literature during lessons and at home. Reading aloud and to oneself are important stages in the aesthetic and philosophical appreciation of an artistic image. A teacher teaches students not only to read but to appreciate. In appreciating subtle nuances of thought and feeling, students participate in a unique school of emotional education.

We attach great significance to reading aloud at lessons when we are studying artistic images that have become immortal incarnations of human virtues and vices: Don Quixote, Hamlet, Othello, Faust, Childe Harold, Till Eulenspiegel, Jean-Christophe, Martin Eden, Tartuffe, Romeo and Juliet, Jean Valjean, Father Goriot, Arthur Burton (*The Gadfly*), Eugene Onegin, Pechorin, Oblomov, Pavel Vlasov (in Gorky's *Mother*), Grigorii Melekhov (*Quiet Flows the Don*) and Pavel Korchagin (*How the Steel was Tempered*). The most striking and expressive passages conveying these characters' aesthetic and philosophical essence are often read multiple times at the same lesson by various students. The process of interpreting and emotionally evaluating such characters is deeply individual. It is crucial that each student understand the author's intention and that an appreciation of the author's text resonates in their personal presentation.

Young men and women should know themselves and their inner worlds and develop their character, willpower and memory. As the study of psychology is not included in the curriculum, we conduct a series of extracurricular lectures on the human psyche for students aged 14–17. Thanks to their self-education and independent reading of literature on thought and speech, emotions, willpower, character and temperament, our students acquire significant knowledge of psychology.

The study of foreign languages occupies a significant place in intellectual education. Our ideal is that students feel the vital essence of a foreign language, that the words and phrases they study should embody the same concepts, feelings and thoughts invested in them by the people who created them. We consider the educational role of foreign languages to be achieved when the words of the foreign language live in a child's thought, and the meaning of what is read or heard does not always require a translation. That is why we try to ensure children acquire words and phrases through living communication in conversation.

How do we approach this ideal? Children approach words via phrases and sentences. The first semester of language study in Grade 5 (we study French) is devoted to conversational language. The children learn how to explain in French what they are seeing and doing, ask questions and reply to them, and memorise proverbs and sayings. During conversation practice, they gradually master phrases that no longer require translation, and the spirit of the language, the emotional colouring of words and phrases, is embedded in their minds. The most capable students achieve this level of knowledge, which is why we speak of aspiring to an ideal. Students in Grades 7–10 who have fallen in love with the French language conduct foreign language groups for students in Grades 1–4. This is a very interesting form of student-initiated school activity.

We attach great significance to practical activities that involve reading, writing and conversation. The foreign language should live in students' thoughts and feelings; only then will it develop the intellect. We encourage students to develop a love for reading literature in the foreign language. To this end, we organise foreign language evenings and publish newspapers. The students have pen friends in France, the German Democratic Republic, Vietnam and African countries where the population speaks French.

Learning and intellectual development

ONE MUST NOT SEE THE AIM of instruction as being to ensure by any means that pupils master the material in the curriculum. One must not assess the effectiveness of the means and methods of instruction only by the quantity of knowledge acquired by the pupils. The aim of instruction is to ensure that the process of acquiring knowledge contributes to the optimum level of general development, and the general development achieved through the process of instruction should facilitate greater success in the acquisition of knowledge. In our school, we assess the effectiveness of instruction methods by the extent to which they facilitate a child's general intellectual development; that is, the extent to which the process of instruction is simultaneously a process of intellectual, moral, philosophical and aesthetic education.

Many teachers are troubled by the question: why is it that a child who studied well in primary school and acquired knowledge without exceptional effort finds study more and more difficult as they progress through the school? Why does the knowledge acquired appear to be a heavy burden requiring ever greater effort to maintain? A gulf forms between the acquisition of knowledge and intellectual development because the teacher sees the aim of instruction as acquiring a certain volume of knowledge and fails to see instruction as a means of educating a developed mind. A developed mind will find studying easier as new knowledge is acquired. Integrating the processes of instruction and intellectual development may well be our most important educational challenge.

The integration of instruction and intellectual development begins with studying a child's development. Our teachers get to know future Grade 1 students long before they begin schooling. During summer and spring, they take them on excursions to the forest, fields and orchards. During winter, the preschoolers play in a room especially allocated for that purpose. The features of each child's thinking processes are ascertained and studied, and their intellectual interests are aroused.

Children's thinking is manifested in their active relationship with the surrounding world. They think about what they see, observe and do. We have several locations that suit our future Grade 1 students where the surrounding environment stimulates thought. We observe how they explore the world, and predict how they will study and where they may encounter difficulties. In one of these locations there are dozens of plants: trees and fruit-bearing shrubs. The children observe their development from spring to autumn, and they have many occasions to ask 'why?' There is also a room with dozens of working models of machines and mechanisms; another location with pictures showing the life and behaviour of animals; and another with pictures showing the life of nations around the world.

This preschool preparation helps us to identify, study and become aware of the specific characteristics of each child's thinking processes. We begin with the idea that studying is an activity of the brain. To understand the individual characteristics of each child's intellectual development, we need to observe that activity long before a child sits behind a desk. The activity of the brain is discrete. The brain instantaneously switches from one thought to another, then to a third, back to the first, and so on. This switching happens instantaneously, and the ability to make sense of the object of cognition depends on the speed with which this switching occurs.

This switching of thoughts occurs in a way that is characteristic for each child: it will be extremely rapid in one child and extremely slow in another. We study all of this, reflecting on how best to develop each child's brain, how to concentrate their thought on one object and switch it instantaneously to another. This is an extremely important process in intellectual development. The ability to rapidly switch thoughts is quick-wittedness, which determines the quality of a developed mind. To develop this ability, we conduct lessons in thought with our preschoolers and then at school. The children investigate and make sense of the objects and phenomena of the surrounding world.

When the children are only five or six years old, we identify a group of children whom we call investigators. They investigate the plant world in the orchard and the vegetable garden. These little children come to school in March, a year and a half before they commence school. They gather again every day or so in the school greenhouse or the orchard. They sow the seeds of grain crops (wheat, buckwheat, barley, millet) and fruit trees (apples, pears, peaches, plums, sour cherries, sweet cherries), and plant grape and rose cuttings. They water the soil with the help of pumps made especially for the little ones. Soon the first shoots of the grain crops appear, then shoots appear on the fruit trees and leaves appear on the cuttings.

The more significant the results of this work, the more questions the children have: why does one plant produce a harvest in the first year, while another takes several years? Why does the peach tree grow a metre over summer while the oak seedling produces only four leaves? Why does an ear of wheat look different to an ear of millet? Why does a watermelon keep its seeds in a 'sweet storeroom' while wheat has no such 'storeroom'? During moments of intense thinking about each of these questions, a child's thought switches thousands of times as the object is studied from all angles. The child learns to think while observing and observe while thinking; this is the essence of these lessons in thought. Before learning to study, a child learns to think.

Another group of children investigates plants in the forest, steppe and meadow. A third group observes life in the pond and the lake; a fourth gets involved with the working models; a fifth constructs little houses, factories and power plants from little wooden parts; a sixth breeds fish in an aquarium; a seventh grows flowers; and an eighth is attracted by unusual phenomena. We have one location where everything is unusual: pumpkins growing on a tomato plant, wheat grafted on to maize. Everywhere they look prompts one question after another: what, how, why? Every child is thinking about something and asking questions of the teacher, club leader or older student. Each one develops an interest in something. Without interest, there is no joy of discovery, no talent or ability, no living soul or human individuality.

Even during these preschool years, theoreticians and dreamers stand out among the children. The theoreticians immerse themselves in the details of phenomena and try to get to the essence. We discern a tendency to reason and seek logical proof in their thoughts. Dreamers and poets see an object or phenomena in its general outline. The beauty of a sunset or a storm cloud makes a great impression on them; they admire the play of colours, while the theoreticians pose questions: why is the same area of sky azure one moment, and then scarlet the next? Why is the sun golden overhead but crimson on the horizon?

Each child's thought has its own path of development; each is intelligent and talented in their own way. There is not a single child who has no ability and no talents. It is important that each child's mind and talents provide a foundation for success in study, so that no child studies below their level of ability. In each class, in each generation of children, we greet the appearance of talented mathematicians, horticulturalists, mechanics and constructors of models and, as they get older, talented chemists, linguists and historians. We try to kindle the spark of these abilities during the preschool years.

Each child produces what they are capable of in their studies. The realisation of this principle allows us to achieve the holistic intellectual development of all students and to prevent failure. We do not allow talented, gifted children to work below their abilities. If a student who should be an investigator of nature, a young experimenter and future scientist descends to the level of an average crammer, those who lack clearly expressed gifts and talents will also fail to fully develop their abilities. To avoid failure among weak students, we consider it necessary for talented and gifted students to go beyond the curriculum in those subjects and spheres of activity for which they have exceptional ability. For example, if a student in Grade 7 or 8 shows a special interest in botany, we do not limit their studies to the secondary school textbook. We encourage them to study biochemistry and investigate the microflora of the soil. This also has a major impact on the weaker students' development of abilities because the intellectual life of the school community is an integrated process. We became convinced that no students will fail physics in a class where several students have gone beyond the curriculum and are studying contemporary problems in science: semiconductors, quantum generators, electronic equipment. When studying literature, even the weakest students are assisted by learning about a difficult area of literature, such as the works of Vissarion Belinsky, whose essays of literary criticism are not included in the curriculum but are studied by their more capable friends who prepare essays on them that contain elements of research. One talented young man studied articles about Belinsky written by Lunacharsky and other scholars and then wrote an essay on the topic 'The evolution of Belinsky's philosophy of life'. Now he is a young scholar and teaches literature at a tertiary institute. The influence of stronger, more mature, more gifted students on weaker and average students is an extraordinarily complex process involving constant spiritual exchange. A major role in this exchange is played by clubs devoted to school subjects and technology, and other extracurricular work such as evenings of science and technology, competitions and quizzes.

Teachers of mathematics give their students problems with several levels of difficulty. Each student is given the opportunity to tackle the level of difficulty that accords with their abilities. But because this work is conducted in a class setting, it takes on a competitive quality. Nobody wants to appear weak; each tries to test their strength on the difficult problem. This competitive atmosphere facilitates the unfolding of talents. In each graduating class of 40 or 50 students, there are two or three talented mathematicians. While still in secondary school, they begin to study material and solve problems from the tertiary course in higher mathematics.

If a teacher can lead the most capable students beyond the curriculum, the intellectual life of the school community becomes rich and diverse. Consequently, the weakest students do not fall behind. Our physics teacher Mr Filippov works on the principle of 'from each according to their abilities'. When studying each section of the curriculum, he plans theoretical questions and problems intended for the most capable students. They are acquainted with this material during lessons and continue studying it during extracurricular work. For example, when studying electricity and molecular and atomic theory, the most capable students were introduced to the following topics:

The production of an electrical current without a generator; thermonuclear reaction; the properties of plasma; the electromagnetic state of plasma; the electromagnetic fields of the planets of our solar system; the electrohydraulic effect (discovered by the Soviet scientist Lev Yutkin); the applications of semiconductors in modern technology; superconductivity of materials; magnetohydrodynamic generators; physical and chemical processes occurring in the deepest layers of the Earth; matter and energy; elementary particles known to science at the present time; light and matter; problems connected with vacuums; the origins of cosmic rays; the structure of the Synchrophasotron; the Van Allen radiation belts and their origin.

In acquainting students with these topics during lessons, the teacher stimulates an interest in extracurricular work and reading. Relevant scientific books and pamphlets are displayed in stands dedicated to new developments in science and technology in reading rooms, the school library and the physics laboratory. Issues in science and technology become topics of conversation and discussion. Truth is born in discussion, and so is intellectual maturity. This is a particularly important extension of the school curriculum. When the teacher is convinced that the ground has been adequately prepared, he encourages the most capable students to prepare talks and essays, to publish a wall newspaper for the science and technology club, and to write abstracts. There are science and technology mornings and evenings and lectures delivered by students. Clubs focus their activities on specific problems. In the atmosphere engendered by this rich intellectual life, even the weakest students hear a lot, learn a lot, and have much food for thought, which motivates them to work more intensely. Thanks to all this extracurricular exposure, it becomes easier for them to understand and master the compulsory curriculum.

It is important that reading gives students the experience of intellectual joy. If students are interested in reading extracurricular material, they will also take an interest in the textbook. While reading, they also stop and reflect on what they are reading. For reading to stimulate a rich intellectual life as early as possible, a person must acquire solid practical skills. In primary school, children must master the skills of reading, writing, thinking, observing and expressing their thoughts.

A child cannot study successfully in Grade 8 if their essays are transcribed sentences learned by heart and not an expression of their own thoughts. In Grades 5–7, we try to ensure children can abstract themselves from the process of writing and concentrate all their attention on the content they are trying to convey. Most creative writing assignments in the primary and middle years are accounts of what children see, observe, think and do.

Reading for interest, with no expectation that the material will be memorised, prevents study overload. Overload is a relative concept. Material is too difficult when a student cannot make sense of it because of limitations imposed by their age. The volume of material that can be absorbed at any age varies greatly depending on the intellectual life of the community and the individual. Even the most insignificant, modest volume of material may be too much for students if the intellectual life that forms a background to study is narrow and impoverished.

We try to ensure that our students read magazines and popular scientific literature. The more they are motivated to read out of interest in books and science, the more easily they master the basics of science and the less time they need to spend on homework.

For our students, reading is accompanied by work in technological or young naturalists' clubs, listening to lectures given by older students, observing natural phenomena, conducting experiments, and other voluntary extracurricular activities. Because of involvement in such activities, students do not encounter insurmountable difficulties in their studies. The more they read, write, think and observe, the less burdensome their studies seem. Overload occurs when intellectual work is too one-sided, and a student spends all their time memorising. Limiting the curriculum is not the best way to avoid overload. Instead, we pay attention to the content and characteristics of students' intellectual life by providing a rich intellectual background to students' studies. Before hearing about the structure of an atom at a physics lesson, our students have already read engaging articles and notes about elementary particles. Even if they have not understood much of what they have read, their interest in the material presented during the lessons is strengthened. Before studying a work of literature in a lesson, they will already have read it, and most importantly, will have experienced the associated moral and aesthetic emotions. We try to ensure the treatment of any difficult topic from the physics, chemistry or geography curricula is always preceded by relevant extracurricular work.

We make sure every student has books that engage their mind and heart and an older friend with whom they can share their thoughts and feelings. For example, if a student shows an aptitude for technological creativity at an early age, they are given popular science books corresponding to their interest by the Pioneer organisation, the Komsomol committee, the principal, or the collective farm management (in the form of a prize or present). By the time they graduate from school, they will have compiled a personal (home) library. These books enrich the spiritual life of the family.

Our science subject-based clubs provide an important avenue for developing intellectual interests in technology, mathematics, chemistry, biology, biochemistry, physics, ethnography and astronomy. We refer to the clubs dedicated to each of these subjects as 'scientific'. This may be a slight exaggeration, but the word does reflect the creative work of our senior students, their experimentation and research. The students are delighted and inspired by the extent to which they experience the scientific approach to intellectual work.

The participants in these clubs are interested in issues that take them far beyond the confines of elementary knowledge and represent the achievements of science. For example, in the scientific biochemistry club, senior students study biochemical processes occurring in the soil and approaches to stimulating the growth of grain and other commercial crops. In the scientific astronomy club, they have been studying theories concerning the formation of stars and the nature of cosmic rays for several years.

The activities of the science subject-based clubs take the form of lively news reports, talks and papers full of interesting, striking facts. Construction and modelling play an important role in the activities of these clubs. During the past five years, members of the automation and radio electronics club have constructed more than 25 devices based on the principles of radio electronics.

At the heart of each science club is a teacher who is deeply interested in the latest achievements of science. One of the technical clubs for automation and radio electronics is led by our physics teacher, Mr Filippov. He does not just supervise the club; he works alongside its members and has his own bench in their workshop.

A student's intellectual immersion in a particular area of science means they acquire considerably more knowledge in the corresponding school subject than is required by the curriculum. The deeper this immersion, the wider the compass of the student's intellectual interests. Moreover, we are convinced that this extended learning by some students in certain subjects is an essential prerequisite for the community's rich intellectual life and the development of each individual's talents. An intelligent, mature student always goes beyond the curriculum in one or more subjects. Deep, substantial knowledge of all subjects, combined with the development of particular interest in one subject, is an important prerequisite for a person's holistic development.

Depending on their individual talents, abilities and interests, students of the same age and in the same year level may master subjects to varying degrees. For those who have no aptitude for the theoretical thought and practical activities associated with a given subject, and consequently experience significant difficulty mastering the material, the compulsory curriculum may be the maximum they can achieve. Conversely, those students who have no difficulty understanding theoretical issues, who show an aptitude for theoretical thought and intellectual work that incorporates elements of scientific research, are exposed to a wider circle of knowledge by the teacher. One of the most significant challenges of the education process is to correctly determine the strengths, abilities, talents and interests of each student, to determine their capabilities.

Developing students' intellectual abilities

ONE OF THE MOST IMPORTANT features of a developed intellect is the power of observation, 'the ability to see, with the eye of intellect, an object *in the centre of all its relationships*'.[40] Closely connected with the power of observation are other features of intellectual development: curiosity (i.e., an active relationship to the phenomena of the surrounding world, striving to learn and know), a systematic approach (i.e., purposeful selection of the objects of cognition, concepts and inferences), capacity (i.e., ability to retain knowledge in one's memory and find one's way among intellectual resources), discipline, flexibility, independence and a critical sense.

Intellectual abilities are developed in the process of acquiring knowledge. But we need to consider the complexity and multifaceted nature of the broad concept of 'knowledge'. First, it incorporates the memory's constant retention of elementary truths (facts, rules, numerical data, various characteristics and causal relationships, definitions) that are continually applied in our lives. Unless we know how to make use of these and can retrieve the necessary information from our memories when required, we are unable to study further, develop intellectually or engage in intellectual work. Second, knowledge incorporates an understanding of things we do not need to retain in our memory and an ability to access the limitless, boundless treasures accumulated by humanity and preserved in books.

These are two interconnected but independent components of knowledge. When dealing with concrete material, it is particularly important to put certain procedures in place. Anything that must be retained in long-term memory, anything crucial to understanding new facts and phenomena, is an essential tool of thought. Such tools must be memorised and, most importantly, used as often as possible so they do not become rusty or a heavy burden. We seek to ensure that those facts, phenomena, definitions and characteristics that need to be retained in long-term memory are imprinted in the memory because they are used and applied in practice to acquire new knowledge and work creatively. Each teacher incorporates the application of knowledge that needs to be memorised in the system of instruction for their subject. The mathematics teachers, Mr Barvinsky, Ms Arishchenko and Ms Vovchenko, have constructed equipment that students use to solve algebraic equations and simultaneously revise the polynomial identities used to solve the problems.

We analyse the curriculum and define the elementary knowledge that must be constantly retained in the memory (formulas, laws, rules, the metric system of measurement; spelling rules; general characteristics of matter, plants and animals; geographic terms, the location of geographic features on a map, etc.).

Such knowledge is memorised through special mnemonic techniques and the application of the knowledge in practical work. To memorise the multiplication tables, we have a special mathematics box that takes the form of an interesting game. To memorise geographical features and distances, we use a series of games that involve a journey through a map. In our experimental plot, the plants are arranged so that transitioning from the care of one plant to another requires the retrieval from memory of certain important plant characteristics. All of these approaches create conditions for involuntary memorisation, the significance of which has been proven by science. Involuntary memorisation is an important means for lightening intellectual work. The effectiveness of involuntary memorisation depends on the type of intellectual work students carry out when they are acquainted with a theoretical issue.[41] For example, if a student has listened to an interesting lecture on the structure of matter and read an engaging book about it, favourable conditions are created for the involuntary memorisation of related material when it is studied during a lesson. We strive to ensure that many concepts (especially abstract concepts such as the state, nation, movement, function, etc.) enter the memory due to involuntary memorisation. The more a child memorises without any particular effort, the easier it is for them to memorise those things that are impossible to memorise without some effort.

Science advances precipitously, and knowledge accumulates, but human memory has its limitations. Today, a person's intellectual development is increasingly defined by their ability to navigate the boundless ocean of knowledge and utilise the storehouse of knowledge recorded in books. We should not expect the impossible of students: that they will retain all the material studied during a course in their memories. We teach students to refer to books when preparing to answer a question during a lesson or when working on an essay.

I emphasise again the exceptional importance of students retaining in their long-term memories those things that definitely need to be memorised at each stage of their studies. We attach special significance to the memorisation of material in the primary and middle years of schooling. Such a strong foundation is laid during the early and middle years that the main feature of study during the senior years is cognitive analysis; that is, the application of existing knowledge to acquire new knowledge. In the primary school, we define a minimum number of spelling words that students should memorise so well that they do not need to remember rules. We attach great significance to this, aiming to achieve a degree of automaticity in writing words and sentences.

In the senior classes, students can only study successfully if they do not need to think about how to spell words and can focus all their effort on thinking about the content of their writing. It is also extremely important to acquire automaticity in reading in primary school. Only those students who can focus on the content of what they are reading, not the reading process, are ready for study in the middle and senior years.

Involuntary memorisation is an important precondition for intellectual development. It frees the powers of the intellect for thought, for deep understanding of the essence of facts and phenomena. Involuntary memorisation prevents one of the most terrible evils of study: cramming. Our teachers are most concerned that students are not led to memorise material they do not understand. When introducing a new mathematical theorem, Ms Arishchenko makes sure students understand the semantic links between the elements, facts, phenomena and laws that constitute the essence of the theorem. Students explain how they understand the theorem using drawings and visual aids. The more students think about the meaning of the theorem, the more easily it is memorised. Memorisation is most reliable when founded on understanding.

Teachers of humanities subjects do not accept students memorising passages from the textbook and quoting it verbatim. That can cripple children's intellectual abilities, especially when developing their first notions of some relationship or law. When students' knowledge is assessed, they are never asked questions that require mere repetition of material from the textbook. The questions require students to reflect, juxtapose, compare and explain. Students do not study one paragraph after another but instead search for knowledge in various sources: the textbook and supplementary literature. For example, they may be revising revolutionary peasant movements, uprisings and wars during a specific historical period. This material is covered in dozens of pages. To read them at one sitting would be beyond students' powers, and therefore meaningless. Taking this into consideration, the teacher suggests students reflect on the following questions: 'What revolutionary and reactionary forces opposed each other during the peasant movements, uprisings and wars we are studying? Why is it that all the peasant movements in exploitative societies ultimately ended in defeat? What demands did peasants make? Who were their main opponents?' During this sort of revision, the students are investigating, reflecting, comparing, juxtaposing. They do not read everything in succession but search for an answer to a question. The answers after such revision are not monotonous retellings but heated debates involving reflection. The students argue with a book in their hands, supporting their ideas with references to sources. When questions are posed this way, it is significantly harder to answer with the aid of a book than without a book.

To know means first and foremost to be able to use knowledge, and this ability is manifested in different ways in different subjects.

At a history lesson in Grade 7, students study the Netherlands bourgeois revolution, while in physics they are studying units of measurement for measuring heat: calories and kilocalories. In both cases a considerable role is played by involuntary memorisation. The more students think deeply about the subject under study, without focusing on memorisation, the more deeply the essence of facts and phenomena and their relationships are imprinted on the memory.

When studying physics, the aim is not only to understand the essence of physical phenomena but also to apply generalisations that must be firmly embedded in one's memory. When studying the Netherlands bourgeois revolution, the ultimate aim is of another order entirely. Intellectual development, understanding the historical process, forming ideological convictions—all of these depend on how deeply students have understood the laws behind this historical event and many others. At the physics lesson, it is only necessary to make a connection between the units of measurement and the phenomenon of heat and not with anything else; the knowledge consists of being able to apply a generalisation in a single context. At the history lesson, it is necessary to consider the decisive significance of a whole range of historical laws that appear to draw attention away from the historical event under consideration. These include the emergence of elements of the capitalist mode of production within a feudal social order; the manipulation of mass discontent by the nascent bourgeoisie in their fight against feudalism, in their own class interests; the growth of labour productivity and increasing exploitation at craft production factories, and so on. The more clearly the teacher explains these historical laws, citing actual historical events and noting the particular characteristics of the Netherlands revolution that distinguish it from other revolutions, the more deeply students understand general historical laws. Consequently, they rely less on rote learning and remember details more deeply of their own accord.

Knowledge of the laws of the historical process is retained in the memory without any special effort at memorisation. Students know that refining the process of production in an exploitative society leads to increased exploitation, just as they know the accumulation of nutrients in the soil leads to increased yields, and carbon dioxide in the air, aided by the sun's rays, is transformed into organic matter in the leaves of plants, and so on.

Causal relationships studied during a physics lesson (heating a body, heat generation, etc.) are also retained in the memory, although the units of measurement themselves may be forgotten. Special work is necessary to ensure they are retained, such as memorising and using the units of measurement for analysing concrete phenomena. The more units of measurement are used, the less work is required to memorise them.

After studying the Netherlands revolution, students learn about many other bourgeois revolutions, and each time they deepen their knowledge of the laws governing the historical process. The deeper their knowledge of these laws, the more easily they find their way around concrete events and the more they know about them, even though they have not set themselves the goal of memorising facts.

The development of curiosity, a systematic approach, and subtlety and independence of thought are facilitated by certain methods that lead a student to investigate a broad range of facts and phenomena as they study an issue. The most effective of these methods is posing problematic questions. Some of the questions posed to students at history lessons when studying the end of serfdom in Russia are:

> What would have happened in Russia if the tsarist government had not granted freedom to serfs? Which social forces supported granting freedom to serfs, and which had an interest in preserving serfdom, and why? What conclusions can we make from a study of the granting of freedom to serfs about the position of various social groups during a time of social conflict? Why is it that after the Russian reforms of 1861, some remnants of serfdom remained? Who had an interest in their preservation, and why? In what ways did future industrial development in Russia depend on the reforms? What pathway would the development of capitalism in Russian agriculture have taken if the large landholdings of landowners had not been preserved? What effect would this have had on the position of peasants? What conclusions can we draw from comparing the liberation of peasants in Russia with the abolition of serfdom in other countries, such as Germany? Why is it that the properties of some landholders fell into decline after the reforms, while the properties of others began to develop quickly? How do you understand Nekrasov's comparison of the reforms of 1861 with the breaking of a 'great chain', that as it broke, hit 'landowners with one end, and peasants with the other'? If the reforms did not improve the peasants' lot, why do we speak of the progressive role played by the abolishing of serfdom?

It is impossible to answer these questions without drawing on a broad selection of material. The more facts that are analysed and compared, the more deeply each problematic issue is understood. When considering an issue, students consider other facts and phenomena from the same field of study. It follows that the teacher must know a great deal more than is dictated by the curriculum. Related analogous facts and phenomena that do not need to be memorised provide a background to the compulsory minimum material and make it easier to memorise that minimum amount. In raising problematic issues, the teacher stimulates thought. Students are enticed to progress from the level of knowledge and intellectual development already attained to a higher level, which can only be reached by acquiring new knowledge. Soviet educational theoretician Mikhail Danilov refers to this interrelationship as a 'contradiction'.[42] In managing students' intellectual development, teachers need to correctly estimate the distance (figuratively speaking) between what has been achieved and what remains to be achieved and set challenges that require the analysis of facts and phenomena.

The study of works of literature offers many opportunities for developing the mind. In studying literature, we prioritise understanding philosophical and aesthetic criteria for evaluating artistic work. The basis of knowledge about literature is a deeply personal, emotional connection with aesthetic values, the life of society and people's spiritual lives. This connection is based on direct perception: the reading of a work of literature. We attach a great deal of significance to collective reading: one student reads expressively while the class listens. Students learn the most striking passages from works of literature by heart. Storing these treasures in their memory enriches the world of thought and feeling, refines their emotional relationship with the surrounding world, and facilitates thought. One cannot imagine the complete intellectual, moral, aesthetic and emotional development of a student if they do not know by heart the monologues of Hamlet and Faust; passages from the poetic works of Heine and Byron; the extract from Gogol's *Dead Souls* in which he compares Russia to a speeding troika; Pushkin's poems 'Songs of the Prophetic Oleg', 'Prisoner', 'I Remember a Magic Moment' and 'When I Wander the Noisy Streets'; the wonderful lyric poems of Koltsov and Nikitin, Shevchenko and Lesia Ukrainka; and passages from the works of Turgenev and Chekhov, Korolenko and Prishvin. In every class in our school, students learn a set number of such texts by heart. From time to time, we conduct evenings and mornings of literary recitals. These take the form of a competition, and the winners are awarded books. When participating in debates, meetings and reading conferences, students utilise what they have learned by heart.

Our literature teachers never set work for study in the textbook if the students have not already read the original. Only after students have read the original, become acquainted with the work's images and developed personal attitudes towards the characters and events portrayed are they allowed to read the textbook. Students cannot complete any assignments by simply memorising passages from the textbook; all the questions set simply require students to be familiar with the original. This is the only way to ensure that literature becomes a textbook of life.

An important prerequisite for developing the capacity and adaptability of the mind is an integration of knowledge and skills, where knowledge is transformed into skill to such an extent that the application of knowledge takes on a degree of automaticity. There are subjects in which knowledge merges with skill and is manifested primarily in skill. This applies especially to grammar. To know grammar does not mean being able to cite a rule for every instance of usage. Many literate people have long forgotten the exact formulation of grammatical rules but write without errors. To know grammar means to comprehend a rule after considering many instances of language usage. If a rule is learned without considering enough instances, students will remember the rule for a short time but will not really know it and soon forget it. Experience shows that the memorisation of grammatical rules must proceed gradually and that rules are involuntarily retained in the memory when they are generalised from many varied examples of living usage.

This is especially important in the primary school. In the junior classes, students spend many lessons completing exercises that aim to analyse instances of living usage. They write words and sentences, think about the laws governing what they write, compare new material with prior knowledge, and carry out creative work. A rule is considered many times based on many new instances. Finally, students reach a point when they remember a rule, not because they have memorised it, but because they have thought about it many times—focused on it, applied it to explain language forms and concentrated on its essence. Reaching this point, where rules are firmly entrenched in students' memories without any particular effort at memorisation, is a highly valued indicator of pedagogical skill. In our primary classes, we do not ask students to memorise rules, and we do not assess students' knowledge by asking them to formulate rules. If a student does not know or cannot remember a rule (without memorising it), they need to complete more exercises and analyse more examples. They need to do this so that when they finally understand the essence of the rule, having really thought about it, they will remember it based on that understanding. Not allowing a student to memorise a rule prematurely is just as important as bringing them to an understanding of the material. Sometimes it is even necessary for a student to forget a formulation they do not understand—get it out of their mind and begin from scratch to focus on the essence of living examples. If this work is conducted well in the primary school, later in the middle and senior years, students will adopt a conscious attitude to the memorisation of generalisations (rules, theorems, formulas, definitions, conclusions). They will not memorise them until they have understood them based on an analysis of concrete examples.

Minimising the role of rote learning places certain demands on lesson structure and a teacher's preparation for lessons. The main type of lesson in the primary classes, and in grammar, arithmetic, algebra, geometry, physics and chemistry in the middle school, is a lesson involving the practical application of prior knowledge to develop new and deeper knowledge. Successful work at this level demands the thoughtful preparation of a series of lessons to study a theme or section. Student work is planned in such a way that from time to time, they return to the analysis of facts and phenomena to gain a deeper understanding of generalisations. In Ms Lysak's mathematics classes, exercises to develop an understanding of polynomial identities are spread over 25 lessons. Several minutes are set aside for these exercises at each lesson. With each new exercise, the students become more independent in applying the knowledge acquired in earlier lessons. Carefully monitoring the work of her students, the teacher sets individual assignments to facilitate reflection and understanding. No program can predict when, how many and which exercises each student will need to complete. Only the teacher can see that, knowing the strengths, abilities and characteristics of each student's intellectual work.

It is essential for active intellectual work to connect thinking and its source—the surrounding world. Study becomes work when the ability to think is developed based on observation of objects and phenomena. Our teachers prompt children who have just started school to think about phenomena, causes and effects, and the characteristics of objects, based on observation.

We set our students special thinking tasks based on observation. This is both a method of studying material and an approach to intellectual development, to the education of reason. For example, the children observe changes in the orchard during autumn, determine the causes of certain phenomena, reflect on consequences and what they lead to, and how the consequences become the causes of new phenomena. Children reflect on cause and effect and begin to understand the interconnectedness of everything in nature. They learn to analyse and synthesise, make hypotheses and test them in practice. For example, children in Grade 2, observing how leaves turn yellow on trees and how trees shed their leaves, reflect on the following questions: why do some trees shed their leaves in September, some in October, and others not until spring? For certain tree species, what connection is there between the shedding of leaves and the time that buds form in spring? The more often thought is associated with concrete phenomena, and the greater the number of phenomena considered, the more deeply the powers of observation are developed. Students who have learned to think carefully while observing their own work (e.g., caring for a tree, constructing a working model) seek to enrich their work intellectually.

For students in the middle and senior years, thinking assignments are linked to work in which results depend on a great variety of objective conditions and causes (e.g., the season or the weather). Students in Grade 7 are asked to think about the factors that increase the viability of seeds and accelerate the development of plants when they bear fruit. The completion of this assignment is linked to work: the children apply fertiliser and treat seeds with chemicals. Yet, this is not just work as it involves research into work processes and the phenomena of nature.

If thought is linked to observation, children develop a certain style of intellectual activity. Children's thoughts are directed to hidden aspects of phenomena they are observing, which may be incomprehensible at first glance. They discover natural laws that cannot be directly observed but can be inferred from observable objects and phenomena. While observing and investigating cause-and-effect relationships, students gradually acquire the ability to think abstractly. Someone who has learned to think while observing is able to mentally analyse facts and phenomena that are not directly perceptible.

Mental analysis of observation results has become part of our system of studying natural science subjects, especially botany, zoology and physics. This analysis can serve two ends. Sometimes it provides new evidence to illustrate laws the students have already studied. Sometimes it paves the way for students to study new laws. When observing phenomena that are soon to be studied, students have many questions. Certain aspects of a subject or phenomenon that a child has previously paid no attention to now present them with a riddle. As questions arise, students discern aspects of a phenomenon that represent something new and unexplained. The process of study becomes one of active intellectual activity, and students experience a deep urge to know. Students have something to think about during their lessons; they generate many ideas about objects and phenomena, and, most importantly, they generate many questions. Without questions, there is no thought.

Observation assignments that precede the study of new material may be given for one or several lessons or for part of a whole course. Students completing Grade 4 observe plants during the summer holidays that they will be studying in Grade 5. They record their observations and any questions that arise during observations and make sketches.

Observation of work, as an interaction between people and nature, and of the operation of machines, mechanisms and technological processes, is highly significant. Before studying the laws of mechanics, students observe the work of tractors, seed drills, cultivators, grain cleaning machines and technology used in construction.

The use of live observation when studying new laws and phenomena of nature helps students become aware of their intellectual effort and its results. They develop an understanding of the quality of intellectual work (and learn that intellectual effort depends on a person's will).

Independence and creativity of thought develop during lessons when elements of investigative research are incorporated into the introduction of new material and the development and deepening of knowledge. For instance, when beginning to study a new geometric shape or solid, students make drawings or prepare schematic models with component parts and study their inter-relationships. We attach particular significance to investigation when students have just been introduced to their first notions of some phenomenon, event or law. The vast majority of lesson time is set aside for reflection. Students consider the relationship between the component parts or elements of the material being studied. They analyse facts and explain cause-and-effect relationships, which leads them further into the material. In considering significant aspects of the new material, students discover new links and relationships. New questions arise, which in turn lead to a deeper understanding of the material.

It takes great pedagogical skill to plan work to promote reflection and analysis of the material and to set independent assignments with this in mind. When experienced teachers prepare for lessons, they analyse the content of the material and identify relationships and links that will provide suitable subjects for reflection following the initial presentation of the material. The teachers do not reveal all aspects of the studied material in their introductory explanations, so something is left for students to investigate independently. It takes skill to leave some significant aspect of the material for reflection.

One of the chemistry lessons on solutions is devoted to heat phenomena that occur when dissolving chemicals: a lowering of temperature in some cases and generating heat in others. In explaining the material, Ms Kolomyichenko characterises the phenomenon as the integration of two processes—physical and chemical—the transition of matter from one form to another. Before conducting experiments in the laboratory, the teacher poses a number of questions that require an explanation from the viewpoint of molecular theory. The teacher deliberately avoids explaining this aspect of the causal relationships during her introduction. As they independently investigate the heat phenomena, students reflect on molecular theory and the law governing the conservation of mass. One of the questions is posed so that in answering it, a new question arises: why is it that when dissolving some substances we observe a lowering of temperature, and in others we observe the generation of heat? The teacher's main aim is to provoke this question. The students begin to investigate the properties of different substances. The students refer to supplementary literature and reference books.

Investigating the essence of facts, phenomena, laws and causal relationships is a particularly important means for stimulating mental engagement. This 'deep thinking' is the ideal approach to studying new material, as it involves the full engagement of one's intellectual powers. The greater the role of thought in the study of new material, the more reflective and thoughtful students' approaches are to everything they observe, listen to, do and see around them. The more students think while investigating and investigate while thinking, the easier it is for them to study as they master new material.

Curiosity, independence, flexibility, capacity and creativity of mind are developed in the middle and senior years as students study some sections of the curriculum independently. This work provides an indispensable avenue for intellectual education. Beginning in Grades 6 and 7, students independently study certain laws of nature, a species of plant or animal, works of literature, formulas, historical events and so on. This work takes place during special lessons that teachers prepare meticulously. They choose topics for independent study that will require students to apply knowledge acquired earlier. Even in Grades 6 and 7, the teacher brings supplementary literature (popular science books and magazines) to lessons set aside for independent study. The older the students, the greater the significance we attach to supplementary literature and the ability to locate and use it. In the school library, there are shelves where supplementary literature about various subjects is located. For example, the physics literature is arranged in several sections: mechanics, gases, liquids, electricity, optics and atomic physics. Before undertaking lessons involving the independent study of new material, students in senior classes are given a list of questions. They then select appropriate resources for each question. This work educates independence of thought and teaches students to immerse themselves in books.

Before independent study lessons in mathematics, students are given practical problems that require them to study a theorem or formula. For example, before studying one of the sections on trigonometric functions, students find the distance to an inaccessible point in the local area (each student is set an individual problem).

When studying mathematics, physics or chemistry, one of the methods for educating creative thought is for students to make up their own problems and solve them. In the middle and senior years, such problems are compiled while undertaking practical activities, drawing on the experience of technical creativity and work productivity. Compiling and solving such problems adds an intellectual dimension to work activities (e.g., students devise problems based on data collected from chemical analysis of the soil).

We give considerable attention to independent study that combines reading scientific literature and carrying out laboratory and practical experiments. For instance, while studying physics in Grades 8–10, students conduct laboratory and practical activities on the following topics completely independently:

> Compilation and reading of graphs, showing the dependence of mechanical work on time; establishing the relationship between force, mass and acceleration; the transformation of mechanical energy into other forms of energy; determining the linear expansion coefficient and volume expansion coefficient of a solid object; determining the latent heat of fusion of ice; investigation of the parallel connection of conductors; determining the heat equivalent of work performed by a current, using the Joule-Lenz law; creating an electrical network with an electromagnetic relay; determining the optical power of a lens; investigating the interference and diffraction of light; investigating the photoelectric effect; the practical application of photovoltaic cells, photoelectric relays and photoresistors; constructing a pocket radio using semiconductors.

Literature and reference books are selected for each of these assignments. Lessons involving independent laboratory work require teachers to prepare meticulously.

As they gain experience studying independently during lessons, our senior students gradually transition to self-education—the independent mastery of theoretical material and practical skills at home, in the library, reading room or study room. Each teacher chooses one theme or section from the yearly program for self-education. In this section, the students select the literature and determine the types of practical assignments. The results of this independent work are presented in papers delivered during special lessons that take the form of seminars. Each student gives an exposition of the content they have studied and explains how they gained their knowledge. For instance, Grade 10 students independently study two sections of the chemistry course ('carbonic acid salts' and 'physical and chemical properties of silicon'), the physics topic 'the internal combustion engine', the algebra topic 'taking the logarithm by parts' and the literature topic 'Aleksei Tolstoy's trilogy *The Road to Calvary*'.

Along with material included in the compulsory curriculum, teachers set some students topics, questions, or problems studied at the tertiary level for their own self-education. For instance, in biology, Grade 10 students may study the following topics independently: the vital activity of the growth cells of agricultural plants during various stages of vegetative growth; the influence of chemicals on the chromosomes of sugar beet, buckwheat and sunflowers; the influence of ultrasound on the seeds of grains and commercial crops; and the viability of wheat seed.

During the final year of secondary school, several days per term are allocated to self-education, and there are no classes on these days. The teachers compile methodological advice for the senior students on the most difficult sections of the curriculum.

Knowledge that is acquired through self-education is firmly imprinted in students' memories. Students actively and consciously make use of such knowledge in their further studies and practical work. We cannot imagine the development of students' intellectual abilities without self-education. During the process of self-education, students develop intellectual traits of character and an individual style in their intellectual work.

In developing children's abilities, it is highly significant that they write compositions about what they see, think, feel and experience. How children write compositions is a universal pedagogical problem. Its resolution affects children's intellectual development and the richness of their spiritual lives.

From their first days at school, we teach children to think about what they see, and talk about the things they are thinking about. Observing the phenomena of nature, children mentally compose and then write down sentences about nature. For example, a teacher may take their students to the riverbank to observe the sun setting on the horizon and the play of colours on the water, fields and meadows. The teacher helps the children find the words they need to express their thoughts and to compose a sentence.

During each year in Grades 1–4, children write five or six compositions from nature; in Grades 5–7, they compose seven or eight, and in Grades 8–10, three or four. They begin composing these during a period of preschool preparation. Writing such compositions down begins during the third quarter of the first year of studies. In Grades 5–7, the children are set composition topics related to the literary works they are studying at school. In these compositions, children express their thoughts and personal attitudes to life, people and the surrounding world.

Some compositions represent a development or extrapolation of a thought expressed by a great person: a writer, artist or scientist. Students love writing compositions in which free rein is given to their fantasy. Every year they write compositions inspired by the pictures of eminent artists.

As we attach exceptional significance to creative writing for the intellectual development of our students, a list of composition topics set in Grades 1–10 is listed in Appendix 2 at the end of this book.

Because we teach children to appreciate the beauty and nuances of words from an early age, our students love to write compositions. In the primary school, such compositions are written amid nature, during journeys to the source of words. The children's emotional response to the beauty of nature is like a stream that carries the beauty of words into their souls. The creative use of language enters children's spiritual lives and becomes as much an imperative as the need to listen to music. Children wish to express as beautifully and as clearly as possible what they see, feel and experience.

Following are examples of some of the compositions recorded in our handwritten journals, *Our Creativity* and *Our Thought*:

When the Sun Goes Behind a Cloud
(Grade 1, Maya Postolova)

The rays of the sun light up a golden field. The ears of grain play, the flowers smile at the blue sky. Sun, you are so joyful and merry! Your sparks are in every flower and every blade of grass. But now a dark cloud approaches and covers the sun. The ears of grain are sad, the flowers are anxious, the blades of grass hang their heads. The field becomes grey, the sky overcast. It is as if someone has covered the golden meadow with a grey blanket. Oh, how I wish that the sun will come out from behind that cloud as soon as possible. I wish it, and so do the ears of grain, the flowers and the blades of grass.

Cranes in the Blue Sky
(Grade 2, Andrei Kravchenko)

The meadows spring to life with spring music. Birds sing, streams babble, ducks quack. The slender branches of the weeping willow show their greenery and bees are buzzing. The sky is a deep blue, clear and bright. Just before sunset a formation of cranes appears in the blue sky. The silver birds are flying and calling. Where have you been, birds, and where are you flying to? You seem to be swimming through the air. A blue wave is caressing you. The setting sun sends you a greeting. Beyond the forest, beyond the primeval forest, is a blue lake with crystal clear water and emerald banks. That is where your nests are. I will go there, and you will give me a drop of water for good luck.

Evening Dusk
(Grade 3, Valya Marchenko)

The sun goes to rest behind a mountain. The fields have grown dark. From a ravine Dusk comes out. It is a little old man, grey-haired, with a stick. It walks quietly over the earth. It looks into huts. It taps its finger on windowpanes. Children go to sleep.

At Night
(Grade 4, Lida Tkach)

The lamp is dim. Two of my dolls are leaning against the back of a chair, dozing. My little bear is sleeping under the table. My tin soldiers are sleeping. Everyone is asleep. Outside it is winter. Beyond the frozen windowpane hoar frost is floating down from a tree. The wind rocks a streetlamp. A shadow creeps quietly over the snow.

When Autumn Begins
(Grade 4, Svetlana Lobar)

I know when autumn begins—when it smells of apples. You cannot smell them in summer, but you can smell them in autumn. The sun does not make you hot, but gently warms. In the garden it is as quiet as can be. In the yard of the collective farm there are mountains of wheat. The fields are ploughed, and green shoots are appearing. Basket loads of fragrant apples are carted from the orchards. Red tomatoes are harvested in the vegetable gardens.

In early autumn the nights turn cool. In the mornings the pond is covered with a thin layer of mist. On quiet autumn days we love to go into the fields. One day we travelled in a truck to the melon plantation. Each of us was given a large watermelon. I brought my watermelon home. Mum cut it up. It was as red as the sun and smelled of the distant steppe.

Storks
(Grade 5, Valya Skripnik)

Long ago, when I had just been born, some storks built a nest on our barn. My mother said it was a sign of good luck for me. Each year two white storks fly from warmer climes. They fuss about and get their nest in order and raise some chicks.

In the evening, as soon as the sun sets behind the mountain, they stand beside their nest and look far off into the distance. They gaze at a distant meadow and at the fields. They seem to be admiring the sunset. Darkness falls over the earth, and the storks seem to be drawn in grey on an ashen sky.

A Night at the Harvest
(Grade 6, Oleg Ryadovoi)

In summer we lived in the hayfields. During the day we helped dry the hay, grazed the calves, and collected wood in the forest for the kitchen. And in the evening—how wonderful it was!—a little campfire burned under the starry sky. Grandpa Grigorii Filippovich told us about the distant past of our village, about rare plants and animals, about how he served in the navy.

Then we climbed onto a haystack to sleep, but we did not feel sleepy. We talked to each other about other worlds among the distant stars. We forgot that we were surrounded by meadows, forests and steppe, and became space travellers. Up there was a small, barely perceptible star, but it was a sun, just like our bright, hot, light-giving sun. And we flew to that distant star. Around us were comets, meteors, constellations. Eight years later we approached the star. It was no longer a little spark in the boundless ocean of space, but a huge, blazing orb.

We approached an unknown planet. It was clothed in a light blue haze. Our spaceship landed amid green hills. Cultivated fields, well-lit buildings—what joy, our brothers in reason were living there…

But then a horse neighed and a dog barked. Our amazing flight ended. The moon rose and illuminated the fields and forest, the wide lake and our hayfield. A white layer of mist covered the lake. Perhaps there is enchanting beauty on distant planets, but nowhere is there any beauty to compare with that on our Earth.

When Our First Astronauts Land on Mars...
(Grade 7, Yurii Morokov)

At last the long-awaited day arrives: I and two of my friends are flying to Mars. Our silver spaceship shines in the sun. We climb into the cabin. The earth shakes. That is our mighty atomic engines starting. We are pressed back into our seats. Then we feel light and float about the cabin, looking out the portholes. We see a huge blue sphere on a black background: our home planet Earth.

With each day Mars draws closer. Now it occupies a third of our field of vision out the porthole. We turn on our braking engines and land smoothly on the planet. Our spaceship is in the middle of a huge plain. The soil is a bluish colour, the sky is dark purple, and the sun barely warms. We leave our spaceship. The whole surface of the planet is covered in little blue bushes with black flowers. Here and there in depressions crystals of ice shine.

Silence. On the horizon we see ruins. We walk towards them through the black flowers. We see the ruins of buildings and wrecked vehicles. It is a dead city. The buildings are covered in ash. In the streets are burned motor vehicles and helicopters. The buildings are covered in a thin layer of dust. We enter one of the buildings. Wide rooms, beautiful windows, bas-reliefs on the walls, wonderful paintings. We shudder when we see the dead people. They appear to have died instantaneously. Each one has died while engaged in some work...

This is a dead planet. The Martians died from atomic radiation. They waged a deadly war. The plants perished as well as the animals. Only blue bushes with black flowers survived, covering the whole planet with a funereal carpet...

We return to Earth shaken. Let the destruction of the Martians be a lesson to us. We must eliminate all nuclear weapons! If war breaks out, we will perish too. The terrible news shocked everyone on Earth. People forced their governments to destroy their nuclear weapons. Eternal peace began.

The Ringing Sound of Spring
(Grade 8, Lena Grinchenko)

The earth has woken from its long winter sleep. The grass shines, and a wave of green mist spreads over the meadow. During the evenings at this time of year I listen to the music of nature. The sky is a gentle blue, the evenings are warm and quiet, the sunset has the colour of the first purple rose. I listen to the quiet of the evening and hear the meadows ringing. Somewhere not far off, as if from the willows leaning over the pond, a barely audible ringing can be heard. The sound floats over the earth: over the green meadows and over the gullies. The willow bushes tremble. What is making that sound? Perhaps a drop of sweet sap has fallen from a birch tree onto the mirror-like surface of the pond, which has rung like a giant bell? Or perhaps the cranes, returning from warmer climes, are singing their joyful song?

A Memorable Day from my Childhood
(Grade 9, Yurii Deineka)

I will never forget that day. I was probably four at the time, or perhaps only three. My father was travelling to get hay from meadows near the Dnieper, and I persuaded him to take me. We arrived at a meadow before sunset. My father unharnessed the horses, and they began to graze on juicy grass next to a lake. The sun set behind the forest. A flock of migratory birds flew overhead. Something rustled in the reeds.

My father loaded the hay and harnessed the horses. It grew dark, and the song of a nocturnal bird carried to us from the forest.

We set off. Stars twinkled in the sky. I felt sleepy. I lay on the hay, and the stars seemed to come closer to me. And then it seemed to me that I was no longer on a cart of hay, but on a ship, sailing through dark blue waves. The waves gently rocked the ship, and the stars twinkled. Suddenly one star trembled and dissolved, and sparks shone in the sky.

The waves rocked me off to sleep. The hay smelled sweet, and I shut my eyes. I saw a meadow bathed in sunlight. Bees were buzzing and clover was in flower. One flower looked like a star that had just fallen to Earth.

I woke up, and for a long time I could not remember where I was. The stars were shining, and I could hear the song of a grasshopper. The cart was standing still. I sat up and looked at the meadow. I saw a big lake on the horizon.

'Is that a fire?' I asked my father.

'No, that's the moon', my father answered.

Then we were off again, and again the field turned into blue waves in an endless sea.

Then I woke up at home. My mother was holding me in her arms. Could I really be that small? My father made a bed for me on the hay. I do not remember falling asleep.

I woke up from the cold. The sky was growing light, with just a few stars twinkling behind the branches of an apple tree. Somewhere sheep were bleating. Again, I fell asleep, and dreamed of a river, a sunny day, waves lapping, so good for swimming.

I woke up again. The sun had risen high above the apple tree and was scorching my face. A wind was rustling the branches. A white cloud was floating in the blue sky.

What a long, long day that was! I will always remember it.

Methods of instruction

MANY YEARS OF EXPERIENCE have led us to conclude that all pedagogical methods of instruction may be divided into two groups.

The first group consists of methods that introduce knowledge and skills to students: an account, explanation, lecture or description; the explanation of a concept, a series of instructions or a talk; the independent reading of a book to gain an introduction to new knowledge; a demonstration or illustration (film, maps, pictures, television, diagrams, tables, models); the demonstration of a work process or skill; independent observation, excursions, practical or laboratory work conducted independently; and the demonstration of physical exercises.

The second group consists of methods involving the interpretation, development and deepening of knowledge: exercises (oral, written, technical); student explanation of facts and phenomena of nature, work or social life; discussions and creative written work (compositions, abstracts, precis, compiling problems, programming); preparing study aids and equipment, geographical projects, laboratory work, experiments (on our experimental plots, collective farm fields, laboratories or workshops); using machines, mechanisms or apparatus to deepen, develop or apply knowledge and skills; and continuous work experience that achieves practical goals while perfecting skills and deepening knowledge (in workshops, our experimental plots, the collective farm fields and the stock breeding farm).

Depending on the specific characteristics of the subject and the content of the material, each method has specific features. A lecture in a literature lesson has certain features, while a mathematics lesson has others. The demonstration of a work process or skill depends on specific links between the work and theoretical knowledge. Observation in the natural sciences differs from observation of a physical process, not only in the means of perception but also in the character of the intellectual work involved. The success of intellectual education depends on the creative application of the methods of instruction, on specific details that are determined by the concrete situation and cannot be foreseen by any theory of instruction. Practice is an inexhaustible source of theory precisely because it is in practice that all aspects of a theory are revealed.

It is extremely important for a proper intellectual education that the methods of instruction, lesson structure, and all its organisational and pedagogical elements correspond to the educational aims of the material, to the challenge of educating students holistically. Knowledge is acquired so that it may be applied in life in some form or other. The convictions formed during the process of instruction should govern students moral, vocational, social and aesthetic relations with others. It is in this application of knowledge that we can integrate moral and intellectual development. When preparing for a lesson, experienced teachers always think about how the knowledge they are presenting will be refracted in their students' minds. This determines a teacher's choice of methods of instruction.

In history lessons in Grade 5, students study the Greco-Persian wars. In this case, knowledge of concrete facts plays a major role in developing views and convictions. But students' further intellectual and moral development—their moral character—does not depend on how reliably they memorise the details of a historical event. The application of knowledge here is indirect. It is not the knowledge of each discrete concrete fact that is applied, but the philosophical, moral evaluation of historical events manifested in a student's subjective attitude towards the surrounding world and their actions.

An experienced teacher tries to ensure that admiration for the Greek's patriotic fight against foreign invaders lives on in students' thoughts and feelings for the rest of their lives. The teacher subordinates their analysis of the facts to an educational aim: that the students develop a strong love for their homeland, and the historical facts are not only viewed in the light of contemporary ideas but deepen those ideas. With this in mind, the teacher includes in their exposition striking facts that the children will not find in the textbook. They do not select events for memorisation and do not resort to techniques that facilitate memorisation (as is sometimes necessary). Instead, they rely on the action of involuntary memory. The more the teacher uses striking supplementary material, the more students understand and remember what is important and basic. To convey a clear understanding of the heroism of the Greeks, who were defending their homeland, the teacher introduces supplementary material about the Spartan warriors' courage and sacrifice during the battle of Thermopylae.

Historical accounts should always be full of striking facts that illustrate political and moral ideas, and there is no need to conduct special work on memorisation when introducing new material, as might be necessary in a mathematics lesson. To do so would weaken the philosophical impact of the material on thoughts and feelings. The more a teacher uses supplementary material when giving accounts or lectures in history or literature lessons, the more deeply political, moral and aesthetic ideas will be understood and responded to emotionally. And whenever ideas induce an emotional response, the teacher's great ally, involuntary memorisation, comes into play.

The idea of defending one's homeland is close and dear to the children, and they want to express their thoughts and feelings. The more historical events are illuminated by moral and political ideas, the greater the opportunity to combine an account with discussion. Generally speaking, experienced teachers of history and language find the discussion method helps them achieve their educational aims. Children express their thoughts and feelings about the courage and heroism of those who defended their homeland. Important political ideas are established in their minds as personal convictions. The children are not passive 'consumers' of knowledge; they are deeply interested in the fates of those defending their homeland. During lessons in history and literature, discussion plays a special role: it facilitates the development of moral convictions.

During such history lessons, there is no need to resort to independent reading of the textbook with a view to memorisation. (You do need to do this when the educational goal demands it.) There is also no need to compile tables, sketches or maps, as that weakens the lesson's philosophical direction. (It makes sense to conduct such activities when revising and systematising knowledge.) In the same way, when analysing a work of literature from a philosophical and aesthetic perspective, it makes no sense to revise other aspects of the curriculum simultaneously.

Methods of instruction at a grammar lesson are determined by quite different circumstances. If students gain knowledge of a given section of the history program during the initial introductory lesson and then go on to develop and deepen that knowledge, the introductory lesson for a grammar topic is something like a plan for many lessons. At each lesson, the knowledge is continually revised, constantly returning to the initial explanation. The process of instruction, and consequently memorisation, consists of gradually coming to understand many related facts that illustrate one and the same generalisation: a grammatical rule. This process of understanding is primarily aimed at memorisation—memorisation for life so entrenched that the formulation of the rule may be forgotten, but the many facts that have passed through the student's consciousness and been understood preserve the rule's essence. For this reason, practical homework assignments play a significant role in studying grammar: reading and regularly completing exercises to reinforce the same rule. The mastery of grammar is a lengthy process of applying the knowledge taught.

At language lessons in the primary and middle school grades, the dominant methods of work consider the lengthy process involved in gradually understanding grammatical rules. The interpretation of rules is combined with exercises and independent explanations of instances of language usage. That is why our methodology emphasises a method like the explanation of facts and phenomena. When using this method, the deepening of knowledge is intricately connected with its application, which strengthens involuntary memorisation. The more deeply material needs to be embedded in one's memory, the longer the time span allocated to its study. If a teacher tries to 'cover' a rule or formula (or some other generalisation used in life to explain or analyse many facts) in a single lesson or in a few lessons, to get students to master it immediately, the inevitable result will be superficial knowledge, the blunting of intellectual abilities, and the shackling of the creative power of reason. The inability to apply a grammatical rule ('the student knows the rule but makes mistakes in their writing') is the result of such rushed coverage of the material.

The main method of work at our grammar lessons is the explanation of the facts and phenomena of language usage while independently completing exercises. As they explain facts and phenomena, the students gradually understand the essence of the generalisation (the rule). For each rule, the teacher compiles a selection of exercises to be completed over a long period of time, together with some individual supplementary work for those who can only grasp the rule after considering a greater number of facts. These students are given cards with text full of relevant examples.

Teachers of language, mathematics, physics and chemistry—those subjects in which rules, laws and formulas learned earlier are used to master new rules, laws and formulas—are especially concerned to see that the main method for revising rules is their practical application.

Aligning the methods of instruction with the challenges of intellectual development also determines the structure of lessons and the relationship between their various stages. Our teaching staff has developed lesson structures for primary, middle school and senior classes, which align with the following principles:

1. Integrate students' practical work with the introduction of knowledge and with its extension, development and application. Consequently, consolidation of knowledge is not a stage in the lesson. Consolidation is a lengthy process that encompasses special exercises, laboratory work and other forms of independent work, as well as the acquisition of new knowledge.

2. The application of knowledge (in a variety of forms) is seen as the main avenue for extending and developing knowledge and also for assessing it. Through the application of knowledge, we seek to ensure constant feedback: information about how students think and what progress each student is making. The teacher's timely collection of information about the intellectual work of each student depends on how well they select tasks involving the application of knowledge, the extent to which they consider individual strengths and abilities, and especially the independent, individual nature of the intellectual work that is set.

3. The acquisition of knowledge is seen as a lengthy and gradual process. If three hours have been allocated to a certain section of the curriculum, that does not mean students will have fully mastered that section in three hours. Knowledge is gradually deepened and developed over a long period of time. The development and extension of knowledge is a lengthy process that takes place during lessons, homework and in the process of self-education (reading literature, preparing talks and abstracts, etc.). The practical work that is required for the consolidation, development and deepening of knowledge is spread over an extended period.

Lessons based on these principles are characterised by a great variety of structures. The overwhelming majority of grammar and mathematics lessons in Grades 1–4 begin with the practical application of knowledge acquired earlier. While doing this work, students gain a deeper understanding of rules, laws, definitions and other generalisations. If students are studying the spelling of unstressed vowels during grammar lessons, the teacher will select a methodological approach that leads students to reflect on the essence of the rule. The students may copy sentences and explain any words with unstressed vowels; they may choose such sentences from a reading book, or group words with unstressed vowels according to their characteristics. Finally, they may independently compose sentences with unstressed vowels.

Whatever approach is selected, practical work involves both the deepening of knowledge and its assessment. Marks are not awarded for answers to individual questions. Experience teaches us that such assessment creates an atmosphere of chance or a lottery. In the early and middle years, marks are only awarded after the teacher has monitored all a student's work over a defined period: classwork, homework and creative work. Some students are awarded a mark after a week's work, others after two weeks (depending on many individual factors). Experience has convinced us that the more visibly and practically students apply their knowledge as they develop and deepen it, the more opportunities there are to assess knowledge, and the less need for special assessment activities. Primary school teacher Ms Zaza has developed a series of about 40 problems that require the practical application of all the knowledge children must master in primary school on measuring length, weight, volume and area. If students find they have forgotten something while solving these problems, they will immediately seek the information they lack.

This is an especially important methodological approach in the junior, middle school, and senior classes. Anything that must be memorised and mastered permanently is recalled and revised not in isolation from concrete, practical knowledge but with an aim in mind, while completing some task or other (solving a problem, creative writing, measuring a locality, etc.). Mathematics teacher Ms Arishchenko has compiled a series of trigonometry problems. While solving them, students learn the trigonometric functions without conscious efforts at memorisation.

The structure of lessons in the primary classes is determined by the characteristics of the knowledge that children must acquire at this stage of their studies. This knowledge is organically combined with skills. The main goal at the primary level of instruction is for children to read, write, think, observe and express their thoughts. Consequently, all stages of a lesson in grammar, arithmetic or language development incorporate active work: children have to be doing something—writing, reading, composing and solving problems, measuring, observing nature phenomena or a work process, or writing a composition. For further studies to be successful, children's writing must become semi-automatic. Their intellectual powers must be directed mainly at understanding the meaning of what they are writing and at reflection, not at the process of writing. Many years of experience has convinced us that if a student is to write quickly, precisely and grammatically, if writing is to become a tool used in intellectual work and not its ultimate aim, a student must write at least 1400–1500 pages in their exercise books during their primary school years. This requires special exercises to develop writing technique and tempo.

Students' creative work has a place at every lesson in which knowledge is being deepened, developed and applied. Students only become literate when they have learned to use language and write compositions. Students will be most successful at learning to solve problems when they know how to make up problems (creativity is most important when making up equations). Our primary school teachers, Ms Verkhovynina, Ms Zaza and Ms Novitskaya, conduct special excursions into the fields or forest with the main aim formulated as 'know how to spot a problem'. We have become convinced that if even the weakest, least successful student in arithmetic has begun to make up their own problems, they will start to find success in arithmetic.

In primary school lessons, an important role is played by types of work characterised by the integration of three things: the teacher's words, a visual image the children can see, and the children's practical activity. Instruction in the primary school is like a window onto the world. Children need everything to be explained, shown, interpreted and demonstrated. We attach great significance to explanation (exposition) with the aim of giving children a concept to describe, an idea to interpret, an action to demonstrate (reading, writing, a work process). Children's vocabularies are enriched during excursions into the natural environment: they learn words that express the subtlest variations of phenomena and characteristics (e.g., shades of colour, scents). The teacher explains the meaning of abstract concepts (each primary school teacher has compiled a glossary of abstract concepts such as nature, organism, matter, etc.), which are continually refreshed as they are illustrated by new facts.

In the primary classes, we attach great significance to the reading technique, seeking to ensure that, while reading, children's intellectual resources are focused on the content of what is read and not on the process of reading. At every lesson, children listen to the emotionally rich, expressive reading of their teacher. Then they read themselves, and not only material set from the textbook, but also books they love. Many years of experience has convinced our teaching staff that if children are to learn to read expressively, fluently and with understanding, focusing on the content of what they are reading and not the reading process, they must spend at least 200 hours reading aloud (in class and at home) and at least 2,000 hours reading silently during the primary school years. The teachers allocate this work over a significant period of time.

In the middle school, there is an increasing role for interpreting, developing and deepening knowledge as new knowledge is acquired. In accounts, descriptions and explanations, we increasingly introduce instructions about how to work independently, and giving instructions begins to occupy a place as a separate method. We attach exceptional significance to the middle school years, as a preparation for further education (especially self-education) and work. An exposition in the middle school may be distinguished from an exposition in the primary school by the teacher's efforts to awaken adolescents' interest in reading literature. As early as Grades 6 and 7, independent reading is set as an introduction to new material. Students are set sections of the curriculum (of medium difficulty) for independent study. Reading is combined with other forms of independent work (experiments in laboratories and experimental plots, observations, examination of additional sources such as diagrams, models and tables).

At lessons in grammar, arithmetic, algebra, geometry, physics and biology, the application of knowledge is an important way of deepening understanding. This is especially so when the very essence of the knowledge to be acquired is the development of skills based on theoretical knowledge. Every teacher working with middle school and senior classes has developed ways of combining studying new material with applying knowledge and skills. The grammar teachers give students individual cards with specially selected factual material, the analysis of which deepens prior knowledge, provides an opportunity to assess knowledge, and leads to the study of new material. The botany teacher introduces the study of a new class or family of plants by examining live samples (stems, flowers, roots, etc.). The physics teacher asks students to think about the essence of some phenomenon or another they have observed, and this analysis of something new and unexplained is combined with the application of knowledge. The history teacher begins a lesson by posing a problem in which something significant remains unexplained but at the same time offers the opportunity to gain understanding by applying prior knowledge.

In the middle and senior years, a special place is allocated to using preparatory observations of natural phenomena and work processes, usually at the beginning of a lesson when students are being introduced to new material. We consider this method exceptionally significant. For example, before studying the roots of plants, children observe the root development of various plants over a comparatively long period. Before studying various types of mechanical movement in physics, they observe the operation of machines and mechanisms at the repair workshop, a road construction site, a home construction site, and the animal farm. Teachers set preparatory observation assignments that prompt students to reflect on causal relationships. These observations are referred to at lessons when teaching causal relationships. The more the known and the unknown are related to each other, the livelier the intellectual work is during the lesson.

In the middle years, work aimed at memorisation takes on even more significance than during the primary years. We seek to ensure that formulas, symbols, units of measurement, properties of substances and other generalisations are revised during practical work that is connected with the deepening, development and application of knowledge and with work. To develop a degree of automaticity, algebra teachers set a series of problems that lead students to revise all the polynomial identities in the space of three or four hours. Grammar teachers set their students a series of creative and visual dictations that lead students to revise the most important spelling rules several times as they progress from Grade 5 through to Grade 8. When conducting these dictations, no time is set aside for revising the actual rules. Preparation for these lessons requires long-term planning, the ability to envisage students' work over the course of a year and distribute it: firstly in time, and secondly between classwork and homework.

At the beginning of each year, language teachers plan how many times per year students in Grades 5–8 will complete exercises for recalling rules and developing automaticity in writing. Every year, mathematics and physics teachers set their students practical assignments on-site, in a workshop, experimental plot or laboratory, during which students revise units of measurement, formulas, properties and other generalisations. These assignments are associated with physical work. Activities such as preparing hotbeds, digging trenches or holes for fruit trees, laying out fruit or decorative nurseries, apart from their productive aims, also have the goal of consolidating knowledge and skills associated with measuring area and volume. At our school fertiliser factory, students independently calculate the relative percentages of the various components of the fertilisers they are preparing. The students who work there have a good grasp not only of biology and chemistry but also mathematics. They are constantly making mental calculations of the quantities and percentages of chemicals. We are convinced that the students who understand percentages the best are those who have to calculate them in their daily work.

In the middle years, we attach great significance to methods involving the demonstration of work and technological processes, the use of machines and mechanisms, preparing study aids and apparatus. Teachers of mathematics, physics, chemistry, biology and astronomy demonstrate how to use apparatus and study aids. Every student is given time to independently set up their apparatus (sometimes disassembling and reassembling). Demonstrations in workshops and on our experimental plot have a special place. The mastery of a work process begins with a demonstration, at which students witness an exemplary model of perfected work. At their work lessons, Grade 8 students attend a special practical class where they learn to use an internal combustion engine, an electric motor and measuring instruments. During their first eight years of schooling, each student prepares a minimum number of visual aids and apparatus in a school workshop or a workspace at home.

We attach major significance in the middle years to creative intellectual work such as the compilation of notes about books students have read, elementary calculations for construction purposes and the compilation of reports (in Grades 7 and 8).

The objectives of the senior years of secondary schooling are to give students a broad polytechnical education, a high degree of skill in intellectual and physical work and well-established practical skills, to educate a love of work and knowledge and prepare students to choose a profession wisely. These goals dictate an appropriate choice of methods of instruction, lesson structure and sequencing; an appropriate amount of independent work at lessons and as part of self-education; and suitable opportunities for the practical application of knowledge. General features of all methods of instruction in the senior classes include a greater degree of independence and reflection when acquiring and applying knowledge (compared with the junior and middle school classes), a variety of approaches to independent intellectual work, and the transfer of knowledge and skills both to their peers and to younger students (this is only expected in the senior classes). The range of theoretical knowledge and practical skills in the senior classes is so broad that if the acquisition of knowledge was not accompanied at every step by its application and transfer to others, and by independent investigation, our senior students would not be able to study successfully.

The main methods of instruction in our senior classes feature the following types of intellectual work:

1 The application of knowledge and skills acquired earlier to 'extract' new knowledge; the independent analysis of facts, objects and phenomena with this goal in mind.

2 The independent development of skill in applying knowledge acquired during lessons; the formation, development and extension

of the skills required for this; the completion of practical assignments (exercises, calculations, problems) with this goal in mind; the construction of working models of machines and mechanisms, etc.

3 Investigation of phenomena and processes in both natural and laboratory settings.

In senior classes, the methods of instruction more obviously depend on the content of the material and the applicability of the knowledge. During the early 1950s, we developed a lecture-laboratory system of lessons for our senior classes.[43] The main feature of this system is the varied combination of methods of exposition (extraction, generalisation) of theoretical knowledge and methods of practical work, with the aim of deepening, developing and assessing knowledge. This combination of methods is planned when a teacher prepares their series of lessons. Here there can be no standard lesson structure. It is impossible to find something that is common to all subjects or all sections of a subject. For example, some topics in literature, history, mathematics or physics require an introductory lesson; that is, a lesson during which students prepare to study all the material incorporated in that section of the curriculum. In another case, there may be no need for such an introductory lesson.

In the lecture-laboratory system of lessons, a major role is played by lectures: historical, literary, geographical or relating to the natural sciences. Depending on the subject and the relative weight given to the practical work necessary for the interpretation, development and deepening of knowledge, the lecture may require one, two or several lessons. The remainder of the time programmed for that section or topic is allocated to independent practical work, the aim of which (I must emphasise this) is not only to deepen and develop knowledge and develop skills, but also to gain new knowledge and pave the way for studying new material. In some cases, the lecture covers all the main issues associated with the topic. In other cases, only part of the material is covered, and the lecture serves to provide students with a model analysis, showing them how to study theoretical issues independently. Lectures of the first sort are typical for the natural sciences (especially physics and chemistry), while lectures of the second sort are typical for the humanities (especially literature).

Our teaching staff give special attention to the connection between the lecture and the independent practical work that follows it. The lecture gives the independent work direction, explaining the theoretical issues raised, the research or experimental methodology to use, and the literature to read. This is especially significant for the basic natural science subjects. For experienced physics and chemistry teachers, part of the lecture is a practical demonstration of the methods for independent work.

Lectures in mathematics have special features unique to that subject. At mathematics lessons, there are hardly any straight lectures in the strict sense of the word. As they listen to an exposition of theoretical material, the students of experienced mathematics teachers relate it to an assignment they have been set requiring them to interpret the principles discussed in the lecture. While working on these assignments, students apply the knowledge and skills acquired earlier. The interpretation of the lecture is thus expressed in independent work, during which knowledge is deepened and developed.

A feature of lectures in the humanities subjects, including history, is the use of generalisation when presenting material. Experienced history teachers choose for their lectures the most important, root issues underlying the topic, an understanding of which is essential for developing a scientific philosophy of life. At this time, students are presented with issues they must investigate and clarify through their independent work. For example, when revising the topic, 'Germany in the 19th century', students independently examine 'the process of eliminating feudal relations in Germany'. During the introductory lecture on this topic, the teacher explains how to work independently on the issue and what literature to consult.

A feature of a lecture on geography is the wide use of supplementary material, characterising the economic and political conditions in which the development of a country or group of countries takes place.

During lectures at literature lessons, we attach great significance to the artistic, emotional and aesthetic elements. At the centre of their lectures, literature teachers place the analysis of a literary image, trying to convey the author's descriptive methods as fully as possible. Their lectures often include a direct appeal to the thoughts and feelings of the senior students. The teacher prompts them to think deeply about certain social phenomena and the psychological relationships between people. Literature lectures often include expressive reading of extracts from the works being studied.

In the lecture-laboratory system of lessons, studying a new topic may begin with practical work carried out both in class and at home, rather than with a lecture. In this case, the teacher's lecture (or a paper delivered by an outstanding student) concludes the unit of study. This approach is sometimes expedient when studying humanities subjects, especially literature. The study of a work of literature often begins with work on the original text. Students re-read the most significant passages of the work being studied and then express their thoughts, views and conclusions concerning the social, political, moral and aesthetic issues touched on in the work. Often the study of a literature topic will begin with a debate or discussion. Teachers of biology, physics and chemistry sometimes begin the study of new material by asking one of the ablest students to prepare an introduction to the course. In this introduction, they review the concepts, theorems, conclusions, rules and laws that lead into the study of the new material.

The practical work that follows the lecture (or introduction by one of the ablest students), or which precedes it, may make use of the most diverse methods and approaches, depending on the content of the material, the nature of the knowledge and the ways it may be applied. At mathematics lessons, it involves solving problems, setting problems, drawing graphs or making calculations; practical measurement conducted in specific locations (in workshops or laboratories); the analysis of various proofs of theorems; programming of automated models; describing the operational parameters of machinery (e.g., based on the indicated rotational speed of an operating shaft, reducing gear, working parts, etc.); the analysis of statistical and other numerical data to determine laws or make conclusions; the preparation of models illustrating the proofs of theorems; and the mentoring of the most capable mathematics students in more junior classes.

The mathematics teachers seek to ensure that every student works independently when they are solving problems, and comes to an understanding of the theoretical generalisations explained in the teacher's lecture or a fellow student's presentation. Several variations of a problem (usually four) are chosen for independent work. The first three, of varying levels of difficulty, are dictated by the curriculum. The fourth problem includes some element that goes beyond the curriculum. It is intended for the strongest, most talented students who are participating in individual work in interest groups, and to foster new talent. This differentiation in the assignments arouses considerable interest among the students, allowing them to demonstrate their abilities, awakening their competitive instincts, and helping the teacher observe and assess knowledge while the students are working. The students try to choose a more difficult variation and solve it in an original way. Often, having solved an easier variation, a student takes on a more complex one, overcomes the difficulties, and successfully completes the work. Thanks to this work with differentiated problems, students develop a sense of competition. The most successful and original solutions to problems are published in our school mathematics journal.

As individual students develop and deepen their knowledge during this practical classwork, the teacher may set two or three students (sometimes four or five) several variations of some problems for assessment. Each student chooses a variation within their level of ability and solves the problem. Sometimes, as well as solving the problem, the assessment assignment includes posing a new problem (or a drawing, chart, calculation, or diagram). The whole class is continuing their studies while a group of students is being assessed. Usually, all the students have been assessed by the time they have completed a unit of work. Those who have already been assessed are set more difficult assignments from previous sections of the curriculum or advised to independently begin studying the next section.

When studying some topics in mathematics, physics, chemistry or biology, the unit of work is concluded with a lesson involving practical application of the knowledge acquired. The aim of such lessons is to teach the students to independently apply knowledge in practical work, in using technology, in gaining new knowledge, in theoretical research, and in experiments or laboratory work. The teachers prepare students for such practical lessons beforehand (sometimes this preparation takes place in practical lessons designed to deepen knowledge). Individuals or groups of students are set assignments that incorporate measurement, calculations, or the description of technological processes. For instance, while studying the topic, 'The cylinder and the cone' in solid geometry, students were set the following assignments:

1. Measure the volume of a water tower; calculate the amount of water that may be pumped into the tower.
2. Measure the volume of earthworks carried out when digging a well of cylindrical shape.
3. Calculate the volume of reinforced concrete columns used as supports in the electrification of a railway line, and having the form of a truncated cone. Calculate the volume of cement and metal required to construct 1,000 cubic metres of such columns.
4. Measure the volume and mass of oil in a tank of cylindrical shape. Determine the loss of oil that remains on the walls of the tank after it is emptied.
5. Calculate the volume of waste metal produced when manufacturing gear wheels from blanks having the form of a truncated cone.
6. Calculate the volume and mass of metal discarded as shavings when finishing parts of cylindrical shape.
7. Investigate the most efficient way to construct a water pressure tank (considering the need for heat insulation in winter); calculate the quantity of various materials needed to insulate the tank.

Completing one or more of these problems (by choice), the students write reports. The best solutions are published in our mathematics journal.

We attach great significance to lessons in the practical application of knowledge in agricultural production. For instance, when studying a unit on 'Nitrogen and Phosphorus', students are set problems involving the selection of a mixture of fertilisers for a given soil while researching the activity of bacteria that fix atmospheric nitrogen in the soil.

In the senior classes, experimentation plays an important role. At the beginning of the year, teachers of biology, chemistry and physics choose the sections of the curriculum for which they will set work of an experimental nature.

For example, when studying the foundations of Darwinism, Grade 10 students conduct experiments on the following topics:

1. The action of chemical elements and alkaloids on the chromosomes of sugar beet.
2. Chemical means for treating the seeds of grain crops with a view to increasing their viability.
3. The role of vitamins, phytoncides, and antibiotics in stimulating vital processes in animals.
4. The dependence of the percentage of fat in cow's milk on the proportion of proteins and carbohydrates in their feed ration.
5. The conversion of artificial urea into protein.

Lessons during which students study new material completely independently occupy a special place in the lecture-laboratory system. Such independent work should refer to several sources. Reading is combined with the investigation of phenomena while completing practical tasks.

The lecture-laboratory system facilitates pupils' active participation in the acquisition of knowledge. Under this system, the student and their inner world are not so much the object of a method of instruction as the prime motivating force.

Participating simultaneously in two or three types of work, each student develops various abilities and skills.

CHAPTER 6

Work Education

Principles of Work Education

WORK EDUCATION IS THE PRACTICAL PREPARATION of the younger generation for participation in the workforce. It is also an extremely important element in moral, intellectual and aesthetic education. Our teaching staff are working to create a system of work education in which work gives shape to the moral and intellectual temper of the personality. We see our educational task as being to ensure work becomes part of the spiritual life of the person we are educating and of the life of our community, that our adolescents and young people should be enthusiastic about their involvement in work.

Our activity in the field of work education is based on the following principles:

1 *Work education is part of a person's overall development: moral, intellectual, aesthetic and physical.*

Work only becomes an educating force when it enriches people's intellectual lives, adding a great variety of content to students' intellectual and creative interests, and when it inspires moral integrity and elevates the aesthetic beauty of the individual and the community.

A person's harmonious, all-round development is only achieved when, along with intellectual, moral, aesthetic and physical development, a person attains a high level of work culture and is creative in their work. In the concept of 'work culture', we include the perfection of practical skills and abilities (a level of mastery that is achieved thanks to the training and skilful supervision of elders). That is just one aspect of work. The essence of work culture is the place work activity occupies in a person's spiritual life, the extent to which creativity in work is full of intellectual challenges, moral significance and civic purpose. Work culture implies a level of spiritual development a person reaches when they cannot live without working for the common good, when work fills their lives with moral inspiration and spiritually enriches the life of the community.

2 *A person's individuality should be discovered and developed in work.*

Work will only become a source of joy when a person sees something more significant in it than just gaining the means to satisfy their material needs. They need to find creativity in work, the unfolding of their abilities and talents. Our ideal of work education is that each person, in adolescence and youth, should discover work in which their natural talents may find the fullest and most vibrant expression—work that will give them the happiness of creativity. When analysing a student's readiness for working life, we consider what they can contribute to society, what their work will add to their spiritual lives, and the extent to which their strengths and abilities will unfold as they find success in work.

3 *Work should have moral significance and benefit society.*

We seek to ensure that children are motivated to work by a desire to benefit society, and we mainly involve children in work that benefits the nation (increasing soil fertility; planting belts of woodland to protect fields against erosion, planting grapevines and orchards; participating in the construction of school and community facilities and roads). Such work for society, for the future, provides the children with a type of moral conditioning. Young people who take social interests to heart in childhood and adolescence develop a sense of honour and duty. Their conscience does not permit them to be indifferent to things that benefit society.

We are in no hurry to involve children in paid work, which may encourage self-interest and avarice. Before receiving their first payment for work, students should acquire significant moral experience in voluntary work that provides substantial material benefits to society. Money that is paid for the collective work of students is spent, in accordance with the wishes of the students themselves, on satisfying the material and spiritual needs of members of the group. In childhood, adolescence and early youth, we show young people the highest beauty in life: serving society with one's work. Hundreds of instances, hundreds of young lives, have convinced us that the more effort a person has dedicated to voluntary work for society in childhood, adolescence and youth, the more deeply they take to heart matters that do not appear to have any direct personal relationship to them.

Another morally significant feature of work is that its material results express a person's intelligence, skill, altruistic love for their work, and willingness to pass on their experience to their friends. We try to ensure that children experience a sense of honour and pride in their success in work.

4 *Early involvement in productive work.*

Even before they understand the social significance of work, a child should feel it is impossible to live without work, that work gives joy and contributes to a rich spiritual life. We strive to ensure that work enters children's spiritual lives at an early age. Analysing the work processes in our productive environment, we identify those that show children the social and creative significance of work in a clear, visible and comprehensible way and convince them they are participating in the creation of things of value to society. The children experience feelings of pride and honour, and work becomes a part of their spiritual lives.

The overwhelming majority of jobs in agricultural production can provide avenues for child participation. At our school, children aged seven and eight already carry out interesting and engaging work of considerable social significance. It is an established tradition that certain types of work are performed only by children. For instance, two months before they commence Grade 1, the little ones collect seeds from trees. In the spring, they perform their first work of major social significance: sowing the seeds of trees on the slopes of ravines and gullies. Then they look after the young trees, creating defensive wooded belts that prevent soil erosion in our fields. The work of the smallest pupils in the fields of the local collective farm has created several major defensive forest belts. Over the course of 10 years, these have prevented soil erosion on an area of 160 hectares. It would be hard to place too high a value on the public wealth saved due to this action, which is augmented by the subsequent work of the very same pupils during their middle school and senior years. Each hectare of fertile soil returned to productive use will give a harvest for many years.

Seven-year-old children lay out nurseries and raise young fruit trees. Caring for fruit trees continues throughout adolescence and early youth. The little children take great interest in work, knowing that the results of older students' activity are to some extent dependent on it. They are allocated a small area of infertile, abandoned land, several dozen square metres in size, and over several years they transform the soil to make it highly fertile. At harvest time, children aged seven or eight collect the best ears of wheat and keep the seed until spring. The little ones are particularly inspired by this work, as the quality of the seeds they collect (these seeds are sown in spring by their older friends) contributes to the quality of the harvest on the experimental plots.

At the age of eight or nine, our students cultivate hybrid seeds of wheat, sunflowers, sugar beet and maize, or work in groups to care for young animals and prepare food for stock. The fact that this simple work is connected with research, experimentation and creativity has enormous educational significance.

The early involvement of children in working with various materials (wood, metal, etc.) using machinery is especially valuable. This is a whole area of work education in itself.

5   *Variety in the types of work undertaken.*

Children naturally seek change. They like to rotate activities and combine two or three types of work activity, each with its own distinguishing characteristics, specific operations and skills. A child who enthusiastically grows plants on the experimental plot or in the greenhouse, and looks after animals, takes no less pleasure in working in a club for young technicians or expressing themselves through artistic creativity. Children find satisfaction in varied activities and in novelty.

Participating simultaneously in two or three types of work, each student develops various abilities and skills. Of the 260 students who graduated from our school over the past four years, 102 participated in two clubs throughout their school years, 89 in three clubs, 44 in four clubs, and 24 in five clubs. Many of them were just as enthusiastic about growing wheat, fruit trees and grapes as they were about constructing radio sets, making working models of machines and equipment, learning to operate an internal combustion engine, or operating metalworking machine tools. Many moved from club to club, taking an interest in new forms of work.

Interest in a variety of work is maintained in the senior years. A student learning how to operate a tractor in the young mechanics club also takes an interest in learning about electronics and biochemistry in clubs devoted to those subjects. The variety of work that senior students participate in is an important precondition for making wise career choices.

It is quite unacceptable to force a child to join a particular club or workgroup, just as monotony in work is unacceptable. The more varied their work is in adolescence and early youth, the more wisely young men and women choose a career, and the more clearly their individual aptitudes are displayed.

6 *Consistency and continuity of work.*

We do not allow work assignments to be allocated to a particular time of the year, month or week. Only constant, daily work enriches one's spiritual life. Children only discover the creative nature of work activity when involved in long-term work that demands daily thought and care.

Our young orchardists raise fruit trees over a period of two or three years while working on some interesting projects. Through experimentation, the students discover which approaches to grafting horticultural varieties to rootstock are most suitable for our locality, the best time to sow the seeds of fruit trees, which fertilisers give the best results, and so on. This is daily work in the full sense of the word: the students work not only in spring and summer, but also in autumn and winter (e.g., trialling various methods for stratifying seed).

The work in our clubs for young plant breeders is just as constant, as the children select the hardiest plants and trial them in various conditions over a number of years.

7 *Children's work should have characteristics of adult work.*

Children's work should have as much as possible in common with adult work in terms of both its social significance and the techniques and technology involved in its processes. The more similar children's work is to that of adults, the greater its educational impact.

Once, we gave a group of seven-year-old children an amusing toy that depended on the use of electricity for operation. At the same time, we gave another group of seven-year-old children a miniature drilling machine, which also relied on electricity—not a toy, but a 'real' one, in the words of the children. It could be used for drilling holes in sheet metal to make models. What was the result? Although the toy was more interesting than the machine tool, the children soon tired of it. It was quite another matter with the machine tool. Once the children had learned to drill holes, they wanted to use it as much as possible. From an adult's perspective, this work was also just a game, but it was genuine, useful, necessary and interesting for the children. The children took special delight in the fact that the machine tool was just like one they had seen in a factory workshop they had visited during an excursion.

We became convinced that we should not hold back children's development. They should use the same tools as adults as early as possible. Of course, the machines, mechanisms and equipment used by children must accord with the limitations imposed by age, school hygiene rules and safety requirements.

The thing that makes children's work most like adult work—makes it serious and real from the children's viewpoint—is the use of internal combustion engines or electric motors. In our school, there are several small engines that are used only by young school children. Special protection features exclude the possibility of accidents. Under the supervision of senior students, the little ones take great interest in learning to operate these engines, taking them apart and putting them together, and learning how to maintain them. We also have low voltage generators and a variety of electrical equipment used in our work and in the maintenance of the school by students, such as pumps for watering flowers.

Experience has convinced us that creating special machines and equipment for children, which as far as possible embody real technology and can be used for real work, is one of our most important educational tasks.

8 *Work should be creative and combine the efforts of hands and minds.*

One of the strongest motivating factors in physical work is having a significant idea behind the work, combining the efforts of intellect and hands. The more significant the idea behind work, the greater the interest with which even the simplest task is performed. Mastering skills, research, experimentation and utilising scientific data in work are all recognised and experienced by the child as an expression of moral dignity.

It is especially important to ensure the coordination of physical effort and intellect in agricultural work, where there are many monotonous work processes. We strive to ensure that any work connected with horticulture or animal husbandry has a creative goal behind it, the realisation of which will stimulate a child's intellectual powers, forcing them to think, observe and study natural phenomena. For example, there are many monotonous, uninteresting work processes in growing sugar beet, but even this work can become creative if a research goal is set. (Our children are researching ways of increasing the sugar content in the roots of the beet.)

9 *Sequential development of work activities, abilities and skills.*

As children mature, we try to develop, deepen, and find wider applications for everything they have learned to do during the early and middle years.

It is very important that work during the years of adolescence should pave the way for learning new skills in the senior years. We do not teach young people aged 15 or 16 to drill holes in metal, prepare soil for sowing wheat or bud graft a fruit tree. They should have learned these skills five years earlier, and the more competently they develop these skills, the greater their all-round development when they enter the senior years.

Early involvement in work activity allows us to ensure that by the age of 10 or 12, children know how to work the soil and prepare it for sowing grains and industrial crops. They know how to grow and harvest these crops, grow fruit trees, prepare fertilisers and apply them to the soil, make infertile soil highly fertile, operate an internal combustion engine, and operate lathes and drilling machines. At the age of 14 or 15, all our boys and girls can drive a tractor and a car. This would be impossible if they did not learn to operate an internal combustion engine at the age of 10 or 12. By the age of 16 or 17, our young men and women not only know how to drive a tractor; they can use one to plough the ground, sow seed and apply fertiliser. Having this skill is not some kind of professional training or early choice of profession, but just a basic work requirement. Everyone in our country should be able to drive a tractor. In this way, thanks to continuity in the development of work skills by our students, by the time they enter the senior years, they have a broad and varied range of abilities and skills.

10 *The universal nature of productive work.*

Whatever talents students manifest for intellectual or artistic activity, their participation in productive work during adolescence and youth is compulsory. Physical work, especially work connected with unattractive or arduous processes, is universal, and all students participate in it. Everyone collectively gathers local manure and applies it to the soil, eliminates crop pests, prepares food for stock, plants woodland belts to protect fields from erosion, and builds sheds. Every student in Grades 1–4 prepares 100–300 kilograms of local manure for use. In Grades 5–7, they prepare 300–600 kilograms and in Grades 8–10, 600–1,200 kilograms. Because of its collective nature, this simple work is carried out with great enthusiasm.

11 *Work activity should be within children's powers.*

We allow healthy tiredness in any work but never the exhaustion of children's physical and mental powers. The appropriateness of children's work is determined by the correspondence of physical demands to children's strength, the judicious alternation of intellectual and physical work, and offering a variety of types of work activity.

We attach particular significance to alternating agricultural work (horticulture and animal husbandry) with technical creativity (construction, modelling and metalwork). Thanks to this rotation, children can manage a workload that would be excessive and exhausting if it were monotonous.

Experience has also convinced us that children's abilities and potential are greatly enhanced when their work does not consist of unrelated operations but is part of a continuous project based on an interesting idea. Let me cite an example. Once, when we were preparing grapevines for winter, a group of 28 children aged 11 years managed to complete the comparatively difficult task of covering 40 grapevines in the space of one and a half hours. This brought the children healthy tiredness, but also moral satisfaction, as they had been looking after these grapevines for three years. It was a different story with another group, which was asked to cover the same number of 'other people's' grapevines. In an hour and a half, they only managed to complete half the work and were so tired they could not continue working.

Any physical work carried out by children needs to be considered in light of their spiritual lives.

12 Work should be part of a multifaceted spiritual life.

People do not live just for work. They only discover the joy of work when they have access to other joys—things of cultural and spiritual value such as literature, music, painting, sport and hikes through their local countryside. In refining human nature and developing the nobility of the soul, these good things also help them understand and experience the joy of creativity more deeply. The more sources of human culture the mind and heart are exposed to in adolescence and early youth, the more work ennobles a person. We try to ensure that a diverse spiritual life continues uninterrupted in our community. In summer in particular, when our pupils are hard at work in the fields for several weeks, we conduct literary and musical evenings at the school, evenings of science and technology, and collective readings.

Success in work education depends on preparing a suitable material base, on judiciously selecting work activities for children, and on pedagogically sound forms and methods of educational work.

Work education infrastructure

CREATING THE MATERIAL INFRASTRUCTURE to allow children's involvement in work at an early age and making available a variety of work activities connected with both agricultural and industrial production is a serious educational issue.

In an earlier chapter, I gave a detailed description of our material infrastructure for work education, our classrooms, workshops, laboratories and greenhouses. I will now briefly examine the pedagogical and educational aspect of these facilities.

All our material facilities are designed so that even young children can learn to use relatively complex tools and equipment. Before being allowed to use mechanical tools, students carry out set tasks with hand tools. For example, students only gain access to an electric bandsaw or circular saw (a disc saw made especially for young children) after they have learned to use a hand fretsaw. They must be able to use the fretsaw skilfully to complete an assignment that confers the right to use their first child-friendly mechanical tool. The boys and girls strive to master handwork skills as well as possible, as a step towards making the transition to machine tools. With the help of a mechanical disc saw, it is possible to cut timber into blocks, boards and slats to provide material for further woodworking. The mechanism is set up so that children may independently adjust the working parts depending on the purpose of the material being cut. Next to the bandsaw and the circular saws are children's planing machines, also fitted with safety features to prevent any accident.

A similar sequence and similar incentives are involved in working with metal, in construction and modelling. Work facilities for our youngest students are equipped with special children's tools (for students aged 7–10). We have metalworking lathes and drills made by our senior students and teachers, allocated specifically for the use of children aged 8–10.

The creation of this equipment solves a major pedagogical problem. What attracts children to our machine tools is they are smaller and slightly simplified copies of real factory machine tools. To earn the right to work on this equipment, the children patiently work at mastering the use of hand tools. As they progress, those who are successful in working on a lathe gain the right to work on a children's milling machine and a lathe made for a factory.

Students in the middle and senior years only gain the right to carry out complex operations on lathes, drilling machines and milling machines intended for factory use after they have made several relatively complex parts and components for smaller children's machine tools. Nearby are assembly benches for young designers. The workspaces at one bench are equipped with more complex tools, while the other bench is for less complex types of work. The young beginner technicians work next to more experienced senior students, learning from them and striving to gain the right to work with more complex tools and equipment.

There is an analogous relationship between the material infrastructure and the level of creative work undertaken during our electronics and radio electronics activities. To gain access to the complex instruments and equipment at our children's electricity generating station, the children need to construct three working models of generators with their own hands (each successive model is more complex than the preceding one). Then, they connect them to small working models of machines like winnowing machines, threshing machines and so on. The right to assemble a transistor radio is gained by assembling a valve radio.

Children aged 10–12 work at our children's power station under the supervision of senior students. They start up and stop the engine, turn on the generator, and connect it to devices driven by the current (a small saw, a miniature metal cutting machine, a mechanical fretsaw). This is all very interesting and gets the children involved, but every child working at the children's power station dreams of gaining the right to move on to the training power station (for the middle and senior years). Here, several internal combustion engines and generators of varying capacity (16 kW, 4.5 kW, 2 kW, 0.5 kW) produce direct and alternating current, and there is a transformer and a station for charging accumulators. Only those who have developed the basic skills in managing the engine and generator at the children's power station are allowed to work at the training (or 'real' as the children call it) power station.

The children patiently develop their skills. This earns them the right to learn to drive a small car with a miniature combustion engine (driven by students aged eight or nine). Having learned to drive the miniature car, students dream of riding a motorcycle, and then driving a real car. The logical progression in work, the logic behind creating and using our material infrastructure, means that all students completing Grades 7 and 8 know how to manage a stationary internal combustion engine, a miniature car and a motorcycle. Approximately 75% of those completing Grade 8 can drive a car and a tractor, and all students in Grades 9 and 10 can drive a tractor and use it in the field. I repeat that this is not a specialisation, but just the ABC of technical training. In our times, the ability to drive a car and a tractor should be just as normal for everyone as the ability to use an electric hotplate.

A school's material base can only really be improved when work is characterised by a degree of reproduction. The harvests produced on our experimental plots, in our orchard and vineyard, and the production of young fruit trees, are all of considerable material value. A proportion is donated free of charge to the collective farm and to parents. A proportion is also sold, generating funds to meet the students' cultural needs (excursions, purchasing musical instruments and literature for reading) and the future expansion of our infrastructure. With the proceeds of sales, the school purchases electric motors, materials for the electronics clubs, and internal combustion engines. The children labour, not only to learn how to work, but also to create the material conditions for more complex, intellectually challenging work. From our funds, the school has also created a fund for providing material assistance to those in need, which is managed by the school's Komsomol committee and Pioneer group committee.

Organising student work activities

TO ORGANISE WORK EDUCATION PROPERLY and take full advantage of the educational potential of work, we classify types of work according to certain attributes.

1 *Social significance.*

   In some types of work, the social significance is obvious; in others, it is more difficult for a child to understand. Students may be involved in planting a woodland belt to protect fields from erosion, or an oak grove, and caring for it for several years, for example, or in sweeping the classroom floor every day and wiping the dust from the desks. In both cases, the students are carrying out work that is essential for society and has great educational significance. But whereas in the first case, the students are directly participating in the creation of society's material and technological base, in the second case, their work does not go beyond self-service. In the second case, the work cannot give rise to the same feelings and convictions as in the first case. At the same time, self-service has its own benefits: educating tidiness and fostering respect for simple work and for people working in humble, unobtrusive professions.

   We seek to include work of varying degrees of social significance in students' lives and ensure work that clearly involves participation in strengthening society's material base enters children's lives at an early age. This is of great significance for the education of feelings of honour and pride in work. At the same time, we attach great significance to any work, however uninteresting and difficult it may be. We try to ensure that from early childhood, every student feels that if they do not collect manure and apply it to the soil, if they do not work hard on a hot summer's day or a frosty winter's day, they will not produce any material and, consequently, any spiritual benefits, and will not find joy in life.

2 *The correspondence between study goals and educational goals (where 'educational goals' refers specifically to moral education).*

   Some types of work are carried out with the primary aim of acquiring knowledge and skills; others are pursued purely for the education of character, to form moral concepts, convictions and habits and to gain moral experience. In the former case, although acquiring scientific knowledge and work skills does contribute to the development of philosophical convictions and, consequently, a student's character is being educated as they study, the primary aim of the work process is to learn, to know and to acquire skills.

Work conducted in the formal classes is always cognitive in nature. The goal of the work is considered to be achieved if the student learns well. Cognitive goals are prominent in classroom work, reading, experiments on the school plots, laboratory work in physics and chemistry, measurements carried out on location, and the collection of plant specimens, etc. It is very important that in all these types of work, the ultimate goal is not just to learn about the world. The experimental work conducted by our students serves dual aims: to know and to create; to discover the laws of nature and make a least one small corner of the world richer and more beautiful. We seek to ensure that as they study and acquire knowledge, our students also create things of material value (mechanisms and tools in the workshop, seeds and fruits on our plots).

Along with work directly connected with study, a major role is played by work that has the principal aim of educating a person's moral qualities, to give every student the joy and happiness of social work and feelings of civic pride. This educational goal is achieved when students create material benefits of great social significance. For example, when our students join the Pioneer movement, they plant an oak grove and then spend several years caring for the young oak trees. By the time they graduate from school, they can see the significant results of their work: the oak grove secures the banks of a gulley against erosion. In this way, we ensure that students' work extends as far as possible beyond the school and beyond school interests, and that each student feels they are participating in the life of society.

3 *The role of work education in intellectual, moral, physical, aesthetic and polytechnical education.*

For young children, the aesthetic and socially useful goals of work are the most accessible. Children affirm their moral worth and take pride in the beauty of the work process and its material results. During early childhood, aesthetic feelings are one of the richest sources of moral feelings. That is why most of our work for young children has a clearly expressed aesthetic dimension: children create beauty. This determines the types of work: growing flowers and caring for them, making things whose practical value is determined mainly by their beauty and role in satisfying aesthetic needs. Little children also try to accurately and beautifully carry out work whose purpose is not primarily aesthetic but experimental or socially useful. We utilise children's aspiration for beauty to enrich their work philosophically and intellectually. Everything that little children do should be beautiful.

There are some types of work activity and long-term work projects that play an important role due to their content. Some play an important role in intellectual education, some in moral education, some in physical education, some in polytechnical education. The all-round development of the personality depends on the extent to which all the component elements of communist education are incorporated into work activities.

4 *The correlation between intellectual and physical effort.*

One of the most important rules of work education is to combine intellectual and physical work. It is unacceptable for some students to have creative ideas and bring them to fruition (e.g., constructing working models) while other students carry out monotonous physical work. Any project involves some physical, monotonous, often unpleasant work, and the person to do this work should be the one who is trying to bring the project to fruition. When physical work is very simple and monotonous, it is especially important that it is not the ultimate goal but a means for realising some ultimate goal, some creative project. When preparing young people psychologically for work, it is essential they do not view simple work in the fields or on the animal farm as no more than an application of physical effort. We seek to coordinate the work of minds and hands so that physical work attracts young men and women as an arena for spiritual growth and development. While creating things of material value, students are simultaneously researching, experimenting, studying the laws of nature and technology, and perfecting technological processes. At the animal farm, where the most difficult and monotonous work is to be found, some most interesting research is being undertaken by senior students into the influence of antibiotics on vital functions in animals.

5   *The tools used in the work.*

Work involving complex technology and processes provides greater opportunities for uncovering talents and abilities and educating high work standards. To prepare young people to use complex technology (machines, mechanisms, installations), we involve them in complex production processes from an early age, especially during the middle school years, teaching them work skills appropriate for a time of rapid scientific and technological progress.

As well as using hand tools, our students use mechanical tools from an early age, especially those driven by electricity (such as an electric bandsaw). This challenges children and leads them into the world of technology. The older the child and deeper their knowledge of science, the more important it is to include ever more complex technology in work processes. In this way, we ensure children learn to consider physical work as an opportunity to utilise machine technology. For example, if Pioneers are requested to move several hundred kilograms of wheat from one place to another, they should ask themselves whether it is possible to use some mechanical means rather than do it by hand. If the adolescents have experience using relatively complex work technology, they will think of a way to set up a conveyor.

The more complex the work technology, the more refined the manual skills required, and the higher the standard of manual work. We educate a high standard of manual skills from an early age. Construction, assembly, fitting parts and assemblies, adjusting and tuning interacting parts and equipment, the diverse creative work carried out over all the years of schooling—all these things lead to a high level of manual skills and develop thinking skills at the same time. Skill in managing complex technology largely depends on developing a high level of manual skills.

6 *The results of the work activity.*

Sometimes material results are created during the process of working and are obvious to the students (such as the articles made by the young technicians' clubs). Sometimes, the work is a preparation for material results that will appear in the not-too-distant future (e.g., harvesting wheat grain and preparing it for sowing). Sometimes, the work provides the conditions for results that will only appear in the comparatively distant future (e.g., agricultural afforestation to increase soil fertility). Sometimes, there are no obvious material results at all, and the work only brings psychological benefits (e.g., helping an old or sick person).

The more significant the material result of the work, the greater the opportunities for forming convictions, and the deeper the feelings that accompany the work process. We plan work activities that require students to work hard over a lengthy period of time to gain a material result in the future, and to overcome difficulties, so this period of sustained effort becomes a stage in their spiritual development. Along with short-term work assignments, there is always work in the life of our community that is calculated to last several years (such as growing trees or caring for a vineyard or orchard).

Sometimes the material results of work are distributed to people, and sometimes the work does not result in anything that can be consumed. Both types of work are equally significant educationally. Students produce goods for individual consumption (bread, vegetables, meat, milk) and things of value that belong to all of society (fertile soil, forest).

7. *Payment.*

Young people are involved in two types of work activity: voluntary and paid. In planning a ratio between these two types of work, we consider the deep changes that are taking place in our society. Workers receive more and more of the good things of life from public funds, independently of their own work. The proportion of such benefits in children's lives is incomparably greater than is the case for adults, which places a great responsibility on us as educators. Students should understand the labour value of the benefits they receive from society free of charge. To this end, we involve them in unpaid work that benefits society. The more benefits the younger generation receives that are not paid for by their own work, the more essential their unpaid work is.

But individual payments, personal wages also have great educational value. During the summer, students in the middle and senior years who work on the collective farm receive individual payments. This is an important prerequisite for educating a feeling of duty towards one's parents. Using all the means at the school's disposal (discussions, lectures), we seek to ensure that after school, as they embark on their independent working lives, young people give a portion of their wages to their mother and father.

Teaching work skills

DURING THEIR ADOLESCENCE AND YOUTH, we need to give people the skills to help them choose a profession wisely, to uncover their talents, abilities and aptitudes. Students acquire such skills in two ways:

1 At the compulsory lessons dictated by the curriculum.

In the primary classes, this is manual work. In Grades 5–7, it is work on the experimental plots and in the workshops. In Grades 8–10, it is work associated with studying the foundations of basic industrial and agricultural production. Work at these compulsory lessons includes using materials (paper, cardboard, plasticine, clay, wood, fabric, metals, plastics), preparing soil and caring for plants, construction and modelling, and operating machines and equipment.

A general secondary school does not aim to provide professional vocational training. Students graduating from secondary school should just be able to navigate their way around the main branches of production and have acquired skills that will facilitate a wise choice of profession. Elementary types of handcrafts in the primary classes are the first important stage of instruction in work skills. The skills acquired during handcraft lessons are a prerequisite for developing other more complex skills that are acquired during the middle and senior years. The ability to use a fretsaw or cut paper prepares students to work with a vice, work metal with a file or a lathe, construct a radio, and so on. In Grades 1 and 2, our children use metal blades to cut paper into lace patterns and cut out wooden models of machines and figures of people and animals. This work develops the ability to measure by eye, persistence and an appreciation of beauty. The children weave and knit little toy bags and purses, make chairs from straw, and mould the figures of people and animals from plasticine and clay.

Along with the simplest handcrafts, children in the primary classes learn to construct and model, assemble toy models of equipment and machines, and take them apart. Work is combined with elements of play. Construction and modelling begin with the use of soft metal wire and plastic discs. The children make wire figures of animals and then progress to models of tractors, cars, aeroplanes, cranes, excavators and transporters. Using wooden, metal, clay and plastic parts, discs and blocks, they construct models of houses and industrial structures. As they get used to working with wood, more and more parts are prepared using glue. At some lessons, children prepare figures of people and animals using papier-mache.

In the primary classes, children begin to use tools. We attach great significance to the children's hand tools. During their work lessons in the metal workshop, middle school students prepare knives and cutting tools for the junior classes to use for wood carving and cutting out paper and cardboard. We have made a special machine tool the little children use to make little clay bricks for building toy buildings. Little chisels, hatchets and hammers are all used by young children. Learning to work with materials, children gradually progress to preparing objects in which the perfection of the whole depends on the perfection of the parts and their interaction.

The precise calculation, accuracy in processing and assembling, the specific interaction of the various parts that make up a whole—these features of work in the primary school are very important for further instruction in work skills. For instance, students in Grade 4 use springs and shears to make tools for cutting branches from little trees.

In life, some professional skills become universal skills (e.g., the ability to use a simple lathe). They become part of the ABC of work.

For this reason, we have added the ability to turn wood or metal on a lathe to our primary school curriculum. Using a miniature lathe, children turn cylinders and bolts from wood and soft alloys.

Working in our experimental plots, young school students learn the skills of creative agricultural work. They do not carry out auxiliary, secondary types of work but initiate and complete work assignments that are comparatively complex for their age, achieving material results. From Grade 1, children begin several cycles of agricultural work (on small plots), preparing the soil and increasing its fertility, looking after trees, growing grain and other industrial crops. One cycle is planned for a year, one for four years, and a third for seven or eight years. During their primary school years, every child produces a high-yielding crop: harvesting two ears of grain where people previously harvested one and developing a conviction that nature's gifts depend upon human reason, will and creativity. Individual work experience plays a major role in developing this conviction. Each student in Grade 2 is allocated a square metre of earth on which they grow 500 grams of wheat, which equates to a yield of five tonnes per hectare. In Grades 3 and 4, they produce an even higher yield: 600–700 grams from one square metre (six or seven tonnes per hectare). The children carefully nurture each plant and count every grain.

By the time they complete primary school, each student has grown some three or four-year-old cuttings (this work begins in the first autumn or spring of their school life). In addition, each student plants a fruit tree during the first autumn of their school studies, which has begun to bear fruit by the time they complete primary school.

In Grades 5–8, the aim of work in our workshops and experimental plots is to develop skills further, strengthen the socially useful and productive aspects of work, and differentiate interests based on developing students' talents and abilities. Students develop skills in metalworking, turning, electrical wiring, horticulture and animal husbandry. Experience has convinced us that it is expedient to transition to studying the foundations of production in Grade 8. (In Grade 8, our students study internal combustion engines, the operational principles of the most common industrial machines, and electrical wiring.)

During the middle years, the study element of work is combined with production to an even greater extent. Not just to learn how, but to actually do something useful and necessary, that is one of the main rules of work education. In our workshops and workrooms, students in Grades 5–8 make study aids and equipment, working models, tools, mechanical implements and equipment for technological processes. Each year every class or group of students manufactures relatively complex mechanical equipment: lathes, drills and milling machines, equipment for working the soil or managing crops, and so on.

All this work has a polytechnical orientation and facilitates the all-round development of the personality. Adolescent students already have some familiarity with general principles of production and have acquired skills common to a number of concrete areas of work.

We pay particular attention to preparing visual aids for mathematics, physics and chemistry classes, manufacturing simple, primitive tools for working on our experimental plots and in our workshops, and simple equipment and teaching aids for mechanics and electrical engineering. However much technology develops, whatever heights technological thought reaches, the pathway to the highest levels of scientific thought and work culture will always be through a mastery of the ABC of technology, through studying internal combustion engines, turbines, band and circular saws, and so on. Just as it is impossible to reach the outer frontiers of science without knowing the alphabet, it is impossible to master complex technology and achieve a high level of work culture without knowledge of simple tools, equipment and mechanisms.

During Grades 5–8, each student completes the following individual assignments on our experimental plots: to grow grain and other industrial crops (from three to ten crops), to graft cultivated varieties of fruit trees to 25 rootstocks, to cultivate young fruit trees, to lay out a plant nursery, to increase soil fertility.

Each assignment has an experimental research orientation. For example, some students will investigate the quality of seed and fertiliser. In this case, work on the experimental plots is combined with work in the nature laboratory. Children and adolescents who are interested in agricultural production take on comparatively large plots (20–100 square metres), and by applying the achievements of science, especially chemistry, they produce yields two, three or four times greater than are achieved on our collective farm fields.

Like the boys, the girls master skills that are essential in an age of highly developed technology, but the work tasks we select for girls require less physical effort and more precision, creativity in design and expertise. For example, if the boys are making a massive metal lathe, the girls are busy making some automatic equipment or a model that involves automation.

Work instruction in Grades 8–10 consists of theoretical lessons and practical work lessons during which students master skills. The theoretical course includes such topics as a general description of the branches of industry in our country, the basic features of the main branches of industrial and agricultural production, a description of energy sources, general principles governing the structure and functioning of engines and industrial machinery, the structure and applications of internal combustion engines and electric motors in industrial machines, and chemical technology used in the most common areas of work.

At practical lessons, students master skills of a polytechnical nature that find application in many branches of production. In Grade 8, students study stationary internal combustion engines, industrial machinery, and electrical wiring and generators. In Grades 9–10, they study tractors, cars and combine harvesters, and continue electrical work. They study radio technology with elements of electronics and automation and learn to work with lathes, drills and milling machines. The acquisition of skills is closely connected with construction and modelling, the repair and restoration of machines and mechanisms, and the manufacture of metalworking tools and measuring instruments. In Grades 8–10, all students study a theoretical course in horticulture and animal husbandry and complete a practicum associated with the course during a specially programmed time during the summer. The practicum in horticulture and animal husbandry is usually conducted simultaneously with tractor work. During Grade 10, students study an 18-hour course in agricultural chemistry and complete practical work associated with that course.

Work instruction in the senior classes is thus built on a broad polytechnical foundation, and theory is closely associated with practice.

There are strong inner links between the theoretical course in the foundations of production, and mathematics, physics, chemistry and biology. Thanks to these links, three hours a week are sufficient for work instruction during the senior years. The theoretical course in agricultural chemistry fits into 18 hours, but only because the teaching is based on the active application of knowledge acquired during the study of inorganic and organic chemistry.

At first glance, it may appear that studying the foundations of production during the senior years places a heavy burden on students. They are studying engines, generators, tractors, cars, electrical wiring, radio technology, horticulture and animal husbandry. This would indeed be an excessive burden if our children had not already been involved in various clubs during the early and middle years. In these clubs, they learned about machinery, used metalworking machine tools and took a keen interest in experimentation. We could not study electrical wiring and radio electronics in such a short time (around 36 hours) if each student in Grades 5–8 had not made a generator and a radio with their own hands in the technology clubs. Early involvement in productive work facilitates polytechnical education in the senior years so that our senior students are able to master a wide range of polytechnical skills.

Thanks to the polytechnical nature of the knowledge and skills acquired, every senior student has the opportunity to choose a profession in which they can display their abilities and talents. We also need to keep in mind that along with the compulsory work instruction lessons, the compulsory range of knowledge and skills, there are extra-curricular activities: clubs that function outside school hours, scientific subject clubs, where everyone is engaged in their favourite activities. These involve reading and work. If not for these intellectual and work activities, successful polytechnical education and work instruction in the senior years would be out of the question.

We make sure that work instruction in the senior classes does not become hackwork. The leading role is played by theory. Theoretical knowledge is made sense of while working, through observation and experience; theoretical generalisations rest upon students' comprehensive work experiences. For example, when describing the role of the energy sector, we utilise the practical experience acquired in the process of managing internal combustion engines and electric motors. We conduct excursions so students can see the technology and work processes characteristic of the main branches of production. When describing what they have seen, students analyse the main common features of machines and equipment, work and technological processes.

Students complete polytechnical assignments that involve identifying practical examples that demonstrate a principle of production or a feature of machine technology. For example:

1. Name a production process in which a mechanical means of crushing or breaking up material takes place. Explain how the characteristics of the material and the final product determine the characteristics of the equipment used to process the material.

2. What equipment do you need to fabricate when using a tractor for loading and unloading sugar beet?

The completion of polytechnical assignments deepens interest in science and technology and educates a culture of work.

During the summer, students completing Grades 8 and 9 spend three or four weeks completing practicums in our school workshops, workrooms and laboratories, experimental plots, repair shops at our maintenance stations, and the tractor brigade on the collective farm. Those who have completed Grade 9 and passed their tractor tests do shift work as tractor drivers. Each collective farm machine operator is assigned a student as a shift tractor driver working six hours a day. An assistant is assigned to each of these shift drivers: a student who has completed Grade 8 and learned to drive a tractor in a club. The students carry out ploughing, cultivation, working the soil between rows, harvesting grain and other industrial crops, preparing silage, seed cleaning, sowing and fertilising.

The electrical practicum includes wiring a circuit, connecting electric motors and heating appliances to it, and manufacturing low voltage, low output, alternating current and direct current generators. The completion of this work requires significant precision and calculation and is a good way of deepening knowledge and skills. As part of their assessment, each student completing Grade 8 submits a working model of an electricity generator to the school physics laboratory. When they complete Grade 10, they make a generator that is used to power a working model. Students repair the electrical components of tractors, cars, self-driven combine harvesters, grain cleaning equipment, electrical milking machines and other machinery. Each senior student spends several days working in teams setting up pumps and irrigation systems on farms.

As part of their studies in Grades 8–10, each student makes simplified models of electrical measuring equipment and mechanical work equipment driven by electricity (a pump, a grinder, etc.). This is not a specialisation, but the ABC of work. Each student assembles one valve radio and one transistor radio. This is compulsory. Boys and girls who develop a special interest in radio technology and electronics master a more extensive range of knowledge and skills independently. Activities are conducted with such students periodically. They make equipment based on principles of automation.

During the past seven years (1961–1967), during practical lessons and club activities at our school, we have made more than 3500 various items of equipment, visual aids for physics, chemistry, mathematics, and astronomy, working models and mechanisms, and various machine tools. (A list of these items of equipment is contained in Appendix 4 at the end of this book.)

Acquiring skills and developing an interest in one type of work or another while at school does play a definite role in finding a vocation but does not predetermine the ultimate choice of profession. Acquiring a broad range of polytechnical knowledge and skills and developing a positive work culture in early youth stimulates a thirst for knowledge and gives rise to inquisitiveness and curiosity. Due to these positive attributes, graduates strive to choose a path in life that will allow them to display their talents and abilities fully. Some go on to tertiary education; others acquire a trade and work in industry or agriculture. The pathways chosen by our graduates are indicated in the following figures.

From 1949 to 1966, 712 students graduated from our school. Among these graduates, 278 received a tertiary education (at institutes and universities) in the following faculties: 94 in engineering, 45 in medicine, 49 in agriculture, 53 in education, 27 in others. The students who went on to work in industry and agriculture upon completing their secondary education are distributed as follows: 73 machine operators, 116 technicians, mechanics and specialist workers, 62 agricultural technicians and stockbreeders. Among these graduates, 68 are working on our collective farm as machine operators, mechanics, agricultural technicians and stockbreeders.

Students in senior classes (beginning in Grades 7 and 8) are also given the opportunity to acquire skills not included in the curriculum. For example, some students have acquired electric welding skills after expressing a desire to do so. Anyone who wishes can take up beekeeping in the school's experimental apiary. During the spring and summer, some students study reinforced concrete construction. Girls can undertake training in the use of electric sewing machines if they wish.

The senior students have made 32 automated machine tools (lathes, milling machines and planing machines). During the past three years (1965–1967) in our automation and radio electronics clubs and electrical and radio technology lessons, our senior students have made 45 electronic calculators for use in mathematics, physics, chemistry and grammar lessons. Together with students from Grades 5–8, the senior students have made two miniature cars, two children's electricity power stations, and more than 40 sets of children's tools for students in the junior classes. For the little ones, we have also made machinery for working the soil, sowing and harvesting: disc harrows, seed drills, a threshing machine, a grain cleaning machine and a mower. All this machinery is driven by electric motors.

After graduating from our secondary school, 42 people have undertaken further specialised secondary education (externally and on-site) in the following areas: 26 in technical and agricultural, six in medical, five in education and five in other specialisations.

Our school staff are proud that our former students are working in many areas of production and culture in our village. Victor Shcherbina, the chief agricultural scientist on the collective farm, is one of our former students. So is Anatolii Makarenko, the chief engineer at our district administration centre for collective farm production. So are three of the doctors at our hospital and more than ten of the machine operators working on the collective farm.

2   *Voluntary activities.*

A second, no less important way of preparing students for working life is work undertaken by choice in accordance with talents and interests.

The compulsory curriculum cannot encompass the diversity of individual differences. Even in the early years, a child often wants to do something of their own as well as what the rest of the class is doing in manual arts classes. The level of achievement and skills achieved by the class may not be sufficient for them, as they strive to master more refined aspects of the work. With age, these aspirations increase. Life demands *extracurricular* work instruction.

Such instruction takes place in clubs. Each year, 40–45 clubs operate at our school. (The number fluctuates depending on the individual interests of students). In some clubs, there are only young children; some involve early and middle year students; only senior students participate in others; and others have senior and middle year students working together. It depends on the participants' level of skill, the extent to which the work approaches that of adults, and the theoretical knowledge required.

Once they cross the threshold of our school, children enter an atmosphere of varied creative work. We do not have a single student who is not participating in at least one technical or agricultural club. The overwhelming majority of children are involved in two or three types of work involving both technology and horticulture. Children in the early years often work alongside adolescents and even senior students, which has great educational significance.

There are some technical and agricultural clubs that nearly all children pass through during the first two or three years of their school lives. These provide stepping stones to more complex types of work. All the boys and girls aged seven and eight work with great interest in the young carpenters' club (working with fretsaws) and the young flower growers' club. At the same time, these children participate in other clubs for young metalworkers and designers and young radio technicians. As the students grow older, shaping wood with a fretsaw and growing flowers may still be the favourite activity for some, but the overwhelming majority move on to other clubs according to their developing interests and aptitude for other forms of work.

In 1967, our students in Grades 1–8 participated in 58 extracurricular activity groups. (These are listed in full in Appendix 5 at the end of this book.)

Among the technical clubs, children are most attracted to the clubs for metalworkers and designers, turners, electricians, machine operators and radio technicians. The older the students, the more they are attracted to work that demands precision, fine finishing and adjustment. In the clubs for young metalworkers and designers, the children make models of machines and mechanisms. The students in Grades 1–6 are especially drawn to work on a miniature lathe. At their lessons, all the children learn how to operate this lathe, but those drawn to technical creativity from an early age perfect their skills in clubs.

In the clubs for young machine operators, students begin at the simplest level: running, disassembling and reassembling small internal combustion engines (initially compression engines, then with carburettors). Then they progress to studying stationary engines, followed by motorcycles and tractors. In our school, we have over 50 internal combustion engines for use in our clubs.

In our young carpenters' clubs, children initially use hand fretsaws, then electric band saws. At first they plane, drill and chisel with hand tools, then with machine tools (planing machines, universal machine tools, milling machines). The young carpenters make rulers, compasses, protractors, set squares and other school equipment, and also wooden models (houses, bridges and other structures).

In the clubs for young radio technicians, the work begins with making crystal radios, then valve radios and finally transistor radios.

The young animal breeders first care for rabbits, then go on to care for calves, sheep and cows.

In the club for young plant breeders, children grow grains, industrial crops and young trees. Each club for young plant breeders supplies biology lessons with some type of material for distribution.

The young flower growers grow flowers for the school and flower seedlings for parents.

In the clubs for young soil scientists, the children study the life of the soil and research the quality of fertilisers.

The young botanists conduct hikes during the summer and collect seeds from interesting varieties of trees, grains and industrial crops.

The clubs are run by the ablest students in Grades 8–10. However, some clubs, such as the automation and radio electronics clubs, are run by senior students and teachers. The teachers meet with and train the senior students running the children's clubs. They suggest ways to sequence practical work and explain how to run club activities and how to combine work with reading.

The children's technical clubs aim to gradually lead children into the world of technical creativity associated with mechanics, electrical engineering, radio technology, automation and electronics. We attach great significance to the role of mechanics in the education of young students as a focus for creative thinking. The young metalworkers and designers not only construct working models of existing machines and mechanisms, they also come up with new ways of combining driving engines with working mechanisms and new ways of assembling working models. For example, the young designers made a working model of a grain cleaning machine, connecting it with several originally constructed transporters, which supplied the uncleaned grain and transported the cleaned grain to a special store (in the model, a box), where it was packed into sacks (little bags). All of this was done with the aid of cleverly designed mechanisms. In another club, children constructed a little hay cutting machine driven by an internal combustion engine. Members of the metalworkers club for students in Grades 4–8 made a semi-automated production line that cut wooden blocks into thin sheets, needed in the construction of various models.

In the clubs for young mechanics, the youngest children (aged 7–10) study compression engines, then progress to studying a small engine with a carburettor. Children aged 10–12 learn to drive a miniature motor car, then a motorcycle. In one section of that club, the most able middle school students learn to drive a tractor.

In the clubs for young plant breeders, children conduct interesting experiments. For several years they studied winter wheat crops and were able to produce grain three times the normal size. The young plant breeders have also cultivated sunflowers with increased oil content and sugar beet with higher-than-normal sugar content. For more than 15 years, the young plant breeders have conducted interesting trials cultivating spring wheat with higher-than-normal protein content. Every year they collect seed from winter wheat that has shown resistance to frosts.

In the technical and agricultural clubs, skill acquisition is associated with interesting projects involving creative thought. For example, in the radio technology clubs, the children construct a radio-controlled device each term.

The creation of a mechanism, especially one used in production that in future will serve to create new material goods, is a higher level of student work that is extremely valuable from an educational point of view. That is why we attach such significance to manufacturing metalworking machines. Such work is a test of skill, and whoever passes such a test experiences feelings of joy and pride.

Creative work elevates children in their own eyes, refining their moral character. Even in the early years, children see the first significant results of their work, which they present to their community, to society: trees for planting, woodland belts to protect our fields, small plots of fertile soil that have been created on barren land. The young horticulturalists present the collective farm with the seeds of maize, cabbages and tomatoes, grown on our experimental plots.

The skills acquired in one club prepare students to progress to another club, from easier work to more complex, from simple tools and mechanisms to more complex machines. Since children have to pass through one stage before they can progress to the next, which they find very attractive, they apply every effort to master the skills that confer the right to such a progression. For example, a student is only permitted to study an engine with a carburettor after they have assembled and disassembled a compression engine and cleaned it several times.

Thanks to the diversity of work in the clubs, by the time they progress to Grade 8, all of our students have already acquired a broad range of skills and are able to find a pursuit to their liking. Students completing Grade 8 are able to work with metal using metalworking hand tools and machine tools; turn wood on a lathe; make simple wooden objects (frames, stools, rulers, compasses); assemble models of machinery from pre-made parts; make metal parts for such models; make tools for working with wood and metal; assemble metalworking machine tools; install electrical cabling, electrical equipment and installations combining an electric motor and working machinery; assemble radios; cultivate soil; sow crops and manage them; harvest a crop; manage animals; drive a car and a tractor; prepare grafted cuttings of fruit trees; and grow grapes and fruits. The mastery of such a broad range of skills enables students in the senior years to master comparatively complex skills within a relatively short time.

The club participation of senior students reflects their aspiration for intellectually stimulating work, their wish to combine the work of thought and hands. There is a more intense differentiation of intellectual and work interests in the senior classes, as each student delves more deeply into a particular area of knowledge. It is very important here that selective interest in science is combined with a high level of work culture.

Our senior students come together in scientific subject related clubs. We do not believe we exaggerate when we use the word 'scientific'. Our country needs hundreds of thousands of scientists, and the path to science must begin with work in early youth. 'Begin your scientific activity as early as possible,' advises academician Sergei Sobelev. 'It does not matter if at 15 or 16 years of age you do not have enough knowledge and experience and are not clear about your desires and aspirations. A scientific life does not have to begin with independent creativity but can begin with a study of what humanity has already accomplished. It is important at this age to develop a thirst for scientific knowledge, curiosity, and a love of science.'[44]

The senior students participating in our science and technology clubs show an aptitude for physics and technological creativity. The problems that engage them are both theoretical and practical. Our club members study a broad range of theoretical issues: the world of elementary particles, thermonuclear reactions, the direct conversion of heat into electricity, quantum generators, the application of semiconductors and ultrasound in technology, the electrohydraulic effect, etc. The students strive not only to understand and interpret the achievements of science but to actively apply them. For instance, our club members designed and constructed a working model of a water main in which the pump is turned on and off automatically. The water mains in our school were then assembled according to this model. They made three automated lathes that are being used to produce parts for children's wind-up toys. They designed equipment to sort the seeds of grain crops (according to the size and weight of the grain), and also a thresher, a grain cleaning machine, a mower and a blacksmith's forge. They helped the collective farm mechanics to make drilling machines and lathes for their repair workshop. Students working in the automation and electronics club designed an automatic batch dispenser for free-flowing dry substances, five electronic calculators, a vending machine for pencils, and an electric smelting furnace for manufacturing parts from nylon-6. They made seven instructional and assessment devices for mathematics lessons and fitted out our language laboratory.

We strive to apply the achievements of chemistry, biology and especially biochemistry to encourage a high level of work culture among our students. We explain to students the biological processes taking place in the soil and the reasons for using antibiotics and growth hormones in stock feed. We teach them how to make poor food nutritious with the aid of the microorganism *Clostridium Pasteurianum*, which is capable of synthesising proteins from nitrogen in the air and carbon in the food mass. We explain the science and technology used in combating weeds with chemicals. The practical application of science is of great interest to the senior students. They understand that in these situations, work and science are closely associated. Participation in the chemistry, biology and biochemistry clubs prepares students psychologically to work in agriculture at an advanced level.

In the chemistry club, our students study the chemical and biochemical means for processing the stems of grain crops (straw). They learn that it is possible to supplement the low protein content of straw with proteins, converting material of little nutritional value into valuable feed. They also master the technology for accomplishing this.

In the biochemistry club, students study the life of the soil. At the school fertiliser factory, they study the microflora of the soil and conduct experiments creating an environment favourable for the vital activity of beneficial bacteria. They are fascinated to learn that dozens of types of microorganisms live in the soil. Some stimulate growth, some accelerate the ripening of fruit and some increase resistance to frosts. By creating an environment favourable for beneficial microorganisms, the students increase yields on our experimental beds by a factor of three, five, sometimes ten. Some types of microorganisms of the genus *Penicillium* (*P. notatum, P. chrysogenum, P. crustosum*) accelerate the conversion of clay soil into chernozem. Club members have developed the technology for laboratory preparation of a nutritious medium for these microorganisms and are now transitioning their experiments from small beds to larger plots.

Students are also breeding bacteria that feed on silicates, applying the research of the Soviet scientist Vasily Aleksandrov.[45] As they break down silicates, these bacteria take ash constituents and combine them with atmospheric nitrogen to produce proteins, creating a nutritious environment for plants.

In nature, there are many substances and microorganisms that act as catalysts for the activity of silicate bacteria. Combining chemical and microbiological fertilisers enriches the soil with nutritious substances. At the fertiliser factory, the club members test the impact of various chemical compounds and organic substances on the vital activity of bacteria. The students are not discouraged by the difficult physical work entailed, as it is the means for achieving significant goals.

In the biology club, senior students study living processes in the plant world. Their experiments involve accelerating vegetative growth in plants and increasing the vitamin content in fruits and vegetables, the protein content in wheat, and the sugar content in beet. Work in this club has convinced students that good quality seed is one of the most important sources of vitality in a plant organism. Selecting strong seeds with high viability, correctly storing the seeds, stimulating the germination energy and the plant's resistance to disease and unfavourable conditions are typical areas for club members' experimentation.

In our scientific subject clubs, senior students are joined by young industrial and collective farm workers—our former students. This provides an important opportunity for strengthening ties between the school and the local collective farm, and strengthening our reputation among the collective farm workers.

Keeping up with science and technology

WE STRIVE TO ENSURE that the work of our students is creative and incorporates the achievements of science and technology. Educating the creative abilities of young inventors and production rationalisers depends on the development of their technical expertise and their ability to grasp the essence of any work. If school students can operate an internal combustion engine and manufacture metal parts using a machine tool at an early age, their development is accelerated by several years. At 17 or 18, they reach a level of technical expertise typical of an experienced worker.

Our aim is that children's thinking should not only take place in their heads but also, figuratively speaking, on the tips of their fingers. The most effective way to educate technical expertise is through invention, the highest stage of children's creativity. To make a working model that is a copy of an actual machine is only the first stage in creativity. It is very important that children, through their own problem-solving, invent new combinations from working models, put together new assemblies and find new applications for mechanisms. For instance, our students made a model of a steam turbine. It powers a small generator, and that generator provides energy for working models. Children find it interesting to connect various models to the generator: a winnowing machine, a mechanical saw, a separator, etc. They are being creative, but the children want more. They are not satisfied just to see moving parts. They dream that their machine will be used to process something. And then they have the idea of changing the construction of the mechanical saw and adapting it for polishing. In the process of reconstructing the model, they have another idea: to combine a saw and a wood lathe in a single mechanism. Creative competition arises between several small groups, each striving to improve their model as much as possible.

As they develop skills in operating machinery, working with metal, construction and modelling, they broaden the areas of physical work in which these skills are not only applied but developed and deepened. Students aged 14 and 15 acquire a range of skills connected with the operation of machines, construction and modelling. The adolescent cohort becomes enthusiastically engaged in work that is enriched by inventiveness and the creative application of knowledge. For instance, students completing Grades 7 and 8 constructed a small building to house our green laboratory: a centre for experimental work. Their productive work became creative as they began to mechanise a sequence of labour-intensive processes and decided to use reinforced concrete blocks in place of timber. Under the direction of the physics teacher, the students assembled a mechanism for preparing cement mortar, set up a crane to lift the mortar, bricks and blocks, made a transporter, and constructed a power-saw bench. All of these mechanisms were significantly smaller than those usually used in construction, but they operated on the same principles.

In this work, we see how a production goal can be approached creatively in perfecting the actual work process. The students not only constructed a building; they created a work process that was new to them. Their experience showed them that it is possible to build a crane from a few dozen kilograms of iron and several metres of cable using an electric motor and a pulley. With the aid of that crane, it is possible to lift heavy items on a building site, load a truck, and move stones and beams. It is possible to make a concrete mixer from several metal sheets. At every stage, they were convinced that technical refinement in work involves assembling, adjusting and harnessing electricity.

We try to continually provide new opportunities for students to apply machine technology, electrical energy and chemistry in simple agricultural work. Experience has convinced us that it is only possible to educate a love for agricultural work when young people have learned to replace manual work processes with mechanised ones; when they have obtained higher yields of grain from the soil not through physical effort but through the application of scientific knowledge. This is what provides a psychological preparation for working life. It is very important that the experimental plot, greenhouse, orchard, nature room, apiary and green laboratory all provide a school in technical training.

Plants in our greenhouse and experimental plot used to be watered by hand. Having learned to view every work process from the perspective of applying machinery and mechanics, the students pondered whether it would be possible to mechanise the water supply and the watering. They laid pipes from the well to the greenhouse and experimental plot and set up a pump. This was fairly heavy work, but it would lighten work in the future, so it was interesting and inspiring. Now, when looking after plants, the most important thing was not physical effort but careful thought. Freeing our students from difficult and monotonous physical work, we strive to ensure their attention and hands are occupied with more refined work. When raising seedlings for vegetables, flowers and grapevines and watering by hand, the care of the plants was dominated by physical work. When watering became a secondary concern, children began to think about how to improve the composition of the soil, how to accelerate the plants' development, maintain a constant humidity in the air, conduct foliar fertilising, etc. They had a new idea: it would be possible to replace watering individual plants with artificial rain. They ran rows of perforated pipes along the ceiling of the greenhouse. By regulating the pressure in the pipes, the children created rain. The senior students began to ionise the water. The ionised water brought the conditions in the greenhouse close to the natural conditions of a stormy summer day (you could even smell the ozone in the greenhouse). Thanks to these conditions, the development of the plants intensified, their metabolism was elevated, and beneficial microorganisms flourished in the soil.

The teachers and students created a machine to loosen the top layer of soil and make it friable. This machine combined a small internal combustion engine with a rotating blade that cut the top layer of soil, turned it and, if required, loosened the soil to the required depth. Depending on how you used and directed this machine (the students called it a mechanical hoe), it could dig furrows or create mounds. This little invention stimulated creative thought and taught us to discover new possibilities for the use of small technology, which should be created not only by engineers and designers but by every worker. The students were enthused by a new idea: to apply electrical energy for trimming branches on fruit trees, and for preparing solutions that their friends used to feed plants. The realisation of all these creative ideas began in the technical clubs when students thought about how to transform hand tools into mechanical tools.

Experience has convinced us that to educate a high level of technical expertise and thought, it is necessary to achieve productive goals, the material results of work, through experimentation. (In a school, that mainly involves constructing new machinery and assemblies.) This is especially important when educating senior students.

The Grade 9 students were cleaning grain on the collective farm threshing floor. The threshing floor was considered to be mechanised, as the two-grain cleaning machines ran on electricity. But 20 male and female students had to carry grain in buckets to supply these machines. The students thought about how to mechanise this manual work. They set up two transporters to deliver uncleaned grain to the machines and transport the cleaned grain to storage. The nature of the work changed dramatically. Before mechanisation, strenuous physical work was required to keep the machines working without interruption, but now all that was required was to monitor the operation of the various working parts. Those who were most successful in handling this new form of work were those with a good knowledge of electrical engineering and mechanics, who could design and connect the universal source of energy, the electric motor, with the various assemblies and mechanisms. The boys and girls were convinced once again that in agricultural production, there are dozens of work processes in which it is possible to create small-scale mechanisation through one's own efforts by connecting machinery to an electric motor or an internal combustion engine.

The senior students working at the animal farm noticed that it took a great deal of effort to cart out the manure. When they studied the situation, which the collective farm workers had become accustomed to, they wondered whether it was really necessary for the straw bedding and animal manure to consist of soggy lumps that were so difficult to transport. Would it not be possible to change the bedding straw so that its removal, a difficult and unpleasant task, could be done by a machine? They came up with a solution. Instead of using normal straw they could use pulverised straw so it could be removed mechanically. This is what they did. It turned out that the pulverised straw absorbed moisture much more evenly, and when spread on the fields, it broke down into humus more quickly.

We want to make sure that our students are capable of embedding mechanical technology more and more deeply in various fields of work. We want them to not only find new applications for existing machinery but also create new assemblies and devices based on existing technology. Preparing the young generation to apply technology creatively to innovate on a mass scale is one of the most important preconditions for technological progress. As technology develops and is perfected, advances in productivity depend on both the inventors of machines and those who work with them.

In modern agriculture, we no longer have the ploughmen and sowers of past centuries. Master horticulturalists and pastoralists need to be good machine operators. And if we cannot dispense with shovels and pitchforks in some places due to tradition and backwardness, that does not mean we need to teach young people a love of shovels and pitchforks to prepare them for agricultural work. A love for agricultural work is impossible without the desire and ability to replace shovels and pitchforks with technology. All collective farm workers must become machine operators. That is the main way of overcoming the difference between the city and the country. There should be no more than ten machine operators for every 1,000 hectares of arable land on a collective farm. Only then will we achieve a high level of work productivity. In the country, we are still trampling wealth underfoot. Many natural resources are not being utilised. We are trying to extract as much as possible from the soil but giving very little back to the soil. On every collective farm, it is possible to produce thousands of tonnes of good quality organic fertiliser that is easily absorbed by plants and could at least double our yields. Every hectare of arable land can feed at least one cow, and if we can achieve that, the nation will be blessed with a river of milk. (Now, unfortunately, we have one cow for every 5–8 hectares.) But all of this will only be achieved if every young person from the age of seven or eight lives in a world of technology; if the practical application of scientific knowledge is considered an important characteristic of intellectual development.

The effective use of machinery depends on the technological literacy of the machine operators. This is especially important for the productivity of machinery like beet and potato harvesters. When adjusting such machinery, it is necessary to consider the various root forms, varying soil densities and the relief of the land. To operate such machinery, the machine operator needs to have the mindset of a designer. That is why we try to develop such a mindset in our students. We teach them not only to get everything out of the machine that the designer put into it, but also to introduce additional refinements and adjustments that may initially appear insignificant but guarantee the machinery's constant successful operation. Let us explain this through examples.

When our students had to monitor the operation of a beet sowing machine (and the successful operation of such a machine depends largely on the relief of the land, characteristics of the soil and quality of the seed), they noticed that the precise planting of a given quantity of seed into each hole depended significantly on the moisture level of the soil.

If they did not consider the daily moisture level of the soil in the area to be sown and adjust the sowing mechanism accordingly, it would begin to function inaccurately within an hour. This was not a defect in manufacture. It is necessary to adjust the interaction of the sowing mechanism with the other parts of the machine each time it is operated, taking into account the moisture level of the seed and the composition and moisture level of the soil. Our students learn to operate the sowing machine with various soil types and in varying conditions. They always manage to get the sowing mechanism to operate with ideal precision, as envisaged by the designer.

A creative approach is required even when using a simple machine like a cultivator. Observation led our students to conclude that when choosing cutting implements (the blades of the cultivator), it is not only necessary to consider the soil and how it is to be worked, but also the speed of the tractor. They learned to select plough blades so that even when working at high speed, not only were weeds destroyed, but soil was earthed up around the cropped plants, and the soil crust was broken up between the rows and around the plants as well.

For the past five years, our agricultural technology club has managed experimental plots of between 0.1 and 0.5 hectares, located directly within the collective farm fields. Here we test various methods of working the soil and managing plants that have proven valuable in our school experimental plot. Here we also continue experimentation begun in our greenhouse and green laboratory, and trialled on our school plot, to test the application of chemicals that accelerate plant growth and development, or stimulate plant metabolism. The fundamental aim of all this experimentation and development is to obtain yields several times higher than normal. Thanks to the introduction of chemical and microbiological fertilisers, the correct soil preparation, and the selection of high-quality seed, our experimental plots have produced outstanding yields of wheat (6–7 tonnes per hectare), sunflower seeds (3–3.5 tonnes per hectare), and sugar beet (65–70 tonnes per hectare).

Our students have conducted interesting experiments to study grain crops and learn to increase yields using advances in chemical science. In our agricultural technology club, we have grown summer wheat by tilling between rows. Seeds are sown in furrows, guaranteeing each row a large area for feeding. The areas between rows are tilled, and chemical fertilisers and growth stimulants are added to the soil. Exceptionally large heads of grain grow, with each grain one and a half to two times the size of a normal grain. We are deeply convinced that these large grains are a natural characteristic of wheat that has not been fully developed. The method of tilling between rows produces a yield five or six times higher than normal. These experimental methods will soon be adopted directly into farm production. We already have machinery in use at our collective farm that could easily be adapted to tilling between rows.

I remind readers that the participants in our agricultural science clubs include young machine operators and agricultural scientists from the collective farm, as well as our students. This association between our students and those working in the field, combined with work experience in collective farm brigades, is the best way of connecting our school with work environments. Students must work alongside members of the workforce.

Developing talents, abilities and a vocation

TO GIVE PEOPLE THE HAPPINESS of finding their vocation in life, we need to help them find, among many possible pathways, that pathway that will lead to the full flowering of their individual creative abilities and personality. There should not be any failures coming out of our schools, people who have not found a vocation. Communism means, above all else, the flowering of gifts and talents. The essence of communist education is to discover that golden vein, that vital spark in each human being, that can be developed to bring them the joy of creativity. The extent to which each student successfully finds their place in their community and carries out their duty to society determines their moral and intellectual fulfilment in life.

There are many facets to the development of a person's creative abilities. Gifts and talents are not only expressed when a person becomes a scientist, engineer or any other sort of intellectual worker. In a society where human beings are put first, any work can be raised to the level of creativity. For any child (we declare this categorically, as it is one of our fundamental educational convictions), work in which they manifest themselves as genuine creators, poets or artists, taking pride in their work and that of their group, can express their inner creativity. Consequently, we do not have a single child who is indifferent to work.

To educate a keen interest in work in each child—to discover their aptitudes and vocation, and develop an enthusiasm for some area of work—is the essence of the individual educational work that demonstrates true educational skill. Each student finds their vocation and path in life. The common view that a human being and their vocation exist independently of each other, that a person's fate depends totally on luck, is fundamentally false. A vocation is developed. And success in educating a vocation depends hugely on how deeply work has entered a person's inner life, how closely work is associated with thought.

We have set ourselves the goal of ensuring there is not a single faceless student at our school who is not interested in anything. A student who gets excellent marks in all subjects but is not excited and enthused by anything, who studies mathematical formulas and lyrical poems, plants a tree and uses a lathe, all with the same indifference, arouses feelings of concern in us. The fact that everything seems to be going smoothly for them presents its own danger, and we consider it essential to awaken some interest and enthusiasm in that successful student so that they leave our school full of love for some area of work and proud of their skill.

The first thing that catches the eye of a child who enters our school in Grade 1 is the array of interesting things with which all, without exception, are busy. Each student has a favourite workplace, a favourite hobby, and an older friend whose work serves as a model. The overwhelming majority of our students who are learning and mastering something are also passing on their acquired skills and knowledge to their friends. A person is only truly educated when they pass their knowledge, experience and mastery on to someone else. One only begins to sense one's creative powers and abilities when one enters into moral relations with another person and becomes concerned about increasing their spiritual wealth. This is how a vocation is born and how self-education occurs. Moral relations arise between people who work together from the moment one begins to see in another their own virtues; when the other person is like a mirror to them. It is on these moral relationships in the community that vocational self-education is built.

In every child sleep the seeds of some abilities. These seeds are like gunpowder: they need a spark to ignite them. Such a spark is provided by inspiration, admiration for the skill of a friend who may be the same age or older. Collective work is not just people acting upon nature, upon the surrounding world, but a social interaction involving hearts, feelings, thoughts, emotions, interest and enthusiasm.

We have special workplaces for children in the early and middle school years to stimulate interest in design and construction. Here students assemble working models from disassembled parts. Those participating solve problems of varying levels of difficulty. The younger students may be assembling a simple crane, adolescents may be assembling a drilling machine or a lathe, while senior students next to them are making a demonstration automated lathe. A new participant arrives who is interested in technical creativity. The child does not yet know how to do anything. They are entrusted with a simple task and then with something more complex. The child very quickly acquires knowledge and skills that are quite complex for their age. Figuratively speaking, the powder in the child's soul has come in contact with a spark: they have met students who are inspired by their work. And this inspiration is the most powerful educator of individual interests and abilities, of a vocation. The tools, machinery and visual aids all remain inert if there is no atmosphere of creatively inspired work and no moral relationships.

We strive to create an atmosphere of inspired creative work in every group. For every ten boys and girls, three or four will be able to disassemble and reassemble a small internal combustion engine and operate it by the time they are aged 10 or 11. In the future, they will be talented machine operators. For every 100 boys and girls aged 10 or 11, seven or eight will know internal combustion engines incomparably better than a final year student for whom technology has not touched the inner recesses of their soul and who will 'find their powder' in something else. These naturally talented young people will become designers, inventors and engineers. We try to ensure that they also provide a spark that kindles the hearts of the friends who work alongside them in our clubs for young machine operators. Without them, our club work would be impossible, and there would be no spontaneous initiatives. Actually, it is with their spark, with their love for their work, that the moral relationships in such groups begin. One of the most important objectives of our educational endeavours is to ensure that, figuratively speaking, no child's heart should remain unkindled, that all talents and abilities should fully unfold and the most talented and gifted children should become educators—only then will they be educated themselves.

The more delicate work is, and the more it relies on an intellectual foundation, the greater the importance assumed by self-education, the transfer of knowledge between members of the workgroup, and the formation of friendships between older and younger students. In every club for young electrical engineers or young radio mechanics, there are one or two students who are complete masters in the field, whose work serves as a model for others. Such talented students will always be found in a school community, as long as the fire of creative inspiration is alive there. Many years of experience have convinced us that in every class of students, there will always be five or six for whom electronics and radio technology have become a special work interest, a hobby. For every 100 students, there are always 10 or 12 who have achieved significant success in automation and radio electronics. Having senior students mentor junior students is especially important in this most refined form of technical creativity. It is thus no accident that in the automation and radio electronics clubs, students from the junior, middle and senior classes work together.

Senior students who have achieved significant success and competence in radio technology and electronics manage clubs for young collective farm workers that meet in the workers' homes. In these clubs, young men and women construct radios and study television technology.

Our staff pay significant attention to the development of artistic abilities in our students, especially in applied arts. We have a small ceramics workshop in our school, where students fashion crockery and the figures of animals and people from clay. There is a special area for the little ones where they can fashion whatever they want and make puppets for our puppet theatre. In the club for artistic pokerwork and fretwork, the children use their imagination to create drawings and plywood figures. Students from Grades 1–10 who have a talent for drawing and painting gather in the painting club. The students' musical abilities are developed in choir circles, our children's folk instrument orchestra and the club for bayan players. There are undoubtedly some future performers, musicians and composers among our children. For these particular students, art may become their main activity, a profession. But whatever our students' future professions, we believe art should be a constant source of spiritual enrichment for everyone.

In the student community, there are always some who find their favourite work on the land, growing crops and caring for animals. These students are the prized assistants of the biology teachers. On our experimental plots, in the orchard, the greenhouses, the green laboratory, the collective farms and our experimental rabbit farm, you will find the favourite workplaces of the young plant breeders, soil scientists, animal breeders and botanists. You will find interesting work in each of these workplaces, with students discovering the secrets and laws of nature, and that spark of enthusiasm, that bright talent that awakens the interest and curiosity of those who cross our school's threshold.

Gifted and talented children, adolescents, and young men and women become the leaders of our clubs. Some of our clubs are led by teachers, but only if they are especially skilled. The more the children see a teacher's mastery, the more they regard them as a friend, and the greater their authority as a teacher.

We take care to ensure that, even at a young age, gifted and talented students pass on their knowledge to their friends. A child who can work on a small lathe, construct a working model of a generator or radio, or graft two or three varieties of fruit tree onto a single rootstock at the age of 10 or 11, becomes in adolescence and youth the leader of children's clubs, where abilities, talents and vocations are developed. But this is a special sort of leadership, the living example of mastery, the ability to inspire with their work. Each gifted and talented student is surrounded by several boys and girls in love with the same pursuit—often simply interested in what the older ones are doing. More often than not, the talented pupil has no thought of guiding others; they are immersed in their work and do not initially notice those who work beside them. Conscious guidance appears later. At first, children and adolescents with varying degrees of preparedness for the work and varying abilities and skills appear to come together chaotically: a Grade 2 pupil is working with a Grade 8 pupil, a Grade 5 pupil is learning from a Grade 10 pupil. But later, this apparent chaos becomes genuinely self-directed: the children are united by their enthusiasm for the work.

For example, a group of 11 students gathers in one of our workshops during the hours set aside for favourite work activities. These are the young metalworkers and designers. What enthuses them is the construction of working models driven by electricity. The most capable of them is Grade 10 student, Sergei V. He and three of his friends (a Grade 7 student, a Grade 8 student, and a female Grade 10 student) are constructing a model electric railway with automatic signalling, several switching points, sidings and extra routes. Next to them, two

Grade 7 students (a boy and a girl), one Grade 8 student and one Grade 5 student are working. They are making a model electric crane, but from time to time, they come over to the model railway, and Sergei helps them construct the crane. Here, in a single club, are two small groups, one involved in more complex work, the other in simpler work. The children in the second group want to work together with their more experienced friends, but the more experienced ones want to keep ahead of them. They are concerned that one of the less experienced ones may soon overtake them. Here, abilities and skills are constantly being developed.

There are another three students in this club: two Grade 2 students (a boy and a girl) and one Grade 4 student. They want to do something, and their older friends have given them some work: the children are polishing metal sheets for the wagons and points, and dismantling and cleaning the parts of an old, rusty electric motor. The little ones are very satisfied, and gradually they begin to take on more complex tasks. Oleg R., the Grade 4 student, is helping Sergei cut out openings in the metal sheets within a month. The older ones see that they will soon be able to trust Oleg to work on the lathe. He has a steady hand, a good eye, and a feel for tools. (The boy has been using an electric jigsaw for 18 months and has made wooden and plastic parts using a lathe.)

Three months pass, and the railway and crane models are complete. Sergei brings plans for a new model to the workshop: a blooming mill. It involves elements of automation and electronics (programmed operation, control of the quality of processed parts). The two groups that have completed work of varying complexity, combine as one. It soon becomes apparent that some of the work involved in making the blooming mill is too difficult for some of those who made the model crane. They do not want to take on secondary tasks, as they also want to demonstrate their skills, so they begin work on a model of an electric motor. The Grade 2 students join them, while Oleg continues working on the blooming mill at the same time as being the most active participant in making the model electric motor. At this time, two new members join the club, a girl from Grade 3 and a boy from Grade 4.

This is how all the children work. As their work is based on common interests and enthusiasm, each one strives to do their work as well as they can. Since nearly everyone is passing on their knowledge to a friend, everyone strives to achieve perfection. This striving involves strenuous mental effort that develops aptitudes and leads to a vocation. We carefully encourage each child, so the light of their inspiration can light the way for someone else at the earliest opportunity.

The more a child gains emotionally from teaching others, the more they want to learn themselves. There are students in Grades 5 and 6 who lead small groups of young plant breeders. While studying in Grades 5 and 6, sisters Valya and Lyuda P. worked enthusiastically with a group of youngsters from Grades 2–4. They produced high yields of vegetables and potatoes. From one square metre of land, they harvested over 10 kilograms of potatoes. The girls gained the inspiration and knowledge for this leadership role from the agricultural technology club that operated alongside and in which they also participated. The girls really wanted to understand the essence of the phenomena that took place in the soil, and such a wish provides the impulse that leads to a new stage of intellectual development and mastery. This complex inner process, in which emotional, intellectual, moral and volitional elements are interwoven, leads to the discovery of talents, the development of abilities and a vocation.

The various types of work that surround a child from the moment they set foot in our school are like magnets of varying strength that attract the sensitive needle of the compass guiding a child on their path. The stronger the magnet, the more interesting the work in which a child becomes involved, the more clearly they develop their abilities, aptitude and vocation for that particular work.

At the animal breeding section of the collective farm, chemistry teacher Ms Kolomyichenko has created a laboratory where students investigate the role of antibiotics in the development of animal organisms. If not for the teacher's example and enthusiasm for the work, the adolescents working with the animals would not find it at all interesting. Educational management of independent work consists of a child feeling the inspiration and enthusiasm of the person next to them. If the teacher's work provides a model for the student and earns their admiration, the teacher will become their favourite person. Experience has convinced us that there is no apathy or indifference towards work that can resist the creative inspiration of a teacher or senior student who is in love with the work they do. If we see that a child is indifferent to everything, not interested in anything, we think hard about which teacher or senior student could mentor that difficult student. That is where our individual approach to the child begins. Every teacher, including the principal and director of studies, mentors two or three difficult children who live in an unfavourable family setting, who do not enjoy a parent's love and affection. We find a way to the hearts of these children mainly because we are their friends in work, because we are excited by the same projects, aims and plans.

We strive to ensure that each pupil achieves significant success in their favourite activity. The path to success usually lies through prolonged trial and error. A pupil tries their strength in a variety of activities, acquiring many skills, but if their success in some activity does not extend far beyond the bounds of what is normal for their age, it means they have still not found their path. Significant success is not merely the satisfactory, good or excellent execution of what is achievable by anyone. Anyone may do an excellent job of making a ruler or assembling a model generator—some just need more practice than others. But for work to become a favourite activity, a passion, success needs to exceed the highest standards achievable by all pupils of a given age. It is such success that we call significant. All students in Grades 6 and 7 are good at grafting the scion of a productive variety of fruit tree onto rootstock, and we do not consider the excellent execution of such work significant success. But if a child achieves mastery of this task in Grade 3 or 4, or even more outstandingly, in Grade 2, that is indeed significant success. By the time they are studying in Grade 6 or 7, such a child will be in a club and conducting experiments in selection and hybridisation that would normally only be carried out by a capable final year student. In their final year at school, the same student will conduct experiments in microbiology, studying the life in the soil and the influence of chemical agents on the development of various plant organs, all of which goes beyond the bounds of the curriculum. Significant success means a student goes beyond their peers. Of course, that does not mean that one or two members of the class go on ahead while everyone else straggles behind. Each student also has their own favourite work, in which they have tasted at least some serious success, if not significant success.

Many students attain significant success in work in the primary school. A Grade 1 student may use a fretsaw better than an average Grade 4 student. A Grade 2 student makes a little wooden house that is so beautiful the whole school admires it. A Grade 4 student grafts bud cuttings to a fruit tree that produce such strong, vigorous branches that the botany teacher wonders how he did it. A Grade 2 student helping young mechanics clean engine parts learns how to disassemble and reassemble a small engine. However, such successes do not mean that all of a child's talents have been uncovered and their abilities definitively established so that they are practically ready to plan their future. A child may later achieve more substantial success in some other area of work. The development of abilities is a living, dynamic process. In the overwhelming majority of cases, people do not become what they dreamed of becoming in adolescence. Nevertheless, achieving significant success is like climbing a small mountain whose summit a child can only reach by making a special effort. When that summit is reached, the child realises how much and also how little they have achieved, as from a small summit, they get a better view of higher, as yet unattainable summits.

I have known more than 20 adolescents and several senior students who were unable to achieve success in any one area for a long time. Some of them were bone lazy. But however little a person wanted to work, we always began with the achievement of success, at first small, then significant. In the case of an idle lazybones who feels no inclination to pursue any activity, we first compel them to work at something where we consider they have a good chance of success.

The best way of compelling someone to work is to involve them in a joint project with a teacher. For several years we educated Igor D., who was lazy and indifferent to everything. At first, he did not even want to learn to ride a motorcycle, and it is very rare for a student to be indifferent to that. We literally had to take the boy by the hand and make him join in an activity that I or someone else might be doing, such as grafting an apple tree or transplanting a sapling, and we had to repeat this dozens of times. But work itself has magical power. Once a person completes a certain amount of work and sees its results, they become enthused with it. Igor became enthused with horticulture.

As soon as a student achieves significant success, we direct their energies to more complex, difficult work. This is very important for discovering talents and developing abilities. Without the opportunity to overcome difficulties, a gift will wither. Talent, skill and perfection come with determined effort to overcome difficulties.

Several years ago, in one of the clubs for young animal breeders, a Grade 4 student, Victor K., was working alongside senior students. He loved caring for small calves. The boy noticed how the senior students paid a lot of attention to the nutritional value of hay. He was entrusted to prepare several dozen kilograms of vitamin-rich hay for the calves. The boy was able to dry the hay in such a way that it became a valuable medicinal feed. For a 12-year-old boy, this was significant success. Victor became enthusiastically involved in the preparation of feed for young cattle and then in the cultivation of feed crops. In Grade 7, he learned how to enrich raw feed with protein, and the milk yield of the cow he was supervising increased. It seemed like the young boy would become an excellent animal breeder, but he was simply involved in what he was doing and had no dreams of the future. In the senior classes, Victor became interested in antibiotics. Together with his teacher, he sought new methods for creating media for the vital activity of antibiotics and conducted experiments. When he graduated from school, he entered university, graduated and became a scientist.

We devote special attention to developing abilities, interests and a vocation in students who display no obvious talents or spark of creative inspiration in their work. Such unnoticeable, faceless students are found not only among average students but also among those who receive excellent grades. Deeply believing that each person can become a poet, an artist in some pursuit, we strive to ensure that these students concentrate all their energies on a single point—immersing themselves in the details and subtleties of some particular pursuit. If success is not achieved at the first attempt, we help them to make a fresh start. If there is failure at the second attempt, we help them to approach the matter from a different direction.

One adolescent showed some interest in growing grape seedlings in the greenhouse. This work requires considerable skill: selecting an appropriate growing medium, correctly placing cuttings in the medium, selecting a well-lit location, maintaining suitable humidity and encouraging the activity of beneficial microorganisms in the soil. Initially, things did not go to plan for the young boy, and he was ready to abandon the activity and try something else. But, knowing that growing grapes was just what he needed to focus on, we showed him how to prepare the soil more effectively, how to fertilise, and so on. The boy began the work again, saw some improvement and was encouraged. But the results were again unsatisfactory: the buds opened slowly, and the shoots were weak. We again examined the work process to find something the boy had missed on his first and second attempts. Again, the same work was undertaken, and because some skills had now been perfected, the result was a bit better. This fact became a stimulus for new efforts: if the result had been improved once, it could be improved again. The boy repeated the work over and over again, perfecting more and more skills along the way, and freeing his intellectual powers to delve deeper into the essence of the process. He began to reflect more deeply on what he was doing and how the results depended on effort and endeavour. At last, the time came when his plants developed significantly better than those of other students. This was true success. Now the boy wanted to become more and more involved in that pursuit, which became a favourite activity because it brought success. Success in this instance was due 99% to effort. Thanks to persistent effort, unremarkable, faceless students can find a passion and develop their abilities.

In developing abilities, we attach great significance to combining physical work and intellectual work. A person can only become a capable and talented turner, mechanic, horticulturalist or animal breeder if they consider everything they do beforehand. If young people show an interest in nature, in the soil, in animals, we seek to ensure that simple, sometimes unpleasant, work processes are always associated with investigative, experimental thought. At our school fertiliser factory, we cannot avoid a lot of spade work, but this work also marks the beginning of interesting research. We prepare fertilisers containing microelements with certain properties. Some fertilisers accelerate the maturation of wheat by 5–7 days, and some by 10–12 days.

Someone who has done a complete work cycle from preparing fertiliser to harvesting a crop that has matured one or two weeks earlier than the rest of the farm will be hard to drag away from the soil, the fertilisers and plants. We have boys and girls who have worked creatively for four or five years at our fertiliser factory. Because this simple physical work is also thoughtful work, the children gradually develop as highly talented farmers. They 'feel' the life of the soil, and they love plants. Their physical work is combined with laboratory research, such as testing the influence of chemicals on plant metabolism. From pitchforks and shovels to microscopes, from chemical reactions to trenches full of humus: this is the way to educate farmer-researchers, thinkers who can work with heads and hands. We are currently establishing a station for young soil researchers. This will be another favourite work club where students can study the soils in our district and region.

To make someone work intellectually is very difficult. To make someone work physically is significantly easier. A combination of physical and intellectual work is a decisive way to educate a love of work in the most neglected, lazy children whose parents have never made them work. We first make such students complete a certain amount of physical work, gradually ensuring that they find a path to knowledge in the work, however insignificant it may seem at first, and a way to harness the forces of nature. Once a person sees work as a way of achieving social and intellectual goals, their laziness is overcome, and the way is clear to educate a love of work.

When educating individual interests and abilities and a vocation, we are simultaneously creating the division of social labour. Marx wrote that 'the necessity for some division of social labour in defined proportions cannot be eliminated by a *given form* of social production. What can change is the way this is *manifested*.'[46] A division of labour based on an advanced scientific and technological foundation will facilitate every person's free choice of a vocation in which their abilities can be fully developed. There will be orchardists and builders, metallurgists and geologists, plant breeders and soil scientists. In many professions, people will be both creators of material goods and thinkers, creating things of intellectual and spiritual value, manifesting their intellect in their work. The simplest task will then become, in Marx's words, 'a devilishly serious business'.

An educator's task is to identify future talented machine operators, plant breeders, designers, theoretical mathematicians, geologists, builders and metallurgists, to awaken talents and kindle the spark of creativity in every student. That is what we aim to do in the coming years.

We aim to involve students more deeply in the practical activities associated with their favourite pursuits and in mastering theoretical knowledge. For example, students who show an aptitude for horticulture will study a more advanced botany course. We are currently selecting suitable literature for them to add to our library collection. Those students will be given more advanced assignments during their lessons, and more will be expected of them. For those with particular talents for working in mechanisation, electronics, design and modelling, we have already supplemented the school physics course with several topics not included in the curriculum, and we are deepening the study of the existing topics with additional material. This extension of the curriculum will take place in lessons (where it is possible to do so without adversely affecting the learning of other students) and more particularly during independent extracurricular work. We have already enjoyed some success in combining studying supplementary theoretical material with students' favourite work activities.

The most gifted mathematics students will start to study the foundations of algebra in Grades 3 and 4, not Grade 6. (Senior mathematics students will work with them during hours specially set aside for this in the timetable.) In Grades 9 and 10, these students will study differential and integral calculus. This is no less achievable than having some students assemble radio sets at the age of nine or 10. We are already creating equipment and visual aids for a room for young mathematicians. A curriculum for gifted mathematicians, including elements of higher mathematics, is currently being trialled, with some students in Grades 9 and 10 successfully mastering the analysis of infinitely small numbers, differential and integral calculus.

In all classes, beginning in Grade 3, the timetable will include an hour devoted to each student's favourite subject (we may call it an hour of creativity). During this hour (one hour per week, although we hope in the future, as we perfect our learning methods, to increase it to two hours in the middle school and three hours in the senior school), each student will study and conduct research into questions that interest them. During this hour, mental and physical work will be combined. The location of each student's activity will depend on the nature of their interest. Some will sit down with a book, some will be looking into microscopes, some will be using spades on the experimental plot, some will be standing at a lathe or an assembly bench in the electronics laboratory or workroom. Grade 10 students will work with Grade 5 students. The organisers of workgroups such as we described earlier will go to work with their young friends.

The hours of favourite work during the second half of the day will become even richer and more diverse. We are already creating new work areas. Our 'difficult challenges' room promises to be interesting. Here we will set children comparatively complex design and assembly challenges that will require deep thought. Here work will involve willpower, failures and disappointments, but this, too, is essential; this is how genuine thinkers and researchers are forged. We have already created a room for small mechanisation projects where senior students reflect on how to create new machines and assemblies that can lighten the human workload.

Manual work and all-round development

HOWEVER COMPLEX MACHINE TECHNOLOGY and technological processes may become, manual work will always be an important part of production. The concept of 'manual work' is not synonymous with 'physical work'. In refined manual work, creative thought shines through. Elementary manual work skills are a prerequisite for mastering complex machine technology and technological processes. As we automate our production processes, an increasingly important role is played by the skills required for adjusting, fine-tuning, repairing, technically inspecting and modernising equipment. Mastery of manual work allows people to be more skilled and confident when managing complex machinery. People who have undertaken lengthy training in manual work are able to operate machinery in a way that ensures the moving parts interact smoothly, without jerks or shuddering. It may be truly said that a skilled person's talent is in their fingertips.

When we begin to acquaint students in the middle and senior years with machine technology, we attach great significance to a particular type of manual work. Before learning to operate a machine, students assemble and disassemble a working model and come to understand how its various parts interact. Then they progress to assembling and disassembling a real machine. Observations have confirmed that if the operation of a machine is preceded by such preparatory manual work, people will truly master the use of the machine. They operate it with confidence and are able to avoid faulty operation and breakdowns.

The educational role of manual work depends on what a person does with their hands, how they do it and how the work process is connected with a worker's train of thought. In manual work, we attach great significance to skill, calculation, and combining precision of movement with physical effort when working with materials and transforming them to create something new. That is why we give so much attention to construction, design and modelling, to working the soil, grafting, planting and transplanting trees. People have to work with materials in all these work processes, either directly with their hands or with tools. In these work processes, we encourage people to work with their left hand and their right so that both hands interact during the work process. This is an exceptionally important issue in work education, but unfortunately, I am not able to dwell on it here.

Manual work also plays an important role in the development of abstract thought. The formation of such generalised concepts as machine, mechanism, technological process and work productivity depend on the nature of the manual work undertaken. Our observation of students aged 12 and 13 when they are disassembling and assembling working models of machinery shows that such work greatly assists them in visualising the interaction of the various working parts, and this understanding has a beneficial effect on their work activity.

For instance, when the children were studying the structure and operation of a small compression engine, they took it apart and reassembled it many times, as they tried to understand the cause of a delay in ignition. Was it a construction defect and a faulty part or an incorrect formulation of the fuel mixture? Visual comparison and juxtaposition gradually gave way to mental analysis. The children drew conclusions not only from direct observation but also from logical deduction. Our observations suggest that the vitality of this thought process depends on how close the link is between direct observation and logical cognition during the work process. A student acquires the ability to reflect on work, to mentally analyse work processes, only after a lengthy period of learning to think while working, while using their hands to work with materials, constructing and modelling.

There are other aspects of thinking that depend upon the depth with which students mentally grasp the essence of the work they are doing, such as mental experimentation (logically checking the validity of an idea based on practical data) and the coordinated activity of imagination and thought. A student whose capacity for mental analysis has not been developed in close association with practical activity will attempt to conduct practical trials even when there is no need for it; when it is possible to think it through and conduct the trial in one's mind. The capacity for mental experimentation is especially important when solving design problems, and also when repairing and restoring machinery. Then it is essential to visualise the interaction of the parts and their interdependence in a given situation or position. The vividness of this imaginative visualisation is directly connected with the extent to which the efforts of hands and mind are combined during work. There are adolescents who can determine from the sound of a tractor engine why it is not functioning properly; consequently, they are able to anticipate a breakdown in a timely way and prevent it.

If the ability to analyse and synthesise has been developed during practice, during work, then people approach work tasks as problems to be solved. They put forward hypotheses and then mentally test them in practice. A valuable characteristic of such people is their ability to see the issues and problems presented by a concrete set of circumstances, which is particularly important when pitting their will against the elemental forces of nature.

Manual work during which an idea is developed and realised facilitates the development of such mental attributes as critical thinking, flexibility, the breadth and vitality of thought and the ability to subject suppositions and conclusions to critical examination. People whose hands have worked in close association with their thinking from an early age are typically able to check the validity of a supposition through work. Based on their own experience and the experience of those around them, children are convinced from an early age that there are varying degrees of skill in any work. The ideal is a high level of skill and creativity. People set high expectations on their work from childhood, never satisfied with what they have achieved. If a child wants to have a second attempt at a task they have already completed, we consider this a significant indicator of success in our educational work.

A critical appraisal of the creative aspect of work is especially important when a person is doing the same work day after day. When preparing for the next work cycle, the best agricultural workers will always analyse the previous work cycle: how the soil has been prepared and how this has catered for plant development, how seeds have been prepared for sowing, etc. We need to establish such an approach to work while children are still at school. In work that repeats itself in the same fashion year after year, children must always see something new. For example, when growing the same crop for several years, students simultaneously undertake selective breeding, choosing seed from plants that have displayed desirable characteristics and sowing this seed in special beds.

To this end, we always strive to vary the conditions and circumstances under which our students work, incorporating new elements into our planning and demonstrating several ways of achieving the same end. Educational considerations such as allowing more scope for consciously changing the situation and creating new conditions largely determine the educational value of work. Creativity begins when new ideas are born during the work process and when plans evolve. In the 'difficult challenges' room we are setting up, we are focusing on children's creativity, their ability to make adjustments in response to new criteria for assessing the results and new technological conditions, such as a new operating regime for a working model.

In agricultural production, there are certain times when the situation does not appear to demand any human input: you can simply wait for the harvest. But people with creative minds will find opportunities for being active at such times. We try to ensure that our students always think creatively while work is in progress. For example, when tomatoes begin to ripen, the children are encouraged to think about ways of increasing the yield.

Educating coordination between hands and minds is especially important for developing the ability to mentally grasp complex work processes and understand the interdependence of a number of circumstances and phenomena.

The breadth of thought depends principally on the extent to which a single person can combine the roles of creating a plan and executing the work, as both a designer and a skilled worker able to bring a design to life. For this reason, we do not allow the less capable students in our technological clubs or those who show less initiative to be assigned the role of mere executors of plans thought out by the more active and capable. Abilities only develop when people bring their own plans to fruition.

It is very important that every student, at a certain stage in their work activity, comes up with an idea for a reasonably complex work process (growing a high-yield crop, making a working model of a machine, etc.). At first, this idea may be general in nature, its details not clearly delineated. Then, during the work process, it becomes more defined and detailed. For instance, when planning to make a working model of an actual machine, at first there is no clear conception of the detailed construction, just a conception of the general principles of the structure and operation. The ability to transfer the design features of the actual machine to the model depends on one's breadth of thought—the ability to mentally grasp the links between various phenomena. That is why we try to ensure that students who wish to construct working models are competent using hand tools. Such competence helps them understand more deeply the working principles and function of the parts that have developed from hand tools. The more competently they use hand tools, the easier it is for them to understand the transformation of manual skills into the working parts of a machine.

With this in mind, we have a great variety of hand tools in our workrooms and workshops. While using these tools, the students come to understand those elements that define the structural characteristics of the tool or instrument, and leave their impression on human work. For example, all cutting tools are characterised by elements such as the angle of the cutting edge, the form and size of the teeth, the size of the gullet, and the length and thickness of the blade. An understanding of these elements and how they may be applied in manual work plays a major role in developing thought and widening a student's horizons.

Self-service

SELF-SERVICE IS THE SIMPLEST FORM of daily work. Work education usually begins with it, and later it becomes the duty and custom of every person, regardless of what productive work they are involved in. Self-service is an important means for cultivating discipline and educating a sense of duty towards others. Meeting one's personal needs with one's own hands from an early age educates respect for parents, brothers, sisters and friends. Self-service makes work an equal obligation for everyone and is universal.

A fully conscious attitude towards such work—to self-service—is only possible when a person has acquired a habitual, internalised intolerance of dirtiness and untidiness from childhood; when this habit has developed into an emotional and aesthetic sensitivity to the surrounding environment.

At every stage in a child's development, we set parameters for their self-service obligations. We teach them how to fulfil those obligations, encourage regularity in performing their duties and instil the idea that self-service is obligatory for all without exception. Wordy explanations are unnecessary here. The important thing is for children to feel their self-service work makes their life better, more pleasant and more joyful. Without this feeling, there can be no conviction or conscious awareness.

Self-service mainly involves maintaining the cleanliness and beauty of the working environment: classrooms, laboratories and workshops.

It is particularly important to include things that make life more beautiful in self-service. Many self-service duties are aimed at meeting the aesthetic needs of the community and creating an aesthetically pleasing environment (growing flowers, creating flowerbeds etc.).

The most strenuous self-service work is usually carried out by boys. This is an important way of educating respect for women.

The role of work in a holistic education

THE METHODS EMPLOYED IN WORK EDUCATION are closely connected with those employed in intellectual, moral, physical and aesthetic education. This connection is determined by the aim of the work. If work conducted in workshops or on our experimental plots aims to impart or deepen work skills, the work education methodology employed is akin to that employed in intellectual education. If the moral element predominates in the work, and it is aimed at forming attitudes and convictions, then the work education methodology takes on features characteristic of methods for influencing moral feelings. To educate a moral preparedness to work for the common good, it is not enough to just have good skills and be habituated to work. The important thing here is the ideal that motivates a person to work. A crucial role is played by the emotions associated with a person's understanding of the role of their work in the life of society.

There is great educational potential in the organisational form students' work activities take and the relationships formed between students. In work aimed at developing character, skills and abilities are not the ultimate goals but a means of attaining social and creative goals. In work education, we consider our philosophical goals to be of prime importance. This does not mean you have to speak endlessly to students about the social and economic goals of their work. Our ideals permeate the work process itself. We seek to ensure students consider their moral worth, honour and pride to be expressed in mastering work skills and working creatively for the benefit of others. To make work a human imperative means to make it a spiritual imperative. We try to ensure that young children develop an emotional and aesthetic sensitivity to how they complete tasks, what others think and say about their work and how their peers evaluate it. Work only becomes part of a child's spiritual life when they appreciate the beauty of what they have created for others. Only then will they feel the difference between good and bad. Every child has a plot of ground in the school grounds, the orchard or at home where they have created something beautiful, where their work beautifies the earth. A student completing Grade 3 is able to admire the beauty of a flowering tree they planted during their first year at school. Every class has a lilac or peach grove they care for year after year.

The role of example in work education

CONSIDERING CHILDREN'S TENDENCY TO IMITATE whatever appeals to them, we try to ensure they can always see examples of interesting, engaging work at school. Even at an early age, it is good for every child to be excited and moved by the skilled work of a teacher or senior student—to see the work and spiritual life of an older person as an ideal, a dream to aspire to. Common work hobbies and spiritual interests shared by students and teachers, by younger and older students, their friendship, and their exchange of information and experience, all leave a deep impression on young hearts that remains for the rest of their lives.

The inner character of a child depends primarily on the kind of teacher that guides them on their early path in life.

Children often hear moral teachings and exhortations from their teachers. Children will only take these seriously if they see their teacher as someone who loves their work and is inspired by it. A teacher's example in work is not only what they can do with their hands (though this is of great significance), but the whole tenor of their spiritual life, their inspiration in everything they do with the children to bring them joy.

Children are irresistibly, powerfully influenced by their teacher being as enthused as them by some work they are doing. In such work, the children's hearts open up, and they become the teacher's friends and comrades. During autumn, our Grade 1 teachers create little nurseries where the children grow flowers. In spring, the children are shown how to transplant these flowers and care for them. They plant trees and admire their beauty. The little children are greatly impressed that their teacher knows how to graft a fruit tree, transplant a tree and create a beautiful flower bed. At this stage, work education consists of the teacher and children working together. We work together on the experimental plots and in the workrooms and workshops, constructing model machines and equipment. Working with the children provides the happiest hours of our educational work.

In the middle and senior years, a teacher's greatest influence on their students comes from work connected with their subject. Students love history when their history teacher lovingly researches their local history and explores their locality. They love mathematics when their mathematics teacher enthusiastically solves problems and finds practical applications for theoretical knowledge. They love biology when their biology teacher is in love with nature. A teacher's work consists primarily in the application of their knowledge and skills.

Students sense rather than understand their teacher's breadth of outlook and the depth and comprehensiveness of their knowledge. Students are powerfully influenced when their teacher has a personal interest connected with their subject that takes the children far beyond the bounds of the school curriculum. For example, a language teacher may have a personal interest in creative writing and writes poetry and short stories, not for publication, but for themself. The children gather at the teacher's home and go with them into the forest, the riverbank or the fields. The teacher reads them their poems and stories. The words go straight to the children's hearts because they are creatively inspired. An indelible impression is made on the children not just by the teacher's words but their whole personality. The children want to imitate the teacher, and they try their hand at writing poems and stories themselves.

A great impression is also made on children by the example of older students' work interests and the example of young adults who have recently graduated from school. They look up to a student who is inspired by their work, absorbed in realising a creative idea, and this provides a vital stimulus for self-education in the student community. We manage student work educationally by ensuring no student who is inspired by their work remains an isolated spark. Current students are not the only ones who pass on their skills and love of work to children. We also involve former students working exceptionally well in their fields, whose psychology we know well and who we can trust with the education of children.

Work exercises

IN EVERY WORK EXERCISE, there are both instructional and character-building elements.

The instructional element consists of multiple repetitions of a work process or operation to establish sound work skills. The character-building element can be seen in a heightened sense of moral worth, a student's feelings of pride when they manage to apply their acquired skills in socially useful creative activity.

While a student's successful acquisition of skills may permit us to consider that the instructional aims of a particular form of work have been achieved, the character-building process has not yet been completed. For example, our students master the technique of grafting fruit trees fairly rapidly; it is not hard to teach them this. But for the purpose of character-building, we continue to ask them to graft fruit trees for several years, as it is the persistent application that is of value in building character.

Repetitive exercises in work skills are valuable from several points of view. First, their character-building significance exists in becoming accustomed to performing the same work operations and processes time after time to achieve the social, creative and aesthetic aims of work. There are many types of work in which the same actions are repeated day after day, for many weeks or months. This repetitiveness is not only a necessity that cannot be avoided; it is an important prerequisite for creativity and a person's all-round development in their work. To understand some important law of nature or work principle, sometimes you have to repeat the same work process thousands of times, and frequently it is monotonous and exhausting. We teach our children to become habituated to performing the same task many times to achieve significant social goals. For instance, children select the best grains of wheat by hand so that through repeated sowings of such seeds, we can attain a high protein content in our grain.

Second, we consider the practical skills that our students acquire not just from the viewpoint of the school curriculum but from a broader life perspective. An excellent grade may be the pinnacle of achievement at school, but there is no limit to achievement in life. When a student completely meets the demands of the curriculum, they step over the 'school boundary' and begin to take their bearings from the demands of life. With such students, we educate an aspiration to achieve continuing success in perfecting their skills. The ideal for such children is to become a person with 'golden hands', a wonderful master of the kind that people commonly refer to as an 'artist in their work'. And we try to help every student to perfect skills that can facilitate the flowering of their individuality to the greatest extent.

Third, the more work becomes habitual, the more opportunities there are for acquiring new skills while repeating familiar operations and processes. A student repeats that which is familiar to learn something new. This is especially significant during the senior years when a person is consciously trying to find their path in life.

Learning to select seeds for sowing is not difficult. If student's work is limited to perfecting this simple skill during the middle and senior years, it may become boring. It is a different matter when a skill that has been thoroughly mastered becomes a means of acquiring new skills. This is what happens if students, for example, select seeds (by hand or using a machine) as part of trials aimed at increasing their viability, or if they have set themselves the goal of increasing the plant's drought tolerance or frost tolerance.

Fourth, repeated performance of the same work can have an aesthetic orientation. Cultivating flower seedlings may be monotonous work, but it is also pleasant and brings aesthetic satisfaction. It is important that students strive to achieve aesthetic perfection in work that leaves wide scope for perfecting their skills (such as design and modelling).

Group work projects

IN THE EARLY YEARS, work projects of short duration are the most valuable from an educational point of view. We begin this collective work with projects that clearly demonstrate each student's efforts, such as digging flower beds or planting trees. During such work, children begin to compete with each other, without any encouragement to do so. Each one tries to make the greatest contribution possible to the collective effort. Consequently, we select types of work in which competition arises of its own accord. Inspiring the children with the social, creative and aesthetic aims of the work, we seek to ensure that completing an individual quota is only one of the child's concerns, and not the main one. Everyone completes the expected quota, and no-one considers that meritorious. Children begin to feel they have made a personal contribution to the collective work if they complete the work better than others. If, in consequence of their work experience, this feeling is developed and deepened in every child, the children begin to spontaneously set new goals for their collective work. They want to think of new and better ways to complete their collective work. For example, the children may be constructing a working model that converts heat energy into mechanical energy. Creative competition, the urge to enrich their work in some way, inspires a new idea. Mechanical energy is converted into electrical energy, and electricity flows from an electric motor to several objects. The working model springs into operation, and an electric light bulb lights up.

In the moral education of adolescents and older boys and girls, a major role is played by completing work projects that demand considerable time and effort and extend beyond the interests of their group, and even of the village and the district. Students create things of value that make a significant contribution to the material and technological base of society and improve people's lives. Several schools in our area took responsibility for creating a defensive forest belt around the Kremenchug hydroelectric power station, which was constructed on the Dnieper River. This work played a major role in the ideological education of the senior students. They had a strong sense of the social and national significance of their work. None of them could remain indifferent to the completion of such an important task.

The role of competition

STUDENTS WHO DISPLAY A TALENT for the same type of work compete to see who can complete work assignments the best. They want to outdo their friends in the creativity, skill and aesthetic value of their completed work. For example, in the automation and radio electronics club, every student makes the same item of equipment: an electronic calculator. The criteria for completing the project are the same for everyone, but the work takes on competitive characteristics from the outset. Each student tries to find a unique way of transforming the concept into a design. The students consider how to make the design more complex, how to broaden the scope of the equipment's application and how to make the interaction between the components more complex. Achieving these goals becomes a matter of personal pride for each participant. Creative thought is coloured by moral feelings, and the students are motivated to read scientific literature. The group lives a rich intellectual life. Each one thinks not only about their own work, but the ideas of others, and tries to learn from the experience of their friends.

Once the work is completed, the calculators are put on display for the whole school community to see. The most perfect piece of equipment becomes an exemplar for future competitions. The club members are set a new challenge: to improve on the exemplar and achieve even better results. A new stage of creative work begins. The participants in the new competition include those who have just completed the project and new students also. New ideas are born, new designs are created, and a new winner emerges, but this victory does not signal the end of the competition, just another stage.

Competition develops in the same way in the radio technology club, where students compete to make working models, and in the young plant breeders club, where each autumn we organise a display of the best fruit tree cuttings at one of our work festivals.

The value of this approach to work education is in each student having an opportunity to achieve significant success in an area of creative work that best corresponds to their individual talents, strengths and abilities.

Work routines

A WORK ROUTINE IS an educationally purposeful sequence of various types of work activity that provides the conditions for the all-round development of students. The criteria for assessing a work routine include the combination and rotation of intellectual and physical work, students' free choice of the types of work that best correspond to their individual talents and interests, and the availability of free time as an essential precondition for such choice.

We consider each student's individual talents and interests and foster their interest in, and habituation to, a certain type of physical work that they can engage in on a daily basis. In the early years, this may be looking after flowers or plants more generally, feeding birds, cutting out and carving. In the middle and senior years, it may be caring for trees and grapevines, technical modelling and design, beekeeping, animal husbandry or preparing local fertilisers and using them to enrich the soil. Our goal is to ensure that during childhood, adolescence and young adulthood, every one of our students becomes habituated to the sort of work that millions of industrial and agricultural workers do every day.

From their first days at school, we teach children to understand the beauty of the surrounding world.

Beauty only ennobles a person when they labour to create beauty.

CHAPTER 7

Aesthetic Education

The appreciation of beauty

BEAUTY IS A POTENT SOURCE of moral purity, spiritual wealth and physical perfection. The most important function of aesthetic education is to teach children to find spiritual refinement, kindness and warmth in the beauty of the surrounding world (in nature, art and human relationships) and, on this basis, to affirm the beauty within themselves.

One of the most important preconditions for deep aesthetic appreciation is a person's deep intellectual development. Consequently, aesthetic education includes acquainting children with the broad achievements of world culture and humanity's cultural values.

From their first days at school, we teach children to understand the beauty of the surrounding world, nature and social relationships. Perceiving and appreciating beauty is the foundation and core of aesthetic education, the heart of that aesthetic refinement without which a person's feelings remain insensitive to all that is beautiful. We strive to ensure that in all areas of a child's spiritual life, in their intellectual and physical work, in their creativity, in their social involvements, in their moral and aesthetic relationships, in friendship and in love, the thought never leaves them that beauty must be valued and preserved. We teach the children:

> Humans were singled out from the world of the animals and became gifted beings not only because they made the first tools with their hands, but also because they saw the depth of the dark blue sky, the

twinkling of the stars, the overflowing rosiness of sunset and dawn, the crimson sky before a windy day, the boundless expanse of the steppe, a formation of cranes in the azure heavens, the reflection of the sun in transparent drops of morning dew, grey threads of rain on an overcast autumn day, the tender stalk and pale blue bell of a snowdrop. They saw these things, were filled with wonder, and set out to create new beauty. If you, too, stop in wonder at beauty, beauty will flower in your heart.

People became human when they heard the rustling of leaves and the song of a grasshopper, the babbling of a spring brook and the silver, bell-like notes of a lark in the limitless summer sky, the patter of snowflakes and howling of a blizzard outside their window, the gentle lapping of waves and the majestic silence of the night. They heard these things and, for hundreds and thousands of years have been listening with bated breath to the wonderful music of life. You can also listen to this music and take pleasure in its beauty.

Children's appreciation of beauty is impossible without a teacher's vivid, emotional description of the beauty of the surrounding world. But words about beauty only have an aesthetic effect on a child when they can see that beauty with their own eyes.

Contemplation and listening, the experience of what is seen and heard, is like a first window onto the world of beauty. We consider it very important to teach children to see and feel beauty, and when this capacity awakens in them, to teach them to preserve this spiritual delight and goodness for the rest of their lives.

An important role in our system of aesthetic education is played by journeys into the world of beauty: excursions and hikes, observation and analysis of natural phenomena. We go with children into fields and meadows, to the lake and riverbank, to a shady oak grove or gulley, or to our orchard. Beauty is everywhere; you just need to expose children to it. We go at various times of the year, in autumn, winter, spring and summer. We show them how beauty is born and how it blooms. Children see the play of colours and listen to the music of nature. From the beginning of autumn to the onset of winter, we take children several times to the same location in the forest. Each time they notice new shades in the colours of the leaves. Moreover, these shades vary depending on the time of day we go to the forest—morning, midday or evening—and depending on the weather, how the sun is shining, what wind is blowing, and so on. For this reason, every journey to the world of beauty brings amazing discoveries. The children see that the richest spectrum of colours among the autumn leaves is found on the maples and oaks that grow in the open, not cramped by neighbouring trees. This peculiarity and how nature creates it needs to be explained to the children. 'The sun illuminates these trees from all sides, and colours their leaves,' we tell the children. 'But even when growing among other trees, some oaks do not shed their leaves until winter, and they are richly decorated with all the shades of the rainbow.' The children stand for a long time in wonder, enchanted by this beauty, and it reaches their hearts when the teacher explains it.

During the quiet, sunny days of an 'Indian summer', we direct the children's attention to the wonderful transparency of the air, the depth of the sky and the clearness of the water in the river. Silver strands of spider web float in the air; formations of cranes cry out in the evening sky as they fly to warmer lands; on a cold morning, the first crystals of hoarfrost appear. The children's attention needs to be drawn to all these things. We show them several shades of green in the shoots of winter crops. The green of rye shoots is not the same as the green of wheat shoots. The children take pleasure in admiring the ripening fruit in the orchards and vineyards, the combination of emerald leaves and amber grapes, the play of sunbeams on apples, pears and plums. In the autumn forest, we listen to birdcalls and the quiet rustling of falling leaves, and watch the mirror-like surface of a pond for the sleepy splashes of fish. And children will only pay attention to all these things, watching and listening with care, when a teacher, through their words, reveals to them the beauty of the surrounding world.

Materialistic aesthetics are based on the objective nature of the beautiful. The source of beauty is the world, which is independent of our consciousness. But this world has to be discovered through the senses and through reason. The activity entailed in knowing and affirming beauty involves many facets of our spiritual lives: apprehending the images and phenomena of nature both intellectually and emotionally, working, and forming moral relationships. The educating of feelings is also impossible without activity. Again, the active, intellectual and emotional perception of the surrounding world's beauty takes prime place.

During the first autumn of their school lives, our children spend a whole day—from morning till nightfall—in the forest, fields and meadows. We choose a warm, sunny day. Before dawn, we walk to the outskirts of the village. We stand, enchanted by the beauty of the dawn. The children appear not to have known that the sky could be so beautiful, that it could be flooded by so many shades of colour. One after another, the stars go out, the day is born, and the sun rises. We listen to the birds awakening, the sheep bleating at the field camp, the rumble of tractors in a distant field. We walk to the forest, where we gather fallen leaves. Each child tries to find leaves with the most striking colours. We stop in a clearing and light a campfire. The boys run to fetch water and gather dry brushwood, and the girls cook porridge.

After sunset, we observe the evening sky, watching how the stars light up and the colours change as we observe the fields, hills, meadows and distant burial mounds on the horizon. We listen to the quiet of the night. The cries of nocturnal birds and the amazingly resonant trill of the grasshoppers carry to us on the night air. This day remains in the children's memories for the rest of their lives, and the impression it leaves enhances the emotional impact of other new encounters with the beauty of nature.

This first autumn in the children's school lives convinces us that beauty is the mother of kindness and warmth. Admiring a dog rose bush with its red berries; a shapely apple tree, on which only a few yellowing leaves remain; or contemplating a tomato plant burned by the breath of the first frost, all awaken in children a tender, solicitous attitude to all living things. To them, a plant is a living creature that feels the discomfort and chill of cold winds and hard frosts. Children want to defend plants from the cold.

The beauty of winter is also unique. The children admire the oak grove, sprinkled with snowflakes, the Pushkinesque 'radiance of pink snows, and gloom of late January evenings'[47], and the February blizzards. They listen to the chirping of winter birds. More than once, we walk out at dawn to the edge of the village to greet the winter sun. We admire the play of colours on the snow dunes, listen to the loud drips of melting snow, and study the diamond icicles hanging from the rooves and sparkling in the sunlight.

In spring, the children witness the awakening of life—the first spring flowers, the first buds opening on the trees, the first tender blades of grass, the first butterfly, the first croaking of frogs, the first swallow, the first thunder. All of these things enter the spiritual life of children as a manifestation of the beauty of eternal life. For several days in succession, as the sap rises in the trees, we go with the children to a hill with a view of a valley overgrown with willows, and witness how the grey branches are covered, almost as we watch, with a green film whose shade changes with each day. We admire the pale blue haze on the horizon and the dark blue burial mounds in the steppe.

The orchard flowering is a truly festive occasion for the children. We assemble at the school grounds early in the morning and walk to the orchard, admiring the white, pink and orange blossom that adorns the trees and listening to the humming of the bees. 'You must not sleep in on days like this,' we teach the children. 'You might sleep through this beauty.' And the children rise before the sun, trying not to miss those moments when its first rays illuminate the flowers, covered in drops of dew. With bated breath, each child is filled with admiration. Children will not pay attention to this beauty if it is not shown to them and if they are not told about it.

On summer days, the children admire the beauty of a sea of wheat, its waves undulating in the wind. We show the children how the wheat swells and ripens, how the sunflowers bloom, the tomatoes redden and the melons turn yellow.

The education of aesthetic culture and refined feelings begins with the perception and appreciation of beauty.

Everything of beauty that exists in the surrounding world and is created by people for each other, must touch children's hearts and refine their feelings. With the children, we read and re-read literary works such as Gogol's *Evenings on a Farm Near Dikanka*, Turgenev's *A Sportsman's Sketches*, Korolenko's *The Blind Musician*, Chekhov's

Steppe, Prishvin's short stories, and poems by Pushkin, Lermontov, Nekrasov, Shevchenko, Lesya Ukrainka, Heinrich Heine and Adam Mickiewicz. We attach great significance to reading literary works that extol the beauty of nature.

For such readings, we choose a setting reminiscent of the images of nature described by the author. Language helps us to feel the subtlest manifestations of natural beauty more deeply. The beauty of nature reinforces the emotional colouring of language and allows its music and flavour to touch the hearts and minds of our young people at all stages of their schooling. For each year of study, we have selected works (or extracts from longer works) that we read in natural settings. Such readings educate sensitivity to the emotional colouring of words and enable language to become more deeply embedded in the spiritual lives of children, to become an instrument of thought.

Aesthetic education and holistic development

AESTHETIC EDUCATION, WHICH GIVES a student's cognitive and creative activity direction and develops and satisfies their spiritual needs in their many involvements, encompasses all aspects of the spiritual life of a developing personality. Aesthetic education is inseparably linked with the formation of a person's philosophical outlook—the aesthetic and moral ideals children develop throughout their schooling.

Beauty is a source of moral wealth. In one of his addresses to readers, James Aldridge said that it is impossible to be a cynic and love Dickens at the same time; the two are incompatible. The task facing a school is to ensure beauty becomes a powerful means of moral education in childhood, during the infancy of the nervous system when a child is very sensitive to the emotional colouring of thoughts and images, to the feelings associated with everything they see, absorb and contemplate.

During the nervous system's infancy (up to the age of seven or eight) and later during its adolescence (from the age of seven or eight up to 10 or 11), when the mind, feelings and will continue to develop, it is exceptionally important that a child senses beauty and takes delight in it. It is crucial they admire and are amazed by the wonderful creations of human hands and the miraculous beauty of nature, of that which is not created by human hands. This experience of amazement, wonder and reverence for beauty during the years of childhood and adolescence makes an essential contribution to human relationships, without which the development of true human culture is unthinkable. Human culture is most subtly expressed in the culture of feelings. We must acknowledge that much of what is studied in school will be forgotten with the passage of time, but all things of true cultural value leave a trace in our souls, especially in our feelings and emotions.

From a child's first days at school, we help them develop the idea of a beautiful, socially oriented human being with refined thoughts and feelings. This concept is clothed in flesh and blood, in living examples of highly moral conduct and heroic deeds.

In our concept of human beauty, we give pride of place to spiritual beauty: being true to one's convictions, showing humaneness and strength in the face of evil. From time to time, we redesign our decorative display on 'Human Beauty'. The display includes accounts of peoples' actions, lives and destinies. These accounts clearly demonstrate the oneness of the moral and aesthetic ideal in a way that is comprehensible to children, adolescents and young men and women. We seek to ensure that children not only read about fine, beautiful people but dream about them and discuss their future pathways in life with their friends.

Among the virtues we emphasise as constituting a person's inner spiritual beauty, we champion integrity—acting and living according to one's convictions. We show that acting for the common good is not a sacrifice but a source of true happiness and a rich spiritual life.

All the rich moral heritage created by humanity in the past, and still being created in our own times, must enter the hearts of children, adolescents and young men and women.

In one of our displays on 'Human Beauty', we posted a portrait of the family of Uzbek blacksmith Shaakhmed Shamakhmudov, who adopted 14 orphans from 12 different nationalities during the years of the Great Patriotic War.[48] Our children were amazed to read about his exceptional humaneness and love for others. In the same display, we posted portraits of heroes who repeated the heroic deed of Aleksandr Matrosov.

These examples of human beauty touch children's hearts and make them think about their own actions. Our students' thoughts, feelings and relationships are inspired by moral beauty.

We are always working to encourage our students in the middle and senior school to hold dear the ideal of a person's spiritual beauty, the beauty of their actions and work for the good of society. It is especially important that spiritually beautiful people excite young people's thoughts and prompt them to think about their own futures.

In early adolescence, each student should already have experienced love and admiration for someone who embodies beauty of soul.

We give every adolescent books to read about such people, their lives and destinies. Our young people fall in love not only with famous people whose names are known all over the world, but also with the spiritual beauty of simple people. In their young hearts, they develop the conviction that moral valour and beauty can be achieved by people in their daily working lives, and not just in heroic circumstances.

The connection between aesthetic and moral education is also manifested in an aesthetic appreciation of work. Exploitative oppression over many centuries perverted people's attitudes to the things of value they created. People only felt responsible for their own property, for what they owned. In the moral make-up of contemporary humankind, this feeling of ownership and possession is one of the most burdensome things we have inherited from the past. Overcoming this relic of the past is essential for the integrity of the moral and aesthetic ideal.

We strive to conduct work education and moral education in such a way that students invest all their best spiritual qualities in their work, expressing themselves in the objects they create, so they love the actual process of work and feel the beauty of creativity. That is why we attribute such great significance to individual work interests in work education and seek to ensure every adolescent or young man or woman creates a favourite workspace and puts heart and soul into their work.

Aesthetic education is closely connected with the education of curiosity and inquisitiveness. The urge to involve oneself in investigative, experimental work is at the same time a way of satisfying the aesthetic urge for beautiful, intellectually fulfilling work. If intellectual work is accompanied by intellectual inspiration, if a person senses their power over nature, they will overcome any difficulties and will not be disheartened by failures. Thought is most inspired by feeling when the mind and hands participate simultaneously in work. That is why it is so important that students are inspired by physical work in which the laws of nature are explored and applied.

An aesthetic orientation when teaching the natural sciences plays a major role in affirming materialist convictions. In teaching humanities subjects, it is important to cultivate feelings of a lofty, heroic and dramatic nature. Such feelings are experienced when a student appreciates the beauty of serving one's homeland, the beauty of a heroic act carried out in the service of the nation. Teachers of humanities subjects seek to present a historical event or social phenomenon as a manifestation of the struggle of progressive social forces for a better future for their people, and the students feel the beauty of this struggle. For instance, when describing the selfless defenders of Thermopylae, the heroic actions of Ivan Susanin, the heroic death of Nikolai Gastello, or the selfless labour of millions of women and adolescents during the years of the Great Patriotic War, we reveal those characteristics of people's spiritual worlds that express devotion to one's convictions and active love for one's homeland. The aesthetic orientation of intellectual education involves throwing light on the historical experience of humanity, affirming the present and awakening dreams for the future. It is important to evaluate the past emotionally as well as intellectually. The emotional and aesthetic evaluation of historical experience determines to an enormous extent which 'spirits of the past' (in Marx's words) we summon to our aid, which things from the past we wish to develop and perfect, and which we think should be discarded.

Aesthetic education is also closely connected with physical education. We seek to promote the notion of the harmonious development of the body, of beauty in work, in movement and in overcoming difficulties. At our school's spring Festival of Beauty, we conduct sporting competitions judged on the basis of beauty of movement. Students in the junior classes present the victors with flowers.

It is a school's task to ensure that the appreciation of beauty—developed over many centuries of human culture—is acquired by every human heart and incorporated into a person's aesthetic make-up and their moral relationships with others.

Aesthetic appreciation and aesthetic creativity

IN DEVELOPING AESTHETIC CULTURE, the interrelationship between aesthetic perception and aesthetic creativity is very important. In childhood, adolescence and youth, every student should take delight in beauty in all its manifestations. Only then will they develop a caring and nurturing attitude towards beauty, an urge to return again and again to that object, that source of beauty that has awakened delight and left a trace on their souls.

In aesthetic perception, as a cognitive and emotional process, there is a close connection between concepts, ideas, judgements—thought in general—on the one hand, and feelings and emotions on the other. The success of aesthetic education depends on how deeply a pupil apprehends the nature of the beautiful. But the influence of the beauty of nature, works of art and the surrounding environment on their inner world depends not only on the objective existence of beauty. It also depends on the character of the student's activity and the way beauty is incorporated into their relationships with those around them. Beauty that enters a person's life as a part of their spiritual world awakens aesthetic feelings.

Every person assimilates the beauty of nature, musical melodies and language. But this assimilation depends on their active participation, by which we mean work and creativity, thought and feeling, perceiving, creating and evaluating beauty. When many objects in nature are humanised and provoke an emotional response, when a person sees beauty all around them, they come more and more under the sway of beauty, both human beauty and natural, primordial beauty. When constant communion with nature has become an important part of young people's spiritual lives, they are deeply touched and moved by descriptions of nature in literary works and depictions of natural scenes in paintings.

We try to ensure that every one of our pupils, from an early age, cherishes and cares for a little tree, rose bush, flowers, birds and all things living and beautiful. Such care must become habitual. That is why every student looks after a plant in their class nook of beauty. Each one has their nesting box for starlings or their tree hollow with a nest of tits; each protects a swallow's nest. This area of aesthetic creativity is deeply personal in nature. Without individual, personal feelings, there can be no aesthetic culture.

Aesthetic creativity connected with the appreciation of literature and art is also highly significant.

The aesthetic perception of works of literature, music and visual arts also requires active participation. This participation consists of aesthetic evaluation, a deep appreciation of those attributes inherent in the object of perception itself. We try to ensure that children appreciate the beauty of the language in a work of literature from an early age, that they are excited by a description of nature and the depiction of the spiritual worlds of characters. A student who has experienced the beauty of language many times in childhood strives to express their innermost thoughts in words. Many years of experience have convinced us that the students who try their hand at literature in adolescence and youth, writing poems, short stories and essays, are the ones upon whom the beauty of language in the works of great writers has left a deep impression in childhood.

Children spend some of their free time listening to the expressive reading of works of literature. In the junior classes, special lessons are devoted to reading favourite works. At these lessons, each one reads the works they like best: poems, extracts from short stories and novellas. The teacher also reads their favourite work. Of course, a single lesson is not long enough, so sometimes we dedicate a whole morning to reading. Then the morning is devoted to one major work.

In the middle and senior years, students read extracts from classical and modern literary works, both national and international.

Experience has shown us that appreciating the beauty of paintings (both originals and reproductions) arouses children's aspiration to express their thoughts and feelings, their attitude to the surrounding world, in colour, line and the combination of various shades. We support and develop this aspiration. The children have albums for drawing, and many children not only draw various objects but also seek to express their feelings.

From time to time our school organises children's art exhibitions. In 1964/65, one exhibition of children's drawings from Grades 1–4 was devoted to the theme, 'Our memories of the summer holidays', another to 'Our orchard and vineyard', a third to 'Golden autumn has arrived', a fourth to 'Winter' and a fifth to 'Dreams of space flight'.

Mikhail Sholokhov's story, *The Fate of a Man*, made a tremendous impression on our senior students. Before reading it, they had already learned about a young man who had performed a heroic deed in our village during the fascist occupation.

After one of their punitive expeditions, the fascists gathered the population of our village and triumphantly announced that all the partisans had been killed. The last of them, taken alive, would confirm this. Indeed, there was a traitor prepared to say what the enemy wanted. Hundreds of village folk stood there, crushed by this news. Then, a young man emerged from the crowd, approached the German officers and requested permission to say a few words to the villagers. They gave permission. The young man said, 'Don't believe the fascists. I am a partisan. There are thousands of us. We are still fighting and will keep fighting. I came here to certain death, but my death is a necessary sacrifice. You must believe that as long as our people live, those who fight for our people, the partisans, are also alive.'

The stunned fascists took a while to come to their senses. The young man was seized and shot on the spot. But his words breathed new strength into those to whom they were addressed.

For our senior students, the picture portrayed by Sholokhov shed new light on the heroic deed of an unknown youth that had taken place in our village a quarter of a century earlier.

Our young Grade 3 students often cry when the teacher reads them *Yanko the Musician*, a story by Polish writer Henryk Sienkiewicz. It is as if they are directly witnessing the events the author describes. The grief he writes of becomes their grief. They realise they have often not paid attention to the small events of their daily lives. They imagine themselves taking the place of the boy in the story and try to decide what they would have done. Of course, Soviet children cannot imagine the living conditions in a society long gone. They mentally transfer their moral and aesthetic criteria into that terrible world. They speak of the exploitative landowner with indignation. Each one declares that they and their friends would definitely punish the cruel landowner.

Lyric poetry particularly enriches our vision of the world. For our senior students, reading Pushkin's poem 'Whether I Walk the Noisy Streets' always conjures up a picture of eternal, immortal life and prompts reflection about the succession of the generations. The students are sad at the thought that human beings are mortal, that young people become old and decrepit, but this sadness casts into even greater relief the beauty of life and its joys. The young men and women experience an urge to live more fully, to know more deeply everything that is connected to creation, the immortal life of nature and the eternal human aspiration for happiness. The poetic words awaken noble impulses of the soul. On one occasion, after a reading of this poem, one of the young men said, 'Let's plant an oak that will live for a thousand years'. We planted an acorn from which a young oak grew, and now it is ten years old. It has barely reached the height of a human being, but we already refer to it as 'the thousand-year oak'. Thus, from generation to generation, our school community will hand on the baton and dream of the immortality of eternal life.

We attach great significance to the viewing of paintings. We do this during reading lessons in the junior classes and during literature lessons in the middle and senior years. Sometimes the same painting is studied several times during the junior, middle and senior years. The first viewing is usually not accompanied by detailed explanations of the painting. The students usually view the painting at the conclusion of a discussion about nature or society, or sometimes after direct contact with nature.

For example, while out walking with the children, we may stop to rest in a sunny clearing in the middle of a birch grove. The children cannot help feeling the beauty of the white trunks against the deep green background and the play of light and shade. The graceful trees, the blue sky, the bright sunshine, the river sparkling in the distance, the green grass, the humming of the bees: all of these are appreciated as personified objects. After returning to the classroom, we show the children a reproduction of Levitan's *Birch Grove*, which makes a very strong impression on the children, even though this viewing is not accompanied by any commentary. It is as if the children discover themselves in the artist's masterpiece. It reawakens the feelings they have just experienced when communing with nature, but now these feelings arise as a memory of the past, a desire to reconnect with nature again and again, to feel and experience its beauty.

For students in the middle and senior years, we conduct evening and morning sessions devoted to particular paintings. After briefly describing the life and work of the artist, we concentrate mainly on the images in the painting, trying to convey its content in vivid, expressive language and to explain the brushwork that characterises the artist's work.

To explain the beauty of a painting to students, the teachers must prepare and constantly improve their knowledge in this area of aesthetic culture. Each of our teachers keeps adding to their personal album of reproductions of pictures by eminent artists. Our staff conduct activities devoted to the visual arts. Over a number of years, we have developed a program for discussing paintings. This program incorporates discussions of a single painting (and sometimes two or three paintings) by an eminent artist: Russian, Soviet or international. Some discussions are devoted to architecture or sculpture.

Music is a very powerful means of aesthetic education. Music is the language of feeling and emotion and can express the subtlest variations in mood. Sensitivity to the language of music and the ability to understand it depend on the extent to which folk music and composers' works have been appreciated in childhood and adolescence. At least half the time set aside for singing and music is spent listening to musical compositions. We teach children to understand a musical melody, then progress to listening to simple pieces. Each piece is prefaced by a discussion, which helps the children form some conception of the image or emotion that is conveyed using specific musical techniques.

Here, as when developing an appreciation of a painting, we attach great significance to nature. We teach children to listen to the music of nature. The children may gather on a quiet summer evening in the orchard or by the bank of a pond. The sun sets, and with each minute, we observe the changing colours of the trees, hills and limitless fields in the distance, with their tall Scythian burial mounds. The children observe the surrounding world and listen to the sounds. It turns out that the quietest of summer evenings is filled with a multitude of sounds. Immediately after listening to the music of nature, the children listen to a recording of an appropriate folk song or composition. The children want to listen to these melodies that convey the beauty of a summer evening again and again. When this listening to a musical work is repeated, emotional memory is developed, and the children acquire a deeper sensitivity to the beauty of the melodies. Gradually children begin to sense the feelings, impressions, mood and experiences expressed in a melody. In this way, even before they become familiar with music terminology, children master a language of images, which is very important for musical education and for the formation and development of feelings more generally. The more comprehensible and accessible this language is for a child at an early age, the greater the role of listening to music in the middle and senior years.

The ability to listen to and appreciate music is one of the elementary marks of aesthetic culture, and a complete education is inconceivable without it. Music's domain begins where speech ends. That which it is impossible to express to another person in words may be expressed with a musical melody because music directly conveys moods and feelings. Music can also be an indispensable means for making an impression upon young people. We try to structure our musical education so that students are exposed to a world of great ideas expressed in music: the idea of brotherhood and friendship between people (Beethoven's ninth symphony), the idea of humanity's struggle against merciless fate (Tchaikovsky's sixth symphony), and the battle of the forces of progress and light against the dark forces of fascism (Shostakovich's seventh symphony). We lead children to an understanding of these ideas gradually. At first, they listen to simple musical works that express wonder at beauty, goodness and humanity, and then they progress to more complex works.

We conduct musical evenings for students in the junior, middle and senior years, where the main activity is listening to music. Our musical education program includes listening to vocal, instrumental, symphonic and operatic works (overtures and arias) by leading Russian, Soviet and international composers.

Each musical evening represents the next step in the students' musical education. To understand music, it is necessary to explain the musical modes of expressing thought and feeling. We begin with an elementary explanation of musical association and analogy, showing how composers borrow sounds from the surrounding world. Gradually we progress to an analysis of the ideas behind a musical work.

Taking pleasure in beauty stimulates students' own creativity. This is particularly noticeable in students' creative writing. The more deeply a student has experienced the beauty reflected in poetry, the stronger their urge to express their own thoughts and feelings in words. In this case, perception and creativity are both interdependent and often combined in a single process of aesthetic evaluation. The creativity begins during the reading of a poetic work. A characteristic feature of students' attempts at literary composition, especially poetry, is that thoughts are conveyed with the aid of the concrete, sensory images associated with the first exposure to a poem or musical work.

During the past ten years, I have read over 100 student poems expressing sadness at the prospect of parting with our school and with friends. The young men and women express their feelings in images such as a distant burial mound, shrouded in mist, that becomes ever more distant and barely perceptible; a withering (or, on the contrary, developing) tree on the bank of a pond (or river), illuminated by bright rays of sunlight; a cloud in an endless blue sky; the rising (or setting) of the sun; the sky at sunset or dawn; the distant smoke of a locomotive (or steamship). The young authors associate such images with the feelings of sadness brought on by the thought of parting.

The deeper and more refined their aesthetic appreciation, the more a student is interested in their personal, spiritual world. Many students keep diaries. Notes in a diary are clear evidence of an urge to be creative. This urge should be developed. The ability to use words creatively—to express one's thoughts, feelings and inner experiences in an artistic image—is necessary not just for a writer but for any cultured person. Developing this ability leads to a higher level of aesthetic and general culture, more refined feelings, deeper emotions and a greater ability to appreciate new artistic values. That is why we attach such great significance to creative writing.

Creative writing does not just develop language; it refines feelings. This work begins with a child's communion with nature. During our journeys to the world of beauty, we reveal to children the wealth of feelings, emotions and thoughts that people have invested in language and carefully handed down from generation to generation. When the children take delight in the beauty of the dawn, we are showing them the emotional colouring of the word 'dawn'. When they admire the twinkling of the stars, we reveal to them the beauty of the word 'twinkle'. On quiet summer evenings, we hold discussions in natural surroundings, developing an appreciation of the words 'sunset', 'dusk', 'stillness', 'whispering grass' and 'moonlight'. In the lap of nature, we read immortal works of Russian and world poetry: poems and poetic prose dedicated to nature that reflects the inner world of a human being.

The urge to be creative in the fields of visual arts and music also depends on aesthetic appreciation. In developing a sense of the beauty of nature, we encourage children to express their feelings in colour and line. Creativity begins when a child expresses their feelings while drawing a forest, mountains, the steppe or a river. Such creativity enriches a child's spiritual life. On excursions and hikes, our children take albums and pencils. When they are particularly struck by the beauty of nature, they draw. Some drawing lessons in the junior and middle years are devoted to drawings on themes chosen by the students: the children draw whatever has left a deep impression on their souls.

A sign of a person's aesthetic and general culture is their ability to see music as a means of expressing their feelings and emotions. Not everyone can create new musical compositions, but everyone can understand the language of music and use musical treasures in communicating with others. We try to ensure that everyone considers a musical instrument essential, and everyone can play some instrument. Playing the bayan is the most common form of musical activity in our village. Many of our students have a library of sheet music and spend some of their leisure time playing the bayan. Students can also go to the music room and listen to works recorded on tape during their free time.

The higher the level of aesthetic development common to all students, the greater the opportunities for developing the talents of those with particular artistic abilities.

The role of the environment and of work

WE TRY TO ENSURE THAT children accumulate many impressions of an aesthetic nature and that this leads to concern for the aesthetic environment. Everything a child sees when they enter our school, everything they come in contact with, is beautiful. The overall view of the school, luxuriating in greenery, is beautiful. The green grapevines with their amber grapes are beautiful. The roses growing along the path between the buildings are beautiful. At all seasons of the year, the crowns of the trees in the school grounds are beautiful. The porch of the main entrance to the school, framed by wild grapevines, is beautiful.

The aesthetic value of the things that surround us does not correspond to their monetary cost. We try to ensure everything that surrounds the children is priceless, in aesthetic terms, that a great deal of work, care and feeling has been invested in it.

Aesthetic perception of the surrounding environment is deeply subjective, depending on active involvement in the aesthetic assimilation of reality. For a child, a simple plant in a clay pot that they have grown themselves from a cutting is of incomparable value. A china vase bought in a shop pales in comparison with a clay vase made with one's own hands. This should not be understood as a denigration of the artistic value of artefacts created by masters: the role of such artefacts in education is enormous. We are merely citing these examples to emphasise the value of work in the aesthetic education of students.

The aesthetic impression created by the environment is achieved by harmony between what is created by nature and what is created by human hands—a harmony that awakens feelings of joy. We try to ensure that children can see the beauty of nature everywhere in the school grounds, which becomes even more beautiful because they (the children) are caring for it.

The objects surrounding a child most effectively create a harmonious expression of beauty when individual objects do not cry out for attention, when one seems not to notice them. For example, if one places several large flowers in a broad, well-lit window looking out on an orchard, the harmony will be destroyed. The flowers will extinguish the aesthetic qualities of the other objects—of the orchard itself. However, if a single cutting is placed in the window, harmonious in form with the trees in the orchard and the time of year (harmony may also consist in contrast), then the cutting, the orchard and the expanses of the distant fields will all be perceived quite differently.

Beauty only ennobles a person when they labour to create beauty. We seek to ensure that a person labours not just for their daily bread but also for joy. We teach the children to create beauty. We are happy for a chrysanthemum to bloom next to an ear of wheat, a rose next to sunflowers, a lilac bush next to potatoes. During the first autumn of their school lives, every class plants a rose bush and cares for it. Every class of little children has their chrysanthemums. When cold weather arrives, the children transplant flowers to the greenhouse or their nature corner. In the places of beauty that each class creates in the school grounds are roses, lilacs, grapes and pears. A concern for beauty is experienced as a concern for a tender, delicate, defenceless being that would perish if people did not care for it.

Children's work involves the creation of necessary things, but it is also a form of aesthetic creativity. The unity of these processes is what is behind the ennobling power of work and altruism. This unity also safeguards against a vile relic of the past: possessiveness. When we prioritise aesthetic creativity in socially useful work, we begin to appreciate the objects around us from an aesthetic point of view and assign moral worth to the people who have created them. Many types of children's work are creative in essence and akin to handicrafts (fretwork, pokerwork, moulding, embroidery etc.). The longer these forms of work are part of a person's life, the more vibrantly the aesthetic element will be expressed in all their work activity.

Aesthetic evaluation of work leads to greater respect for the moral value of a worker's contribution. Along with the technological demands of work in our experimental plots, greenhouse, workshops and fields, we also expect students to give attention to beauty. Any work assigned to students has an aesthetic significance (connected with developing a sense of beauty) in addition to any economic significance.

The aesthetic environment includes a sense of air, light, space and perspective. Everything on the walls of our classrooms has the effect of moving the walls outwards, filling the room with the expanses of fields, forests and meadows. When the students see a picture showing an orchard in autumn, it reminds them of the real orchard on the other side of the wall.

The school grounds provide a setting for our students' childhood, adolescence and youth. Everything here develops an aesthetic appreciation of nature and work. The green lawn in the courtyard leads to the beehives, which bring to mind constant, meticulous work. Whatever part of the grounds a student may find themselves in, they can see fruit trees: apples, pears, cherries, plums, apricots. They are beautiful throughout the year: when they bloom, in summer, and in deep autumn, first with their fruit, and then with their many-coloured foliage, which blazes against the autumn sky. The beauty of their branches in winter is unique, covered in snow and frost. The orchard is an expression of both natural beauty and the beauty created by human hands.

In the centre of the school grounds, next to our sports area, are our grapevines. Their external appearance is attractive due to the natural beauty of the vigorous vines, winding along their trellises, and bunches of fruit (visible for three months of the year). Their beauty is enhanced because of the work that has gone into them. The children create this beauty and live and breathe it. During their first autumn at the school, they plant cuttings and then take care of them. Grapevines clad the walls of the rabbit farm, the green laboratory and the toilets. Near the beehives are nectar-bearing plants. From early spring to late autumn, you can hear the sound of the 'bees' music' (in the children's words). The children come here with their teachers on quiet mornings and evenings to listen to the music of nature. This is where they learn to appreciate musical melodies.

In the school grounds are several green bowers of wild grapevines.

The dense foliage creates a living roof, similar to a sunshade. During spring, summer and autumn, nature changes the colouring of this foliage five times. This play of colours delights the students and provides an object for observation. The students observe the same play of colours on the vines that clad the green laboratory.

The environments in the experimental plots, greenhouses and nature rooms all have an aesthetic aspect. Every class in the junior and middle years has their own plot for growing grains and other crops. The crops are chosen so that each class plot is green until late autumn. Autumn flowers bloom until the frosts arrive. Sometimes they peep out from under the first carpet of snow. In the greenhouse, flowers bloom all winter: chrysanthemums, snowdrops and lilies. Among our experimental plots are several nursery beds where we produce fruit trees for planting. The beauty created here is distributed widely and helps beautify the whole village.

We give considerable attention to creating an aesthetic environment in the classrooms, workrooms and workshops. Each class group strives to ensure their room is distinguished by something special. The uniqueness of the aesthetic environment is created by a plant placed next to the blackboard. It may be a lemon tree in one class, a rose in another, a little pine tree in a third. This plant sets the tone for the aesthetic ambience of the whole room. On one of the windowsills, a small flower or piece of greenery reminds us of the school grounds' beauty. The important thing here is not the quantity of greenery (windows are for light) but the striking shape of the stem and leaves silhouetted against the sky.

In every class, there are reproductions of paintings. They are changed depending on various circumstances (the season, the content of class discussions, etc.). Some classes have a picture gallery: a series of reproductions the literature teacher uses to conduct discussions about art. On the teacher's desk is a clay vase into which the pupil on duty each day places a fresh flower or twig from a decorative plant (in spring and autumn, from the experimental plots, in winter, from the greenhouse). This flower not only corresponds to the season, it also expresses the class's mood and the nature of their interests at that time. In the greenhouse, green laboratory and nature room, we cultivate flowers for the classrooms and create a beautiful display. We assign flowers a significant role in aesthetic refinement.

A significant role in aesthetic education is also played by dress, and the external appearance of students and teachers in general. Here the most important thing is simplicity and elegance. We are against having a single uniform for all pupils. (The current uniform is no good at all, especially for the girls. It is hideous, and it is no wonder the young Pioneers in their newspaper recently requested the Ministry of Education give them a new form of dress.) We encourage clothing that emphasises and draws attention to each individual child's aesthetic features. We adhere to those essential requirements of clothing that develop aesthetic appreciation. This is primarily that the colour of the material and cut of the garment should suit the student's individual features. Clothing should be simple, elegant, not too eye-catching, not revealing too much of the human body, but suggesting its beauty (when necessary, softening any shortcomings in physical development). A loud clash of fabrics should be avoided. We recommend soft colours, with half-tones predominating. The main expectations regarding the cut of clothing are that it should be fluid, with soft lines and no sharp angles or tightness. Similar aesthetic recommendations apply to hairstyles. It should not be a requirement that boys' hair is cut with clippers. Our expectations for haircuts are that they are modest, simple, elegant and suit the person's individual features. Our class coordinators and teachers conduct discussions with the older students explaining how to meet these expectations and the meaning of true elegance. We draw particular attention to the fact that the crowning feature of beauty is a correspondence between outer elegance and inner refinement, between outer modesty and inner worth. The educational work we have conducted in this area has produced significant results. Our students, including our girls, have highly developed aesthetic tastes. Each girl sews her own dresses. A significant place is occupied by Ukrainian national dress, which is successfully combined with elements of modern dress.

* * *

We thus conclude our account of how we teach and educate the young people who enter the walls of our school. Our experimental educational work is not something frozen and immutable, repeated from year to year without any change. We are constantly enriching it with new creative experience, painstakingly selecting, bit by bit, the most valuable aspects of someone's initiatives over the past year.

We hope that staff at other schools who wish to apply our experience will not mechanically copy its details. The creative application of others' experiences involves developing educational ideas and forming one's own educational convictions. This is the only way we can improve the work of our secondary schools so they can meet the challenges presented by life.

APPENDICES

Appendix 1
Treasures of Russian and World Literature Recommended for Students

Literature of Russia and the nations of the USSR:

The Tale of Igor's Campaign; *The Knight in a Panther's Skin* (Rustaveli); *Daredevils of Sassoun* (Armenian epic); Ukrainian epic poems; *Kalevipoeg* (Estonian epic); *The Minor* (Fonvizin); *A Journey from St. Petersburg to Moscow* (Radishchev); *Svetlana* (Zhukovsky); *Woe from Wit* (Griboyedov); *Eugene Onegin*, *The Bronze Horseman*, *Poltava*, *Ruslan and Lyudmila*, *Lyrical Poems* (Pushkin); *A Hero of Our Time* (Lermontov); *Songs* (Koltsov); *Evenings on a Farm Near Dikanka*, *Mirgorod*, *Dead Souls*, *St. Petersburg Tales* (Gogol); *Letter to Gogol* (Belinsky); *Fathers and Sons*, *Rudin*, *A Nest of the Gentry*, *Torrents of Spring*, *A Sportsman's Sketches* (Turgenev); *Who is to Blame?* (Herzen); *Who is Happy in Russia?*, *The Railway*, *Russian Women*, *Lyrical Poems* (Nekrasov); *What is to be Done?* (Chernyshevsky); *What is Oblomovism?* (Dobrolyubov); *The Golovlev Family*, *The History of a Town* (Saltykov-Shchedrin); *The Storm* (A.N. Ostrovsky); *Lyrical Poems* (Tyutchev); *Crime and Punishment* (Dostoevsky); *War and Peace*, *Anna Karenina*, *Resurrection*, *The Death of Ivan Ilyich* (Tolstoy); *Kobzar* (Shevchenko); *The Cherry Orchard*, *The Three Sisters*, *Uncle Vanya*, *The Steppe*, *In the Ravine*, *Ward No. 6* (Chekhov); *The Blind Musician*, *The Wood Murmurs* (Korolenko); *Layla and Majnun* (Nizami); *Farhad and Shirin* (Nava'i); *Borislav is Laughing* (Franko); *Blow, Wind!* (Rainis); *Wandering Stars* (Sholem Aleichem); *Forest Song* (Lesya Ukrainka); *Fata Morgana* (Kotsiubynsky); *The Poor Man* (Ayni); *The Lower Depths*, *Mother*, *My Childhood*, *My Apprenticeship*, *My Universities*, *The Old Lady Izergil* (Gorky); poems by Aleksandr Blok; poems by Sergei Yesenin; *Moloch*, *The Duel* (Kuprin); *Songs* (Musa Cälil); *And Quiet*

Flows the Don, Virgin Soil Upturned, The Fate of a Man (Sholokhov); *How the Steel was Tempered* (N. Ostrovsky); *The Young Guard* (Fadeyev); *The Road to Calvary, Aelita* (Aleksei Tolstoy); *The Fisherman's Son* (Lācis); *The Spring of Light* (Prishvin); *The Russian Forest* (Leonov); *Vladimir Ilyich Lenin, All right!* (Mayakovsky); poems by Hovhannes Tumanyan; *The Riders* (Yanovs'kyi); *The Flagbearers* (Honchar); *The Death of the Squadron* (Korniychuk); *At the Crossroads* (Yakub Kolas); *A Pedagogical Poem* (Makarenko); *Tsushima* (Novikov-Priboi); *Sevastopol Labours* (Sergeyev-Tsensky); *The Story of a Real Man* (Boris Polevoi); poems by Suleyman Stalsky; poems by Jambul Jabaev; poems by Galaktion Tabidze; *Distant Countries, The Blue Cup, The Drummer's Fate* (Gaidar); *The Story of My Childhood* (Gladkov); *An Unusual Summer* (Fedin); *The Living and the Dead* (Simonov); *Plutonia* (Obruchev); *The Andromeda Nebula* (Yefremov); *Jump into the Void* (Belyaev); *Argonauts of the Universe* (Vladko); *Daytime Stars* (Berggolts); *Silence* (Bondarev); *Cruelty* (Nilin); *Vladimir Villages* (Soloukhin); *Not to their Liking* (Tendryakov); *Tanya* (Arbuzov); *The Ice Book* (Smuul); *Zoya* (Aliger); *Dark Blue Hussars* (Aseyev); *Blood and Ash* (Marcinkevičius); *Man* (Mieželaitis).

World literature:

The Iliad, The Odyssey (Homer); *Prometheus Bound* (Aeschylus); *Oedipus Rex, Antigone* (Sophocles); *Medea* (Euripides); *The Knights* (Aristophanes); *The Ramayana* (Indian epic); *The Song of Roland* (French epic); *The Song of the Nibelungs* (Old German epic); *Kalevala* (Finnish epic); *Edda* (Icelandic epic); Irish sagas; *Shahnameh* (Ferdowsi); *The Divine Comedy* (Dante); *The Romance of Tristan and Iseult* (Bédier); *Gargantua and Pantagruel* (Rabelais); *Don Quixote* (Cervantes); *King Lear, Hamlet, Othello, Romeo and Juliet* (Shakespeare); *Sonnets* (Petrarch); *Emilia Galotti* (Lessing); *Fuenteovejuna* (Lope de Vega); *Le Cid* (Corneille); fables of La Fontaine; *Tartuffe, The Miser, The Bourgeois Gentleman* (Molière); *Paradise Lost, Paradise Regained* (Milton); *Robinson Crusoe* (Defoe); *Gulliver's Travels* (Swift); *Faust, The Sorrows of Young Werther* (Goethe); *The Robbers, Intrigue and Love, William Tell, Wallenstein* (Schiller); *The Sin of M. Antoine* (George Sand); *Songs* (de Béranger); *Ivanhoe, Quentin Durward* (Walter Scott); *Childe Harold's Pilgrimage, The Prisoner of Chillon, Don Juan* (Byron); *Les Misérables, The Hunchback of Notre-Dame, The Man Who Laughs, Toilers of the Sea* (Hugo); *The Red and the Black, The Charterhouse of Parma* (Stendhal); poems by Freiligrath; poems by Weerth; *Gobseck, Father Goriot, The Magic Skin, Eugénie Grandet* (Balzac); *The Pickwick Papers, Oliver Twist, David Copperfield* (Dickens); *Vanity Fair* (Thackeray); *Pan Tadeusz* (Mickiewicz); *Under the Yoke* (Vazov); *Book of Songs, Germany* (Heine); *Brand, The Doll's House, Peer Gynt* (Ibsen); *The Blue Bird* (Maeterlinck); *John the Valiant* (Petőfi); *The Legend of Thyl Ulenspiegel and Lamme Goedzak* (Charles De Coster); *Ancient Bohemian Legends* (Jirásek); *Emperor and Proletarian* (Eminescu); *Sentimental Education, Madame Bovary* (Flaubert); *The Wandering Jew* (Eugène Sue); *Pillar of Fire* (Kinoshita Naoe); *Germinal, L' Assommoir* (Zola); *A Life, Bel Ami* [Dear friend], *Dumpling* (Maupassant); *Tartarin of Tarascon* (Daudet); *Nobody's Boy* (Hector Malot); *The Adventures of Tom Sawyer* (Mark Twain); Hans Anderson's fairy tales; *Uncle Tom's Cabin* (Beecher Stowe); poems by Walt Whitman; *The Deerslayer, The Pathfinder, The Last of the Mohicans, The Pioneers, The Prairie* (Cooper); *The Headless Horseman, The Boy Tar* (Mayne Reid); *A Captain at Fifteen, Twenty Thousand Leagues Under the Sea, Captain Grant's Children* (Jules Verne); *Treasure Island* (Stevenson); *Pan, Victoria* (Knut Hamsun); *The War of the Worlds* (Wells); fairy tales by Charles Perrault; *Children's and Household Tales* (brothers Grimm); *Fairy Tales* (Wilhelm Hauff); fairy tales by E.T.A. Hoffmann; *The Wreck* (Rabindranath Tagore); *The True Story of Ah Q* (Lu Xun); *The Gadfly* (Voynich); *The Song of Hiawatha* (Longfellow); *An American Tragedy* (Dreiser); *The Loyal Subject* (Heinrich Mann); *Penguin Island* (Anatole France); *The Buddenbrooks* (Thomas Mann); *The Forsyte Saga* (Galsworthy); *Morten the Red, Ditte, Child of Man* (Nexø); *Martin Eden, An Odyssey of the North* (Jack London); *Jean-Christophe, Colas Breugnon* (Rolland); *Under Fire* (Barbusse); *The Good Soldier Švejk* (Hašek); *The Mother, War with the Salamanders* (Čapek); *Playing with Fire* (Pujmanová); *The Oppermanns, The Jew of Rome, The Judean War* (Feuchtwanger); *The Seventh Cross, The Dead Stay Young* (Anna Seghers); *Notes from the Gallows* (Fučík); *The Old Man and the Sea* (Hemingway); *Spartacus*

(Giovagnoli); *Ballad to Him Who Sings While being Tortured [Gabriel Péri]* (Louis Aragon); poems by Pablo Neruda; poems by Nicolás Guillén; poems by Johannes Becher; *A Heart Entrusted to Storms* (Khosro Roozbeh); *The Adventures of Werner Holt* (Noll); poems by Julian Tuwim; *The Germans* (Leon Kruczkowski); *The Good Person of Szechwan* (Bertolt Brecht); *Three Comrades* (Remarque); *Wind, Sand and Stars* (Saint-Exupéry); *Georgia Boy* (Caldwell); *The Winter of Our Discontent* (Steinbeck); *Catcher in the Rye* (Salinger).

Appendix 2
Composition Topics Set in Grades 1–10

Grade 1. The school orchard. The flowers next to the school. When the sun goes behind a cloud. Our walk to the forest. Sunset. Who lives in our pond? The first spring flower. How pigeons, swallows and sparrows fly. Dusk. Fish in the aquarium.

Grade 2. Summer and autumn. Cranes in the blue sky. The starlings fly south. The hedgehog prepares for winter. The swallow makes a nest. How we attract birds. When the sun warms us up on a winter's day. In the forest there is even life under the snow. The watermelons have ripened. Our grapevine. How grain becomes bread. The sunset before a windy day. The sunset before a clear day. A gentle breeze. A cold wind. The gentle spring sun. The hot summer sun.

Grade 3. How wheat forms ears. The buckwheat is in flower. Sunrise. Autumn in the orchard. The bees at work. Field and meadow (a comparison). Birds are our friends. Spring flowers. Summer flowers. Autumn flowers. A world of flowers in the middle of winter (in the greenhouse). The first snow. Evening dusk. Snowflakes are drifting in the air. A woodpecker in the oak tree. A rainbow. When the apple trees flower. Our peach grove. Birds return from warmer climes. My puppy. My kitten. My aquarium. A composition inspired by Shevandronova's painting *In a Rural Library*. Spring rain. The blue sky on a clear day, and the cloudy sky before rain.

Grade 4. The pond and the river (a comparison). When autumn begins. A sunny clearing in the forest. Outside a cold wind is blowing. The first ice on the pond. Leaves are falling from the trees. A fledgling fell from its nest (recollections of our summer holiday). A blizzard begins. Snowdrifts at sunrise. 'Fear has big eyes', 'As you sow, so shall you reap' (compositions inspired by proverbs). If I became invisible… (fantasy). What is truth? If I had a magic wand… (fantasy). At night. A family of sparrows. Where does hoarfrost fall from? The most beautiful thing and the ugliest thing. Phenomenon, cause and effect (an exercise in logic). High water in spring. Where are the storks flying? Evening falls. My village. A composition inspired by Vasnetsov's painting *Bogatyrs*. The sort of person I want to become.

Grade 5. Who is punished in the story *Morozko*, and for what? How does Pushkin condemn evil and injustice in *The Tale of the Dead Princess*? A summer morning (after reading Nikitin's poem 'Morning'). What misfortune did the landowner's wife bring upon Gerasim in Turgenev's story *Mumu*? Dawn and sunset. Autumn rain outside the window. The trees are covered in hoarfrost. What did the first rays of the sun illuminate? A crimson sunset. Cutting hay (recollections of the summer holidays). The first autumn frost. Birds fly away to warmer climes. Evening in the forest. Storks. Phenomenon, cause and effect (an exercise in logic). What people live for. The world seen through a drop of water. The world seen through a piece of blue glass. A composition inspired by Levitan's painting *March*. A composition inspired by Savrasov's painting *The Rooks have Returned*. 'A friend in need is a friend indeed' (composition inspired by a proverb). A letter to a child my age overseas (after reading an article or report in a newspaper). May the sky always be clear: may there never be war.

Grade 6. Who does the legendary bogatyr Ilya Muromets defend, and who does he fight? What I find attractive about Dubrovsky (after reading Pushkin's story *Dubrovksy*). Ostap, a true son of his homeland, and the traitor Andrei (after reading Gogol's *Taras Bulba*). 'A lazybones thinks the sun rises too early', 'No water flows under a motionless stone' (composition inspired by proverbs). The sort of person whose example I would like to follow (my ideal). What shades of colour do fallen leaves take on? How the steppe changes in late autumn. The forest in winter. 'There is in early autumn a short but wondrous time...' (Tyutchev). Spring torrents. A lilac grove. Composition inspired by Kuindzhi's painting *Ukrainian Night*. Composition inspired by Perov's painting *Troika*. Composition inspired by Pryanishnikov's painting *Children Fishing*. A night during the hay cutting season. Composition inspired by Baksheyev's painting *Blue Spring*. Is it possible to display strength and courage during times of peace? What is dearer to a person than anything else in life? Who I consider to be the most evil person. Dreams of space flight. The children of workers all over the world are my friends.

Grade 7. How Grinev understood duty and honour, and how we understand them (after reading Pushkin's *The Captain's Daughter*). How Gogol depicts the dull-wittedness, ignorance, bribe-taking and obsequiousness of officials in the play *The Government Inspector*. How Nekrasov depicts the fate of the peasants Prokol and Daria in the poem 'Red-Nosed Frost'. Are there still chameleons today? (after reading Chekhov's story *Chameleon*). The colonel at the ball and after the ball (from Tolstoy's story *After the Ball*). How the apples ripen. An Indian summer. A winter's day in the forest. The steppe in autumn. We reach a city on the Dnieper at night. The first frosts. 'Now the north, driving the clouds before it, breathes and howls, and now winter herself arrives in all her beauty' (Pushkin). Sunset on a winter's day. Composition inspired by Venetsianov's painting *Peasant Girl with Cornflowers*. Composition inspired by Repin's painting *The Barge Haulers*. Composition inspired by Makovsky's painting *At Night*. My thoughts on people who have died for the freedom and independence of their homeland (Spartacus, Joan of Arc, Sándor Petőfi, Ivan Susanin, Aleksandr Matrosov, Zoya Kosmodemyanskaya). On the heroism of a Pioneer who died during the Great Patriotic War. 'You cannot hide an awl in a sack',[49] 'Strike while the iron is hot' (a composition inspired by proverbs). What do we need knowledge for? When our astronauts first land on Mars (fantasy-dream). Who is Don Quixote? (from extracurricular reading). May there never be war.

Grade 8. 'Without a mother there can be no poet and no hero.' (Gorky) 'One who is born to crawl can never fly!' (from Gorky's *Song of the Falcon*). 'Only the strong in spirit are victorious.' (N. Ostrovsky) What attracts and inspires me in the image of Pavel Korchagin (a character from Nikolai Ostrovsky's *How the Steel was Tempered*). For what cause did the young guardsmen sacrifice their lives? (from Fadeev's *Young Guard*). 'Life without an aim is like a boat without a rudder.' (Indian wisdom) My thoughts on people who gave their lives for their convictions (Giordano Bruno, Aleksandr Ulyanov, Nikolai Kibalchich, Sergei Lazo, Julius Fučík, Ernst Thälmann). The image of a Soviet man in Sholokhov's story *The Fate of a Man*. 'Human will and labour can perform miracles.' (Nekrasov) 'It is worth living, so that one can leave a mark behind, deeper and more visible, so that one's work lives on, like a thousand-year oak.' (Musa Cälil) 'From idleness comes mental and physical flabbiness.' (Pisarev) A rainbow. Apple trees in flower. A summer night. A lark in the blue sky. How grass grows. My thoughts after reading Voynich's novel *The Gadfly*. Composition inspired by Grabar's painting *Azure Sky in February*. Who I want to be like (my ideal in life). My favourite hero in literature and in life.

Grade 9. The characters of Igor and Svyatoslav in *The Lay of Igor's Host*. The cruelty, arbitrariness and ignorance of the landowning class in Fonvizin's comedy *The Minor*. What did Radishchev see on his journey from Petersburg to Moscow 200 years ago, and what will a traveller see in our times? 'A true man and true son of the fatherland are one and the same thing.' (Radishchev) The reasons for Chatsky's disillusionment with his homeland in Griboyedov's play *Woe from Wit*. Why were Onegin and Pechorin unhappy people? We are adults, too. 'My friend, let us devote our finest impulses to the fatherland.' (Pushkin) Do we still encounter Chichikovs and Plyushkins in our times? (After reading Gogol's *Dead Souls*). Do we still encounter Oblomovs in our times? A ray of light in a dark kingdom (after reading Aleksandr Ostrovsky's play *The Storm*). What is the nature of conflict between fathers and sons in our times? (After reading Turgenev's *Fathers and Sons*) My thoughts on the 'new people', the heroes of Chernyshevsky's novel *What is to be Done?* What did the defender of the people, the hero of Nekrasov's poem 'Who is Happy in Russia?' live and fight for? Why are there still 'wise gudgeons' in our times? (After reading Saltykov-Shchedrin's story *The Wise Gudgeon*). 'One who lives without an ideal is to be pitied.' (Turgenev) 'The closest thing to greatness is honesty.' (Victor Hugo) 'The truth will be victorious, but it needs decisive help.' (Julius Fučík) 'One person alone, even if they be great, is still too little.' (Gorky) Autumn in an orchard. Ancient burial mounds in the steppe. A sunny winter's day. 'No great victory is possible without first achieving the minor victory over oneself.' (Leonov) 'Claes' ashes are beating in my breast.' (My thoughts on Charles de Coster's novel *Thyl Ulenspiegel*) A memorable day from my childhood. Where is happiness to be found? A composition inspired by Kuindzhi's painting *Birch Grove*. Jack London: the celebrator of courage. When people fly to the stars (fantasy). Who I strive to emulate in life (my ideal).

Grade 10. Who is the main hero in Tolstoy's novel *War and Peace*? (Reflections on the nation and the individual) The destruction of the cherry orchard represents the destruction of the gentry... But why are we saddened by it? (After reading Chekhov's play *The Cherry Orchard*) In what did Faust see the meaning of life? Larra the egoist, and Danko who sacrificed himself for his people's happiness (after reading Gorky's *Old Izergil*). Why did intelligent, talented people find themselves at the depths of society? (After reading Gorky's play *The Lower Depths*) How a simple Russian woman became a revolutionary (the character of Nilovna in Gorky's novel *Mother*). Lenin as a leader and Lenin as a human being (Mayakovsky's poem *Vladimir Ilyich Lenin*). Semyon Davydov and the chairman of our collective farm (after studying Sholokhov's novel *Virgin Soil Upturned*). What can we learn from the lives of writers who fought for the happiness of the people? (Radishchev, Shevchenko, Byron, Chernyshevsky, Sándor Petőfi, Hristo Botev, Gorky, Musa Cälil, Julius Fučík). 'The brave are recognised in battle, family and children in trouble, and friends in misfortune.' (Indian wisdom) 'The elimination of loafers and the glorification of labour: this is the constant trend of history.' (Dobrolyubov) 'I swear to you that I would not wish to have any other history or any other homeland for anything in the world.' (Pushkin) 'Guard your honour from youth.'

(Composition inspired by a proverb) 'There is nothing higher and more beautiful than to give happiness to many people.' (Beethoven) My ideal in life. What I live for in this world. What I love and what I hate. Composition inspired by Serov's painting *Girl with Peaches*. Composition inspired by Ioganson's painting *Interrogation of Communists*. Spring thaw. Birds fly to warmer climes. Nightingales in a lilac grove. The first day of the harvest. The steppe on a summer's day. Summer dawn. 'People are born, not to drag chains, but to spread their wings wide and soar above the earth.' (Victor Hugo)—young people's reflections on the fate of humanity. 'People are judged not by what they say or think, but by what they do.' (Lenin) 'Any idle citizen is a thief.' (Rousseau) 'Russia can manage without any one of us, but none of us can manage without her.' (Turgenev)—reflections on the eve of the first steps of our working lives.

Appendix 3 – Topics of some of Sukhomlynsky's compositions about nature

'Drops of Dew at Sunrise', 'Sunbeams in the Blossoming Branches of a Peach Tree', 'A Peach Orchard', 'The Opening of the Sunflowers', 'The Flowering of the Flax', 'A Field of clover', 'Bees Leave their Hive', 'The Fading of Nature in Autumn', 'The Rustling of Leaves in the Forest', 'The River at Dawn', 'Sunset Before Rain', 'A Thunderstorm in the Forest', 'A Hot Summer's Day', 'A Lark in the Deep Blue Summer Sky', 'Distant Azure Hills Beyond the Dnieper', 'High Water During the Spring Thaw', 'Ripening Wheat', 'Several Encounters with Levitan's Painting *The Birch Grove*', 'A Sunny Autumn Day', 'The First Signs of Autumn in the Forest', 'The Quiet of Evening in the Steppe', 'The Music of the Grasshoppers', 'The Song of the Nightingale', 'Blizzard in the Steppe', 'An Overcast Autumn Day', 'An Overcast Summer Day', 'Life Under a Carpet of Snow', 'The Awakening of the Forest at Dawn', 'A Forest Path', 'Lillies of the Valley', 'A Summer Day on the Banks of the Dnieper', 'Kyiv Chestnut Trees', 'Taras Shevchenko's Grave', 'A Bouquet of Wildflowers', 'Young Botanists in Search of Plants', 'Starry Night', 'The First Autumn Frost', 'Hoar Frost on the Branches of a Willow Tree', 'The Weeping

Willow by the Pond', 'A Night by the Campfire', 'How a Boy Saved a Puppy', 'Bunches of Grapes in the Greenhouse', 'A Cold Morning Frost', 'Rowan Trees from Belarus are Growing on Ukrainian Soil', 'A White Acacia has Flowered', 'An Apple Tree in Flower', 'A Night in August', 'The First Autumn Rain', 'Young Pine Trees on the Bank of the Dnieper', 'A Memorial to Fallen Warriors on an Ancient Scythian Burial Mound', 'Meeting the Mother of a Hero', 'A Lilac Grove in a Ravine', 'Ravines are the Earth's Wounds', 'A Child's First Step is a Mother's Joy', 'How My Children Found a Chick in the Forest', 'Good People are Everywhere Around Us', 'How I Unintentionally Offended a Boy', 'Joy and Sadness During a Graduation Party', 'Meeting Former Students', 'Books are My Friends', 'Reverie by My Bookshelf', 'Plant Your Tree', 'Leave Behind a Positive Trace on the Earth' and 'What is True Friendship?'

Appendix 4 – Equipment Manufactured at Pavlysh Secondary School 1961–1967

The equipment we produced from 1961 to 1967 has included 35 spirit levels, 35 plane tables, 36 vertical goniometers, 15 classroom (large) abacuses, 75 classroom set squares, 50 pairs of compasses, 63 protractors, 26 universal goniometers, 26 astrolabes (with tripods), 7 film strip projectors, 430 working models of electric motors, 4 sets of demonstration dynamometers, 25 devices for demonstrating the action of a screw, 20 demonstration braces and bits with brakes, 6 demonstration jacks, 17 model transmissions, 15 carts with wind-up mechanisms, 7 model centrifuges, 5 aquariums, 6 sets of communicating vessels, 12 model pumps, 12 devices for demonstrating the heat conductivity of various metals, 18 devices for demonstrating convection in liquids, 25 devices for demonstrating the expansion of water when frozen, 350 test tube holders with metal clamps, 15 cross-sections of steam cylinders with slide valve boxes, 26 cross-sections of internal combustion engines, 25 jet-propelled carts, 15 models of water turbines, 37 working models of steam engines and steam turbines, 8 working models of wind power stations, 7 working models of hydroelectric power stations, 6 Wimshurst machines, 37 electrical knife switches, 10 electrical wiring plans for a domestic building, 1,360 single-valve or double-valve radios and 270 transistor radios, 26 two-way radio transmitters, 57 working models of machinery controlled by radio, 43 working models of a telegraph apparatus, 40 working models of a telephone, 360 electromagnetic ammeters, 440 voltmeters, 160 plug-in rheostats and 25 slide rheostats, 270 bimetallic strip relays and 270 electromagnetic relays, 6 electric sirens, 18 revolution counters, 5 models of an electric arc furnace, 25 Franklin wheels,[50] 25 devices for demonstrating the rotation of an electrically charged frame in a magnetic field, 160 model periscopes, 190 working models with photorelays, 64 thermal ammeters, 160 devices for refracting and reflecting light, 35 devices for receiving actual images with the aid of a lens, 35 photometers, 45 measuring instruments with solenoids, 27 simply constructed telescopes, 5 Liebig condensers, 28 hydrometers for determining the specific gravity of a liquid, 65 collections of metals and alloys, 55 miniature metalworking lathes for students in the junior and middle years, 25 woodworking lathes, 25 drilling machine tools and 12 milling machines, 4 universal woodworking machines, 7 sets of metalworking tools for tractor brigades, and a large number of tools and equipment for school activities: flat and round-nose pliers, hammers, planes, jointers, soil sieves, sieves for cleaning seeds, spades, rakes, shovels, watering cans, workbenches, tables, stools, etc. During those seven years, we presented other schools with 16 metalworking lathes, 8 woodworking lathes and 12 drilling machine tools for their work classes.

Appendix 5 – Extracurricular Activity Groups at Pavlysh Secondary School in 1967

In 1967, our students in Grades 1–8 participated the following extracurricular activity groups:

Activity	Grade levels participating	Number of groups
Young metalworkers and designers	1–6	2
Young metalworkers and designers	3–4	3
Young metalworkers and designers	4–6	3
Young builders	1–3	2
Young carpenters	1–2	4
Young carpenters	3–4	3
Young turners	3–8	2
Young turners	7–8	1
Young machine operators	1–6	1
Young machine operators	5–6	1
Young machine operators	6–7	1
Young machine operators	7–8	2
Young electricians	3–5	2
Young electricians	5–8	2
Young radio technicians	4–6	1
Young radio technicians	5–8	2
Automation and radio electronics	4–10	2
Young orchardists and foresters	5–8	1
Young animal breeders	1–4	1
Young animal breeders	5–8	1
Young plant breeders	1–5	1
Young plant breeders	4–5	1

Activity	Grade levels participating	Number of groups
Young plant breeders	5–6	1
Young plant breeders	6–8	2
Young flower growers	1–2	3
Young flower growers	3–4	2
Young flower growers	5–6	1
Young flower growers	6–8	1
Young beekeepers	1–4	1
Young beekeepers	5–8	1
Young soil scientists	3–5	1
Young soil scientists	5–8	1
Young botanists	1–4	1
Young botanists	3–5	1
Young botanists	5–8	1
Young aeromodellers	1–10	1

Translator's note: The above list omits some other clubs that Sukhomlynsky describes on page 348, where he mentions a ceramics workshop, a puppet theatre, a club for artistic pokerwork and fretwork, a painting club, choir circles, a folk instrument orchestra and a club for bayan players. Clubs and activity groups are also mentioned on pages 56–77, where Sukhomlynsky describes his staff and their interests. These include mathematics clubs, embroidery clubs, drama clubs, creative writing groups, a local history group and a society for nature conservation.

ENDNOTES

1. Translator's note: See T Lovat, *The art and heart of good teaching: values as pedagogy*, Springer Briefs in Education, Singapore, 2019.
2. The term 'infancy of the nervous system' was introduced by corresponding member of the USSR Academy of Sciences VL Ryzhov, in his article 'The molecular basis of memory', *Priroda [Nature]*, 1965, vol. 7, p. 2.
3. Translator's note: The school council (*pedagogicheskii soviet*) included all the staff working at a school and thus, was a larger and more inclusive body than is typically the case in English-speaking countries today.
4. K Marx & F Engels, *Sochineniya [Works]*, vol. 23, p. 378.
5. Translator's note: Sukhomlynsky's school enrolled children from Grades 1–10, with ages ranging from seven through to 18. Most secondary schools in the Soviet Union incorporated primary classes on the same campus.
6. Translator's note: It would appear that Sukhomlynsky is referring here to his combined educational experience, spent predominantly at Pavlysh Secondary School (1948–1970), but also at seven-year schools in Vasylivka and Zybkove (1935–1938), secondary schools in Onufriivka (1939–1941) and Uva (1942–1944), and in the Onufriivka district office of education (1944–1947).
7. Translator's note: In 1933 a Soviet expedition aboard the ship *Chelyuskin* attempted to sail from Murmansk to Vladivostok through the polar ice. They were trapped by the ice in February 1934 and rescued by Soviet pilots.
8. Translator's note: At the time when this book was written, children enrolled in Soviet schools at the age of seven. Primary school encompassed Grades 1–4, and secondary school Grades 5–10, with primary and secondary sections often housed on the same site under a single principal. Sukhomlynsky himself experimented with a preschool year, working with children aged six. This work is described in his most famous book, *My Heart I Give to Children*.

9 AN Leontiev, *Problemy razvitiya psikhiki [Issues in the development of the psyche]*, Moscow, 1965, pp. 532–540.
10 Translator's note: The bayan is a type of chromatic button accordion.
11 Translator's note: The Zaporizhian Sich (or Zaporizhian Host) was a semi-autonomous Cossack proto-state that existed during the 16th–18th centuries.
12 Translator's note: In Soviet schools it was quite common for a primary school teacher to stay with the same group of children for the four years of their primary schooling.
13 Translator's note: The Little Octobrists (*Oktobryata* in Russian) bore a similar relationship to Pioneers that Cub Scouts bear to Scouts in the Scouting movement. Children in the Little Octobrists were aged seven to ten, with each class in the junior primary school constituting a Little Octobrist group.
14 Translator's note: 'Supportive peer groups' is a liberal translation of the word 'collective', but one that is justified by what Sukhomlynsky has written elsewhere about the development of a 'collective' in the context of junior primary school classes, particularly in the article 'Idti vpered!' [Let us go forwards!], published in the journal *Narodnoe Obrazovanie [National Education]*, 1989, vol. 8, pp. 70–78.
15 Translator's note: 'Heuristic discussion' is a translation of the Russian term *evristicheskaya beseda* and refers to something quite like a Socratic dialogue. Rather than presenting knowledge 'on a platter', the teacher encourages students to discover the truth themselves, posing a series of questions that students attempt to answer on the basis of their prior knowledge. This sequence of questions leads to new understanding and new knowledge.
16 Translator's note: The reader will find a much more detailed account of this approach to outdoor learning in Sukhomlynsky's *My Heart I Give to Children*.
17 Translator's note: *Kobzar* was Shevchenko's first collection of poetry, published in 1840. Shevchenko is regarded as a founding father of Ukrainian literature and enjoys a similar status in Ukraine to Pushkin in Russia or Shakespeare in England.
18 Translator's note: Zoya Kosmodemyanskaya was executed on 29

November 1941 after being arrested for setting fire to buildings in a village occupied by German soldiers.
19 See V Muntyan, 'Priroda v opasnosti' [Nature in danger], *Literaturnaya Gazeta*, Kiev (in Ukrainian), 1961, 5 May; *Bol'shaya sovetskaya entsiklopedia [The Great Soviet Encyclopedia]*, vol. 15, pp. 327–329.
20 Translator's note: According to the *Great Soviet Encyclopedia*, phytoncides are biologically active substances secreted by plants and capable of suppressing the vital activity of microorganisms and insects.
21 Research method: We measured the dust on a square metre of cereal crop. To do this, the plants were cut and weighed in the evening, before dew fell. In the morning, after the dew had evaporated, we cut the same number of plants from which the dew had washed the dust, and weighed them. The difference in weight showed us how much dust had been washed away.
22 Translator's note: Volodya is an affectionate form of the name Vladimir, and Ulyanov was Lenin's original surname, so Volodya Ulyanov is what Lenin would have been called in childhood, and the bust is most probably of Lenin as a child.
23 Translator's note: The Russian term is *zamedlennoe myshlenie*, which is sometimes translated as 'bradyphrenia'.
24 Translator's note: In November 1966 the Central Committee of the Communist Party and the Council of Ministers decreed that by 1970 all Soviet primary schools would institute a three-year primary program, with secondary subjects introduced in year four. (Students graduated from secondary school at the end of Grade 10.) At the time, children entered Grade 1 at the age of seven. In 1986, when the school entrance age was reduced to six, the primary school once again adopted a four-year program, with students now graduating from secondary school at the end of Grade 11.
25 Translator's note: During the post-war years, when school buildings could not always accommodate all the students in a single shift, it was not uncommon for schools to operate in two or even three shifts. When Sukhomlynsky was principal of the school in Uva (in

the Urals) during the war, the school operated in three shifts from 8:00 am to 7:15 pm.

26 We observe this rule strictly in our after-school groups. Students in Grades 1–4 who remain at school after classes spend no more than 20–30 minutes on intellectual work in classrooms. The remainder of the time they spend outdoors.

27 *Zmina*, a publication of the Central Committee of the Komsomol of Ukraine, 1961, no. 8. (In Ukrainian.)

28 *Izvestiya*, 1961, 25 June.

29 The school is in regular contact with Dmitrii Kruzhilin.

30 *Pravda*, 1960, 19 October.

31 K Marx & F Engels, *Sochineniya [Works]*, vol. 19, p. 20.

32 AV Lunacharsky, *O vospitanii i obrazovanii [On education]*, Moscow, 1976, p. 306. (This footnote added by editors of a 1980 edition.)

33 I Pavlov, *Pavlovskie sredy. Protokoly i stenogrammy fiziologicheskikh besed [Pavlov Wednesdays. Minutes and stenographic records of physiological conversations]*, Volume 1, Minutes 1929–1932, Moscow-Leningrad, 1949, p. 268.

34 VG Belinsky, *Polnoe sobranie sochinenii [Complete works]*, vol. 2, Moscow, 1953, p. 47.

35 K Marx & F Engels, *Sochineniya [Works]*, vol. 3, p. 36.

36 See 'Marks, Internatsional, Rossiya' [Marx, The International, Russia], *Pravda*, 25 September 1964.

37 AP Pinkevich, *Vvedenie v pedagogiku [Introduction to pedagogy]*, Moscow, 1930, p. 58.

38 VI Lenin, *Polnoe sobranie sochinenii [Complete works]*, vol. 45, p. 391.

39 Maxim Gorky, in his *History of Russian literature*, wrote: 'What is literature's strength? Clothing ideas in flesh and blood, it gives them greater clarity and makes them more convincing than is possible for philosophy or science'. (AM Gorky archive, vol. 1, Moscow, 1939, p. 1.)

40 KD Ushinsky, *Sobranie sochinenii [Collected Works]*, vol. 8, Moscow-Leningrad, 1950, p. 356.

41 PI Zinchenko, *Neproizvol'noe zapominanie [Involuntary memorisation]*, Moscow, 1961, pp. 13–137.

42 MA Danilov, 'Umstvennoe vospitanie' [Intellectual education], *Sovetskaya pedagogika [Soviet pedagogy]*, 1964, vol. 12, p. 81.
43 The general features of this system are described in my book *Systema roboty dyrektora shkoly [A school principal's system of work]*, Kyiv, Radyans'ka shkola, 1959. (In Ukrainian)
44 SL Sobelev, 'Molodost' i nauka' [Youth and science], *Tekhnika – molodezhi [Technology for young people]*, 1961, vol. 9, p. 10.
45 VG Aleksandrov, *Anatomiya rastenii [The anatomy of plants]*, Leningrad-Moscow, 1939.
46 K Marx & F Engels, *Sochineniya [Works]*, vol. 32, pp. 460–461.
47 Translator's note: The 19th-century Russian poet Alexander Pushkin enjoys a similar status in Russian literature to that enjoyed by Shakespeare in English literature. The words quoted here are from the fourth stanza of the fifth chapter of his masterpiece *Evgenii Onegin [Eugene Onegin]*.
48 See *Pravda*, 1958, 17 August.
49 Translator's note: As an awl is sharp, and will inevitably stick out of a sack, this proverb suggests that 'the truth will out'.
50 Translator's note: A type of electric rotational device invented by Benjamin Franklin.

RESOURCES

Books

Vasyl Sukhomlynsky, *My Heart I Give to Children*, EJR Language Service Pty. Ltd., Brisbane, 2016.

Vasyl Sukhomlynsky, *A World of Beauty: Tales from Pavlysh*, EJR Language Service Pty. Ltd., Brisbane, 2013. (This book is also available in Russian, Ukrainian, Japanese and Chinese language editions.)

Alan Cockerill, *Each One Must Shine: The Educational Legacy of V.A. Sukhomlinsky*, EJR Language Service Pty. Ltd., Brisbane, 2017. (Originally published by Peter Lang, New York, 1999.)

For more information about the above publications, please visit:

https://ejr.com.au/publications.

Website

https://theholisticeducator.net/sukhomlynsky/

(This website includes a page with links to the resources listed below, as well as to some Ukrainian language sites.)

YouTube video 'Sukhomlynsky Lesson'

https://www.youtube.com/watch?v=eCksMOPYzas

ABC Radio podcast and associated article

https://www.abc.net.au/radio/programs/conversations/conversations-alan-cockerill-rpt/9611188

'Vasily Sukhomlinsky: Educating the Heart, Head and Hands' – Alan Cockerill in conversation with Richard Fidler. (podcast)

https://www.abc.net.au/radionational/programs/archived/conversations/vasily-sukhomlinsky-educating-the-heart/7878410

'Vasily Sukhomlinsky: The Teacher who Changed the World' (article)

Online Articles

https://www.rosejourn.com/index.php/rose/article/view/331/315

'Sukhomlinsky and Steiner: A Comparison'. – An article written for the RoSE Journal (Research on Steiner Education).

https://www.msvu.ca/wp-content/uploads/2020/05/International20Conversations20of20Teacher20Educators20Dec2013.pdf

'Education for the Anthropocene: The Contribution of Vasily Sukhomlinsky' – Chapter 7 (pages 94–110) in the online publication 'International Conversations of Teacher Educators: Collaborations in Education'.

Blogs

http://insearchofsukhomlinsky.blogspot.com.au/

'In Search of Sukhomlinsky' – This blog was written by Alan Cockerill, and records his activities during a ten day research trip to Ukraine in October 2009. The final post summarizes the contents of archives in Pavlysh and Kyiv, and may contain useful material for anyone interested in researching Sukhomlynsky's legacy.

https://discoveryandwonder.com/category/vasilii-sukhomlinsky/

Blog comments by Robert Weiss, an American scholar who has been interested in Sukhomlynsky for many years. His blog 'Site of Discovery and Wonder' contains several interesting posts about Sukhomlynsky.

Monthly newsletter

https://theholisticeducator.net/Sukhomlynsky/newsletter/

Readers can subscribe to this free monthly newsletter, which contains new translations of extracts from the works of Vasyl Sukhomlynsky, and updates about any new English language publications.

OTHER PUBLICATIONS

http://www.ejr.com.au/publications

MY HEART I GIVE TO CHILDREN

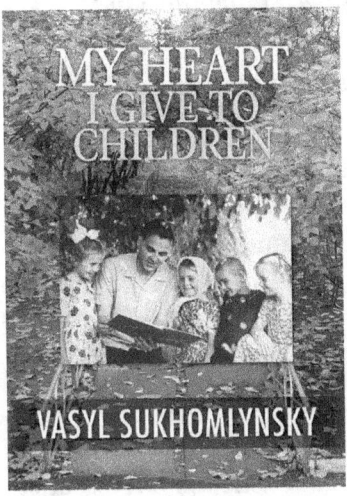

'Now I see the secret of the making of the best persons,

It is to grow in the open air and to eat and sleep with the earth.'

With these words from Walt Whitman's 'Song of the Open Road', Sukhomlynsky closes his account of how he educated young children in a Ukrainian village during the aftermath of the Second World War.

Sukhomlynsky's masterpiece was many years ahead of its time. It addresses issues such as our relationship with nature, how to nurture children's souls in the face of the sometimes negative influences of mass media, how to help children develop empathy for others, how schools can develop strong relationships with families, how children's brains function and develop, how to foster an intrinsic love of learning, and how to support children who struggle to acquire skills in literacy and numeracy. This classic work is addressed to school principals, teachers, and anyone interested in the upbringing of children.

ISBN: 978-0-9805885-7-6
Available from major online retailers.
It can also be ordered through your local bookshop.

EACH ONE MUST SHINE

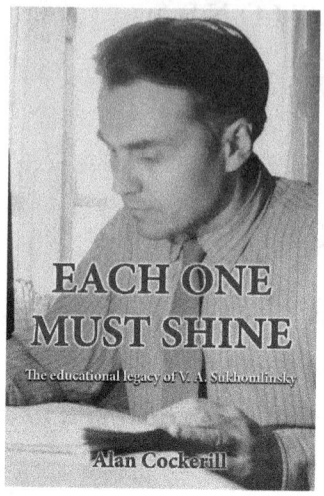

The definitive English language study of the educational legacy of Vasyl Sukhomlynsky.

There should not be any nobodies—specks of dust cast upon the wind. Each one must shine, just as billions upon billions of galaxies shine in the heavens.

Each One Must Shine is an account of the life and work of Vasyl Sukhomlynsky (1918–1970), one of the most influential educators of the twentieth century. Sukhomlynsky's writings inspired millions of Soviet school teachers, and continue to inspire educators in Russia, Ukraine, and China, where he is one of the most influential foreign educators.

Sukhomlynsky's idealistic vision of human development and his deep love for children led him to develop a holistic system of education that emphasised the moral and aesthetic dimensions of a child's development as well as the physical, intellectual and vocational. He was the principal of a rural school in Pavlysh, in central Ukraine, for twenty-two years, and wrote about his experience in numerous books and articles. His school was visited by thousands of educators from the length and breadth of the Soviet Union and beyond, and his books have been read by millions. *Each One Must Shine* is the first major study to present Sukhomlynsky's legacy to an English-speaking audience. It is addressed to parents and educators, as well as specialists in the field.

ISBN: 978-0-9945625-9-3
Available from major online retailers.
It can also be ordered through your local bookshop.

A WORLD OF BEAUTY: TALES FROM PAVLYSH

A selection of Sukhomlynsky's little stories for children, beautifully illustrated by students from Ukraine and Belarus.

The lovely illustrations in this book show beauty through the eyes of children. In 2013, thousands of school students in Ukraine, Russia, Belarus and Kazakhstan submitted illustrations for this selection of stories.

Note: This title is also available in Russian, Ukrainian, Japanese and Chinese editions. (For ISBN numbers and searchable English titles, see our website: https://www.ejr.com.au/publications)

www.ingramcontent.com/pod-product-compliance
Lightning Source LLC
Chambersburg PA
CBHW050258010526
44107CB00055B/2082